Early U.S. Navy Carrier Raids,
February–April 1942

ALSO BY DAVID LEE RUSSELL
AND FROM McFARLAND

David McCampbell: Top Ace of U.S. Naval Aviation in World War II (2019)

Eastern Air Lines: A History, 1926–1991 (2013)

Oglethorpe and Colonial Georgia: A History, 1733–1783 (2006; paperback 2013)

The American Revolution in the Southern Colonies (2000; paperback 2009)

Early U.S. Navy Carrier Raids, February–April 1942

Five Operations That Tested a New Dimension of American Air Power

DAVID LEE RUSSELL

McFarland & Company, Inc., Publishers
Jefferson, North Carolina

LIBRARY OF CONGRESS CATALOGUING-IN-PUBLICATION DATA

Names: Russell, David Lee, 1947– author.
Title: Early U.S. Navy carrier raids, February-April 1942 : five operations that tested a new dimension of American air power / David Lee Russell.
Description: Jefferson, North Carolina : McFarland & Company, Inc., Publishers, 2019 | Includes bibliographical references and index.
Identifiers: LCCN 2019035880 | ISBN 9781476678467 (paperback ; acid free paper) ♾ | ISBN 9781476638614 (ebook)
Subjects: LCSH: World War, 1939–1945—Campaigns—Pacific Area. | Aircraft carriers—United States—History—20th century. | World War, 1939–1945—Aerial operations, American. | World War, 1939–1945—Naval operations, American. | Air power (Military science)—Case studies. | Raids (Military science)—Case studies.
Classification: LCC D773 .R86 2019 | DDC 940.54/26—dc23
LC record available at https://lccn.loc.gov/2019035880

BRITISH LIBRARY CATALOGUING DATA ARE AVAILABLE

ISBN (print) 978-1-4766-7846-7
ISBN (ebook) 978-1-4766-3861-4

© 2019 David Lee Russell. All rights reserved

No part of this book may be reproduced or transmitted in any form or by any means, electronic or mechanical, including photocopying or recording, or by any information storage and retrieval system, without permission in writing from the publisher.

Front cover photograph: Wake Island Raid, 24 February 1942, view showing Douglas SBD-3 Dauntlesses on deck with a variety of markings styles on USS *Enterprise* (CV-6); USS *Northampton* (CA-26) is visible in background (National Archives and Records Administration, College Park, MD: Catalog #: 80-G-66038)

Printed in the United States of America

McFarland & Company, Inc., Publishers
Box 611, Jefferson, North Carolina 28640
www.mcfarlandpub.com

To all those who served in U.S. Naval Aviation
and my shipmates of Patrol Squadron Four
during the Vietnam War, formerly homeported
at Naval Air Station Barbers Point, Hawaii

Table of Contents

Introduction	1
1 • War Begins in the Pacific	5
2 • Marshall and Gilbert Islands	17
3 • Rabaul	66
4 • Wake and Marcus Islands	83
5 • Lae and Salamaua	107
6 • Tokyo	127
7 • Aftermath	164
Appendix A: Marshall and Gilbert Islands Raid, U.S. Navy Task Forces 8 and 17, February 1, 1942	169
Appendix B: Rabaul Raid, U.S. Navy Task Force 11, February 20, 1942	170
Appendix C: Wake and Marcus Island Raid, U.S. Navy Task Force 16, February 24, 1942	171
Appendix D: Lae-Salamaua Raid, Allied Task Force 11 (TF 11, TF 17 and ANZAC Squadron), March 10, 1942	172
Appendix E: Tokyo Raid, U.S. Navy Task Force 16, April 18, 1942	173
Chapter Notes	175
Bibliography	183
Index	187

...with nothing but indomitable courage and hope to support us, we left our mark on a cruel and treacherous enemy.
—Vice Admiral William F. Halsey, Jr., August 15, 1945,
on the deck of his flagship, the USS *Missouri*,
off the coast of Japan

Introduction

> Such remarks as I may have to make as to the nature and extent of the air force required by the Navy will be based upon the assumption that the airplane is now a major force, and is becoming daily more efficient and its weapons more deadly, ... that therefore even a small, high-speed carrier alone can destroy or disable a battleship alone, that a fleet whose carriers give it command of the air over the enemy fleet can defeat the latter, that the fast carrier is the capital ship of the future. Based upon these assumptions, it is evident that our policy in regard to the Navy air force should be command of the air over the fleet of any possible enemy.[1]

These were the words of Admiral William S. Sims, USN, on October 14, 1925. The reality of his assertions came true in the Pacific War in 1942 as carriers raided islands and projected sea power wherever they sailed.

The early sign of the naval significance of air power as the future dominant weapon over the battleship was demonstrated in July 1921 with Billy Mitchell's sanctioned demonstration test off the Virginia coast. That event sent the "unsinkable" surplus World War I German battleship *Ostfriedland* to the bottom of the ocean in 21 minutes with only six bombs dropped from Martin twin-engine MB-2 bombers. The U.S. Navy's leadership was horrified by the tests, but it was simply a matter of time before planes flown off carriers would rule the seas. That time had arrived with the stark reality of the Japanese attack on Pearl Harbor.

Even before the first appearance of the fast carriers *Lexington* (CV-2) and *Saratoga* (CV-3) in late 1927, the Navy senior leadership had clashed between the new naval aviators and the non-air battleship admirals on the question of the proper operational role of the carrier. Various annual Fleet exercises were held in the Atlantic and Pacific to simulate operational battle scenarios. Fleet Problem VII, held in the Caribbean in 1927 using the USS *Langley*, revealed the need for carrier mobility during changing weather and enemy fleet movements. This led to the recommendation that the admiral in charge of carriers, the Commander Aircraft Squadrons, be given "complete freedom of action in employing carrier aircraft."[2] In Fleet Problem IX in 1929, Vice Admiral Pratt allowed Rear Admiral Reeves to send the *Saratoga* at high speed for a surprise attack on the Panama Canal defended by an opposing fleet with carriers. The *Saratoga* attack achieved complete success, but when the carriers got within range of the big guns, the battleship sank the carriers. The battleship admirals felt they had proven their point.

Perhaps the most revealing of the exercises in the context of demonstrating the threat of carrier power was with the infamous Fleet Problem XIII. In this mock attack by a "militaristic, Asian island nation against the base at Pearl Harbor," the "Blue Forces" under the command of Admiral Richard Leigh had directed Rear Admiral Harry Yarnell to attack with his Advanced Raiding Force consisting of the carriers *Lexington* and *Saratoga* and seven destroyers. The "Black Forces" were logically expecting the attackers to engage them with his battleships and cruisers, but they were left behind.[3]

After sailing westward from the West Coast on February 1, 1932, at dawn on Sunday, February 7, Yarnell launched a force of 152 planes from his two carriers at a point 40 miles northeast of Oahu in rough seas. His attack, executed between 0600 and 0700, was a total surprise and great success. The airfields (Wheeler, Luke and Rogers) were destroyed with not a single plane getting airborne. The attackers strafed Ford Island and dropped sacks of flour to simulate bombs on the battleships, scoring multiple hits. The exercise umpires declared Yarnell's attack a complete success and made him the clear winner. The Army and Navy senior officers complained that Yarnell had cheated, calling a Sunday morning attack "inappropriate" and maybe even "illegal." The Navy argued that low-level precision bombing of battleships at anchor in Pearl Harbor was unrealistic. Under great pressure from the War Department, the umpires ultimately reversed their decision to declare that the defenders (the Black Forces) had won the exercise.[4]

Although an acknowledgment of the power of the fast carriers was growing among the admirals, policy was still lagging behind. In the 1934 edition of the Navy's War Instructions Manual, carriers were described as "simply mobile airplane bases and their use depends upon the employment of their aircraft."[5]

This new and most effective weapons system, the fast carrier task force, came on the scene in the Pacific War during a most awkward moment for the U.S. Navy. The Navy expected a Pacific War to be led, yet again, by the mighty battleships, with carriers making their important, yet secondary, airborne contributions. Noel Gayler, the highly decorated World War II Navy fighter pilot ace in the Pacific who rose to the rank of admiral, explained:

> The naval theory of the day was that of fleet in being. The decisive encounter was to be between the battle lines. The destroyers were ancillary to that. The aircraft were very much ancillary to that. Even the very terminology—Aircraft Scouting Force—relegated aircraft to scouting.... I think that far more than either failures of intelligence or failures of awareness ... to me the 90 percent explanation of how something like Pearl Harbor could happen devolved from the mind-set of the commanders, all of whom had been brought up in the big-gun Navy.... I don't think any of them actually imagined that an air attack could be more than a raid.[6]

But with five of eight battleships sunk or damaged and out of commission at Pearl Harbor, carrier airpower would take on the supreme offensive role against Japanese forces in the first phase of the war. The tragic sinking of the British battleship *Prince of Wales* and her escort, the cruiser HMS *Repulse,* on December 10, 1941, by Japanese Imperial Navy land-based bombers and torpedo bombers, confirmed Mitchell's argument of 1921 of the vulnerability of the battleship to air attack at sea without sufficient air cover.

Though there was no history of American carrier warfare as the conflict began, in the Pacific the carrier task force admirals would quickly be called upon to demonstrate their skills at conducting carrier attacks against the advancing Japanese forces on islands recently taken by invasion units. Their success was anything but assured as they took on the daunting task of defeating a motivated enemy fresh from victories throughout the Pacific. If they failed to stop the Japanese advance, the Hawaiian island chain would eventually fall, and the entire West Coast of the United States would be open to attack.

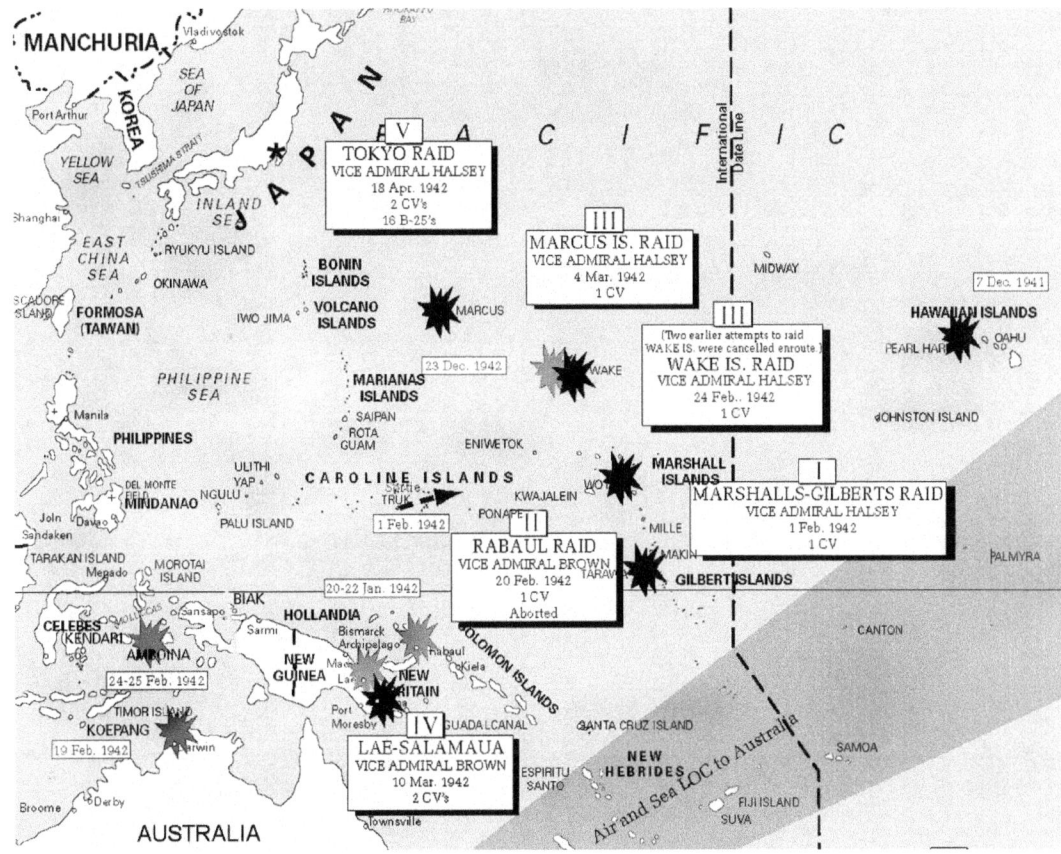

Map of Pacific carrier operations, December 7, 1941–April 18, 1942 (courtesy United States Military Academy, Department of History).

America's fast carrier task forces, with their aircraft squadrons and powerful support ships including heavy cruisers and destroyers, were as prepared as they could be for the war they trained for, but unfortunately, they were in short supply. The Pacific Fleet carrier force had only three U.S. carriers in the Pacific on December 7: *Enterprise*, *Lexington* and *Saratoga*. The *Enterprise* and *Lexington* were operating out of Pearl Harbor on separate missions to deliver much-needed aircraft to island outposts on December 7, and *Saratoga* was at San Diego. Thankfully, none of these carriers were at Pearl Harbor on the day of the Japanese attack.

This book reveals in detail the events of the early carrier raids against the Japanese in the first half of 1942 in the Pacific War, carried out by the officers and men of the U.S. Pacific Fleet. These brave and skilled men would turn carrier task force warfare from an untested "novelty" to the premier strategic naval weapons system that it remains even today.[7]

Chapter 1

War Begins in the Pacific

I have no doubt as to the ultimate outcome.

In the early morning of Christmas Day 1941, the incoming Commander in Chief Pacific Fleet (CINCPAC) Admiral Chester W. Nimitz's Catalina PBY descended out of the clouds over Molokai, Hawaii, and was joined by a fighter escort. The escort led them to the next island, Oahu. As the rain fell, Nimitz could see the bleak scenery out his window. The East Loch anchorage at Pearl Harbor was filled with black oil. The *Utah* and *Oklahoma* were upside down and the battleships *California*, *West Virginia*, and *Arizona* were blackened, with only their top decks above the waterline.

The Catalina made its water landing exactly at 0700. When the plane's door had been opened, Nimitz could smell the nasty mix of the odors of oil, charred wood and dead bodies. Still in civilian clothes and fatigued from little sleep, the admiral stepped aboard a dirty whaleboat to be greeted by handshakes from Rear Admiral Husband E. Kimmel, Vice Admiral William S. Pye, Vice Admiral Patrick N.L. Bellinger, and Captains William W. Smith (chief of staff to Kimmel) and Harold C. Train (chief of staff to Pye). Now reduced to his permanent rank of rear admiral, Kimmel had been relieved of duty as CINCPAC on December 17 by Vice Admiral Pye, who was serving as the Commander Battleships, Battle Force. Vice Admiral Bellinger was commanding officer of Task Force 9, comprising the patrol planes of the Pacific Fleet.[1]

In the choppy water, with the rain refusing to let up, the group stood to avoid soiling their clothes as they moved to the shore when Nimitz asked his first question: "What news from Wake?"[2] The news was bad. After an incredibly heroic resistance to a fifteen-day siege by Japanese forces under Rear Admiral Kajioka Sadamichi and the loss of 47 Marines killed or MIA, 3 Navy personnel killed, and at least 70 civilians dead, the Japanese captured the remaining American forces under Navy Commander Winfield S. Cunningham at Wake Island, totaling 433 military and 1,104 civilians. Left with no other alternative, at 2100 on December 22, Vice Admiral Pye had recalled Rear Admiral Frank Jack Fletcher's Wake Relief Force (Task Force 14) made up of the *Saratoga* (with 81 aircraft including VMF-221), three heavy cruisers, nine destroyers, one seaplane tender, and one fleet oiler.[3]

Nimitz was without words for a short while and then asked about the situation at Pearl. Captain Smith explained that they were still fishing bloated bodies out of the wreckage. After a long pause, Nimitz told Smith to "call Washington and report my arrival." He turned back toward the East Loch and said, "This is a terrible sight, seeing all these ships down."[4]

The whaleboat landed at the submarine base wharf, where Admiral Pye had a car waiting to take Nimitz to his new residence at Makalapa. Nimitz wanted breakfast and convinced Pye to join him. Rear Admiral Kimmel came by for breakfast with them too. Nimitz was "shocked at his old friend's appearance" as they exchanged handshakes, and said to Kimmel, "You have my sympathy. The same thing could have happened to anybody." With the shortage of available quarters, Nimitz offered to have them stay with him, but they declined, agreeing only to have meals with him. Later, Nimitz, Pye, Kimmel, and Mrs. Pye had Christmas dinner together. It was a sobering time for them all.[5]

Nimitz could now see with his own eyes the results of the Sunday, December 7 attack by the six carriers of the Imperial Japanese Navy (IJN) at Pearl Harbor. The first wave of 189 enemy planes under Commander Mitsuo Fuchida had launched by 0630 and set a course to Oahu, with 50 horizontal bombers, 40 torpedo bombers, and 54 dive bombers, accompanied by 45 Zero fighters for air protection. They dropped their first bombs just before 0800 on Wheeler Field, followed shortly by dive-bombing attacks on Hickam Field and the bases at Ford Island. The attacks on Battleship Row, with explosions, fire and smoke everywhere, created shock waves. Commander Fuchida wrote, "As the bombers completed their runs they headed north to return to the carriers. Pearl Harbor and the air bases had been pretty well wrecked by the fierce strafing and bombings. The imposing naval array of an hour before was gone."[6]

At 0715, the second wave of 171 planes, under Lieutenant Commander Shimazaki, launched skyward with 54 Kate horizontal bombers, 81 Val dive bombers and 36 Zeke fighters. After the launches, Admiral Nagumo turned the fleet south at 180 miles from Oahu's northern tip. At 0854, twenty-five minutes after the first wave had left Pearl Harbor, the second wave attacked. The Kate horizontal bombers hit aircraft and hangars at Kaneohe, Ford Island, Hickam Field, and Barber's Point. The Val dive bombers focused their attacks on the battleships, while the Zeke fighters strafed and provided protection against what few American fighters there were. The Japanese planes returned to their carriers immediately after rendezvousing with their fighters at a point about 20 miles bearing 340° from Kaena Point. The aircraft carriers were already underway for Japan. Ninety minutes after it began, the Japanese attack on Pearl Harbor and the Pacific Fleet had ended.[7]

The American losses were devastating. Though the few carriers available in the Pacific were thankfully not at Pearl Harbor, the Pacific Fleet was temporarily crippled. The Japanese sank three battleships (*Arizona*, *West Virginia*, and *Oklahoma*), caused the USS *California* to capsize, and severely damaged the other four. The USS *Helena*, a light cruiser, was torpedoed with a blast that capsized the nearby minelayer *Oglala*. The light cruiser *Raleigh* was hit with a torpedo, while another light cruiser, *Honolulu*, was damaged, but remained in service. The dry-docked destroyers *Cassin* and *Downes* were hit and destroyed by bombs that hit their fuel bunkers. Another destroyer, the USS *Shaw*, was hit by two bombs in her forward magazine. Moored alongside the USS *Arizona*, the repair ship *Vestal* was heavily damaged and breached. The seaplane tender *Curtiss* was also hit.

Aircraft fared no better than the ships. Of the 402 American aircraft on Oahu before the attack, the Japanese destroyed 177 (100 Navy, 77 Army) and damaged 159 (31 Navy, 128 Army), with 155 of them destroyed on the ground. Of 33 PBY patrol planes, 30 were destroyed, with the 3 on patrol returning unharmed. Unfortunately, friendly fire shot down some U.S. aircraft, including the 5 that had been inbound from the carrier USS *Enterprise*.[8]

At Pearl Harbor, the Navy suffered 2008 deaths and 710 wounded, while the Marines lost 109 killed and 69 wounded. The Army lost 218 killed, 364 wounded. Civilian losses were 68 killed and 35 wounded. Japanese losses at Pearl Harbor were very light. They lost 29 aircraft (9 in the first attack wave, 20 in the second wave), and six submarines. Sixty-eight Japanese airmen and nine submariners were killed in action, and one was captured.[9]

Back on December 9, Navy Secretary William Franklin Knox had flown to Hawaii to personally inspect the Pearl Harbor damage and confer with military officers there. When he stood in front of Admiral Kimmel in Hawaii on the 11th, Knox asked bluntly, "Did you receive my message on Saturday night?"[10] The historic warning message of the eminent Japanese attack had never arrived. Knox listened and observed, and by the time he was flying back to Washington, he was agitated by all he had heard.

When he returned on to Washington on Monday, December 15, Knox met with President Franklin D. Roosevelt in the evening to make his recommendations based on his visit to Hawaii. Knox suggested that Kimmel was so identified with the defeat at Pearl Harbor that he should be replaced. He also recommended that the Commander in Chief U.S. Fleet (CINCUS) position be separated from the area commands and be given the independent command over the entire Navy. Roosevelt agreed to Knox's recommendations, and they both felt Admiral Earnest King should take on the new post of Commander in Chief U.S. Fleet (COMINCH).

The next day Knox went back to the White House and, with Roosevelt, concurred that Kimmel would be replaced by Admiral Chester W. Nimitz as Commander in Chief Pacific Fleet (CINCPAC). Roosevelt told Knox, "Tell Nimitz to get the hell out to Pearl and stay there till the war is won." Knox hurried back to the Navy Department and sent for Nimitz.

The admiral strolled wearily into the secretary's office and before he could sit down, Knox asked, "How soon can you be ready to travel?"[11]

Nimitz, who was tired from all the hours he had put in keeping the Navy Bureau of Navigation (later known as the Bureau of Naval Personnel) above water, replied, "It depends on where I'm going and how long I'll be away."

Knox declared, "You're going to take command of the Pacific Fleet and I think you will be gone for a long while." Nimitz was shocked because the year before he had turned down the appointment because he did not want to leapfrog so many more senior naval officers. There were 28 flag officers more senior than him. But this time he could not turn down the position. There was a war on.[12]

Who was this vigorous 54-year-old man heading out to take over the Navy in the Pacific War at its lowest point, as battleships lay at the bottom of Pearl Harbor? On February 24, 1885, Chester William Nimitz was born across the street from his grandfather's Hotel Nimitz in Fredericksburg, Texas. His father had been rather frail and died before Nimitz was born. His mother, Anna Henke, was the daughter of the town butcher. Young Chester had aspirations to attend West Point, but when there were no appointments available, he applied for Annapolis. After outscoring others in the Naval Academy examination in April 1901, he was selected.

Nimitz entered the Naval Academy Class of 1905 the following September and turned out to be an excellent student, with his best subjects being mathematics, modern languages, navigation, and his practice cruise. Nimitz had entered the Naval Academy during a time of expansion and rebirth of the Navy itself. Americans leaders, including President

Theodore Roosevelt, were caught up in the imperialistic concepts expressed in Mahan's books on the influence of sea power.[13]

The eventual U.S. naval leaders of World War II were in attendance while Nimitz attended the Naval Academy. The class ahead of his included Ernest King and William Pye, and his classmates were soon to be household names: William Halsey, Harold Stark, Husband Kimmel, Frank Fletcher, Raymond Spruance, Milo Draemel, John S. McCain, and Wilson Brown. Sixteen members of Nimitz's class made rear admiral or better. He was a top midshipman and graduated 7th in a class of 114. He was described in the Academy yearbook as a man "of cheerful yesterdays and confident tomorrows."[14]

Nimitz's first tour was aboard the USS *Ohio* cruising in the Far East, where he earned favorable comments from Captain Logan: "Midshipman C.W. Nimitz is an Excellent Officer and I cheerfully commend him to the very favorable consideration of the Academic Board."[15] In September 1906, he was transferred to the cruiser *Baltimore*, and in January 1907, with two years' sea duty (then required by law), he was commissioned an ensign. He took his first command of a gunboat, the USS *Panay*, and simultaneously commanded the tiny naval station at Polloc, Mindanao, in the Philippines, where 22 Marines were stationed. At the unheard-of age of 22, Ensign Nimitz was given command of the four-stack, 420-ton destroyer USS *Decatur*. His command duty had been going extremely well when, on the evening of July 7, 1908, Nimitz made a careless mistake and grounded the *Decatur* on a mud bank entering Batangas Harbor south of Manila Bay. He was court-martialed for the grounding and, after receiving a reduced charge, returned from the Philippines to Boston as a watch officer aboard the gunboat *Ranger*, arriving in early December.[16]

After visiting his family, Nimitz reported for instruction at the First Submarine Flotilla on January 25, 1909. Though disappointed not to be given duty on battleships, he worked hard in his new assignment. In May of that year he was given command of the flotilla and the submarine *Plunger*. Nimitz worked his way up the career ladder serving in various submarine command positions as the skippers of the *Snapper*, *Narwhal*, and *Skipjack*, and as commander of the Atlantic Submarine Flotilla. In March 1912 Nimitz rescued Fireman 2nd Class W.J. Walsh from drowning in a strong tide and received the Treasury Department's Silver Lifesaving Medal. He became an expert in diesel engines on a shore assignment to build them for the fleet oiler USS *Maumee*.

Admiral Chester W. Nimitz, USN, Commander in Chief Pacific Fleet. Photographed circa 1942 (photograph #: 80-G-466244, official U.S. Navy photograph, National Archives).

During World War I, Nimitz served as aide and chief of staff to the Commander, Submarine Force Atlantic (COMSUBLANT). In September 1918 he was transferred to the Office of the Chief of Naval Operations and later served additional duty as senior member of the Board of Submarine Design. The next year he finally got his duty on capital ships as executive officer of the USS *South Carolina*. In June of 1920 he was sent to build a submarine base at Pearl Harbor from surplus World War I materials. He completed this challenging assignment in 1922. That summer, Commander Nimitz attended the Naval War College at Newport, Rhode Island.

A year later he became the aide and assistant chief of staff to the Commander of the Battle Fleet, and later took over that command. In August 1926 Nimitz headed to the University of California at Berkeley to establish the Navy's first Naval Reserve Officer Training Corps unit. He was promoted to the rank of captain in June 1927. He then progressed through assignments as Commander Submarine Division 20, commander of the destroyer tender *Rigel* and the out-of-commission reserve destroyers at San Diego, captain of the flagship of the Asiatic Fleet, the heavy cruiser *Augusta,* and assistant chief of the Bureau of Navigation in Washington, ending with his promotion to rear admiral. His next sea command was as Commander Cruiser Division Two, and then as Commander Battle Division One until 1939, when he was appointed chief of the Bureau of Navigation.[17]

It was not hard to see why Nimitz was the right man for his new command. He had come with an excellent background in a vast array of senior naval billets at sea and ashore. He was perhaps the most skilled administrator of men and training in the Navy. He was the leading U.S. Navy authority on submarines. Nimitz was a soft-spoken man, a team player, and a well-liked leader respected for his "intelligence, experience, and hard-working nature." He was a good-looking man of five feet nine inches tall and 180 pounds, with blue eyes and white hair, and projected a look of self-control. He stayed fit by exercise from long walks and the game of tennis. He never lost his temper and maintained his personal control while taking on the most challenging role in the U.S. Navy as the war began. He was a man of character who came to face America's enemy with his skills, experience, and inner confidence.[18]

Several hours before Nimitz had arrived at Pearl Harbor, Vice Admiral Pye and his staff created a comprehensive, 30-page assessment of the Pacific Fleet situation (*U.S. Pacific Fleet, Estimate of the Situation*, dated December 24, 1942). Pye's report opened with the following summary:

> The War, having been opened by Japan's surprise air attack on Pearl Harbor has existed for 17 days. This attack reduced our battleship strength for the time being to almost nothing, laid up two light cruisers for a long period and destroyed two destroyers. Our ally, Great Britain, has lost two of the five heavy ships she planned to station at Singapore. Japan's losses in battleships are uncertain. She may have lost one but, it is more probable that one or two are damaged and not sunk. In all, her losses have been comparatively small. They will be enumerated, as known, in a detailed comparison to be made later. It is sufficient to say that Japan has: twice as many battleships as we have available, even counting our reinforcement (3 BB) from the East Coast; over twice as many carriers, counting our reinforcement of one [*Yorktown*]. In other types, the comparison is not so unfavorable if we include our Asiatic fleet and allies in the Western Pacific.[19]

Though the Japanese attack on Pearl Harbor was a short-term tactical success, it was not a significant strategic victory. The loss of the Pacific Fleet battleships forced the hand of the United States Navy to put their focus on carrier task force aviation and the use of submarines. Pearl Harbor marked the emergence of the aircraft carrier as the center of naval power. The age of the fleet battleship had ended.

Now beginning to settle into his new life on Oahu, Nimitz quickly began inspecting the local facilities and salvage operations with the damaged ships. From his inspections and analysis, he concluded that the damage could "very easily have been devastatingly greater."[20] He also began receiving status briefings from the senior staff of each division of the command. Captain W.A. Lee, Jr., gave his briefing on fleet readiness, and revealed that general gunnery was good. The gunnery proficiency of the six-inch, 10,000-ton cruisers was excellent, while the smaller eight-inch armed cruisers were not as well tuned. The destroyers' gunnery and torpedo proficiency were very good, with the battleships that remained shooting quite well. The carriers were deemed fairly good in the daytime. Submarine proficiency was very good.

There was a real shortage of .50 caliber ammunition, bombs and torpedoes, as well as rapid-fire automatic machine guns like the Oerlikon and Bofors 20mm and 40mm. The situation with Navy pilots was serious. There was a major shortage of trained pilots in the fleet, and there were no spare aircraft for the carriers in Hawaii. They were considering moving one Marine air group, if they were allowed, to fly from carriers. The carriers had radar, but it was still somewhat experimental and yet to be fully utilized with proficiency. The aircraft did not have IFF (identification-friend-or-foe) equipment, which often led to the shooting down of our own planes, as was sadly in evidence at Pearl Harbor. The flight crews were not proficient in gunnery, bombing or dropping torpedoes because they had not been allowed to train with live ordnance due to prewar shortages.

After the full briefings on the eye-opening and rather depressing state of the Naval resources at his disposal, Nimitz and the staff expressed their opinions regarding what actions should be taken. Admiral Pye seemed to feel the critical problem was protecting the shipping between Hawaii and the West Coast. He had lessor concern about the traffic along the Australia–New Zealand shipping corridor. Pye proposed pressing more offensive submarine action, while the surface and air forces were to be employed with great care. Pye presented his position as follows:

> We have forces available—carrier and cruisers—well suited for this work and a judicious choice of objectives and timing will do much to make our defense effective and should help to improve our relative strength. We cannot afford to accept losses on a ship for ship basis, but will have to take some risks in order to strike the enemy a blow from time to time. The morale of the Fleet and of the nation demands it, and it is only in this way that we can keep some of the enemy diverted to the defensive instead of permitting him to take offensive measures against us at will. Aside from raids on positions, we should make sweeps in force (not less than two carrier groups) in areas where inferior enemy forces and supply ships are likely to be. As our battleships become available they can be advanced as supporting "strong points" on which the fast groups could retire.[21]

These leaders were resigned to accept the reality that the Philippines and South Pacific were lost, at least for now. Rear Admiral Milo F. Draemel, the Commander Destroyers, Battle Force, said, "We were to fight a holding war—but there was little to do the holding with…. The crucial and critical time of the Pacific War would be when the Japanese attempted to take the North Pacific and it was necessary to husband every ounce of strength to meet that challenge. If we should fail in that challenge, the whole Pacific—our West Coast—would be open to them."[22]

With such a dismal command situation, it was no surprise that at first Nimitz did not sleep well, and wrote, "To me it seems like I am on a treadmill—whirling around actively but not getting anywhere very fast."[23] Nimitz soon settled into a routine, getting up at 0630, eating breakfast at 0715, and then heading off to his Pacific Fleet headquarters at the submarine base. He lunched at the BOQ with one or two officers and then returned to the office until 1800. At home he ate with Kimmel and Pye, and then relaxed with them in a game of cribbage or the like. Though Kimmel and Pye were tainted by their unfortunate fates, Nimitz maintained his friendship with them.[24]

At 1000 on December 31, on the deck of the USS *Grayling* moored alongside the submarine wharf, Admiral Nimitz took command of CINCPAC as his 4-star flag was hoisted up the mast. He was wearing his submariner's dolphins as he delivered a short speech to the officers and newsmen in which he said, "We have taken a tremendous wallop, but I have no doubt as to the ultimate outcome."[25]

Later that day, Nimitz held a conference with the staff officers of Admirals Kimmel, Pye, and Draemel. With gloom in the air as the attendees anticipated being relegated to backwater billets, Nimitz surprised the group by saying that he had complete confidence in them and wanted them to stay on because he did not blame them for what happened at Pearl Harbor. He had selected Rear Admiral Milo F. Draemel as his chief of staff, and he retained Captain Charles H. McMorris as war plans officer and Lieutenant Commander Edwin T. Layton as head of intelligence.[26]

Nimitz's boss began to engage formally with him. Shortly after taking his oath as COMINCH on the 30th, Admiral King issued the following message to the Navy: "The way to victory is long. The going will be hard. We will do the best we can with what we've got. We must have more planes and ships at once. Then it will be our turn to strike. We will win though in time."[27]

On the 31st, Admiral King issued Nimitz his first orders. Nimitz was directed to defend vital military areas, halt the Japanese advances, keep the lines of communication with Australia open, and mount offensive attacks against the Japanese with his three aircraft carriers, *Enterprise*, *Lexington* and *Saratoga*, and other warships available to him in the Pacific. King also recommended to Nimitz that he stage raids against the Gilberts and the Mandates (after World War I, the League of Nations had granted Japan a mandate over the Caroline, Marshall, and Mariana Islands in the central Pacific). Taking aggressive action, Admiral King had already ordered the carrier *Yorktown*, 3 battleships, 9 destroyers, and 12 old submarines to end convoy duty in the Atlantic and rejoin the Pacific Fleet. The *Yorktown* had sailed into San Diego Harbor on December 30.[28]

On January 2 COMINCH sent Nimitz message 021718 stating, "Urge your thorough consideration of expedition of raid in character against enemy bases in Gilbert Islands probably Makin and or in Ellice and Phoenix Groups either as separate operation or preferably coordinated with Samoa reinforcement expedition in order to first cover latter second check increasing enemy threat to Samoa dash Fiji area third undertake some aggressive action for fleet on general morale." CINCPAC fired back his response (message 022235) "Operations proposed your 021718 contemplated and under consideration."[29]

The CINCPAC staff published on January 2, 1942, a secret document titled *Employment of Carrier Task Forces in January*. It was compiled from Pye's previous "Estimate" that had been prepared on December 24 and corrected on the 28th. The enemy situation from the latest intelligence revealed:

(1) The Far East offensives are occupying practically all of the amphibious forces of the enemy plus 3 or 4 carriers, 2 BBs, about 13 cruisers, about one-third of his destroyers, some submarines and many auxiliary types.

(2) Since the Pearl Harbor raid on the 7th the Japanese First Fleet units and carriers have apparently remained west of the Eastern Marshalls.
(3) Carrier air groups are being refitted or exchanged.
(4) There are about fifteen submarines at sea from the Hawaiian area to the West Coast.
(5) The enemy is consolidated at an air base at Makin and is extending his air activities to New Guinea and, at one time, to the Ellice Islands. He has bombed Ocean Island several times and Nauru at least once.
(6) There are increasing indications of converted raiders and tenders being at large. Known enemy action since the raid on Oahu has been:
(7) The sustained bombing and capture of Wake—with at least one carrier.
(8) Surface ship shelling of Midway and Johnston, and submarine shelling of Johnston, Palmyra, and outlying main islands of the Hawaiian Group.
(9) Sinking of three cargo ships in this general area and three or four on the West Coast.

The U.S. Pacific Fleet situation was stated as follows:

(1) Battleships:
   a. *Pennsylvania* will be ready in mid–January,
   b. *Maryland* about 20 January,
   c. *Tennessee* about 5 February,
   d. *Colorado* 1 February,
   e. Batdiv Three probably by the end of the month. This means that no battleships will be available during the greater part of the month.
(2) Carrier Task Forces:
   TF 11 *Lexington* Vice Admiral Wilson Brown
   Departed Pearl Harbor Dec 29 covering Johnston-Palmyra line; returning Jan. 3.
   TF 14 *Saratoga* Vice Admiral Fairfax Leary
   Departed Pearl Harbor Dec 31 covering Midway area; returning Jan 13.
   TF 8 *Enterprise* Vice Admiral William F. Halsey Jr.
   At Pearl Harbor. Planned to depart Jan. 3 remaining in Oahu vicinity from 3–7 Jan.
   TF 17 *Yorktown* Rear Admiral Frank Jack Fletcher
   At or near San Diego. Departing S.D. for Samoa about 6 Jan. escorting 3 AP, 1 AK, 1 AE, 1 AO. Arriving Jan. 20, Some covering operation has been tentatively planned.
   Other Pacific Forces are engaged in escort, and local anti-submarine operations; 1 on defensive patrol, 3 to Marshalls, 3 off Japan; patrol planes engaged in patrols from Oahu. Some unit must keep and others engaged in some training. The US Asiatic Naval Forces have been retired to the Malay Barrier and are preparing to move to Darwin [Australia] if necessary.
(3) The primary mission from directives that have been issued is: "To safeguard our territory and communications lines." COMINCH stressed the statement and indicated the first priority to the Midway-Hawaii and Hawaii-Mainland lines, and only slightly less to the Hawaii-Samoa line, extending to Suva as soon as practicable.

The estimates of enemy intentions in this report were displayed in order of priority as follows:

(1) The prosecution of the offensives in the Far East until all of Malaysia, Philippines, and N.E.I. have been captured. In this will probably be included Rangoon.
(2) Consolidation of this territory.
(3) Advance upon Australia.
   While these are going on:
(4) Continue submarine raids on our forces and communications, minor attacks against outlying islands and Alaska.
(5) Cruiser raids against the routes to Australia, and possibly to the Mainland.
(6) Capture Samoa.
(7) Capture Canton.

(8) Capture Suva.
(9) Attack with strong forces, including carriers, for demolition Johnston, Palmyra, Midway.
(10) Sweeps in force along our communications to outlying islands; along our route to Mainland.
(11) Carrier raids on West Coast; Attacks for capture of Midway, Palmyra; main Hawaiian Islands; Oahu.

The next section of the report listed the expected "courses of action" that would be taken during the month of January by the Pacific carrier forces. On September 24 an update was provided with the actual final decisions by CINCPAC regarding the employment of the carrier task forces:

> Task Force Eleven sailed on January 7 to cover the Johnston-Midway line; returned on 16th; sailed again on 19th to cover Christmas-Palmyra line; was on January 21 ordered to attack Wake; then, when Neches was sunk, was ordered to return to Pearl.
> Task Force Fourteen carrier, Saratoga, was hit by one torpedo; returned on 13th; out of action for several months.
> Task Force Eight sailed on 11th to cover Samoa; then to make an attack on the Marshall-Gilberts after the reloading was completed.
> Task Force Seventeen was to make an attack in conjunction with Task Force Eight. Final order to depart Samoa for attack just as troops were disembarked. This will make the attacks (Jaluit, Mille, Makin) about January 31.[30]

Nimitz and his new boss would now have to work together to defeat the Japanese war machine. Admiral King had attended the Washington Arcadia Conference meeting, which began on December 23, 1941, where Roosevelt and British Prime Minister Winston Churchill had confirmed the standing "Germany First" policy. Admiral King was strongly opposed to relegating the Pacific War against Japan to a secondary theater. As it turned out, King was fairly satisfied with the actual wording of the Arcadia Agreement, which had authorized that he could "safeguard vital interests" and seize "vantage points" in the Pacific from which a counteroffensive against Japan could be developed. In King's mind the interpretation was that the U.S. Navy could go on the offensive against the Japanese with the limited naval resources that were available.

If Roosevelt had any thoughts that Admiral King would relegate the U.S. Navy into a purely defensive role after the likes of the Pearl Harbor attack, he had selected the wrong man. Although not a warm person, Ernest J. King commanded the respect of all those he had worked with. One day someone asked King if he had said, "When they get in trouble they send for the sonsabitches." He responded that it was not his quote, but he indicated he would have said it if he had thought of it. It was Navy Secretary Frank Knox who wrote on December 23, 1941, of King, "Lord how I need him."[31]

While the other British and American planners would not dare to go on the offensive, King lobbied for just such a move. It was King who wrote, "No fighter ever won his fight by covering up, merely fending off the other fellow's blows. The winner hits and keeps on hitting even though he has to be able to take some stiff blows in order to keep on hitting."[32] This was the man who would lead the American Naval Forces with his audacious strategy.

Ernest Joseph King was born in a Calvinist home 100 yards from Lake Erie in Lorain, Ohio, on November 23, 1878. His father was in shipping in Great Lakes schooners, which influenced his like of the sea. As a boy of 10 he became interested in a Navy career from an article in the *Youth's Companion Magazine* about the Naval Academy. He graduated from Lorain High School in 1897 and was appointed to the Naval Academy by Ohio Representative Kerr. When he was leaving home, his father, a railroad mechanic, gave him a round-trip ticket just in case he wanted to change his mind. He never did.

As a Naval cadet in the summer of 1898, he served aboard the USS *San Francisco* during the Spanish-American War. King graduated from Annapolis fourth in the Class of 1901 and served two years of sea duty before being commissioned an ensign on June 7, 1903. He next served in various sea and shore commands. In 1914 he got his first command as captain of the destroyer *Terry* with the rank of lieutenant commander. In 1918 he was promoted to the rank of captain, and the next year commanded the Postgraduate School at the Naval Academy. After more successful commands, in 1923 he began a 3-year tour as the commander of the submarine base at New London, Connecticut. By this point in his career he had commanded destroyers, submarines, and battleships.

Believing in the future of naval aviation, in May of 1927, at age 50, King earned his aviator wings at a shortened course at NAS Pensacola. The next year he served as assistant chief under Rear Admiral William A. Moffett, who was known as the "Air Admiral" for his leadership of the Navy's Bureau of Aeronautics. King took command of the Navy's first carrier, the USS *Lexington*, in June 1930. After several senior aviation commands, in February 1941 he was promoted to the rank of admiral as Commander in Chief Atlantic Fleet.[33]

Though a brilliant military strategist and organizer, King developed a well-deserved reputation for being rude, abrasive, and argumentative, and was loathed by many officers with whom he served. He was called "an egotist, intellectually arrogant and supremely confident in his ability to distinguish truth and righteousness and to reduce the complex to the simplest terms."[34] A Naval Academy professor noted his weaknesses to be "other men's wives, alcohol, and intolerance." At work he "seemed always to be angry or annoyed." One of his six daughters confirmed that opinion of her father as "the most even-tempered man in the Navy. He is always in a rage." Roosevelt said King was as a man who "shaves every morning with a blow torch."[35]

Back on December 30 there was a change in command on the *Saratoga*. Rear Admiral Frank Jack Fletcher left his flagship *Astoria* for the new *Yorktown* Task Force 17 assembling at San Diego. Rear Admiral Fairfax Leary, a non-aviator, broke out his two-star flag aboard the *Saratoga*. Admiral Fitch reluctantly went ashore as Halsey's administrative representative for Aircraft, Battle Group. His important role was to take on handling of supplies and material for all the carrier squadrons based on Oahu.[36]

Until the *Yorktown* arrived, Nimitz had his three carrier task groups to use for any immediate Pacific operation: the *Saratoga* (Task Force 14), commanded by Leary; the *Lexington* (Task Force 11), commanded by Vice Admiral Wilson Brown; and the *Enterprise* (Task Force 8), under Vice Admiral William F. Halsey, Jr.

By early January 1942, U.S. submarine and other intelligence had revealed a pattern to the movements of the Japanese Fourth Fleet based in Truk in the Mandates. That fleet had been reinforced by the Eighth Cruiser Division and the Second Carrier Division. The Japanese fleet submarine commander based at Jaluit in the Marshall Islands had a significant number of submarines operating near Hawaii and in the eastern Pacific. Also, there were reported raids by cruisers and converted merchantmen vessels against four islands in the Gilbert Islands. Makin Island had been taken unopposed by the Japanese on December 9 and was being used as a base for reconnaissance seaplanes. There were even indications that a full air base was being developed there.

While the Japanese Navy was engaged in attacks against Borneo, the Celebes, and other islands to the west and southwest Pacific, there were clear indicators that they would attack to the southwest of the mandated areas like Samoa, Suva in the Fijis, or Canton Island. If the Japanese were successful in such operations, northeastern approaches to Australia would be threatened and a potential invasion of Australia was eventually possible.

At this point Nimitz had intelligence that two airfields had been constructed on Enybor Island north of Jaluit in the Marshalls, each with a hangar capable of housing 20 medium-sized planes. There were camouflaged storehouses, as well as gasoline and fuel-oil storage tanks at these two fields. Next to the administration buildings there were shore batteries running three-quarters of a mile along the waterfront street called Marine Parade.

After evaluating the intelligence, Admiral Nimitz concurred with Admiral King's recommendation that it was time for an aggressive attack against the Marshall Islands before the Japanese gained more strength in the Mandates. In response to Admiral King's directive to protect U.S. shipping between the U.S. and Australia as far south as Samoa, 5000 Marines were embarked aboard transports in San Diego harbor, bound for Samoa. Nimitz ordered the *Yorktown* to escort the transports.[37]

Portrait of Admiral Ernest J. King, USN. Photograph taken in 1945 (official U.S. Navy photograph, now in the collections of the National Archives, Catalog #: 80-G-416886).

On January 2, Nimitz's staff submitted plans for carrier strikes against the Marshalls and Gilberts. Vice Admiral William S. Pye, the former commander of the Battle Fleet, discussed the assumption that the Japanese, "by means of agents communicating via Mexico,"[38] knew about the reinforcement expedition for Samoa, which would necessitate the need for a second carrier to cover the arrival of the Marines on Samoa. Once the Marines were safely landed on Samoa, the two carriers could head to attack the Marshalls and Gilberts.

In developing war plans, Nimitz listened to the advice and opinions of his senior officers. While some felt the planning conferences were too divided and loudly defended, Rear Admiral Raymond A. Spruance strongly approved of the sessions and said the change in atmosphere was "like being in a stuffy room and having someone open a window and let in a breath of fresh air."[39]

The proposed attack plan for the Marshalls and Gilberts was opposed by most of the officers on the grounds that carriers should not be sent against land targets. There would be no element of surprise such as existed at Pearl Harbor, because certainly the Japanese knew the U.S. would counterattack the nearest bases to Pearl Harbor. The most vocal opposition of the raids was from Rear Admiral Claude Bloch, the commandant of the 14th Naval District. He had been passed over for Kimmel, who lost the Pacific Fleet battleships, and now he was unhappy to see another CINCPAC named Nimitz pushing a plan that could lose the Pacific carriers.

When Halsey's *Enterprise* Task Force 8 returned to Pearl Harbor on January 7 from an uneventful patrol to the west, Halsey was astonished at the opposition to Pye's plan. Barging into the CINCPAC conference, he cleared the air and was openly passionate in his support of the plan and volunteered to lead it. Nimitz was endeared to Halsey for his open support. Much later, when Halsey was being criticized, Nimitz said, "Bill Halsey came to my support and offered to lead the attack. I'll not be party to any enterprise that can hurt the reputation of a man like that."[40]

In response to King's request (081856) for the estimated date of the reinforcement expedition to Samoa, on January 9 Nimitz answered in his 090445 message that the target date of 20 January was set for the reinforcement. The CINCPAC also related that Task Force 8 would depart Pearl Harbor on 11 January to operate in coordination with Task Force 17 to cover the arrival at Samoa. Afterwards both the task forces would make simultaneous air attacks on the Gilberts and the Eastern Marshalls during the first week of February. Nimitz assured King that the offensive operations would not begin until the expedition was ensured and thus "to avoid [a] serious situation that would arise if one carrier were damaged 2,000 miles from the base while operating without other carrier support."[41]

On January 9, Halsey was called by Nimitz to meet at CINCPAC headquarters. At the session Nimitz discussed the implementation of Pye's plan. After he covered the attack plan, Nimitz asked Halsey, "How does that sound? It's a rare opportunity." Halsey agreed to the plan, but he recalled that he answered with "something less than enthusiasm." With Nimitz's gratitude, Halsey, with his *Enterprise* task force, would escort the *Yorktown* group to Samoa, and then proceed to raid the Marshall and Gilbert Islands. Nimitz also tasked the *Lexington*, under Vice Admiral Wilson Brown, to strike Wake Island, while the *Saratoga* would watch over Hawaii. The next day Halsey dropped by the CINCPAC headquarters to see Nimitz. Nimitz walked Halsey down to the wharf. As Halsey stepped into the barge, Nimitz said, "All sorts of luck to you, Bill!"[42]

The plans were now set for the first American carrier raid in the Pacific against the Japanese since the war began only 31 days before.

Chapter 2

Marshall and Gilbert Islands

I must say that the enemy's attack was bold and audacious...

With orders issued by Admiral Nimitz in hand, Admiral Halsey was taking his *Enterprise* carrier Task Force 8 and Fletcher's *Yorktown* Task Force 17 to raid the southern Marshalls and northern Gilbert Islands. Halsey would be able to utilize his air attack and ship bombardment assets to engage in priority sequence combatant ships, aircraft (especially those on the ground or in the water), tenders, other ships, aircraft support facilities, fuel tanks, power stations, radio installations, troop concentrations, and storehouses.[1]

There was no more qualified carrier commander in the U.S. Navy to lead the Marshall and Gilbert Islands raid than Vice Admiral William Frederick Halsey, Jr. He was the man for his time and this place. He would soon become the most acclaimed American admiral in the war for his extremely aggressive drive based on his instincts. He was unique and a sailors' sailor.

Halsey was born into a Navy family in 1882 and, like many others of his background, followed in his father's footsteps to attend the Naval Academy in Annapolis. While there he excelled in athletics, lettering in football, and served as the president of the Athletic Association. But he was no scholar, and he graduated 42nd in a class of sixty-two. In the years from 1909 to 1932, Halsey gained an incredible amount of sea time serving as captain of 12 different torpedo boats and destroyers, commander of three destroyer divisions, and executive officer of the battleship USS *Wyoming*. His shore duty assignments were in the Office of Naval Intelligence in Washington, and as naval attaché at the American Embassy in Berlin, Germany, with additional duty as naval attaché in Christiana, Norway; Copenhagen, Denmark; and Stockholm, Sweden.

In 1932 Captain Halsey was a student at the Naval War College. In 1934, at age 52, he made a major career change within the U.S. Navy by reporting to Naval Air Station Pensacola for flight training. He gained his wings as a naval aviator on May 15, 1935, and became captain of the USS *Saratoga* for two years. Next, he was the commanding officer of Pensacola Naval Air Station in 1937.

Finally elevated to flag rank in 1938, Halsey commanded carrier divisions in the Atlantic and Pacific. He received his third star as vice admiral in June 1940 and became Commander of the Fleet Aircraft Battle Force based at Pearl Harbor.[2]

On his new mission, Halsey first had to screen Fletcher's escort, Task Force 17, carrying the Marine transports to Samoa before dealing with the planned raid. The *Enterprise* crew carried supplies onboard, as one Scouting Six pilot remarked, like they were "loading for bear," until they sailed out of Pearl Harbor at noon on Sunday, January 11, 1942.[3]

Since departing Pearl on December 31, Rear Admiral Fairfax Leary's Task Force 14 had been on patrol in the Midway area with 2 heavy cruisers and 6 destroyers. The ships with *Saratoga* had been enduring a mainly boring mission, zigzagging at 7 to 12 knots. Boredom would soon turn to stark terror on the flight deck. On the afternoon of January 10, the task force was steaming on a southeasterly course towards a rendezvous with Halsey when a TBD from Torpedo Squadron Three had a spectacular landing approach. As the *Saratoga* was pitching steeply in the high seas, the stern rose abruptly just as the TBD, flown by Ensign Earle C. Gullen, reached the rear of the ship. His plane was torn in half when it hit the stern, leaving the back half of the plane in the sea and the engine and cockpit spinning down the desk. Incredibly, Ensign Gullen sustained only a broken leg.

The next day, January 11, was not so lucky for the *Saratoga*. As the carrier bounced in the waves 420 miles southwest of Pearl, at 1915 there was a terrible explosion from a torpedo launched by a Japanese submarine, the *I-6*. The torpedo had slammed into the port side of the *Saratoga*, causing a list to port. The ship's damage control team soon had the situation under control. Leary had to cancel his rendezvous with Halsey and set a course toward Pearl, making 16 knots. A CAP (Combat Air Patrol) was launched the next morning at dawn. Although three firerooms had been flooded, killing six sailors, the carrier reached Oahu under her own power on the 13th. Subsequently, the *Saratoga* sailed to the Bremerton Navy Yard in Puget Sound for permanent repairs. The *Saratoga* was unavailable for active service until her return to Pearl Harbor on June 6, 1942.[4]

Portrait of Fleet Admiral William F. Halsey, USN. Photograph dated 6 February 1946 (official U.S. Navy photograph, now in the collections of the National Archives, Catalog #: 80-G-701920).

The first day out of Pearl, Halsey received the news that the *Saratoga* had been hit. Nimitz was down one carrier. The initial days out of Pearl were not good ones as mishaps and accidents were prevalent aboard the *Enterprise*. On the 13th a pilot broke radio silence, putting the task force at risk of detection, and on the 14th a sailor was lost overboard on the destroyer *Blue*. Two days later a sailor was killed by accident on the *Salt Lake City*; a Dauntless aircraft crashed on landing, killing ACMM George F. Lawhon; and a Devastator from Torpedo Squadron Six vanished. Miraculously, the crew of 3 from the Devastator had crash-landed at sea and finally washed ashore on Pukapuka Island (which was 750 miles from where they had ditched the plane) after 34 days.

Despite the unfavorable start, the *Enterprise* and TF 8 arrived on Monday, January 19, and took up their station 100 miles north of Samoa as scheduled. They sailed back and forth for five days as air patrols were launched to the northwest for any sign of the Japanese, and to the southeast looking for the *Yorktown* TF 17 and her Marine transports.[5]

The U.S. Navy aircraft carrier USS *Saratoga* (CV-3) in 1943/44. The photograph was taken from one of her planes of Carrier Air Group 12 (CVG-12), of which many aircraft are visible on deck: Douglas SBD Dauntless dive bombers (aft), Grumman F6F Hellcat fighters (mostly forward), and Grumman TBF Avenger torpedo bombers (U.S. Navy National Museum of Naval Aviation photograph No. 1977.031.085.056).

The transit of the *Yorktown* with Task Force 17 under Rear Admiral Frank Jack Fletcher had not gone without its share of problems. At San Diego a 4,798-man force of the 2nd Marine Brigade had embarked aboard former Matson liners *Monterey*, *Matsonia*, and *Lurline* and sailed on January 6 at 1045. With support ships including oiler *Kaskaskia* (AO-27), ammunition ship *Lassen* (AE-3) and cargo ship *Jupiter* (AK-43), the *Yorktown* sailed with her other task force vessels *Louisville* (CA-28), *St. Louis* (CL-49), and the destroyers *Russell*, *Walke*, *Hughes*, and *Sims*.

After only one day out of San Diego, problems had just begun for fighter squadron VF-42. First, Ensign Edgar R. Bassett put his F4F into the barrier. Then, on the 8th, Ensign William S. Woollen lost power on takeoff and crashed into the sea. He was rescued by the *Russell*. The 12th saw Ensign Walter A. Haas crash into the sea, to be picked up by the *Walke*. On the morning of the 14th, Ensign Richard L. Wright crashed on takeoff, likewise picked up by the *Walke*. Thankfully, there were no pilots lost, but the mishaps had resulted in the loss of three fighter aircraft.

One man was lost overboard on the 12th from the *Yorktown*. Later, on January 17, there were serious problems during refueling operations between the oiler *Kaskaskia* and the *Yorktown*. The two vessels scraped sides on two occasions that day, causing damage to both the carrier and the oiler. Subsequent refueling operations were improved as Task Force 17 headed toward Samoa.[6]

Commanding Task Force 17 was one of the most unusual naval leaders in the service. Frank Jack Fletcher was born on April 29, 1885, to an upper-middle-class family in Marshalltown, Iowa. He grew up in a 6,000-square-foot house at 202 Church Street built by his grandfather. He attended public schools and played football for Marshalltown High School, graduating with a class of 29 students. He was appointed to Annapolis in 1902 by Senator Jonathan Dolliver and graduated from the Naval Academy on February 12, 1906, ranked 26th in a class of 116 midshipmen. After serving his required two years at sea, he was commissioned an ensign on February 13, 1908.[7]

Vice Admiral Frank Jack Fletcher, USN, photographed on board ship, 17 September 1942 (official U.S. Navy photograph, now in the collections of the U.S. National Archives, Catalog #: 80-G-14193).

In November 1909 Fletcher served aboard the USS *Chancey*, part of a unit in the Asiatic Torpedo Flotilla, followed in April 1910 as the commanding officer of the destroyer USS *Dale*. In the spring battle practice in 1911, his destroyer placed first among 22 destroyers and won the gunnery trophy. His uncle, Captain Frank Friday Fletcher, wrote his father, "I am more proud of his having won this trophy than if I had won it myself."[8] In March 1912 he was assigned back to the USS *Chancey* as its commanding officer. That December he was transferred to the battleship USS *Florida*. During the occupation of Veracruz, Mexico, in April 1914, led by uncle Rear Admiral Frank Friday Fletcher, Lieutenant Frank Jack Fletcher commanded the SS *Esperanza*, a chartered mail ship, which evacuated 350 civilians to safety while enduring gunfire. Later on he ran a train that brought foreigners from the interior, negotiating safe passage with the Mexican authorities. He was cited for gallantry by his uncle and in 1915 the Navy upgraded the award to the Medal of Honor.

In July of 1914 Fletcher became aide and flag lieutenant on the staff of the Commander in Chief U.S. Atlantic Fleet. The following year he returned to the Naval Academy for duty in the Executive Department. With the outbreak of World War I, he served as gunnery officer for the USS *Kearsarge* until September 1917, when he took command of the yacht *Margaret* (SP-527) of the Scout Patrol, which was a collection of converted civilian ships known as the "Suicide Fleet." He was towing another ship that was in worse shape than his *Margaret*. One of the officers observed that Fletcher "was the kind of officer to say 'orders are orders' and fight a rowboat against a sixteen-inch gun, trusting to his own skill to pull him through. And that skill was superb. Many a time, save for his flawless seamanship, the *Maggie* might have ended her career as a warship a good deal earlier than she did."[9]

In February 1918 he was assigned to the USS *Allen*, and in May took command of the destroyer USS *Benham* on convoy duty in the North Atlantic. On July 22 the *Benham* was damaged in a collision with the destroyer *Jarvis*. Fletcher was cleared of any blame in a court of inquiry. In 1920 he received the Navy Cross for his gallantry and distinguished service. In the early 1920s as part of the Asiatic Fleet, Fletcher commanded the old gunboat *Sacramento*, two sub tenders, and the Cavite submarine base. For two years beginning in 1929 he was the executive officer of the battleship *Colorado*. During his tour the ship collided with a passenger steamer. The steamer's skipper was declared at fault.

While serving aboard the *Colorado*, Fletcher curiously enrolled for flight training. As a solid black-shoe officer, he might have felt there was a possible chance that promotion was faster going with naval aviation than climbing up the always-crowded "black-shoe" battleship route. Fletcher had been around aviation earlier in his career. As a lieutenant at Veracruz in 1914, he had observed the first American aerial combat missions. In 1919, commanding the destroyer USS *Gridley*, he served as one of the many ships along the route of the transatlantic flights of NC flying boats. Off the Azores on May 17, his destroyer helped to direct the NC-4 by signals, the only plane to reach the Azores. He later acted as the guard ship for the final leg of the flight of NC-4 to England. Fletcher's eyesight was too poor for pilot training, so he did not end up as a naval aviator or an observer.

In June 1930, Fletcher completed the senior course at the Naval War College in Newport, Rhode Island, and completed the Army War College the following year. In August 1931, Captain Fletcher was named the chief of staff for the Commander in Chief of the Asiatic Fleet, Montgomery Meigs Taylor. In September that year, the Japanese invaded Manchuria and soon began an incursion into southern China. Fletcher experienced firsthand the Japanese actions and gained valuable naval diplomacy skills. In 1936 Fletcher reached the much sought-after battleship command of the *New Mexico*. With the help of subordinates like Lieutenant Hyman G. Rickover, Fletcher received the engineering trophy for the second and third years in a row, while taking two of the three top prizes in gunnery. He received commendation for refueling destroyers with oil during a severe storm in the Aleutian Islands, earning praise in a "smart seamanship manner." One of his former officers called him a "very, very fine naval officer."[10]

In November 1939, Fletcher was promoted to rear admiral, the 8th member for his class of 1906 to be "frocked." He was assigned as commander of Cruiser Division (Crudiv) Three, part of Cruisers, Battle Force, U.S. Fleet, based on the West Coast. In June 1940, Fletcher moved up to Crudiv Six, one of three heavy cruiser divisions in the Scouting Force, U.S. Fleet. This division was made up of the *New Orleans*, *Astoria*, *Minneapolis*, and *San Francisco*, powerful ten-thousand-ton ships commissioned in 1934.

As December 1941 came around, 56-year-old Jack Fletcher had already served the Navy for 39 years, with 22 of those years at sea. He was described as being of medium height, slender, fit, with a ruddy and weathered complexion, black hair, high forehead, "smiling brown eyes," and a "sunny disposition and hearty laugh."[11]

As a complete surprise to almost all of his senior naval peers, on December 15, the very day that the USS *Saratoga* finally reached Pearl Harbor from San Diego, Admiral Kimmel with CINCPAC Op-Ord 39-41 placed Fletcher in command of Task Force 14, the Wake Island relief force.[12]

On January 19 at 0300, Fletcher detached the troop liners to sail to Pago Pago, Samoa, at 20 knots escorted by destroyers *Walke* and *Hughes* under air patrol cover. The next day at 1230 he received word that the Marines were commencing disembarkation. After providing daily air patrols and covering the Marine disembarkation, the *Yorktown* Task Force 17 departed Pago Pago on January 25 to join with Halsey's Task Force 8. Fletcher's Task Force 17 with the *Yorktown* was positioned 150 miles astern of Halsey's Task Force 8 with the *Enterprise*.

The first day out leaving the Samoa area, Lieutenant (JG) C.T. Fogg of Scouting Six from the *Enterprise* sighted a four-engine flying boat on his patrol. Though the contact displayed no enemy markings, since Japanese planes of that type were known to be in the area, Fogg flew up next to the flying boat, but received no answer to the recognition signals. He fired a burst of warning shots cross the contact s path, but still no response. He then fired on the "enemy" target. When the first bullet had entered the fuselage, the hatch was quickly opened, and the flag of New Zealand was streamed out. The friendly crew showed the "V" for Victory sign from other ports. Thankfully, Halsey's force had not been spotted.[13]

Now the *Yorktown* and *Enterprise* carrier task forces were sailing northwest toward the Marshalls some 1600 miles away. They would soon be engaging the Japanese garrisons of Vice Admiral Shigeyoshi Inoue, commander of the 4th Fleet. Inoue had command over all the Japanese naval forces in the Marshalls and the Gilberts, better known as the South Seas Force. The aircraft in these islands belonged to the 24th Air Flotilla under Rear Admiral Gotō Eiji.[14] The flotilla had 33 carrier fighters, 9 land attack planes, and 9 flying boats. The rest of the aircraft of the air flotilla were operating from Truk and Rabaul to the south to provide air support for the invasion of the Bismarck archipelago. These assets conducted daily long-range patrols from the major bases for early warning protection.

The two principal aviation units of the 24th Air Flotilla were the Chitose Air Group and the Yokohama Air Group. The authorized inventory of the Chitose Air Group was 36 obsolete twin-engine land attack Mitsubishi G2M2 Type 96 medium bombers and 48 Mitsubishi A5M4 Type 96 carrier fighters. The Yokohama Air Group was equipped with large Kawanishi H6K4 Type 97 flying boats used for long-range patrol.

The distribution of Japanese aircraft at their attack locations was as follows:

Roi in Kwajalein Atoll at the Chitose Air Group headquarters commanded by Captain Ohashi Fujiro—18 Type 96 carrier planes led by senior pilot (group leader) Lieutenant Commander Igarashi Chikamasa.

Taroa in Maloelap Atoll with a detachment of the Chitose Air Group under the command of Lieutenant Kurakane Yoshio (division leader)—15 Type 96 carrier fighters (under direct control of Kurakane), 9 Type 96 land attack fighters led by Lieutenant Nakai Kazuo (division leader).

Jaluit (Emidj) with a detachment of the Yokohama Air Group—6 Type 97 flying boats led by Lieutenant Commander Koizumi Sanemiro (division leader).

Makin Atoll in the Gilberts at a detachment of the Yokohama Air Group—3 Type 97 flying boats led by Lieutenant Sakaki Usamu (division leader).[15]

The final Marshall-Gilbert attack plans as they developed for the operation were intricate in their detail. Aboard the *Enterprise*, Halsey and his chief of staff, Commander Miles Browning, developed the plan for the raid. From Samoa the two task forces would sail to the vicinity of Howland Island for refueling on January 28. Task Force 8 with *Enterprise* would launch attacks in the northern Marshalls against Wotje Island in the Wotje Atoll, Taroa in the Maloelap Atoll, and Roi and Kwajalein islands in the Kwajalein Atoll on February 1 at 15 minutes before sunrise. Their bombardment group (TG 8.1) commanded by Rear Admiral Raymond Spruance, made up of the *Northampton*, *Salt Lake City*, and *Dunlap*, were to shell Wotje, while Maloelap and Taroa were to be shelled by the *Chester*, *Balch*, and *Maury* (TG 8.3 under Captain Thomas M. Shock).

Admiral Fletcher's Task Force 17 organization consisted of the Striking Group (17.1) of the *Yorktown*, *Louisville*, and *St. Louis*, with the Support Group (17.2) of destroyers *Hughes*, *Sims*, *Russell*, and *Walke*, and the Fueling Group (17.3) *Sabine* and escorting destroyer *Mahan*. They were ordered to launch an air attack against Japanese forces on Makin in the Gilberts and the islands of Jaluit and Milli in the southern Marshalls.[16]

Back on December 24 at 0930, Lieutenant Commander Gordon Benbow "Dizzy" Rainer took the submarine USS *Dolphin* out of Pearl Harbor on its first war patrol to Area 21, the East Marshall Islands. The *Dolphin* was on-station by January 1 and began reconnoitering the islands of the atolls at Jaluit, Namorick, Ailinglapalap, Arno, and Maloelap. Though continuing to gather critical intelligence of Japanese activity in the Marshalls, the *Dolphin* experienced significant mechanical problems. Plagued by 38 reported equipment defects, on January 24 the *Dolphin* sent this message to the Commander Submarines, Pacific Fleet, Rear Admiral Thomas Withers, Jr.: "Radio trunk is flooded and using jury rig antenna. Vessel is unable to carry out orders having reached limit of material endurance. Attempting to make repairs."[17]

After receipt of the message, Withers ordered the *Dolphin* back to Pearl. Having endured the strain of the war patrol and the frustration of equipment failures, Rainer suffered a nervous breakdown and informally turned over command to his executive officer, Lieutenant Bernard Ambrose Clarey, for the remainder of the patrol. The *Dolphin* departed for Pearl at 1906 on the 27th.[18]

The day after Christmas 1941, the submarine *Tautog* departed Pearl Harbor for the

Marshalls under the command of Lieutenant Commander Joseph H. Willingham, Jr. After making observations of eight atolls, the *Tautog* reported significant Japanese air and ship activity in the Kwajalein Atoll. On January 13 at 1115, some 15 miles off Kwajalein Island, the submarine attacked a Japanese minesweeper at 1800 yards, firing three torpedoes, but apparently missed. The sub was running low on fresh water, so the patrol was ended early and returned to Pearl on February 4.[19]

On January 27, new intelligence from the Marshall Islands from the submarines *Dolphin* and *Tautog*, detecting significant enemy air and shipping activity at Kwajalein Atoll, reached Halsey. Adding Kwajalein within range of American bombers, the *Enterprise* would have to operate dangerously close to enemy land-based bombers on Wotje and Taroa. It would be a primary objective of Halsey's carriers to destroy the enemy airfields and aircraft on these two islands to protect the vulnerable carriers. Although Kwajalein was only 150 miles west of Wotje, Commander Browning, the brilliant tactician, convinced Halsey to add this to the target list.[20]

The two carrier task forces sailed together for two days to the vicinity northeast of Howland Island to their refueling events on the 28th. At daybreak the smaller gray ships of Task Force 8 refueled from the tanker *Platte* with hoses rigged between the ships. It was not until 2000 in the evening that the *Enterprise* was able to take her turn with the hose to take on the black oil. No heavy ship had ever fueled at night in the open sea. The *Enterprise* was about to conduct the first night refueling of any capital ship in history. To accomplish this task, the 15,000-ton *Platte* steamed in parallel with the 25,000-ton *Enterprise* carrier with just 50 feet separating the two ships, running at speeds between 7 and 12 knots. They had to maintain this operational configuration for 5 hours until the carriers' fuel tanks were full at 0130.

On completion of refueling operations for both task forces, the *Platte* and the *Craven* proceeded to Pearl Harbor, while the *Sabine* and *Mahan* headed eastward in time for a second fueling rendezvous at a point about midway on the return trip, scheduled for 2000 on February 2. The *Sabine's* approach to the second fueling point was to be from the southeastward to avoid possible contact with other units of the task forces during the preceding night.[21]

The next day the two carrier groups separated, and the next morning they moved across the International Date Line into January 31, 1942.

Enterprise Task Force 8 Action

The task forces prepared for the upcoming attack. The *Enterprise*'s Fighting Six installed homemade armor (boilerplate) behind each seat on their Wildcat fighters. Each of Halsey's ships was ordered to be rigged for being towed and for towing. In each of the carriers at 30 knots their four 13-ton propellers revolved 275 times per minute approaching their respective launch points.[22]

Aboard the *Enterprise* the squadrons prepared for the upcoming battle, including the Fighting Six (VF-6). The squadron consisted of 19 pilots and 120 enlisted men with 18 F4F-3s and 3 F4F-3As. The squadron became the first to transition from the Grumman F3F-2 biplane to the Grumman F4F Wildcat in May 1941. The squadron, like all naval aviation squadrons, had two forms of organization, one for flight operations and another for administration on the ground. In 1941 such squadrons maintained a usual strength of 18 fighters, divided for flight duties into three divisions of six planes each. The squadron was led by a commanding officer, an executive officer, and a flight officer. Each division was divided into three sections of two aircraft. The section of two aircraft had a section leader and his wingman.

The rank of the officer did not always determine the section leader, which was determined by flying experience and skill. The commanding officer of VF-6 was Lieutenant Commander Clarence Wade McClusky. He was somewhat old to be on active status in a fighter squadron at age 39. McClusky was a 1926 graduate of the Naval Academy, earning his Navy wings of gold in 1929. His first squadron was VF-1B, the "High Hats" (later renamed Bombing Three, VB-3), stationed aboard the *Saratoga*. He served in several staff positions and taught at the Naval Academy before reporting aboard VF-6 with the *Enterprise* in June 1940. He soon became the executive officer of Fighting Six and the following year took over as commanding officer (CO), responsible for all squadron operations and activities. Like all Navy COs, he was called "captain." McClusky was known as a "level-headed, personable, and direct" officer who was well respected.

The executive officer for VF-6 was Lieutenant Frank Corbin from the 1927 class at the Academy. Corbin started out on submarines, but transferred to aviation, obtaining his wings in 1936. He served in the Training Command, teaching new pilots at NAS Pensacola until he reported to VF-6 in mid–1941.

The third in the squadron hierarchy was the flight officer, Lieutenant (JG) James S. Gray, Jr. He was a civilian pilot and a 1936 graduate of the Naval Academy. In July 1939 he earned his wings and reported to VF-6.

Of the 19 pilots in VF-6, nine had attended the Naval Academy. Of the remaining ten, four were veterans of the aviation cadet program and already held commissions. The squadron had six reservists, and all but one had been aboard the squadron for at least six months. Lieutenant Commander McClusky was proud of his premium squadron and knew they were ready to take on the mission before them. Like all *Enterprise* squadrons, as with those of the *Yorktown* and all Navy carrier squadrons, taking the battle to the enemy was what they were trained for and served to define the very reason for their existence.[23]

The *Enterprise* plan of attack on Roi and Kwajalein called for Scouting Squadron Six VS-6 SBDs to strafe and bomb using a glide attack with 100-pound bombs on the airfield, planes on the ground, hangars, fuel tanks, etc. If there were additional shore facilities, they were to make a second attack, divebombing with 500-pound bombs. The primary objectives for the Air Group Commander and the VB-6 SBDs were any ships discovered at Roi. If none were found, they were to proceed to Kwajalein Island for ship targets with the support of the first division of VT-6 Devastators conducting horizontal bombing. If suitable targets were found or remained for torpedo attacks after the horizontal and divebombing had been completed, the ship was notified and the second division of VT-6 torpedo bombers were to be sent in to attack.

A secondary mission of taking photographs was to be made, if possible, at both locations by two photographic planes with built-in camera (SDBPs) and the Air Group Commander with a small hand-held camera. The remainder of the attack group (12 VF-6 fighters) was directed to attack airfields at Wotje and Maleolap islands (six planes assigned to each airfield), while the remaining six were to maintain combat patrol over the ship. Any other attacks by all planes were to be made if required, depending on the situation.[24]

Halsey's *Enterprise* task force arrived near their attack area and sailed at reduced speed throughout the daylight hours of the 31st. The executive officer of the *Enterprise*, Commander T.P. Jeter, added a little verse to the header of the ships' Plan of the Day: "An eye for an eye, A tooth for a tooth, This Sunday it's our turn to shoot. Remember Pearl Harbor."[25] The task force was alerted to an unknown aircraft that day at 1350 when it passed 34 miles astern and to the south of the rear ships of the task force. Thankfully, the aircraft did not detect the fleet units. Halsey composed a sarcastic note to the Japanese thanking them for missing his task force and arranged to have it dropped the next day.[26]

After sunset the cruisers and carrier separated as the forces increased speed to 25 and 30 knots, respectively. Halsey wrote of his feelings prior to the raid:

> As a commanding officer on the eve of his first action, I felt that I should set an example of composure, but I was so nervous that I took myself to my emergency cabin, out of sight. I couldn't sleep. I tossed and twisted, drank coffee, read mystery stories, and smoked cigarettes. Finally, I gave up and went back to flag plot. There, at about 0300, less than 2 hours before we were due to launch, I received a terrifying report. The staff duty officer, Lieutenant Commander S. Everett Burroughs, Jr., came in from the bridge and announced, "Sir, sand has just blown in my face!"
>
> I have already said that the Marshalls area had long been kapu [tabu, forbidden, keep out]. We knew that our charts were old and we were afraid that they were incomplete and inaccurate as well. (Of course, even the best navigation charts don't show mine fields.) When sand blows onto a ship, there is a strong suggestion that land is close aboard; and when the ship is making 25 knots, there is a further suggestion that the situation will clarify quickly and violently. I could do nothing but tell Evvie to go out and investigate. He returned in a moment, grinning. Suddenly inspired, he had licked his fingers, pressed them against the sand on the deck, and licked them again. The "sand" tasted sweet. On the range-finder platform forward of the bridge, he could dimly make out a sailor stirring a cup.[27]

USS *Enterprise* underway on 12 April 1939 (official U.S. Navy photograph 80-G-463246, U.S. National Archives, National Archives Identifier [NAID] 520587).

As Halsey came to the designated launch point (latitude 10° N, longitude 170° W), the weather and sea state were ideal. At 0300 the aviators of the *Enterprise* were awakened and served a special breakfast. At 0445, located 156 miles off Kwajalein Island, with no wind and a full moon, the *Enterprise* first launched the CAP of 6 F4Fs led by Frank Corbin. They were followed at 0500 by a total of 36 SBDs from VS-6 and VB-6, each loaded with one 500- and two 100-pound bombs. At 0510, nine torpedo bombers (TBD Devastators) from Torpedo Squadron Six (VT-6), loaded with three 500-pound bombs, and one SBD headed down the carrier deck for takeoff. All these aircraft were heading to the Kwajalein and Roi Islands in the Kwajalein Atoll under Commander Howard L. Young, the *Enterprise* Air Group Commander (Young was piloting an SBD-3). At 0610, 6 F4F-3s from VF-6 were launched to Taroa in the Maloelap Atoll. Just six minutes later, another 6 fighters were launched to attack Wotje Island. By 0620 there were 58 aircraft from the *Enterprise* in the first attack wave en route to make sunrise attacks.

At 0645 the Roi Island attackers were some 20 miles northeast of the island at 15,000 feet as the sun rose above the horizon with the full moon setting. The visibility should have been perfect, but the morning mist shrouded Roi Island. The naval aviators did not identify the small strip of land called Roi Island on their small photostatic maps until 0705, ten minutes after sunrise.

The first division of VS-6 planes, led by the squadron skipper, Lieutenant Commander Halsted L. Hopping, began their strafing and glide-bombing attack from 15 miles north of Roi Island at 0705 from 14,000 feet, followed immediately by like attacks by the second and third divisions in succession. There was no prior intelligence of the Roi installations, so target selection was left up to the individual pilots. Apparently the first division came in too slow, considering the amount of heavy antiaircraft fire coming up from the enemy shore batteries. A Japanese Type 96 fighter was able to get under Hopping's plane as he completed his glide-bombing run and shot him down for a sea crash, killing

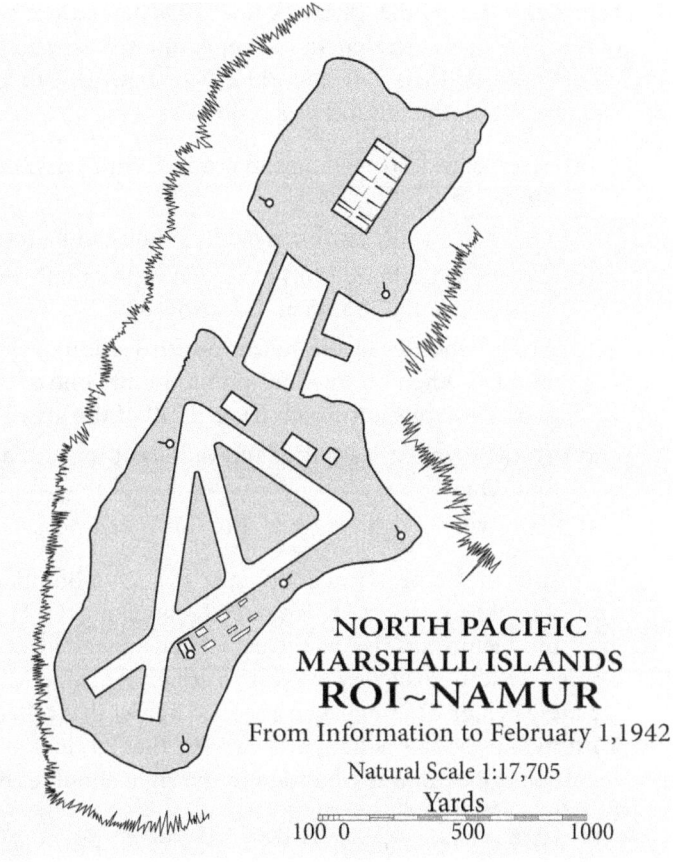

Map of Roi-Namir Island. Image redrawn based on *Early Carrier Raids in the Pacific Ocean, February 1 to March 10, 1942* (Publication Section, Combat Intelligence Branch, Office of Naval Intelligence, United States Navy, 1943, 34).

Hopping and his gunner RM1c H.R. Thomas. Another Japanese fighter shot down in flames a second SBD fighter flown by Ensign E.R. Donnell, Jr., with gunner AMM2c A.J. Travis. A third SBD piloted by Lieutenant (JG) C.T. Fogg, with gunner RM3c O.L. Dennis, was hit by flak in the dive attack and was unable to recover until the plane crossed the island to ditch a half mile north of Roi. A fourth SBD piloted by Ensign D. Seid, with gunner AMM3c D.F. Grogg, was lost either from AA fire or enemy fighter action and believed to have made a controlled, extremely fast, downwind landing at sea a mile north of Roi.

The second division of VS-6 planes had to make a full circle at 10,000 feet to allow the planes from the first division to clear the area before attacking. They came in at 200 knots, followed closely by the third division. All fighters were dropping their 100- and 500-pounders on individual targets as the Japanese fighters engaged. The Americans shot down 3 Japanese fighters, but had lost 4 scouting bomber planes. From 0709 to 0730, VS-6 had encountered 10 Japanese Type 96 fighters. Some aircraft were able to make second attack runs on island shore installations.

Communications were lost between the division attackers during the second and third division attacks. Some planes were engaged with enemy fighters that had taken off before and during the attack. A few SBDs made their second attack runs. The majority of the VS-6 planes strafed and dropped their 100-pound bombs during the attack, while others released their 500-pounders. The damage inflicted on the Japanese installations and aircraft on the ground was as follows:

(a) Six planes destroyed on the ground, with possible others hit in the hangars and strafed area.
(b) One hangar totally destroyed by bombs and another seriously damaged.
(c) One large building (80ft by 200ft) in the southwest section of Roi Island was hit by a 500-pound bomb and destroyed.
(d) Six storehouses in the southwestern section of the island were hit by numerous bombs. When hit by a 100-pound bomb, one of the storehouses blew up with a massive explosion which leveled "all of the area."
(e) In the town on Namur Island (adjacent to Roi), a fire started in one of the large buildings.
(f) Two type 97 fighters were shot down near Roi.

After their Roi Island attack, the five VS-6 bombers flown by Lieutenant (JG) P.L. Teaff, Lieutenant (JG) B.H. Troemel, Lieutenant (JG) H.D. Hilton, Lieutenant F.A. Patriarca, and Lieutenant (JG) E.T. Deacon had expended all their bombs and returned to the carrier. At Roi, Ensign W.F. West's gunner, AMM3c Milton Wayne Clark, shot down a Japanese fighter. They engaged a second fighter that rolled over on its back, forcing Ensign West to take evasive action, and causing them to lose sight of the fighter. In the engagement, Ensign West was wounded in the right shoulder by gunfire, and he and Clark had to return alone to the carrier.[28]

After the completion of VS-6 attacks on Roi, Ensign C.J. Dobson and Lieutenant (JG) N.J. Kleiss, led by Lieutenant C.E. Dickenson, Jr., proceeded to Kwajalein Island. From 8,500 feet at 0743, a divebombing attack was made on ships in the lagoon. Dickenson scored a direct hit on a Yawata class ship with his 500-pound bomb, while Dobson made his 500-pound bomb attack on a submarine tied up alongside a tender, likewise making a direct hit. Kleiss dropped his 500-pounder on a cruiser, scoring a direct hit, and after pulling out of his dive, he strafed a radio station on Enubuj Island. The three SBDs then returned to the *Enterprise*.

Another four VS-6 planes headed to Kwajalein Island after completing their Roi attacks. Led by Lieutenant W.E. Gallagher, with Ensign P.W. Forman, Lieutenant (JG) J.N. West and Lieutenant R. Rutherford, a divebombing attack was begun from 12,000 feet on shipping. Gallagher attacked a cruiser and scored a direct hit with his 500-pound bomb. Forman attacked a supply ship, but his bomb missed. West targeted a large tanker with his 500-pound bomb and made a direct hit. Rutherford also targeted a large tanker with his 500-pounder, but his possible bomb hit was not confirmed. Rutherford followed up his attack with a strafing run on the radio station at Enubuj Island. These four SBDs headed back to the carrier.

At 0905, Lieutenant Hilton, Ensign West, Lieutenant Patriarca, and Lieutenant Deacon landed aboard the *Enterprise*. Because their SBDs had suffered damage from gunfire, Hilton's and Deacon's planes were sent below for repairs. The other planes were reserviced and rearmed. At about 1000 the remaining ten planes landed.[29]

While Scouting Squadron Six was first commencing their attack on Roi Island, Bombing Squadron Six was flying down the center of the lagoon looking for ships. At 0705 the Enterprise Air Group Commander (CEAG) ordered Bombing Squadron Six southward to Kwajalein Island. CEAG Young had received word from the *Enterprise* that Lieutenant Commander Eugene Lindsey's VT-6 aircraft over Kwajalein Island had encountered numerous enemy naval vessels including two carriers. Young immediately sent his squadron of 9 SBD bombers toward Kwajalein.

At 0725, nine VB-6 planes arrived in the Kwajalein area at 14,000 feet altitude. They saw no carriers, but did sight several large ships among the other vessels there. As the squadron approached the target area ready to engage, a barrage of 3-inch and 5-inch antiaircraft fire came up at them, covering the ships in the anchorage like "an umbrella" at 10,000 feet. The attackers also noticed heavy machine-gun fire which was, of course, "an utter waste of ammunition." There was some large caliber AA fire coming from shore batteries, but the clear majority of the AA was from an antiaircraft cruiser in a central anchorage location. This cruiser was equipped with 12 or more large-caliber guns and numerous small-caliber AA guns, as well as at least one multiple pom-pom gun.[30]

The VB-6 SBDs came into the area in their three-division attack formation. With a single signal at 0727, the three divisions separated, and each section chose a target. The standard divebombing approach was utilized as they dropped their 500-pound bombs. Some bombers had to sidestep heavy machine-gun fire, while others pulled up out of their dives to select a different target. But in general, the majority of the VB-6 attackers conducted their normal divebombing approach. Subsequent attacks were made, glide-bombing with their 100-pound bombs or strafing the smaller ships, large seaplanes, and shore installations. The group was not engaged in the air by enemy aircraft.

The damage inflicted on the Japanese by VB-6 was as follows:

(a) One 2500-ton submarine sunk.

(b) A large cargo ship was set on fire.

(c) A large cargo ship was damaged.

(d) A large transport was set on fire.

(e) Antiaircraft cruiser damaged.

(f) Two four-engine patrol seaplanes sunk.

(g) Four buildings on Gugegwe Island were destroyed.

(h) Two small storehouses on Kwajalein Island were destroyed.

(i) Three submarines, several ships, radio installation, and shore facilities were strafed. A motor launch full of men was strafed. All hands jumped into the water, leaving the motor launch running about in circles.

There was minor damage to six VB-6 bombers from antiaircraft fire and shrapnel. No VB-6 personnel were injured, and no planes were lost. The attack was ended at 0745 and the planes returned to the carrier in small groups, joining up as they retired en route.[31]

After the nine planes from Torpedo Squadron Six had launched at 0510 from the *Enterprise*, each loaded with three 500-pound bombs, fused with a $\frac{1}{100}$ second delay, they headed to attack the ships and shore facilities at Kwajalein Island. The weather was good with low scattered clouds at 3,000 feet, an unlimited ceiling, and winds from the east-northeast at 15 knots. Lieutenant Commander Lindsey's attack group made landfall and released their first bombs at 0658. The number of targets at Kwajalein was sufficient to warrant the use of additional aircraft loaded with torpedoes for use in attacking ships at anchor in the lagoon. A voice radio report of such intelligence was made to the *Enterprise*.

The antiaircraft fire was heavy and constant, and more accurate than expected. Under heavy antiaircraft fire, they attacked 9 cargo ships, 2 four-engine aircraft, and a large compound area. No enemy aircraft were encountered. At 0711 the last bomb was dropped, and the group departed Kwajalein at 0717, landing aboard at about 0935, except Lieutenant Ely, who landed earlier at 0915. No personnel were injured, and the aircraft were undamaged.[32]

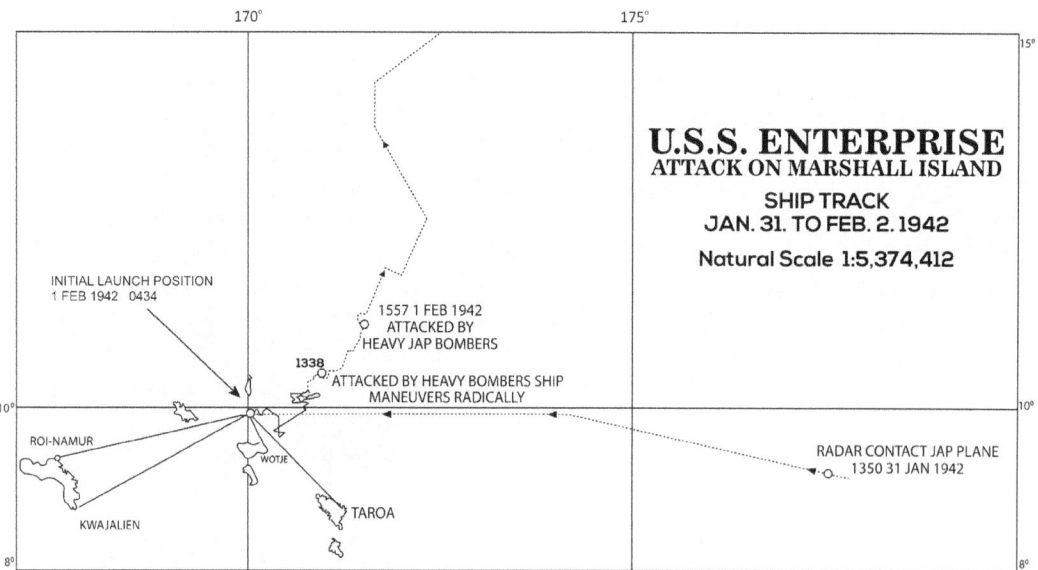

USS *Enterprise* track—Marshall Islands raid. Image redrawn based on *Early Raids in the Pacific Ocean*, 20.

As a result of the intelligence received from that first Kwajalein VT-6 Attack Group, the second division of 9 VT-6 planes, under the command of the executive officer, Lieutenant Commander Lance E. Massey, were directed to attack Kwajalein. At 0731 the nine torpedo bombers launched from the *Enterprise* to attack a probable Japanese carrier and several large auxiliaries anchored in the lagoon off Kwajalein Island. The TBDs set a course of 245°T straight to the island at a distance of 180 miles. At 0800 they received a message from Lieutenant Ely indicating that they should attack from the north. They changed course to reach the atoll some five miles north of Bigej Channel. CEAG Young informed them that there was no carrier at Kwajalein, but that there were nine auxiliaries in the anchorage.

The torpedo planes arrived off Bigej Channel at 0905 in a close echelon of vees at 1,200 feet and were immediately engaged by 3-inch and 5-inch AA fire. The layout of the anchorage revealed the large auxiliaries anchored in parallel lines lying about east and west, with oilers on the northernmost line. The next line contained cargo vessels and troop transports close to the island, with light vessels and patrol craft moving in the lagoon to the north of the oilers.

By decision, the first plane was directed to attack the first large ship to the east, with the rest of the planes hitting the large vessels "working toward the west in rotation."[33] The plane formation was a right echelon of echelons at 500 to 700 feet passing over the reef bordering the lagoon to the north of Bigej Island. Heavy AA fire and pom-poms were coming up at the TBDs. The antiaircraft fire forced the attacking formation to break up. The planes had to pass over numerous small patrol vessels and beached craft along the lagoon. The vessels fired up intense machine-gun fire.

A light cruiser was seen "limping" out of the anchorage in the direction of the southern pass. The sixth section was directed to concentrate on the cruiser. The TBDs began to attack the first line of ships, releasing their torpedoes at 400 to 500 yards from the target ships. These planes departed to the east. The planes targeting the second line dropped their torpedoes after they had maneuvered over and through the first line and then retired to the east. The sixth section of planes released their torpedoes and then headed off to the north.

The heavy antiaircraft firing was constant, but it was random and seemingly "haphazard." The flight crews believed that the first-line ships were firing their AA at the second line of their own ships, inflicting considerable casualties. It was noted that when the TBDs were diving aggressively on the enemy ships, their gun crews dispersed even when the plane was not firing on them. One plane attempted to strafe patrol planes and facilities on Ebeye Island but failed with a jammed gun. The radiomen in the TBDs kept up a constant fire with their free guns during the approach and retirement.

The torpedo planes rendezvoused some 10 to 15 miles east of Kwajalein Island. As the planes were circling to join up to retire, they noticed shells from large-caliber shore-based gun batteries falling into the water below them. The group returned to the carrier for landing at 1130. Bullet and shrapnel damage were found in three planes. There were no injuries from the mission.

After the attack, Lieutenant Commander Lance E. Massey made a quick circle outside the lagoon to survey the damage inflicted. Three tankers had large quantities of oil around their north sides. The light cruiser was dead in the water and down by the bow. A Yawata class ship was down by the stern and was swung some 90° to the south and heading for the beach. One of the planes engaging the light cruiser reported that one of his torpedoes exploded before reaching the ship. It had probably hit a coral head.[34]

The skipper of VT-6, Lieutenant Commander Lindsey, reported that "it is considered that this torpedo attack was the most remarkable of the entire day's activities. The attack was vigorously pushed to close range in the face of withering anti-aircraft fire. Absolutely no diversion or support, such as a coordinated bombing-torpedo attack, surprise factor or smoke screen was available. That a majority of these planes were not lost may be regarded as a minor miracle. Every pilot in this group is worthy of commendation in that each one individually took his torpedo into point blank range of the target in the face of such anti-aircraft opposition that a successful retirement was highly improbable."[35]

The attack on Taroa Island in the Maloelap Atoll began at 0610 with the launch of 5 fighter planes of VF-6's 3rd Division under Lieutenant James S. Gray from the *Enterprise*. The F4F-3s were armed with two 100-pound bombs, one under each wing, and a full load of .50 caliber bullets, ball, armor-piercing, tracer, but no incendiaries (which had not yet been sent out to the fleet). The 6th fighter, piloted by Ensign David W. Criswell on his first night launch, apparently became disoriented as he passed over the bow and swerved violently to the left. As he tried to correct, he stalled the fighter and crashed into the sea. He sank with his plane.

Gray's VF-6 group, with Lieutenant (JG) Wilmer E. Rawie, Lieutenant (JG) Harold N. Heisel, Ensign Ralph M. Rich, and Ensign William M. Holt, reached what they thought was Taroa in the faint light. Gray rocked his wings and pushed over in a steep dive as he moved down the tranquil, plush lagoon, dropping one of his 100-pound bombs. His wingman Rawie followed his leader and expended a bomb. Gray realized this was not Taroa and climbed back to 5000 feet. As it turned out, they had attacked the uninhabited island of Tjan, located 15 miles northwest of their objective.

Gray raced to Taroa off to the southeast to observe a new airfield with a 5,000-foot runway. It was not the sleepy seaplane base that Intelligence had told them, but a well-equipped airfield resembling Ford Island. Gray dived from 8000 feet, aiming his bomb on the airfield, and then strafed the parked bombers. Rawie likewise dived from 6000 feet to release his bombs at 1,200 feet. Seeing two airborne Mitsubishi A5M4 Type 96 fighters, he attacked with his four .50 caliber guns blazing and shot down one. He was nearly rammed when he made a head-on run at his other attacker, denting his fuselage and shearing his antenna. Rawie then dropped low, preparing to strafe, but all his guns jammed. He withdrew along the island chain and returned to the carrier.

The Japanese were now alerted to the attack as Lieutenant Kurakane's Chitose Air Group detachment responded. Kurakane and two other pilots ran to their fighters while the mechanics warmed up the remaining fighters. Lieutenant Nakai's land attack plane crews began to assemble around the headquarters. The Japanese CAP had already been airborne since before sunrise at 0620 with two Type 96 fighters. They sighted the warships of Captain Thomas M. Shock's Taroa Bombardment Group off Taroa (one heavy cruiser and two destroyers) coming in from the east and headed out to sea to inspect them.

Attackers Heisel, Rich and Holt headed in behind their two lead planes and dropped their bombs into the hangars and parked planes. They all wished they'd had incendiary rounds to use against the planes. Rich was the only one to flame one of the bombers. The Japanese pilots and mechanics labored under fire to get three more Type 96 planes aloft. At 0715 five more Type 96s were airborne, making a total of eight. Rich raced out of the area with guns jammed. Heisel and Holt were chased away from the attack by the Japanese fighters. Heisel's main fuel tank was hit by a 7.7mm bullet but was not leaking gasoline or igniting. He was lucky, since their VF-6 F4Fs were not yet equipped with self-sealing tanks.

Gray was all alone now. Though he had only one of his .50 caliber guns working, he attacked a low-flying Type 96 over the runway and caused serious damage. When he noticed that 8 enemy fighters were heading his way, he fought to exit the area with the enemy doing all they could to shoot him down. Gray returned to the waiting carrier by 0800 with 30 to 40 bullet holes in his fuselage.[36]

As soon as the Kwajalein bombing group had landed back at 0935, they had been reserviced and rearmed. At 1035 nine VT-6 planes were launched from the *Enterprise* for their third mission of the day. Each plane was loaded with three 500-pound bombs and heading for Wotje Island in the Wotje Atoll to attack airfield facilities and surface ships. The first bomb was released at 1220. They received only minor AA fire from a single battery on the airfield. No enemy aircraft were encountered. The bombing group released their last bomb at 1235 and returned to the carrier to land at 1325.[37]

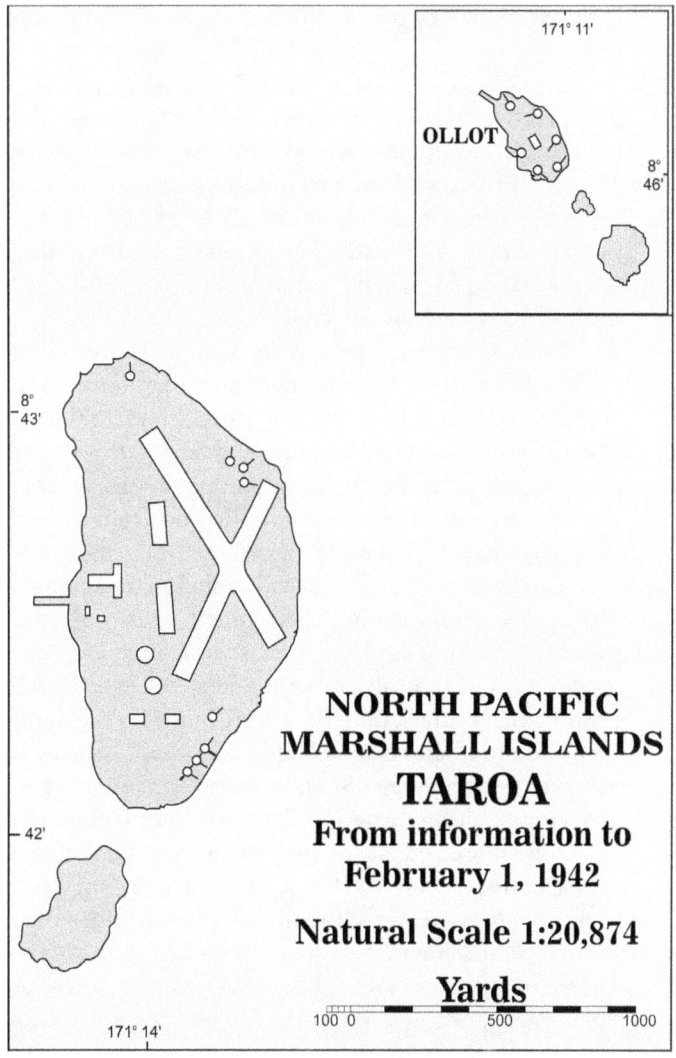

Taroa and Ollet Island maps. Image redrawn based on *Early Carrier Raids in the Pacific Ocean*, 34.

Led by Lieutenant Commander W.R. Hollingsworth, the VB-6 skipper, at 0935 nine SBDs (7 planes from VB-6 and 2 from VS-6) were launched for a second attack on Taroa without fighter escort. The carrier was then 95 miles from the island. At 1032 the attack group in 3-plane formation was up-sun some 30 miles to the southeast of Taroa at 19,000 feet. At 6 miles from the target airfield from 13,000 feet with flaps opened, they nosed over and began their deep vertical dive approaches in a north to northwest direction.

The attackers observed no enemy fighters or antiaircraft fire as they dived. Curiously, there were no signs of the previous attack as they noticed hangars and buildings were new and undamaged with the enemy planes lined up in neat rows. On the field were 12 two-engine bombers, 5 fighters parked in front of the north hangar, 6 fighters parked at the south end of the north-south runway, and 2 bombers to the northeast of the runway.

In a classic air attack on airfield parked planes, the first attacking section leader dropped two 100-pound bombs and one 500-pound bomb on the line, destroying two large Japanese bombers, while setting two others on fire, plus three smaller fighter planes. The second attacker dropped his 500-pound bomb on the south hangar, scoring a direct hit and causing a major gasoline explosion. They headed off to Ollet Island and attacked radio towers, a radio station, an administrative building, and a powerhouse. A third scout bomber dropped his 500-pounder and two 100-pounders about 20 feet in front of the north hangar, destroying 3 fighter planes.

From 9,000 feet the second section leader dropped his 100-pounder on parked planes, destroying a large bomber and 2 fighter planes. Continuing on, he used his 500-pounder to hit and destroy the oil storage tank to the southeast of the hangars. His section likewise moved to Ollet Island and dropped their bombs on the antiaircraft battery and barracks, and strafed a small boat sailing toward a pier on Ollet. An enemy fighter attacked one of the scout bombers as it pulled up from a strafing run, but it was able to evade undamaged as the Japanese plane fired out of range.

The third section made its bombing run against the north and south hangars and planes parked on the line. Their attack yielded mixed results as they retired northward. At 6 miles out, a Japanese fighter dove against one plane, taking a few bullet holes in the process, but did not drive home the attack. Sections two and three saw no antiaircraft fire during the attack until they joined up with the flight leader to retire, when all sections found the fire had become "fairly accurate." As they dived for a lower altitude, the fire became ineffective again, and ceased altogether at 8 miles from the island. The nine attacking planes returned to *Enterprise* and landed after 1000.

Nine more SBD scout bombers were launched at 1036 under Lieut. Richard H. Best, the executive officer of VB-6, for a third attack on Taroa. That group climbed and moved to the east to come out of the sun and downwind. At 15 miles from the target, they leveled out at 13,000 feet and were gaining speed toward the south. It was then that a two-plane section of Japanese fighters turned toward the American bombers as they started to begin their glide down at 200 knots. The enemy fighters followed the bombers down as the antiaircraft bursts were encountered between 12,000 and 10,000 feet. They were still 8 miles from Taroa.

North of the field the flight noticed the antiaircraft fire was directed in a "fixed umbrella" formation and was not directed at the individual fighters. Just as the attackers were about to push over for the run, they were attacked by the trailing fighters. One of the Japanese fighters was shot down in the exchange. The American bomber aircraft attacked the hangars and large bombers on the field. As they came out of their dives, they were engaged in dogfights with Japanese type 96 and 97 fighters and Zeros coming from low altitude. All the American bombers were attacked at least once by Japanese fighters in the attack, with their only natural defense being the cloud layer from 2,000 to 4,000 feet. The American F4F fighter planes from Fighting Six made no attempt to engage in dogfights with the Japanese fighters when they saw how highly maneuverable they were compared to their own aircraft.

The first attack on Wotje Island, only a 40-mile flight from the *Enterprise*, began when six fighter planes launched from *Enterprise* at 0616 under the command of Lieutenant Commander McClusky. Accompanying McClusky were Lieutenant R.W. Mehle,

Lieutenant (JG) R.J. Hoyle, Lieutenant (JG) J.G. Daniels III, Ensign W.J. Hiebert, and Radioman Electrician E.H. Bayers. As planned, the attack on the Japanese facilities was to be handled by the bombardment group of the *Northampton*, *Salt Lake City*, and *Dunlap*, but preceded by air strikes. With the first light coming from the eastern horizon, the VF-6 pilots made out Wotje Island with ease. At 0658 McClusky took his fighters into a high-speed glide-bombing run into the lagoon just west of the island as several naval auxiliary and merchant ships came into view. The first fighters released their 100-pound bombs with no opposition from antiaircraft fire, but the second attackers met AA fire. The fighters strafed buildings and shore batteries and departed before the bombardment began just after sunrise at 0714. They destroyed several buildings and hangars and started numerous fires. As they departed, the pilots looked back with satisfaction to see columns of smoke.[38]

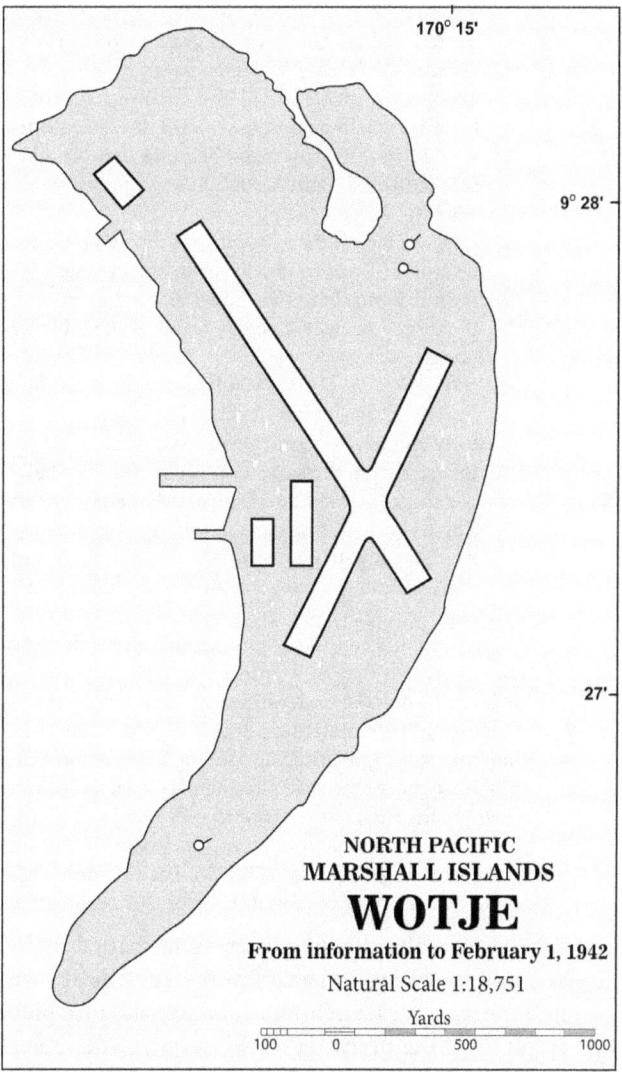

Wotje Island map. Image redrawn based on *Early Carrier Raids in the Pacific Ocean*, 34.

WOTJE BOMBARDMENT GROUP ATTACK PLAN

As a result of prior study it was believed that all Japanese shore installations would be found on the island of Wotje and that enemy vessels inside the atoll would probably be in the anchorage immediately to the westward of that island. This did not, however, preclude the possibilities that shore batteries might be located on outlying supporting islands, such as Egmedio, Ene Cherutakku, or Ormed, and that ships might be found using other anchorages, such as Ormed and Christmas Harbor, or attempting to leave or enter the lagoon.

In selecting the point from which to commence the bombardment and the courses to be steered during it, the following factors were given considerations:

(a) *Priority of Objectives*—Enemy ships were given first priority; they might get underway and move out of range. Aircraft on the ground were obviously important, but these were assigned to the *Enterprise* fighters. Also, the possibility of being able to bring enemy aircraft under effective fire from ships' guns during the early stages of the bombardment seemed unlikely, as the location of the landing field was unknown. Wind data available for the Marshall Islands showed prevailing winds from northeast to east. If these data were accurate, the necessity for a good east-west runway would have placed the landing field on the north end of the island. Shore installations were thus given second priority after ships.

(b) *Location and strength of shore batteries*—it was believed that the largest caliber gun likely to be found on Wotje would be 6-inch with a maximum range of 20,000 yards; that the shore batteries would be on the seaward or eastern side of the island; and that enemy fire control would be most accurate on bearings between northeast and southeast and least accurate to the southward. Batteries might exist, however, on Egmedio, Ene Cherutakku and Ormed Islands.

(c) *Range of own batteries*—Our cruisers' 8-inch guns would be effective to 30,000 yards, destroyer 5-inch to 15,000 yards, and cruiser 5-inch (dual purpose) to 12,000 yards. Concerning our 5-inch batteries, however, consideration had to be given to the difference in ranges to the shore line, where enemy batteries probably were located, and to the positions of shore objectives.

(d) *Navigational and other conditions involved in the approach*—The sun would rise at 0702, bearing 110°. Cruiser aircraft should be launched as late as possible in order to conserve fuel, but early enough to permit them to be on spotting stations by 0715, yet not so close to Wotje that the flash from the catapult powder charges would alert the enemy. It was also undesirable for our ships to be silhouetted from Wotje on the eastern horizon before our fighters attacked. These considerations, the proximity of Erikub and Maloelap Atolls to the southward of Wotje Atoll, the low-lying nature of all land in these atolls and the fact that rather strong ocean currents were known to exist, all would require exceptional accuracy of navigation during the night.

The foregoing considerations resulted in the decision to approach Wotje from the southeastward, and to arrive at 0715 at a position 20,000 yards from probable shore batteries whence ships at the anchorage would be under direct observation; to maneuver by turn movements on courses to close the range while maintaining broadside fire, firing deliberately with 8-inch partial salvos on enemy ships and at the same time developing the location and strength of the shore batteries; and, finally to shift fire to shore objectives, closing the range, if possible, to permit the cruiser 5-inch to fire effectively. An approach from the southward of Wotje Island, rather than the northward, was selected because this covered Schischmarev Strait, the principal entrance to the lagoon, and the channel to it from Wotje anchorage. Moreover, for fire against shore objectives a position to the southward of Wotje Island was desirable because the major axis of the island is north and south.[39]

The bombardment group, commanded by Rear Admiral Raymond Spruance, had sailed toward Wotje on a course of 258° true at a speed of 17.3 knots until the ships turned into the wind for launching the reconnaissance planes of the *Salt Lake City* and *Northampton* at 0620 the morning of February 1. The Japanese on the island were first alerted by a rocket fired from an 800-ton patrol craft that was being chased by the *Dunlap* as it zigzagged away. The gun on the bow of the destroyer was the only gun able to bear on the low target as she fled, making it hard to hit.

The cruiser reconnaissance planes rendezvoused and headed north of Wotje. The spotter planes then broke off to the south to photograph the straits and the atoll. The Japanese antiaircraft fire had shifted from the VF-6 F4F fighters to the spotter planes.

At 0655 the group sighted land on the starboard bow. Only the two medium-height Wotje radio towers and ship masts from the lagoon were seen. There was black smoke, which confirmed that the Japanese ships were getting underway. The reconnaissance planes initially reported "three ships and no shore batteries," but later it was learned that there were eight ships in the lagoon and five shore batteries present. Such mistaken reconnaissance was a serious issue.

As the range closed in to 24,000 yards off Wotje, three large freighters were seen. The leftmost ship was assigned to the *Northampton*, while the right-hand auxiliary was designated by the *Salt Lake City* control officer for his target.

After the VF-6 fighters had cleared the area at 0715, the bombardment group initiated their attack by passing the island on course 270° in a column formation. The destroyer *Dunlap* worked independently, screening ahead, and sank the patrol craft before heading westward looking for two submarines reported to be in the lagoon. The *Northampton* fired its full salvo first, followed 20 seconds later with a full salvo from the *Salt Lake City*. The subsequent salvos were single-turret salvos to conserve ammunition.

The cruisers continued the shelling of the Japanese cruisers in the lagoon for the next 55 minutes. Targeting proved to be a problem for the control officers as the enemy ships in the harbor were partially blocked from view by high ground at certain spots, and the enemy ships were getting underway and shifting positions, nullifying rangefinder data. The air spotters had issues as they dodged antiaircraft fire and flew around clouds.

At 0803 the American cruisers reversed course from 270° to 060° and continued the shelling of enemy ship targets. The targets came into clearer view for the cruisers, and the spotter planes were able to finally locate good spotting positions over the lagoon to report back to the control officers. After the course change, one direct hit from the *Salt Lake City* at 13,850 yards sank a target ship at 0812. Both cruisers then shifted their fire to shore targets on the island. Identifying the shore targets was difficult because gasoline storage tanks were painted deep green and covered on top with sod, while other buildings were painted to look like sand dunes. Some of the buildings were discovered only by the shadows they cast on the ground in the sunlight.

Lack of prior detailed intelligence about the targets to be bombarded creates considerable problems for attacking surface ships. The account that follows, regarding the shelling of enemy aircraft installations by the cruiser *Salt Lake City* at Wotje, provides just such an example:

> A group of buildings, some of which appeared to be hangars, were observed some distance from the beach. Eight buildings, painted to resemble sand dunes, were counted by the spotter with no trouble. However, the director pointer and trainer, with lower powered optics than the spotter, could not pick up any of these buildings through their telescopes. To the right of these sand-colored buildings was a group of smaller buildings painted a deep green. Since the director pointer and trainer were able to see these green buildings, they were ordered to use the left group of the green buildings as a point of aim. An arbitrary spot of left 5 was put on the rangekeeper to cause the shots to fall in this aviation center. But, the rangekeeper operator was not notified that the target had been shifted, and the left 5 was applied to a left deflection accumulated spot remaining from the previous target, so the first salvo landed well to the left of the hangars. There was no observation on that salvo. Another was fired with the same set up and a rich orange flame leaped into the air from among the palm trees to the left of the aviation buildings. Then the error on the rangekeeper was corrected and the next salvo was a little off to the right and another heavy fire was observed to start. The control officer next ordered full 10-gun salvos. The first landed among the aviation buildings followed by another salvo close to the same place, and it is believed considerable damage was done. A spot of right 03 was given, and our shells landed among the green buildings that were being used as the point of aim. The gun range at this time was averaging 11,800 yards. Later reports from the aviators revealed that this salvo did immense damage to industrial plants.[40]

The enemy had initially opened fire on the American cruisers at 0721, but their accuracy was poor until 0842 when shells exploded close to the *Salt Lake City* from shore batteries. The cruiser increased her speed and turned away, but the shells from two guns burst just astern of her. At 0848 the *Northampton* was "straddled" by shells, but although the Japanese continued to fire for another hour, they were "ineffective."

At 0852 Spruance ordered "Cease Firing" and the planes from the *Northampton* and *Salt Lake City* were directed to drop their remaining 100-pound bombs on enemy targets.

The bombardment task group withdrew and began to recover their aircraft at 0955. On recovery, one plane crashed into the side of the *Salt Lake City*, with the pilot and radioman surviving to be rescued by the *Dunlap*. Their spotter plane was sunk by machine gun and rifle fire. The bombardment group rendezvoused with the *Enterprise* at 1230 on a course of 070° moving at 25 knots. The task group later fired on enemy planes at 1335 and 1535 during an air attack on the *Enterprise*. The task group received no battle damage from enemy action. The *Salt Lake City* had its 5-inch No. 8 gun damaged by a shell that burst in the muzzle, and the 5-inch No. 6 gun was found to have a "slight bulge" in it when a gun bore was gaged on February 2.[41]

At 1116 a group of 8 SBDs from VS-6 and 9 TBD planes from VT-6 were launched on the second attack on Wotje Island led by CEAG Commander Young. With VS-6 were Lieutenant W.E. Gallagher, Ensign C.J. Dobson, Lieutenant R. Rutherford, Lieutenant (JG) J.N. West, Lieutenant (JG) Perry L. Teaff, Lieutenant (JG) B.H. Troemel, and VB-6's Lieutenant (JG) E.L. Anderson. VT-6's nine TBDs, each loaded with three 500-pound bombs, were led by the Executive Officer, Lieutenant Commander Massey, accompanied by Lieutenant (JG) Eversole, Ensign Severin Rombach, Lieutenant White, Lieutenant (JG) Thomas, Ensign Heck, Lieutenant Riley, Ensign McPherson, and Ensign Hodges. The purpose of the attack was to hit island targets not already destroyed by the shelling, as well as any enemy ships in the lagoon.

The VT-6 planes encountered heavy and constant AA fire as they attacked. During the first mission that morning, the plane of Ensign Rombach had been given a "down," so this was the first chance to see combat that day. Rombach flew over the bow of an enemy merchant ship when his rear gunner, ARM2c Ronald Graetz, saw a deck gunner on the ship begin to turn his antiaircraft gun toward their plane. Graetz immediately fired a long burst of machine-gun fire toward the gunner to "discourage the Japanese AA man." Graetz recalled, "I really did not feel that I was nervous, at any time, over the flight, but I used the 'P-tube' and relieved myself four times on the way out and five times on the way back. I guess I was more nervous than I had realized."[42]

On arrival at a position about 10 miles southeast of Wotje at 13,000 feet, the CEAG turned the lead over to Lieutenant (JG) Gallagher. At 1215 a high-speed approach began to the island, and at a point 5 miles south of the Wotje, a large cargo ship was sighted at anchor close to shore inside the lagoon. Gallagher, along with Dobson, Rutherford, Anderson, and West, swung around and made a divebombing attack on the cargo ship toward the southwest. Each plane released a 500-pound bomb and four of them hit the mark, while the 5th bomb scored a near-miss.

CEAG Young, Teaff and Troemel saw the direct hits and looked for an alternative target. Teaff and Troemel dropped their bombs on a cargo ship off Wotje, with no hits observed. The CEAG released his bombs on a building on the south side of the island believed to be part of an antiaircraft installation. Damage was not observed. Gallagher climbed with the five planes up to 8,000 feet and began a glide-bombing attack on the same cargo ship and harbor vessel inside the lagoon, each dropping two 100-pound bombs, and strafing as they went. The cargo ship was in flames, and still burning when they rendezvoused and headed back to the carrier, landing at 1315. The VT-6 bombers landed about 1325.

There were no enemy aircraft at the airfield except two small seaplanes. The airfield was totally destroyed and only two ships out of the original nine were still visible: one small auxiliary was aground and seriously damaged, and a larger ship was damaged, but still afloat. Two AA batteries and a 6-inch shore battery were silenced.[43]

Taroa Bombardment Group Attack Plan

The attack on Taroa was to be carried out by a task group consisting of the *Chester*, *Balch*, and *Maury*. It was the intention of the group to pass through the initial point, bearing 116°, distant 10 miles from the center of Taroa Island at 0715, February 1st. The approach was to be made with the *Balch* as guide, followed by the *Chester* and *Maury* at distances of 1,000 yards, on course 236° at a speed of 20 knots. The ships were to continue on that course with the *Chester*'s main battery firing for about 20 minutes. Thereafter, if practicable the group was to close the range to permit effective fire of all 5-inch batteries. The priority of objectives would be as set forth in Admiral Nimitz's order. If any enemy surface vessels were present and attempted to escape, the group was to maneuver to cover the entrance to Enijun Channel.[44]

The Taroa Bombardment Group of Task Force 8 began their attack operations at 0600 with the launch from the heavy cruiser *Chester* of two planes for spotter operations, while the other two were to conduct reconnaissance. The planes sighted Taroa Island forty-nine minutes later at 28,500 yards. Two enemy dive bombers attacked the *Chester* ten minutes later, and at 0710 the shore batteries began firing. The enemy firing could not be determined, but the shell splashes indicated they came from 5- and 6-inch guns.

As the *Enterprise* fighters strafed the island, at 0715 the *Chester* opened fire with the main battery salvo, using the towers at the northwest corner of the island as the primary aiming point. The spotter planes were unable to help direct salvos because they were under attack at the time. A second Japanese dive bomber attack occurred as the shore batteries continued to shell the *Chester*.

In response to the shelling from the shore batteries, the *Chester* turned its aim point 30° to a range of 12,000 yards, pointing at the shore batteries. Five more salvos from the *Chester* silenced one enemy battery as the air attack continued. While in range of the shore batteries and with only two small auxiliaries seen in the lagoon, the *Chester* reversed course at 0731, firing at the shore batteries as they moved north toward the airfield and hangar. Eventually the destroyer *Balch* was fired on by the enemy shore batteries from the center of the island.

At this point in the attack, some nine minutes after the course change, eight enemy twin-engine bombers were seen taking off from the Taroa airfield. The bombardment group immediately began to retire, and the course was changed to 130° and then 184° with their speed increased. The crew from the main battery was moved to the antiaircraft battery in anticipation of a bomber attack.

There were numerous divebombing and strafing attacks against the bombardment group by the Japanese until 0900. At 0820 the *Chester* was hit by a 134-pound bomb in the well deck near the port catapult tower, but at 0841 the cruiser was able to avoid major damage when the eight enemy bombers dropped 500-pound bombs from 12,000 feet. These bombs fell some 100 yards astern.

As the Japanese attacked the *Chester*'s reconnaissance planes, they maneuvered to position themselves directly overhead, then they executed a half-roll and steep dive. They pulled out too early and abruptly at a high altitude, causing their machine-gun fire to be scattered and inaccurate.[45]

As the group retired from Taroa at maximum speed, the air attack eventually dropped off. At 1130 the *Chester* recovered its 4 planes. The damage against the Japanese forces at Taroa were 3 shore batteries and one antiaircraft battery, one plane by dogfight, several buildings, an observation tower, and a radio tower. The Taroa Bombardment Group sailors suffered 8 killed, 34 injured. The *Chester* bomb blast made a 9 × 4-foot

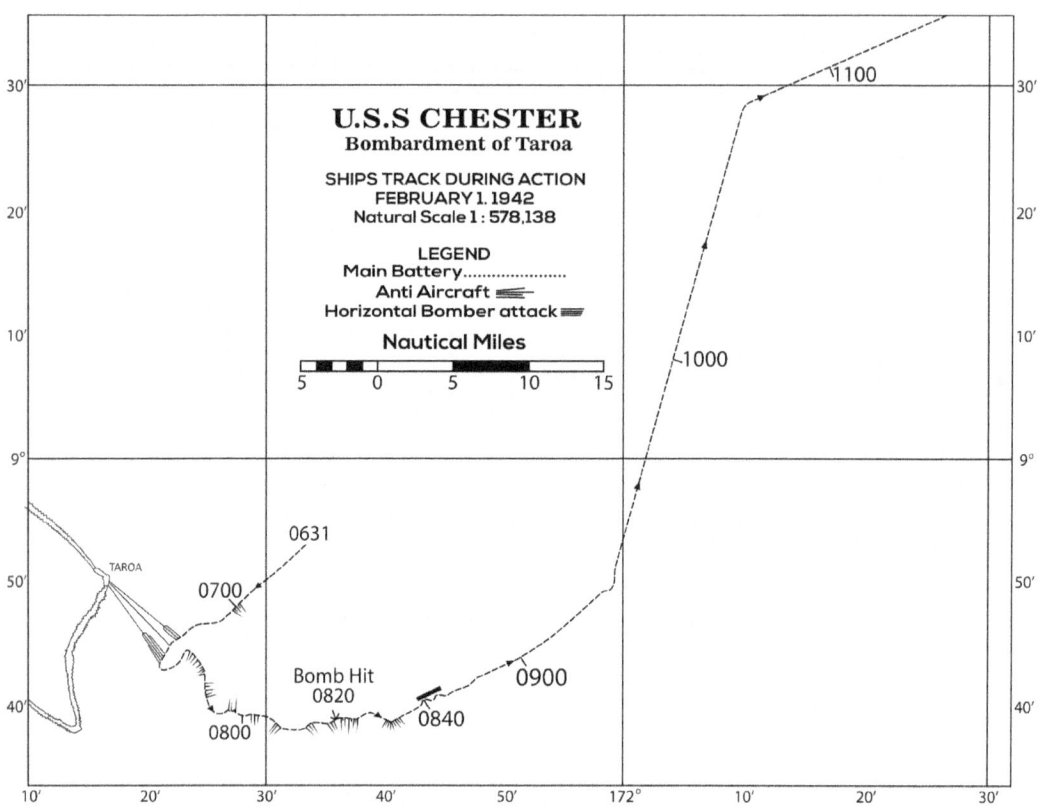

Track chart of bombardment of Taroa by USS *Chester* on February 1, 1942. Image redrawn based on *Early Raids in the Pacific Ocean*, 21.

hole in the main deck and significant superficial damage to ship infrastructure, including blower screens, ventilation trunks, catapult catwalk, deck stanchions, and nearly all of the light bulkheads. It also "dished in the catapult foundation about 1 foot, seriously damaged the port motor, whaleboat, and started a fire in the cork insulation of the exhaust duct from the forward engine room." It was noticed that the Japanese air attackers "lacked aggressiveness and failed to press their attacks home." Their dive-bomber attacks were at a 45-degree angle and they released their bombs at the high altitude of about 4,000 feet. The enemy planes used the cloud layer at 8,000 feet effectively to conceal themselves.[46]

The *Enterprise* would launch 14 combat patrols all day over the task force, involving 58 aircraft. At 1255 the *Enterprise* launched four VF-6 F4Fs led by Corbin and six SBDs from VB-6 to provide anti-torpedo plane patrol. Once the eight SBDs landed aboard after their attack on Taroa and the four VF-6 CAP fighters with low fuel had landed, the CAP consisted of 7 F4Fs and six SBDs.

The surprise attack on that Sunday had shocked the Japanese as they regrouped. Lieutenant Nakai of the 24th Air Flotilla radioed Captain Ohashi at Roi requesting permission to take his eight land attack planes. Ohashi refused Nakai because his facilities had been damaged by the American bombers. Thus, Nakai just circled off Taroa until after the SBDs left the area. His land attack aircraft finally were able to land at 1130, allowing the ground crews to quickly started rearming the aircraft. All 8 of his bombers were damaged in some way and one was unserviceable.

Anxious to engage the Americans, at 1210 Nakai took five of his G3M Type 96 land attack planes airborne and headed off to find Halsey's task force. The scattered clouds made locating the carrier force difficult, but just after 1330 Nakai's Type 96 land attack planes found Task Force 8 northeast of Wotje. At the time, the assigned *Enterprise* fighter director officer (FDO), Lieutenant Commander Leonard J. Dow (staff communications officer), continued to have trouble determining if the air contacts on his radar screen were friendly or not. None of the carriers' planes were equipped with IFF (Identification—Friend or Foe) gear.

Meanwhile, Rawie saw the enemy bombers coming in toward the carrier from a distance out and contacted Corbin. Then Nakai's planes moved into the cloud cover to hide. Dow sent two sections of F4Fs out toward the Rawie contacts. The fighters located the bandits at 10,000 feet some 15 miles from the carrier. They attacked, but they suffered gun failures. Rawie had only one of his four Browning machine guns working on the first pass.

The five enemy bombers emerged from the clouds at 6,000 feet at 1335 in sight of Halsey's ships. Their approach was made on the carrier "about broad on the starboard bow from a position angle of 25°" 3,500 yards away. The enemy planes came in at 1338 at 250 knots in a shallow glide-bomb attack, each releasing its three 100- to 200-kilogram bombs at 3,000 to 4,000 feet altitude. They passed over the carrier at 1,500 feet. One of the enemy bombers peeled off from the formation as it passed over the ship, either to strafe the planes on the flight deck or crash into them. The Japanese pilot ran into heavy 5-inch AA gunfire from the *Enterprise*, crashed into the port side of the flight deck in flames, and fell over the side. That enemy plane was that of Lieutenant Nakai, which had been shot up by Lieutenant (JG) Frank B. Quady and Ensign Norman Hodson earlier. The right wing of Nakai's bomber had struck the tail of one of the SBDs, which caused so much damage that the plane was pushed overboard. Nakai's crash also spread his gasoline over the flight deck and put bullets into the left-wing fuel tanks of two planes.

Lieutenant Commander E.B. Mott, the *Enterprise*'s gunnery officer, viewed Corbin's F4Fs attack on Nakai's bombers and saw that his ship's AA gun bursts were behind the bombers. The gunners had obviously underestimated the speed of the incoming bombers. During the attack, Captain Murray had increased the carrier's speed to 30 knots and ordered the rudder to be positioned hard left; he then reversed it in order to move the ship out of its former track. Due to Murray's skill, most of the enemy bombs fell to the starboard side, but one 250-kilogram bomb landed 30 feet from the port side and put 9 holes in the gasoline fuel line. Other damage included dents and puncture holes in the deck of the .50 caliber ammunition room, a gasoline hose destroyed by a fire that set off a few rounds of .50 caliber on the gun platform, wiring and cable burned, and deep gashes in the hull plating below the main deck.

The surviving four enemy bombers moved away from the carrier at low altitude and headed home to their base. At 1405 McClusky's four F4Fs launched as the relief CAP. A few minutes later, three F4Fs landed to refuel and rearm. This left 8 CAP planes aloft. At 1500 the FDO saw a radar contact and sent McClusky's second section with Lieutenant Roger Mehle and Lieutenant (JG) Rhonald J. Hoyle to investigate. Worried about a second carrier attack, Dow sent five more F4Fs aloft led by Gray, increasing the CAP to 13 fighters.

Mehle sighted an enemy twin-float seaplane and made his first pass, killing the rear gunner, but the plane escaped into the clouds. McClusky's wingman, Bayers, located the floatplane and engaged, making two passes, but it evaded him. Finally, Mehle found the floatplane, an Aichi E13A1 Type 0 reconnaissance floatplane (JAKE) from the 19th Air Group based at Ebeye Island in the Kwajalein Atoll, and shot him down in flames.[47]

At 1430 Nakai's two remaining twin-engine land attack bombers took off from Taroa heading to the last location of the *Enterprise*. An hour later the planes were seen as radar contacts off 25 miles to the east of the task force. Nine F4Fs were aloft from McClusky's and Gray's divisions. The Chitose flight crews approached in a standard horizontal bombing formation at 14,000 feet cruising at 140 knots on the port quarter, off 50,000 yards. McClusky led his fighters out to attack the raiders, but just as they were ready to intercept, the task force ships opened up firing their 5-inch AA fire at the attackers. The VF-6 fighters had to bear away from the enemy planes according to standing orders to avoid being hit by the AA fire.

The two enemy bombers were tracked and eventually made their attack from the sun position and through scattered clouds at a slant range of 6,500 yards. At 1557 both planes dropped their two 500-pound bombs simultaneously. The bombs fell about 125 yards from the ship abreast the forecastle, causing no reported damage. Once the attackers were clear of the AA fire, the F4Fs moved in to attack the retreating bombers. Lieutenant Mehle and Lieutenant (JG) Daniels headed after the trailing bomber and made several passes on the plane. Finally, Daniels closed in tighter, firing his bullets into the silver tail of the Mitsubishi and setting it on fire. Over the radio Daniels was heard yelling, "Bingo! Bingo! I got one!"[48] as the bomber hit the water.

McClusky, Mehle, and Hoyle took off after the remaining plane, which was still trailing smoke from an earlier AA hit. They had to disengage and turn back when they were getting too far away from the carrier. They claimed a probable kill, but actually the enemy bomber made it back to Taroa.[49]

The *Enterprise* replaced part of the CAP with a launch at 1641 of 4 F4Fs. Still airborne, Rawie saw a Japanese floatplane "lurking in the clouds" off 12 miles from the carrier on a bearing of 240°. Rawie took off after the bogey, but he had propeller and fuel pressure problems. Captain Murray was concerned about the enemy attacking at dusk and directed some of the CAP to land early to refuel, and then sent them back up. Gray's division landed just after 1700. Gray's own Wildcat had a problem with its landing gear, which collapsed on landing. The carrier launched its last 8 CAP fighters at 1753, providing a dusk combat patrol totaling 14 F4Fs. The sunset came to the *Enterprise* Task Force 8 at 1835 and the last combat patrol fighter landed at 1902. The attack mission of Task Force 8 had now ended.[50]

The damage inflicted by Halsey's Task Force 8 on the Japanese were extensive and included 13 vessels and 35 planes as confirmed losses. Between four and seven ships were believed to have suffered damage of indeterminate degree. An indeterminate number of enemy planes were destroyed in the hangars and dispersed parking areas next to the airfields at Roi and Taroa. The damage reported by island targets were as follows:

> *Wotje*: All facilities were destroyed including two hangars, fuel oil tanks, gasoline storage, warehouses, shops and barracks. Also destroyed were two antiaircraft batteries and all coastal defense guns. Four or five auxiliaries or cargo ships of 4000 to 5000 tons, along with 3 or 4 small "bird" class ships sunk or damaged.
>
> *Taroa*: Two hangars were destroyed, several buildings hit and afire in the industrial area. The radio

station on Ollet Island was also destroyed. Two submarines sunk by 500-pound direct hits. One large "Yawata" class ship sunk by three 500-pound bombs and one torpedo. One cruiser sunk by two 500-pound bombs, and one confirmed torpedo plus one possible torpedo. Three large AO's sunk by four direct hits from 500-pound bombs and 3 torpedo hits. Two AK's damaged by near misses from 500-pound bombs, and one torpedo. The ship was beached. One PG patrol craft was damaged and ran aground.

Roi: Destroyed two hangars, the ammunition dump, the radio building, all stores and warehouses, and set the town east of Roi on fire.

Kwajalein: Large compounds received 3 direct hits.

Gugegwe: Destroyed four buildings.

The losses sustained by Task Force 8 were 11 airmen killed and 4 wounded. One enlisted man was killed, and an officer and 5 sailors were wounded on the *Enterprise*. On the cruiser *Chester*, 8 men were killed and 34 wounded. Ships damaged included the *Chester* and superficial damage on the *Enterprise*. Air losses were one VF-6 F4F-3 fighter (crashed on takeoff), one VB-6 SBD-2 bomber, and four VS-6 SBD scout planes shot down. Damaged planes included 7 fighters, 3 torpedo planes, 11 bombers, one reconnaissance plane, and 12 scout planes.[51]

Halsey provided miscellaneous notes regarding the Japanese forces the task force attacked:

(a) Both Roi and Taroa had complete air bases of recent construction. Wotje also had a new installation. Pilots report Taroa base better equipped than Ford Island.
(b) A.A. batteries present on Roi, Kwajalein, Taroa, Wotje and Olliot [*sic*]. Guns of 3", .50 and .30 caliber.
(c) Kwajalein apparently used as submarine base.
(d) A.A. fire of umbrella type-apparently not well controlled.
(e) Enemy VF of Type 96 or 97 with possibility of "OO" [zero] being present.
(f) High degree of maneuverability of enemy VF and good climb but not as fast as F4Fs.
(g) Twin-engined bomber; tactics of bombing and VF attack described elsewhere [in Action Report].
(h) Apparent reluctance of VF to engage VSB.

Of the attack on the Marshalls, Halsey provided his overall assessment:

It is my considered opinion that the enemy has been struck an extremely heavy blow in the Mandated Area. The action embraced, to the best of my knowledge, the first instance in history of offensive combat by U.S. carriers. The performance of the *Enterprise* justifies the highest hopes heretofore held regarding the effectiveness of these vessels when properly employed. This action, likewise, was the first offensive operation by Task Forces of the Pacific Fleet in the current war. The results must speak for themselves. I am proud and grateful for the high privilege of having commanded Task Force Eight in these operations.[52]

Captain Murray, as the commander of the *Enterprise*, provided his recommendations in his Action Report:

(a) That every effort be made to improve and increase AA batteries, at earliest date.
(b) That gunnery Radar installations be provided immediately.
(c) That AA Gunnery Practices be scheduled when opportunity offers, with ship steaming at not less than 25 knots. If adequate safeguards can be introduced, ship should be required to make radical changes of course.
(d) That own carrier is and will continue to be principal objective of enemy effort in any air attack at sea. Although it will always be true that the most vigorous aggressive action on the part of the carrier air group may largely nullify the amount and degree of enemy air attack against the carrier, the need for providing carriers with the best anti-aircraft batteries, including the latest

Radar fire control installation, and adequate fighter protection with friendly aircraft identification equipment is apparent.[53]

Murray commented, "It is believed a serious and perhaps vital blow has been dealt enemy installations, ships and aircraft in the Marshalls." He gave the air group positive marks for "the greatest vigor and determination" and declared, "It is the considered opinion of the Commanding Officer that pilots and gunners taking part in these operations lived up to the highest traditions of the Naval Service and all merit the warmest praise from their seniors for their exemplary performance of duty."[54]

Murray continued with his praise for the ship's company, calling the conduct of both officers and men subjected to enemy air attacks "inspiring." He indicated that the reports he received from his department heads "universally held [the] view that all hands eagerly carried out their duties with the greatest amount of determination and spirit." He gave to those who promptly fought the gasoline fire on the flight deck and gun gallery on the port quarter special praise.[55]

The *Enterprise* Air Group Commander Young documented his recommendations regarding the raid on the Marshalls:

(a) That damage to ships would have been greater had the 500 lb. bombs on the VSB been fitted with delayed action fuses instead of instantaneous fuses.
(b) That more damage would have been inflicted during the strafing attacks—especially on airplanes on ground if incendiary bullets had been available.
(c) That our type airplanes, with exception of the F4F-3s do not have sufficient performance in their present overloaded condition.
(d) That armor and leak-proof tanks are a vital necessity. VF-6 made up and installed their own armor aboard ship prior to this action, using 3/8" boiler plate behind the pilot's seat. This saved one pilot from certain destruction. No leak-proof tanks were installed in any type.
(e) That the oxygen equipment in the SBD type is not satisfactory. The face mask does not fit properly, deteriorates rapidly and is uncomfortable.
(f) That "IFF" equipment is necessary. Considerable voice radio communications for identification of friendly planes and confusion would have been eliminated.
(g) That the number of VSB planes be reduced to permit operating 27 VF. Fighter protection for VT is mandatory. Fortunately in this action VT-6 encountered no air opposition, but it is certain that their mission would not have been accomplished had they been intercepted by enemy fighters which were in the near vicinity.
(h) That at least 50% spare qualified pilots are necessary for any prolonged operations lasting longer than a period of one day. It must be remembered that the Enterprise Air Group participating in this operation, with a few exceptions, is considered a thoroughly trained and experienced one. With less experienced groups, as will be the case in the future, more losses will be incurred in action, deck landing accidents, and minor casualties. Fighter squadrons will require more replacement or relief pilots than other types due to constant combat patrols that must be maintained in addition to any other missions that may be assigned to them."[56]

Commander Young praised the air group, indicating that "they accomplished their missions and performed their duties in a superlative manner and carried on like veterans from the instant the first bomb hit. There was no confusion at any time. Each squadron commander and flight leader in every case I witnessed, displayed the proper initiative and judgement [sic] to handle every situation that arose. All attacks were well executed and pressed home without question. The dive bombing was exceptional in spite of the general lack of information on targets and the opposition encountered. The Torpedo attack is considered exemplary."[57]

Yorktown Task Force 17 Action

YORKTOWN ATTACK PLAN

Admiral Fletcher's orders to his task force required that the striking group, which consisted of the *Yorktown*, *Louisville*, and *St. Louis*, and support, consisting of the destroyers *Hughes*, *Sims*, *Russell*, and *Walke* proceed in company to latitude 5° N., longitude 175°25' E., arriving at 7 o'clock on the evening of the 31st. From this point the striking group was ordered to proceed at 25 knots on course 270°, while the support was to follow at a speed of advance of 15 knots until rejoining the striking group.

The striking group was to launch an air attack on Jaluit, Makin, and Mili from the *Yorktown*. The attack was to be launched at latitude 5° N., longitude 171°50' E., after which the *Yorktown* was to retire eastward at 25 knots on course 090°. The attack was to be executed to strike about 15 minutes prior to sunrise; however, launching times could be advanced to permit attack and recovery of aircraft prior to daylight if weather conditions were propitious.

It was provided that if the support failed to contact the striking group at the expected time and place, support would continue on 270° for about 1 hour unless otherwise directed, and endeavor to locate the *Yorktown*. This search was not to proceed further west than 172°00' E. Should the search fail to locate any units of the striking group and should no further orders be received, the support was to retire toward latitude 4°40' N., longitude 170°00' W., where it would pick up the fueling group, *Sabine* and *Mahan*, and return to Pearl Harbor.[58]

Fletcher's Task Force 17 tactical organization was established in his Operation Order No. 2-42 on January 25, 1942, as follows:

(17.1) Striking Group				
	(17.1.1)	*Louisville*	Captain Nixon	1 CA
		St. Louis		1 CL
	(17.1.2)	*Yorktown*	Captain Buckmaster	1 CV
		Air Group		17 VF, 31 VSB, 12 VT
(17.2) Support Group			Captain Fahrion	4 DD
		Hughes, *Sims*, *Russell*, *Walke*		
(17.3) Fueling Group			Commander Maples	1 AO
				1 DD
		Sabine, *Mahan*[59]		

Fletcher's Task Force 17 with the *Yorktown* and cruisers *Louisville* and *St. Louis* approached their attack point between the Marshall and Gilbert Islands on a course of 270° true at 25.5 knots. Their four destroyers moved at a slower 15 knots. Barometric pressure continued to fall heading into a tropical low and bad weather. Flight quarters sounded at 0415 on the *Yorktown*. At 0452 on February 1, they reversed course and first launched the 4-plane CAP at their attack point 140, 127, and 71 miles respectively from Jaluit, Makin, and Milli islands. There would be no fighter escorts for the attacking groups, with VF-42 assigned to provide CAP protection for the Task Force 17 fleet.[60]

Jaluit Attack Group Action

The planes for the Jaluit Island attack were then launched into moonlight, with high overcast, threatening dark clouds, and lightning toward Jaluit. Under Commander Curtis S. Smiley, the commander of the *Yorktown* Air Group in his SBD, 11 TBDs from VT-5 and 17 SBDs from VB-5 were launched. The planes were spotted for the attack in order

USS *Yorktown* (CV-5) underway 21 July 1937, U.S. National Archives photograph, ARC Identifier 513026/Local Identifier 19-N-17424, arcweb.archives.gov.

by tactical organization. The TBDs were armed with three 500-pound bombs and the SBDs were loaded with one 500-pound bomb.

With his tail and formation lights set on dim, Lieutenant Commander Robert G. Armstrong's SBD-3 was launched first at 0455 on a normal run ahead for four minutes. He made a wide sweeping turn to the right to allow the rest of the first division of VB-5 to join with him in a loose formation, and completing the turn running parallel to the starboard side of the *Yorktown*. Armstrong noted a group of lights ahead and to the starboard of the track of the carrier.

Armstrong made a second turn to the right and circled the carrier with what he thought were 15 planes from the VB-5 attack group. He and his radioman J.W. Trott were somewhat unsure of the exact count. A few more easy right turns around the carrier were made to pick up more planes. The Torpedo Squadron Five planes were supposed to rendezvous on the port side of the *Yorktown*, but Armstrong was unable to sight them. Realizing that VB-5 was ten minutes past the planned departure time, he led his planes on a wide sweep to the left to come up the port side of the carrier, hoping to locate the VT-5 aircraft. They saw some lights they believed to be VT-5 planes. Having been unable to rendezvous with the Torpedo Squadron, at 0535 Armstrong departed with his planes from the *Yorktown* to the target objective.

In company with Armstrong were some 22 to 23 planes, including Air Group Commander Smiley. At 0540, after seeing lights astern that might be torpedo planes, Armstrong yet again made a wide left sweep to no avail. He completed his turn, reset his course, and rejoined his attack group. Since Armstrong still believed there were additional

VT-5 planes astern, he set the approach speed to 110 to 115 knots to accommodate the slower TBDs. He also needed to conserve fuel. With the dark scattered clouds low at 1,000 feet and the moon nearly down, he maintained the altitude between 400 and 600 feet off the water.

At about 0627 Armstrong felt he should have reached the southern tip of the Jaluit Atoll. As dawn began to break, he saw the planes of the 2nd division and decided to climb above the thin overcast to avoid being detected by enemy forces on the island. He ran into a heavy thunderstorm and continued to climb for about two minutes until he saw two bright flashes of what he thought were lightning. He then decreased speed to descend at 150 knots. Three minutes later he broke through the clouds at about 700 feet altitude and saw three planes from Lieutenant Adam's section. He tried to call the second division leader, Lieutenant Bellinger, by radio, but his radio did not work.

The southern tip of Jaluit Island was sighted off a half mile on his starboard bow, and he began to turn to the left, away from land. The visibility was now clear and unlimited area some five miles wide as dawn arrived. He began to climb and continued to call Bellinger. Armstrong's radio began to function again, but one of the wingmen told him that his transmitter was not working. Actually, it was the wingman's receiver that had malfunctioned. Armstrong tried multiple times to contact his group to reassemble his division at the navigational objective, but it was no use. He continued to climb, heading to the southeast for 7 to 8 minutes, and then reversed course to position himself over the western part of the atoll before attacking.

At 8,000 feet on a northwest course, Armstrong saw two additional planes flying together at 6,000 feet. He later learned that it was Lieutenant (JG) Christie's section. Christie did not hear or see him but was seen astern of him during several attacks. At 0700 in high winds, the planes made contact over the western part of the atoll. A course was set for the anchorage at Jaluit. It took great effort to locate and reach the target because of the thunderstorm and heavy overcast. Once they reached the anchorage, they saw one large 8,000-ton freighter or tender in the center of the anchorage that was painted a dark color and was on fire at its stern. There were many small fishing or patrol type vessels anchored in the harbor. Diving from 9,000 feet from the south to the north, Armstrong's first division began their attack at about 0725. Armstrong's bomb missed the vessel on the port side some 100 feet. He and the others experienced fogging of the windshield and partial fogging of the telescope during the dives.

He recovered from the dive to the northeast and headed at high speed towards Kabbenbock Island just inside the channel mouth, planning to strafe any AA installations that could be found. At 1,000 feet from the island, flying at low altitude, he did not see any activity. He changed the course toward the tip of Enybor Island, where two airfields were supposed to be found. At the end of the island in a clear area, a structure was sighted to the east that could be a dirigible hangar estimated to be 200 feet long. On the southeast part of the clearing were four structures that appeared to be wooden buildings not over 50 feet square set on stilts about 50 feet in the air. Observation of the targets was difficult due to the foggy windshields and high-speed search, but they were all destroyed by some 100 rounds of .50 caliber fire.

After strafing on the south tip of Enybor, Armstrong's division moved along the atoll as planned to destroy the seaplane facility and aircraft at Emidji Island. No targets were of interest until they reached the seaplane base on the lagoon side of the island. Three small hangars deemed too small to hold four-engine patrol planes were on the

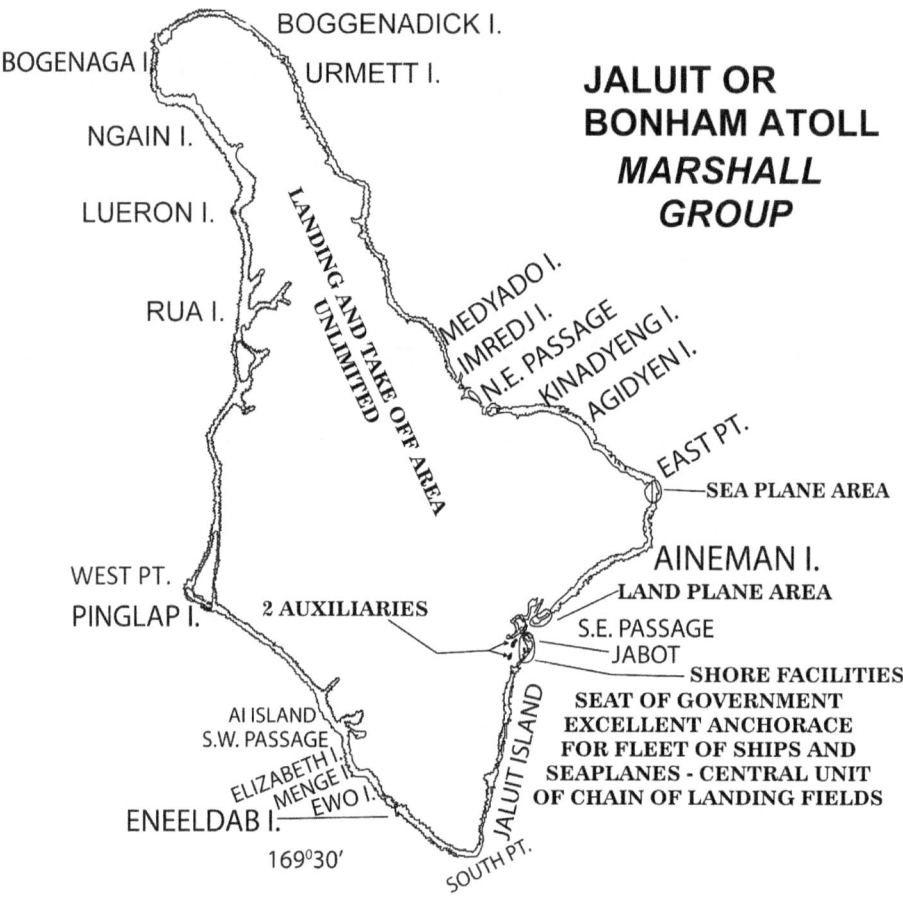

Chart of Jaluit Atoll for the Task Force 17 (USS *Yorktown*) raid on February 1, 1942. Image redrawn based on *Report of Attack of Yorktown Air Group on Jaluit, Milli and Makin in Marshall and Gilbert Islands*, Enclosure F, dated February 5, 1942 (NARA, College Park, Maryland).

lagoon side of the island. In front of the buildings were three L-shaped breakwaters projecting out about 50 yards from the buildings. There were circular clearings 20 feet in diameter scattered around the buildings, appearing to be gun emplacements among the palm trees. No activity was seen as they passed over the facility. A small ship of some 200 feet long was anchored 500 yards off the seaplane base in the lagoon. Armstrong fired 200 rounds of .50 caliber ammunition into the freighter lying broadside to him. His tracer bullets were ricocheting from the water on the far side of the vessel as he flew just 50 feet off the water and within 200 feet of the ship; he then pulled up and passed overhead. His gunner, Radioman 1c J.W. Trott, noted AA fire as the wing planes maneuvered to strafe the ship as they were moved a good ways northward.

Armstrong continued up the islands at 100 feet altitude, seeing only occasional thatched huts surrounded by palm trees. He passed to the north of Agidyen Island, then turned east into a small rainstorm and circled, waiting for his trailing wingmen to join him. He contacted them on his radio, but after 5 minutes they had not arrived. He then headed to the east of south point and saw Lieutenant Adam's section located 10 miles east of the island. He joined them at 0740 and headed back to the carrier.

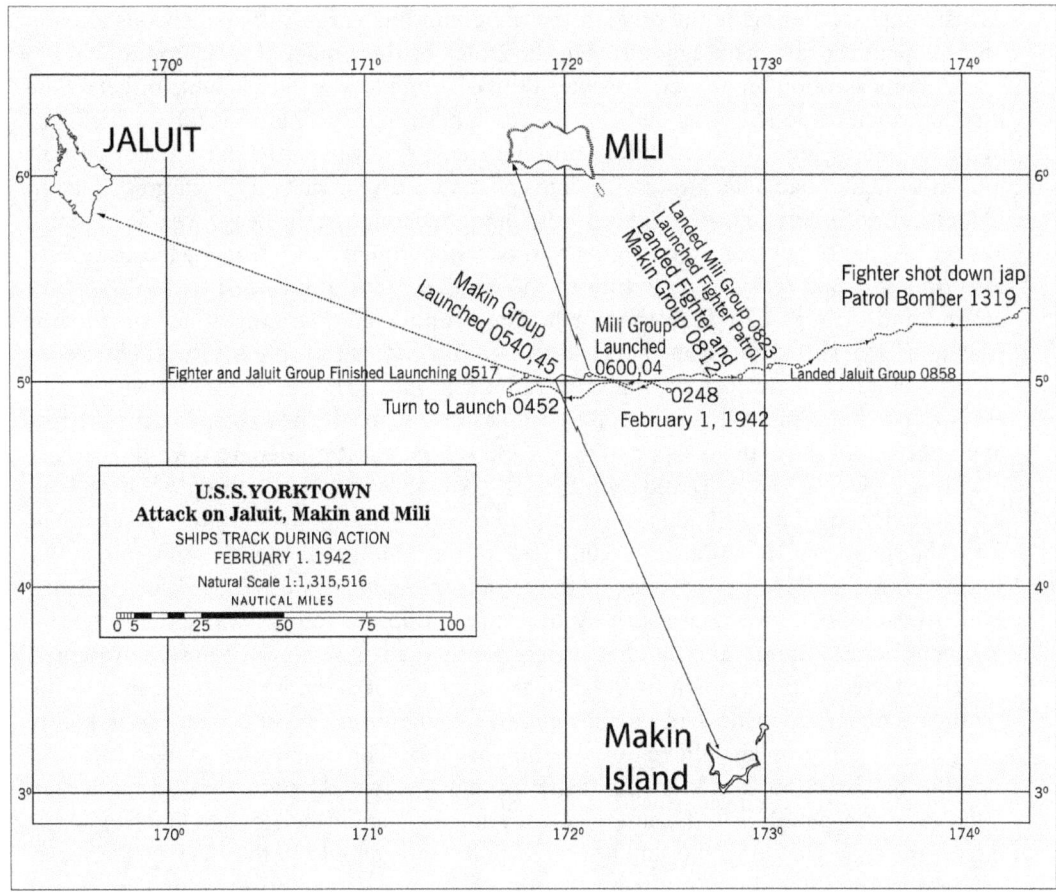

USS *Yorktown* attack track—Marshall Islands raid. Image redrawn based on *Early Carrier Raids in the Pacific Ocean*, 27.

Armstrong's two wingmen, Lieutenant J.L. Nielsen and Lieutenant J.J. Powers, experienced the same action as he did. Lieutenant Nielsen started his dive on the transport at 0720, but his bomb missed. His windshield had fogged up at 4,000 feet in his dive. He strafed the barracks on the extreme south end of Enybor Island, the lookout and radio towers on Agidyen Island, and a junk he sighted west of Emidji Island. Powers had sighted Jaluit at 0640 and circled until 0700. The target was obscured by clouds, but eventually he was able to see the Jaluit anchorage through the clouds. As the third plane in the section, he dived on the transport in the anchorage on a heading 030°, experienced the same windshield fogging, and dropped his bomb, which landed close aboard. Powers then moved at 200 feet altitude for 5 minutes toward the northeast, strafing a three-story building, a radio station tower, and a water or oil tank on Agidyen Island. At 0730 he joined with Lieutenant Nielsen and they headed back to the carrier.

VB-5 pilot Lieutenant S. Adams led his section, which included wingman Ensign H.L.A. Berger and Ensign David R. Berry, to Jaluit and began action at 0715. Berry saw just six planes at daybreak when he first sighted Jaluit Island. The six-plane group consisted of Squadron CO Armstrong and his two wingmen Powers and Nielsen, and his section leader Lieutenant Adams's section with wingman "Duke" Berger and himself. After

Armstrong's section made the dive on the merchantman cargo ship, which was already on fire, he never saw them again during the attack or the results of their bombing.

Adams's section made a circle around the island to assess the available targets. One merchantman cargo ship was on fire with a bright orange glow at the stern, which was being fanned by high 20-knot winds. Another cargo ship was in the harbor that did not look as though it had been attacked. Adams began his dive attack on the cargo ship from 10,000 feet, with Berry close by to keep from being separated in the heavy weather. Adams almost lost his target from the fogging windshield at 4,000 feet but managed to release his bomb at 2,500 feet. He pulled up to the southeast and proceeded with his section around and through clouds to the north. They conducted a strafing attack on Enybor Island, firing at sheds, tanks, and barracks. Adams noted that the only AA fire encountered was at 3,000 feet below him during the strafing action. As the section was about to join at about two miles east of the island, Berry got a glimpse of a torpedo plane in the process of bombing, but the plane disappeared. At 0735 Adams's section departed for the carrier.

Ensign B.G. Preston arrived with the VB-5 squadron at the south tip of Jaluit Atoll and started their climb. At 1,500 feet he entered a heavy rain cloud and came out separated from the squadron. He climbed to 6,000 feet to break out of the clouds some four miles south of the island. He circled to locate the squadron. A few minutes passed and he heard over the radio, "Circling over south tip of island, 3 minutes to go."[61] Since the radio did not mention the altitude, and the clouds were dense, Preston was unable to see any planes.

He started to move down from 8,500 feet and at 4,500 feet he sighted a ship to the northeast steaming upwind and heading for a heavy rain area. On his way to the ship, Preston saw a monoplane above him on the port side. The other pilot spotted him and dived in his direction. Not knowing if the contact was friend or foe, Preston moved up into the nearest cloud. Later he emerged from the cloud and descended to 600 feet, looking for the ship. He found the ship after 5 minutes and came in to the stern of the vessel heading in the same direction as he at 065°. He noticed a fire off the ship's starboard quarter from his position four to five miles away. The ceiling was 600 feet altitude as he approached the target, a tanker of between 5,000 to 7,000 tons. He waited for a break in the clouds to allow him to climb and make a dive on the tanker. During that time, he strafed the broadside of the ship with machine-gun fire and received .30 caliber return fire from the ship.

As the time passed, the tanker continued to maneuver in order to stay in the heaviest rainstorms. After 45 minutes, a slight break in the clouds opened up. Preston climbed to 1,500 feet and pushed over to release his bomb at 900 feet in this shallow dive. He lost sight of the ship for about 10 seconds in the thick fog and, when he recovered it, saw that his bomb had landed ahead of the ship. He strafed the tanker and then headed to Point Option alone. The attack had occurred some three to four miles off the island.

While he was climbing through dense clouds, Lieutenant K.E. Taylor's engine completely cut out momentarily, and he dropped below the formation, losing it in the clouds. He regained power and came on top of the clouds ten minutes later at about 4,500 feet, moving toward Jaluit. After 15 minutes had passed, he sighted the island off five miles ahead through the cloud cover. He was at 7,000 feet one point off his starboard bow. Taylor circled over the island to join the rest of the squadron. He saw one of his friendlies above him at 10,000 feet to the south. He headed up to join the other plane when it disappeared into the clouds.

Circling back toward the island, he still was unable to find the plane. Descending to 200 feet altitude, he tried to locate any land, but failed. Climbing back up, he saw a TBD plane piloted by Lieutenant (JG) R. Denniston in the open space. Taylor saw a flash in the clouds to the south and headed in that direction, thinking it was perhaps AA fire over Jaluit. It must have been lightning because he found no land. Starting down under the clouds, he spotted Lieutenant Commander Jon Taylor's TBD and Dennison's torpedo bomber and headed back to the carrier at 0725. En route, the three planes jettisoned their bombs. Later they were joined by two SBDs piloted by Lieutenant (JG) Christie and Ensign L.M. Bigelow. They landed aboard the *Yorktown* at 0950.

Ensign Bigelow had sighted the island at about 0705 on the southwest corner and circled it at 7,000 feet. Weather was extremely cloudy with occasional glimpses of the surface. At 0714 he saw two ships in the anchorage: one large AK and a small one. A fire was seen burning on the stern from the larger ship. He climbed to 11,000 feet, dove on the larger vessel, and released his bomb. It landed about 75 feet from the ship on the aft port quarter. He strafed both ships on the way back and fired some 150 rounds on a pier nearby. Through close observation of the beach, Bigelow noticed three large mounds of dirt that looked like possible ammunition depots. Poor visibility made it difficult to recognize targets. He received AA fire from 5-inch rounds, but it was not close. He headed back to the ship around 0730 in company with Lieutenant (JG) Christie.

VB-5 Lieutenant Christie launched at 0455 from the *Yorktown*. At 0658, in company with Ensign Bigelow, he first sighted the objective from 12,000 feet. They circled Jaluit to select targets, and at 0705 began a dive through the overcast on a cargo ship of some 9,000 tons that was already burning on the stern. Some AA fire was encountered during the approach and dive. The bomb missed the target. He swung around and strafed the ship, expending 400 rounds of .50 caliber ammunition. He saw 5-inch batteries and machine gun fire from the ship. The damage to the ship was unobserved. On departure there were still three other ships that showed no fire or serious damage in the lagoon. He left for the carrier at 0730 and joined with Lieutenant Commander Taylor en route.

At 0701 VB-5 Lieutenant W.S. Guest, in company with Ensign H.M. McDowell, attacked the infamous large transport during a divebombing attack from 5,000 feet. One of the bombs hit the stern, blowing up approximately 30 feet of the ship, and damaging the propellers, stopping the ship's progress as the fire burned "furiously."[62] The second bomb overshot the ship. They both proceeded to Enybor Island and were unable to locate any airfield as previously reported by intelligence. They strafed what appeared to be storehouses and ammunition dumps. No enemy aircraft were seen. They headed back to the anchorage and strafed the other large ship and a tug. The harbor had only fishing boats remaining. Guest had expended all his ammunition, but his gunner, Radioman 1c O.R. Phelps, strafed the barracks with his free gun. McDowell also strafed the barracks, a group of houses (buildings) and antennae masts. The two SBD bombers departed the island at 0712, landing aboard the carrier at 0904.

At 0706 VB-5 Ensign O.I. Houghton arrived over the northwest tip of Jaluit Atoll in company with two TBD planes from VT-5 piloted by Lieutenant (JG) R. Denniston and the executive officer of VT-5, Lieutenant Harland T. Johnson. He dove under the 4,000-foot ceiling on a small building or lookout station in among trees on a small island. His bomb landed between a road and the building. Then he climbed to attempt to rejoin the TBDs, noticing that their bombs landed along the shoreline. Unable to find the torpedo planes, he moved to the rendezvous point and did not find other friendlies, so he headed back to the carrier at 0710. When he landed, he learned that the TBDs he had flown with had conducted forced landings on Jaluit. It was a mystery to him what caused them to be forced down.

Ensign J.T. Cranford from VB-5, in company with two TBDs piloted by Lieutenant A.H. Furer and Lieutenant (JG) T.B. Ellison, saw Jaluit Island at 0715. The three planes climbed to gain sufficient altitude to execute a bombing attack. As they neared the island, they sighted one plane circling above the northern tip of the island and also several planes down at low altitude conducting strafing runs. They lost sight of the planes as clouds ascended to as high as 15,000 to 20,000 feet. At 7,000 feet it was decided that it would be impossible to bomb at high altitude. The TBD pilots decided to descend and conduct a glide-bombing run. Cranford lost sight of them until he saw the third bomb descend. He observed the harbor area and saw the largest supply ship on fire burning at the stern.

There was a large fire to the northwest part of the island that looked like an oil fire. He spotted what he recognized from drawings as the administration building and immediately made a 180° turn back and started to climb up, immediately signaling to a TBD to circle, while he went "aloft" to execute a dive. Cranford climbed to 8,000 feet, then pushed over into a 60° angle dive to release his bomb at 2,000 feet. Looking back as he recovered, he saw that he had "scored a hit on this building or one of the barracks very near." He noticed debris, smoke, and flames ascending skyward. Close to the target was "a clearing which appeared to be a parade ground, and a white ribbon, possibly a road, running from the clearing to the end of the island." He continued down and passed over the ship and strafed the area. At this point he climbed to rejoin the TBDs but was unable to find them. He circled the island for 15 minutes, seeing no planes, and then started back to the carrier at 0815. He was forced to stay below the 400- to 500-foot ceiling and landed aboard at 1015. He encountered no other planes on his trek home.[63]

The Torpedo Squadron Five commanding officer, Lieutenant Commander Jon Taylor, was launched from the *Yorktown* at 0505 and proceeded ahead for 7 minutes. He then turned on the opposite course to rendezvous with his squadron planes. Turning to the left, he passed one mile off the port beam of the carrier, running 105 knots at 1,000 feet. In the darkness and poor weather conditions, none of his planes joined with him. He circled the carrier until 0530 with his running lights on and then decided to head toward Jaluit on a course of 294° to allow his planes to join en route. Taylor remained on the same course and varied altitudes between 500 and 7,500 feet until 0700 but could not find Jaluit. At 0750 he joined with VB-5 Lieutenant K.E. Taylor as they headed back toward the *Yorktown*. Just afterwards VB-5 Lieutenant J.J. Powers joined them and revealed that he had been unable to find Jaluit and had used nearly half his fuel. When one of them used up one of his tanks, the group jettisoned their bombs and continued on to the carrier. En route, two more VB-5 planes, Lieutenant (JG) Christie and Ensign L.M. Bigelow, joined.

Taylor located the carrier off 150 miles away using the ship's YE and, based on that course, assumed he must have passed over Jaluit on the way out. Passing through several rain squalls, they reached the *Yorktown*, landing at 1010. After his landing, he learned the other planes of his squadron had reached Jaluit either alone or in company with VB-5 planes.

VT-5 Ensign G.E. Bottjer was launched in his TBD at 0505 and flew for 30 minutes before rendezvousing with his section leader. The Radioman 3c C.L. Smith noticed the lead plane was signaling "wheels" several times. He contacted the pilot, who indicated that he was having trouble retracting the landing gear. He directed Smith to send the following message via blinker, "Hydraulic system busted." The section leader ordered Bottjer to return to the carrier, and he landed at 0845.[64]

At 0500 Lieutenant E.B. Parker launched in his TBD and joined up with Lieutenant (JG) T.B. Ellison and Lieutenant A.H. Furer. Furer was leading and refused to turn the lead over to him. An SBD came in to join but left immediately. At 0545 he headed on instruments for over an hour toward Jaluit alone. At about 0700, flying at 8,800 feet, he sighted land and decided to descend on instruments to the south through the clouds. At 100 feet altitude, Furer broke into the clear but had lost the island. He took to a course to the north and found coral reefs and small isolated land areas. At 0725 he again came into a clearing with a ceiling of 2,000 feet and found Jaluit Harbor. He saw one ship burning and spotted what he thought was a dirt field serving as an airfield, but with no planes or activity.

Parker saw two or possibly three other planes diving at the field. He selected the mole and town as his targets. One of his bombs missed, falling into the water, and the second hit in the mole, where many fishing boats were anchored. One bomb hit near the barracks, with damage unknown. AA fire of perhaps 20mm was encountered close by. They felt a concussion from what they believed was a 3-inch gun that fired at them. Parker departed the area at 0745 on a course back to the carrier.

At 0811 Parker's Radioman 1c A.M. Shirah heard on the radio the following announcement from the executive officer of VT-5, Lieutenant Harland T. Johnson: "This is 5-T-7. 5-T-7 and 5-T-6 [Ensign Herbert R. Hein] are landing at Jaluit. Are landing alongside one of the northwestern islands of Jaluit. That is all."[65] Both planes landed in the water and their crews were able to get aboard their rubber boats. They landed ashore and were hidden by the local natives, but were captured two days later by a Japanese patrol boat. All six of the men became prisoners of war. For most of the trip back, Parker was on instruments. He landed at 1025 with only two gallons of gas in his fuel tanks.

VT-5 Lieutenant A.H. Furer launched at 0504 and saw the tail light of the plane ahead piloted by the VT-5 CO, Lieutenant Commander Taylor. The plane's light quickly faded away in the darkness as he approached. He never saw his plane again during the engagement. Furer continued on for several minutes, and then turned back toward the ship. Two other TBDs joined him. He tried to locate the ship with no success, and then attempted to hear the YE signals to no avail. He requested the carrier to turn on the YE and soon the signal came in. He circled the sector and called out his position on the radio to Taylor. Lieutenant Parker, in company with him, signaled "Join up,"[66] but he was unable to see his lights and he lost Parker.

Furer decided to return to the ship to set for departure to the objective. Then he was joined by VT-5 Lieutenant (JG) Ellison and VB-5 Ensign J.T. Cranford. They were now 45 minutes late in departing. He requested Cranford to take the lead and fly on automatic pilot to Jaluit. En route they maintained a slow high-pitch climb at 100 knots to conserve fuel, to arrive at 0725 at the western tip of Jaluit Atoll at altitude of 6,000 feet. Furer turned the lead over to Ellison, who flew along the west fringe to find a "hole"[67] in the clouds to locate the objective.

They could not execute horizontal bombing. Furer took the lead back and signaled for glide bombing on two ships in the anchorage. At 0740 they came over the ships and flew down through the clouds, coming out at 1,500 feet, where they pushed over and dropped their bombs. Furer's two bombs (one from the left wing and one from the right wing) fell short of the merchantman, which was already burning at the stern. Ellison released one bomb, which was also short, but closer than Furer's had been. Furer moved back into the clouds to avoid AA fire and lost Ellison. He emerged from the clouds and made a horizontal run on a pier and marine railway (objective six) as best he could, having no bombsight in his plane. He was unable to see the results of his rear bomb due to cloud cover. Ensign Cranford was still with him as he withdrew to the southward. Cranford had not released his bombs yet, so Furer directed him to make his attack.

At 0750 Furer departed from the area with 78 gallons in his fuel tanks. He flew at 95 knots with his carburetor set to lean on a course of 089° at 600 feet. He flew on autopilot about half the time. At 0948 he reported his position as 18 miles from point "TRUK" bearing 290° and requested change in point option, if any. The carrier replied and directed him to "Vector 100" which was 091° magnetic. Ten minutes later Furer picked up the YE signal.[68]

At 1015 he saw a TBD afloat with flotation bags functional. Radioman thought he saw occupants in a rubber boat nearby. Furer reported by radio to the carrier that the TBD was located on bearing 290° at 20 miles. Five minutes later a destroyer was seen heading to the contact. The destroyer signaled, "Int Corpen" by light and Furer replied "Corpen 290," assuming that he wanted to know the direction of the plane. Furer landed aboard at 1030 with 10 gallons remaining. In his opinion, the attack was unsuccessful for the TBDs because the ceiling was extremely low over the targets, and because of the lack of gasoline.[69]

At 0500, Lieutenant (JG) T.B. Ellison took off from the *Yorktown* in his TBD to rendezvous with Lieutenant Furer and then with Lieutenant Parker and Ensign Cranford. Parker soon departed after trying to take the lead from Lieutenant Furer. They were unable to join with the Air Group in the darkness, and decided to proceed to Jaluit independently. Ellison departed at 0600 and arrived at Jaluit at 0718. The overcast was heavy, making targets difficult to locate. The primary objectives were abandoned, and the group separated to make glide-bombing approaches on the two ships in the harbor. Ellison began a shallow dive at 0740 and dropped a single bomb a few hundred feet astern of the cargo ship furthest from the harbor entrance. He attempted to strafe during his glide in, but it was ineffective.

He then pulled up into the clouds as he opened the bombing windows in preparation for the next bomb release. Using a low horizontal approach and not using his bombsight, Ellison pulled up sharply, waited until the ship was visible in his bombing window, and dropped the two bombs simultaneously at 2,500 feet on the second ship, already burning from the stern, located close in to the channel leading through the island. One of his bombs hit on the starboard side, aft of amidships. He did not see where the second bomb landed, but they left the ship in flames from the amidships to the stern.

Ellison turned for home with less than the usual amount of fuel needed to reach the carrier. They flew following the Fox-George sector of the YE towards the carrier. At 1020, some 20 miles from the ship, the crew spotted a TBD in the water, with three men waving at them from a rubber boat. They dropped a smoke flare at the site and Ellison radioed the carrier. Having difficulty seeing the carrier, Ellison requested a radar bearing from the *Yorktown* and finally was able to land at 1035 with two gallons of fuel remaining.

Ensign A.J. Schultheis in his TBD had trouble with the wing pins not locking in place and was late for takeoff at 0515. He was the last plane to launch from the *Yorktown*. He had difficulty locating the rest of the squadron. When he joined up with what he thought was the first division of VT-5, the second division was about a half mile behind him. He formed up loosely with the first division and waited until the second division moved up. His course varied from 287° to 300° flying at 120 knots at an average altitude of 600 feet.

When the second division had not moved up after 30 to 40 minutes, Schultheis closed on the first division until he could barely make out two silhouettes of two planes. He positioned his plane third in the right echelon on them. After flying for some fifteen minutes, at 1,300 feet they encountered a heavy rainstorm and immediately he lost sight of both of the planes. A few seconds later he noticed three abrupt flashes of light that had "a slightly red tinge" to them. He continued on his course of 287°T for four minutes as he moved down to 150 feet. With visibility near zero, he executed a "slow climbing turn to the right," completing a full circle. Realizing he was "still in the soup," he turned left 180° and flew for about five minutes before finally emerging from the rainstorm.[70]

After circling, he did not see any planes, and decided to head back to the carrier on a course of 115°T. When fifteen to twenty minutes had passed, Aviation Ordnanceman 3c H.E. Sybrant was directed to clear the bomb racks. Sybrant dropped the third bomb, but stopped when he heard the pilot say he thought he saw three TBDs flying in the opposite direction. Schultheis circled back but was unable to find them. He cleared the remaining two bombs using his emergency release, and twenty minutes later he directed Radioman 3c F.J. Chantiny to send the carrier the message, "ZED YOKE EASY." After sending another three or four times, they received the ZB signals "DOG" and "FOX." Flying on the ZB course for 45 minutes to an hour, they sighted the ship, exchanged recognition signals, and landed aboard at 0845.[71]

After launching at 0505, Lieutenant (JG) R. Denniston was unable to rendezvous with his group. At 0530 he decided to proceed independently to the objective. At around 0625 he noticed a bright flare burning momentarily and headed off to find it. He lost sight of it in the rain squall. Five minutes later he saw a small island. Since he thought he was perhaps the only plane not in company with his attack group, he reentered the rain storm to remain undetected and avoid giving away the surprise attack. With poor visibility and not sure the small island was Jaluit, he proceeded to try to locate other islands of the atoll. He was unsuccessful and could not even find the first island he had already encountered. At about 0720 he saw Lieutenant K.E. Taylor of VB-5, but they became separated. He gave up trying to find the objective and headed toward the carrier. At 0735 he joined with Lieutenant Taylor and the VT-5 CO Lieutenant Commander Jon Taylor. CO Taylor directed them to clear their bomb racks. An hour later two more SBDs joined the group and they returned to the carrier, landing at 0810.[72]

The damage inflicted on the Japanese during the Jaluit Atoll attack did not involve enemy aircraft. No enemy planes were observed or encountered. Intelligence reports had indicated the existence of a landplane base on Enybor Island, but there were only two short dirt runways noted. The action report filed by the *Yorktown* Air Group Commander, Commander C.S. Smiley, recorded the following surface craft and shore installation damages:

Surface Craft.

(1) One auxiliary, underway when attack commenced, was hit directly on stern and set fire. It stopped immediately and dropped anchor. Later another direct hit was obtained by TBD-1 with a two bomb salvo. As no splash was observed both bombs may have hit. When last observed was burning fiercely. Repeated strafing attacks directed at this ship.
(2) One auxiliary, at anchor, suffered at least three near bomb misses and repeated strafing attacks. Only superficial damage may be assumed.

(3) One auxiliary, underway at sea, attacked by one SBD-3, bombing and strafing. Bomb missed; damage by strafing considered negligible.
(4) Other small craft were strafed with undetermined results.

Shore Establishment.
(1) Several bombs were dropped in the administration building and barracks area and near the mole on Jabor Island causing extensive damage. This area was subjected to heavy strafing by .50 caliber fixed and .30 caliber free guns.
(2) At least two bombs were dropped in the vicinity of Enybor Island landplane facilities and the area strafed. Damage undetermined.
(3) The buildings indicated as seaplane facilities on Emidji Island were strafed. Damage undetermined."[73]

The *Yorktown* Air Group losses were substantial: four VT-5 crews and planes, and two VB-5 crews and planes.

Torpedo Squadron Five
Lieutenant H.T. Johnson, USN
ACMM(PA) C.T. Fosha, USN
RM1c J.W. Dalzell, USN

Ensign H.R. Hein (AVN), USNR
AOM3c J.D. Strahl, USN
Sea1c M.E. Windham, USN

Lieutenant J.C. Moore, USN
AOM1c H.F. Omo, USN
RM3c H.C. Schonberg, USN

Lieutenant F.X. Maher, USN
AMM1c (NAP) J.C. Chitwood, USN
RM3c R.L. Ayers, USN

Bombing Squadron Five
Lieutenant G.L. Bellinger, USN
RM1c D. MacKillop, USN

Lieutenant (jg) M.P. Fishel, USN
RM1c L.W. Costello, USN[74]

Commander Smiley summarized the results of the Attack on Jaluit Atoll: "The successful accomplishment of the mission assigned was greatly hampered by extremely adverse weather conditions. It is believed that our losses would have been little or none under more favorable circumstances. The condition of one auxiliary when last observed would tend to indicate its eventually becoming a total loss. Damage on two other auxiliaries may be assumed from near bomb misses and intensive strafing. The damage inflicted on the shore establishment is incalculable but may be assumed to have been severe."[75]

Makin Attack Group Action

The commanding officer of Scouting Squadron Five, Lieutenant Commander William O. Burch, Jr., launched at 0550 from the *Yorktown* with nine SBDs, each armed with one 500-pound bomb. At 0630, flying at 1,000 feet in better weather but under a rain squall, the attack group sighted Makin Island. They climbed to 12,000 feet to begin their divebombing attacks on an 8,000-ton aircraft tender, *Nagata Maru*, and two four-engine Kawanishi H6K Type 97 flying boats (seaplanes). The ship was in the harbor and the two flying boats were anchored on the far side of the lagoon to the south.

At 0658, Burch attacked from 12,000 feet, encountering antiaircraft fire that was fortunately inaccurate. He scored a direct hit on the stern of the ship. Lieutenant Stockton B. Strong, behind the leader, also hit the ship. The squadron closed up and proceeded in a large circle around the southwest corner of the island to make strafing attacks on the two seaplanes in the lagoon. They came in from 3,000 feet on a northerly heading. In the lead, Burch fired on the left seaplane, and started a fire. The remaining attackers fired on the right seaplane, hitting it many times. Burch ordered Lieutenant T.F. Caldwell, "Get that plane." Caldwell came in heading to the west, and "in bursts ... fired a string of about 20 shots into the plane, which immediately burst into a large ball of fire."[76]

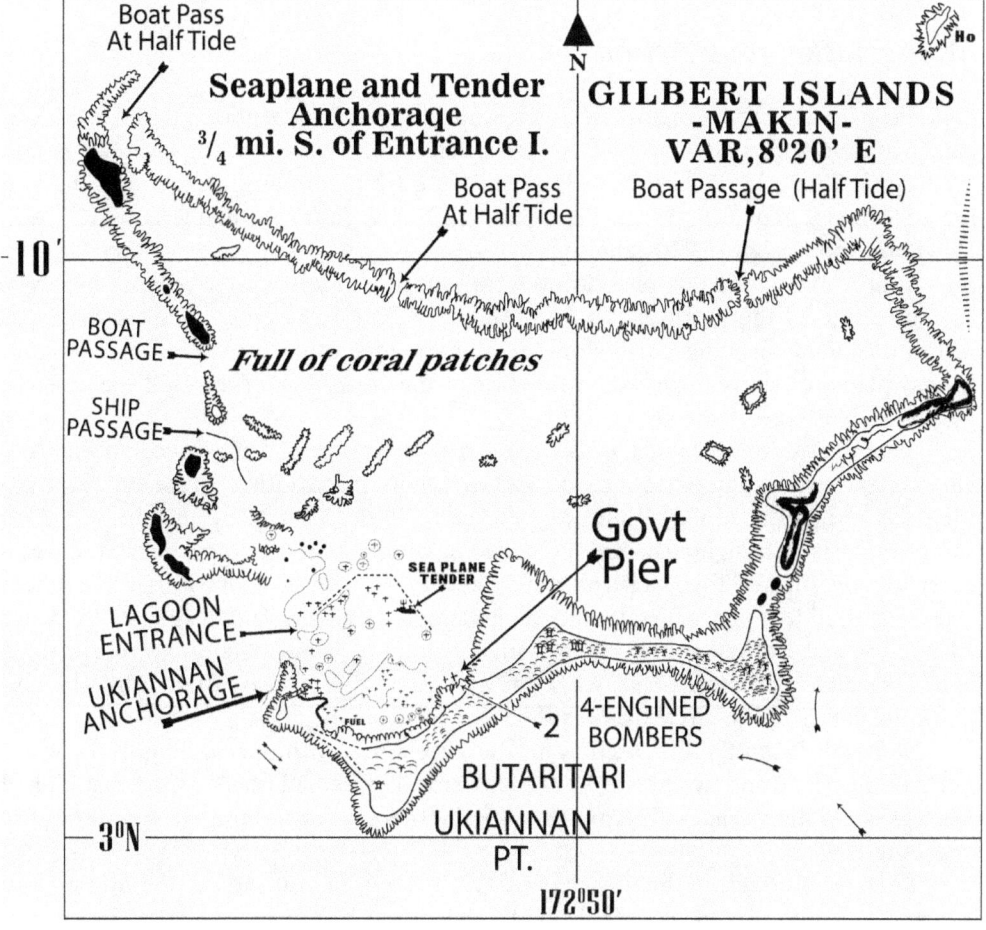

Chart of Makin Island, in the Gilbert Islands, for Task Force 17 (USS *Yorktown*) raid on February 1, 1942. Image redrawn based on *Report of Attack of Yorktown Air Group on Jaluit, Mili and Makin in Marshall and Gilbert Islands*.

Lieutenant R.B. Woodhull "sighted off Butaritari two fairly large wooden hulks very close inshore and one small two-masted schooner. One rectangular barge was alongside Government Pier. There was a large two or three story red wooden building at foot of Government Pier."[77]

After all the squadron attackers had bombed the ship and strafed the seaplanes one or more times, at 0730 the squadron rendezvoused west of Ukiannan Point, and then on a north heading flew back to the ship, landing between 0815 and 0820.

There were no personnel or aircraft lost during the Makin Island Attack. The Japanese lost two four-engine Kawanishi H6K Type 97 flying patrol boats destroyed by strafing at anchor in the harbor near Butaritari. A large auxiliary ship received two direct hits plus seven close misses and was "set on fire." The air group commander noted the destruction of the two patrol planes and concluded that "the damage incurred by the auxiliary may be assumed to have resulted in its total loss. An apparent attempt to beach it was made but when last seen was stopped in deep water, on fire and with a large oil slick astern."[78]

Milli Attack Group Action

The Milli Attack Group of five SBDs, armed with one 500-pound bomb each, was launched at 0610 in good weather led by the executive officer of Scouting Five, Lieutenant Wallace C. Short, Jr. The other SBD pilots were from Bombing Squadron Five and included Lieutenant C.R. Ware, Lieutenant (JG) E.V. Johnson, Lieutenant (JG) A.L. Downing, and Ensign H.W. Nicholson.

At 0635 flying at 2,000 feet altitude, running at 140 knots on a heading 345°, the squadron sighted the southeastern tip of the Milli Atoll. The group climbed to 12,000 feet in the clouds heading north along the eastern edge of the atoll, keeping a lookout for any planes or ships anchored on this side of the area. Most of the atoll was covered by clouds. No targets were seen.

At 0645 at altitude 12,000 feet, the group arrived at the northeast corner of the atoll, where they turned westward toward the northwest corner (Port Rhin) of the atoll, arriving there five minutes later. Port Rhin was believed to be the most likely anchorage, but no ships or planes were sighted. They descended to about 3,000 feet to get below the cloud cover and investigated Tokowa Island. Only a small 75-foot by 50-foot barn-shaped brown warehouse building with a metal roof was sighted on the small island just west of Tokowa Island. The first section of three planes with Short, Johnson and Nicholson were ordered at 0720 to attack the storehouse, while the second section of two SBDs with Ware and Downing continued to circle overhead looking for a better target.

No bombs from the first section hit the warehouse, with one landing in the water north of the island and two hitting on the west side of the small island near "what looked like a group of native shacks."[79] They then strafed the warehouse with no antiaircraft fire encountered.

After reconnoitering the western area of the atoll, the second section located and attacked a warehouse and water tank on Milli Island. At Milli they found a "village fronting on the lagoon with a wooden pier built out about 100 yards to moderately deep water."[80] Nearby was a long, low building of new construction sized 200 feet by 50 feet, which could have been a barracks. Next to the building was a large lumber store and the

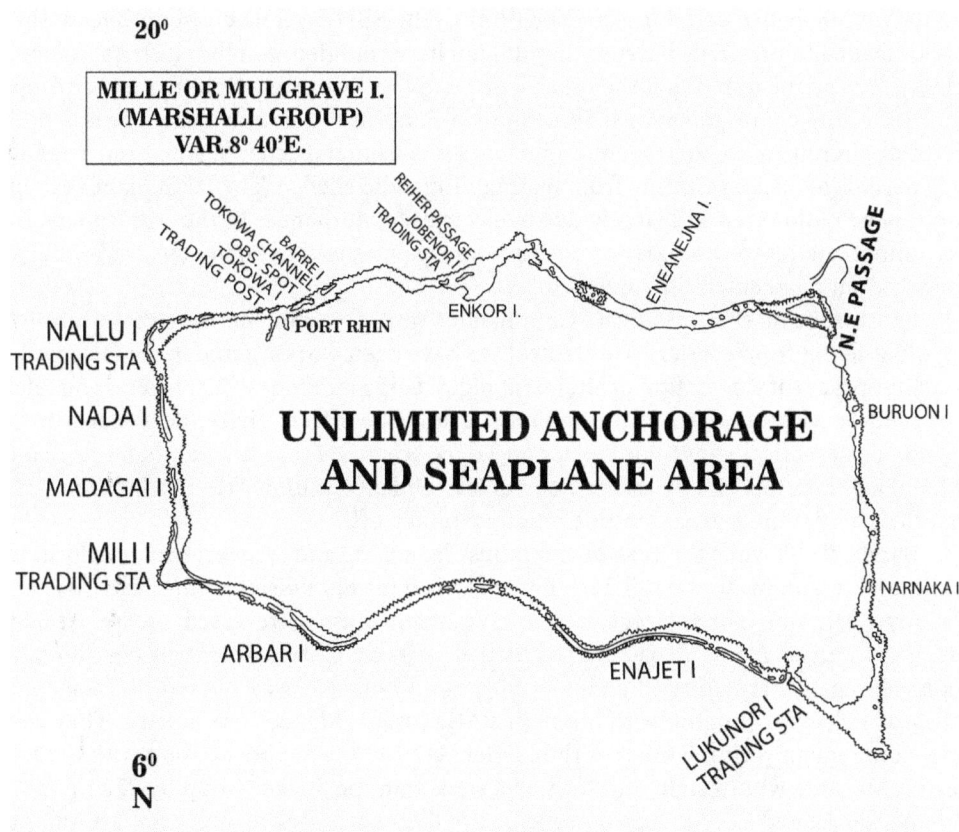

Chart of Milli Island, in the Marshall Islands, for Task Force 17 (USS *Yorktown*) raid on February 1, 1942. Image redrawn based on *Report of Attack of Yorktown Air Group on Jaluit, Milli and Makin in Marshall and Gilbert Islands*.

beginning of another building. Out to the north of the village was a cleared strip of uprooted coco palms. Though no construction had been started yet and no heavy machinery was seen, it was probably to be an airfield.

At 0725 Lieutenant Downing from the second section did not attack the barracks but decided to use his 500-pound bomb on a few small tanks at the back of the village, destroying what he assumed were fresh water tanks. Ware's bomb was a dud, but he had strafed while he dove from 3,000 feet on the target.

All five planes of the attack group rendezvoused over Knox Island and departed at 0810 for the *Yorktown*, landing at 0845. No planes or personnel were lost in the Milli attack. The damage inflicted on the Japanese during the attack on Milli Atoll was "negligible" at best. There was no evidence that the atoll was being used as a base.[81]

Yorktown Air Group Commander Smiley's action report, summarizing the Jaluit, Makin and Milli attacks, provided several useful comments. Regarding ordnance, he noted that the 500-pound Mark-12 bombs using Mk. 21 and 23 fuses functioned well. The Jaluit bombs hit the water in shallow dives, exploded on or close to the surface, and threw up columns of smoke and fragmentation. The Makin bombs, dropped at steep angles, submerged deeply before exploding, which produced a "mining effect."[82] A number of stoppages and jams with .50 caliber fixed guns installed in SBD-3 planes were found, with defective cartridges and belt links. The SBD-3 pilots chose to release their bombs manually, primarily because they did not have confidence in the electrical solenoid release. Smiley suggested that the pilots be able to test the installation in practice drops.

Regarding communications, Smiley noted that this mission had again revealed the fact that aircraft radio equipment could not be considered reliable when not used for long periods of disuse resulting from maintaining radio silence. The Jaluit planes experienced poor radio reception largely due to electrical disturbances in the atmosphere, but transmitter failures were also reported. They also experienced failure to receive YE signals when the ship had entered a rainstorm.

Perhaps the most interesting of Commander Smiley's comments were those concerning night flying from carriers. He wrote, "We have been working under the false premise in our peace time operation of aircraft at night. Large numbers of airplanes, completely darkened or with only dim running lights, cannot be effectively rendezvoused in the vicinity of a practically invisible carrier on a dark ocean. It is considered that nine planes is the maximum that can be assured of a quick rendezvous under these conditions, and that then only if there are no undue holdups in take off."[83]

Back at 0500, while the *Yorktown* was busy launching and recovering planes to attack Jaluit, Makin and Milli, the full Task Force 17 (*Yorktown, Louisville, Salt Lake City*) and Destroyer Division Three (*Hughes, Sims, Walke* and *Russell*) reversed course. At 0642 the heavy cruiser *Louisville* catapulted their Curtiss SOC-3 floatplane to port on antisubmarine patrol armed with a single 100-pound bomb. It was piloted by Lieutenant Edward Hicks Worthington with observer RM1c Joseph Alonzo Barr aboard. They were briefed to remain within 5 miles of the carrier. At 0700 the Support Group with the four destroyers came within sight and formed a screen on the Strike Group by 0720.

As the rotated CAP planes patrolled, at 0903 the weather turned even grimmer as the carrier pitched and rolled. The carrier launched 14 SBDs from VS-5 on an antitorpedo plane patrol as the *Yorktown* continued to land returning planes. Twenty minutes later, Captain Buckmaster suspended flight operations temporarily when the visibility was reduced to 100 yards in wind gusts to 50 knots.

At 0936 the heavy rain squall came in that reduced visibility to between 100 and 500 yards. At 0943 the destroyer *Walke* received a message via voice radio from the *Hughes* that a plane had crashed in the water on the *Hughes* port bow quarter. A minute later the commander of Destroyer Division Three ordered the *Walke* to proceed to rescue the crew of the crashed plane. Ensign T.A. Reeves with Seaman 1c Lonnie C. Gooch from VS-5 in his SBD had flown into the sea off the carrier's port beam. A motor whaleboat was used to recover the crew. Ensign Reeves suffered a severe scalp wound and Gooch had an internal injury. They were treated by the pharmacist's mate aboard the *Walke*. Later, at 1108 they were transported via whaleboat to the waiting *Louisville* for further medical treatment. At 1128 running at 30 knots, they rejoined the formation.[84]

With weather conditions so poor, Captain Buckmaster ordered all planes to land. At 0945 the six-fighter plane CAP and two strike planes landed aboard the *Yorktown*. Between 1015 and 1030 all the remaining planes aloft landed aboard the *Yorktown* to ride out the storm. With so many planes and crews still aloft or missing from the Jaluit attack, at 1040 Fletcher detached destroyers *Hughes*, *Sims* and *Russell* to look for missing aviators. The three destroyers headed west in a scouting line while the rest of the fleet sailed eastward at 20 knots.

Meanwhile, a Japanese Kawanishi flying boat, one of the three that had taken off after the American attackers had departed Jaluit, was out searching for the Task Force in the rough weather. At 1110 they reported sighting two American destroyers bearing 105° some 230 miles from Jaluit. The *Hughes* first saw the enemy intruder and requested air support. The *Yorktown* had spotted the flying boat on radar at 1117 bearing 270° just 32 miles from the carrier. Captain Buckmaster launched six F4Fs from the third division of VF-42 toward the target, led by Lieutenant Vince McCormack. After searching in and out of the clouds in the rain, the fighters never found the Japanese intruder. Likewise, the Kawanishi crew from the Yokohama Air Group lost sight of the destroyers and returned back home to Jaluit at 1610.[85]

At 1257 the relief CAP of six fighters under VF-42's executive officer, Lieutenant Commander Charles R. Fenton, took off, and Fletcher broke radio silence to instruct his destroyers to rendezvous. At 1305 the *Yorktown* picked up a second intruder at 1,000 feet under low clouds. The intruder turned out to be another Kawanishi Type 97 flying boat. Meanwhile, at 1313 the *Louisville* began calling out to Lieutenant Worthington's Curtiss SOC-3 but received no reply. Ensign E. Scott McCuskey and Ensign John P. Adams engaged the target as the intruder nosed down to gain speed. The two fighters silenced the tail gunner, and during the second pass they split up, with McCuskey moving below the plane and firing at the keel and the wings, as Adams continued firing at the tail from behind. The fighters destroyed the Kawanishi as it "exploded in midair and broke into many fragments." This action occurred in full view of the *Yorktown*. At the sight of the burning Kawanishi, newly promoted Captain J.J. ("Jocko") Clark grabbed a microphone and yelled out, "Burn, you son-of-a-bitch, burn!" On his radio McCuskey radioed to his fellow Yorktowners his reaction, "We just shot his ass off!"[86]

At 1325 the Task Force commander informed the *Louisville* that if the pilot did not answer, he thought the SOC-3 "went into a spin" because of the bad weather. The *Louisville* ceased calling to Lieutenant Worthington and the crew and plane were assumed to be lost. Fletcher considered sending a second raid to Jaluit, but with overdue planes, the poor weather conditions, and the late hour (which would require the planes from a second attack to return in darkness), he decided to retire from the area. Halsey gave orders to withdraw "not later than the ensuing night."[87]

Captain Frank G. Fahrion, the commander of Destroyer Division Three (Task Group 17.2), noted that his ships "carried out their assignments in a satisfactory manner. Conditions were such that the battery could not be used effectively. The action emphasized the importance of radar and the necessity of having fire control radar on our destroyers."[88] The commander of Strike Force 17.1.1 and captain of the *Louisville*, Captain Elliott B. Nixon, commented that "the installation of radio receivers and transmitters capable of voice modulation carrier transmission and reception is urgent. The standard receivers (code) used eliminate much of the voice band necessary for intelligibility especially on plane circuits where fast speaking is necessary. Model TBS and TBX or equivalent sets are recommended."[89] He also noted that since 5-inch and 3-inch guns are too slow to follow fast planes like a dive bomber, it was vital that 20mm and 40mm AA guns be installed. He recommended that submarine detection gear be installed. Cruisers like the *Louisville* that conducted escort duty were often called upon to detach and attack submarines with no detection capability.[90]

In his action report, *Yorktown*'s Captain Buckmaster wrote that "the conduct and spirit of all personnel upheld the highest traditions of the service. The younger and less experienced pilots of the Jaluit attack group are to be especially commended for their spirit and initiative in pressing home individual attacks after they had become separated from their leaders due to bad weather." Buckmaster gave special commendation to Lieutenant Commander William O. Burch, Jr., for leading his squadron in the Makin Island attack, as well as scoring a direct hit on an enemy seaplane tender and sinking one four-engine patrol seaplane on the water with machine-gun fire. Ensign E.S. McCuskey and Ensign J.P. Adams were commended for "destroying a Japanese four engine patrol bomber seaplane in the air which was attempting to attack the ship."[91]

Retirement

Vice Admiral Halsey retired with his two task forces from attacks in the Marshall and Gilbert Islands on February 1 with fuel problems. Having departed while evading Japanese bombing attacks, the carrier forces had burned excessive fuel. Halsey requested emergency fueling arrangements from Nimitz.

While Halsey was concerned over fuel during retirement from the raids, Vice Admiral Wilson Brown, in command of Task Force 11 with the carrier *Lexington*, four cruisers, and ten destroyers, departed Pearl Harbor on January 31, heading southward to begin a new patrol mission. Nimitz changed Brown's orders and directed him to proceed to the Marshalls and cover Halsey's withdrawal and provide fuel if required. Brown's orders were first to escort the tanker *Neosho* to a rendezvous with Admiral Halsey's returning force, then to head south to escort a convoy to Canton Island. As it turned out, Nimitz changed Brown's orders two days out of port, as Halsey was able to return to Pearl without emergency refueling.[92]

In the morning on Thursday, February 5, the *Enterprise* Air Group flew through heavy rain to land at NAS Pearl Harbor on Ford Island. Word came that they had a 48-hour pass to rest at the Royal Hawaiian Hotel on Waikiki. The aviators' only impediment to a good time was the Army's ban on hard liquor in the islands. This barrier was soon overcome.[93]

When Halsey's task force sailed into Pearl Harbor later that day flying their largest colors, the men on the ships in the harbor cheered. Every ship in the harbor blew its siren. As ship crews cheered, civilian shipyard workers along the shore looked on and applauded. "The troops at Hickam Field cheered … all the way to our mooring." The *Enterprise* tied up at the wharf at berth F-2 at 1053. Nimitz was so anxious to see Halsey that he did not wait for the gangway to be lowered and was hoisted aboard using the bos'n's chair. He shouted out, "Nice going!" as he grabbed Halsey's hand. Rear Admiral Robert A. Theobald, the commander of destroyers for the Pacific, who had opposed the raid, shook a finger at Halsey and said, "Damn you, Bill, you've got no business getting home from that one! No business at all!"[94]

Halsey later wrote of the raid: "The reason we brought off these early raids is that we violated all the rules and traditions of naval warfare. We did the exact opposite of what the enemy expected. We did not keep our carriers behind the battle; we deliberately exposed them to shore-based planes. Most important, whatever we did, we did fast. I have heard that there was a popular saying on the *Enterprise* at this time, 'The Admiral will get us in, and the Captain will get us out.'"[95]

When Fletcher's *Yorktown* Task Force 17 with escorts arrived at Pearl the following day, there seemed to be little cheering left over for them, as they only attracted moderate interest. The reporters wasted little ink printing the few words they had for Frank Jack Fletcher or Raymond Spruance. The *Yorktown* Air Group had flown into the Marine airfield at Ewa. The aviators soon headed off for their 24 hours at the Royal Hawaiian Hotel.

With both carrier groups now back at Pearl, Nimitz's public relations officer arranged a press conference for Halsey and Fletcher for the afternoon. Fletcher was rather quiet, but Halsey was the delight of the newsmen and photographers. Nimitz turned Halsey over to the reporters and moved out of the way. Halsey, with a big smile on his face, showed what "a charming, genial, approachable fellow" he was as he was besieged by reporters and photographers. With salty language and his boy-like charm, Halsey told of his adventure as their national hero, a man who fit his nickname, "Bull Halsey." The newspapers heralded the success of the raid with headlines like "Pearl Harbor Avenged!" America was starved for good news and something to raise its morale, and they found it in Halsey.[96]

Admiral Spruance did not attend and remained aboard his flagship, *Northampton*, discouraged over what he felt was a poor showing in the Marshall Raid. Though a friend of Halsey for many years, Spruance did not like the way Halsey loved publicity. Halsey praised the effort of all those who participated in the raid and recommended many medals. Stressing the role of Miles Browning in planning the raid, Halsey was able to get him promoted to captain. Halsey also saw to it that Spruance received the Navy Commendation Medal.

In an impressive ceremony on the flight deck of the *Enterprise*, with everyone wearing full dress whites, Halsey pinned on the medals. Admiral Halsey was likewise awarded the Distinguished Service Medal from Nimitz. Later that evening the carrier crew gathered in the hangar deck for a movie. Suddenly, Admiral Halsey entered the deck as the men stood in silence. He barked out, "Carry on," and the men settled down and took their seats. Just before the movie was about to start, Halsey stood up and faced the crowd. He then held out the medal he had won and said in a loud voice, "Men, this medal belongs to you. I am honored to wear it for you." After pausing, he continued, "I am so damned proud of you I could cry." He then turned and sat back down. After a moment of silence, the entire complement of men broke out in loud cheers that roared for 5 minutes. Here was a real naval leader and his men would follow him anywhere.[97]

In Admiral Nimitz's letter to the Secretary of the Navy (*Report of Action, Marshall-Gilbert Islands raids, by Task Forces "HOW" and "FOX"*), he noted that the Marshall-Gilbert Islands raid "is considered to have been well conceived, well planned and brilliantly executed. It is noted that heavy rain interfered with the attack on Jaluit." He revealed the raids were the more noteworthy considering that the submarine intelligence of land facilities and forces was lacking, while the shipping data were "fairly accurate." Nimitz deemed the gunnery performance against land and surface targets "generally excellent," but antiaircraft batteries did not provide satisfactory results. He also considered the losses to be small considering the magnitude of the operations. The words of Halsey regarding this operation were relevant: "It was one of those plans which are called 'brilliant' if they succeed and 'foolhardy' if they fail."[98]

In truth, the Marshall-Gilbert Islands Raid had no discernible impact on the enemy advances. It did not stop the Japanese from pushing ahead in the Philippines in driving the American and Filipino solders into the Bataan Peninsula and nearby Corregidor Island. The enemy attacks in Rangoon, Singapore and the Netherlands East Indies revealed no letup. But the raid did raise the Japanese awareness of the tactical American threat and the type of risks that the U.S. Navy would take to engage them. Halsey summed up the results this way: "When our task forces sortied for the Marshalls raid, you could almost smell the defeatism around Pearl. Now the offensive spirit was reestablished; officers and men were bushy-tailed again. So, presently, was the American public. At last we had been able to answer their roweling question, 'Where is the Navy?'"[99]

The personal war diaries of Yamamoto's chief of staff, Rear Admiral Matome Ugaki, and his operations officer, Commander Yoshitake Miwa, provide the written details of the inner thinking of the command. From aboard Yamamoto's flagship *Yamato*, moored at the fleet anchorage at Kure, Ugaki recorded his thoughts on the American carrier attacks on the Marshall and Gilbert islands on February 1, 1942:

> Urgent messages report Wotje, Tarawa and Kwajalein in the Marshall Islands under attack by enemy force of one aircraft carrier, three cruisers and several destroyers. Wotje and Tarawa are also under cruiser gunfire bombardment.... Another carrier is attacking Jaluit in the south ... counterattack force of all available bombers and flying boats now speeding from Truk to the Marshalls at high speed. The old axiom says, "Beware in the north when the enemy attacks in the south." Have ordered alerts for East Coast of Japan and all forces in that area. The emphasis on our current Southern Operations (Malay, Philippines, Netherlands East Indies) has left the Marshalls area with insufficient forces, so this was the enemy's opportunity and he seized it. He not only held our forces in check, but was able to obtain some significant results. This attack was "Heaven's admonition for our shortcomings."
>
> I must say that the enemy's attack was bold and audacious, but bringing his aircraft carriers and cruisers in so close to our shore bases was stupid. That foolishness cost him a bomb hit on a cruiser, reducing its speed, but it escaped any further damage.
>
> It is mortifying that our aircraft from Truk were too late; that the contact with the enemy force was lost, that our carrier strike forces had too far to go and that the enemy carriers escaped. I am chagrined by the carelessness and stupidity that allowed the enemy to get so close without being sighted. To be so completely surprised, long after the beginning of the war is incredible.[100]

The attack on the Marshalls prompted Yamamoto to send a replacement air unit of 21 Navy shore-based bombers to hurry the move from Taiwan to Truk. Only 19 arrived in Rabaul after two collided in midair over Truk.[101] The American attack did have the immediate effect of drawing two Japanese carriers from Truk to chase Halsey's task forces, but they were recalled on February 4.[102] The Japanese were beginning to see the fallacy of attempting to provide perimeter defense using dispersed island garrisons that were too far apart to provide mutual support to prevent penetration by American carrier forces.

The American naval operation yielded some valuable lessons for the U.S. Navy. Certainly, having two carrier task forces working in proximity was successful, and though it was not yet an American doctrine, it would become the norm in further attacks. It was a risky operation for Halsey as the *Enterprise* steamed in a 5 × 25 rectangle off Wotje Island within striking distance of three Japanese airfields. But taking some level of risk was the reality of the U.S. naval forces in the Pacific in February 1942.

The actual attacks disclosed numerous detailed operational requirements including the need for all aircraft to have self-sealing fuel tanks and IFF (Identification Friend or Foe) gear. A contingent of 18 fighter planes per squadron was considered insufficient. The skipper of *Enterprise* Air Group 6, Commander Howard Young, wanted at least 27 fighters. Young remarked, "Fortunately in this action, VT-6 encountered no air opposition, but it is certain that their mission would have [failed] ... had they been intercepted by enemy fighters which were in the near vicinity."[103]

Perhaps the most important result of the raids was the positive impact in morale of the American public and the men of the U.S. Navy. This was the first attack against the

Japanese since Pearl Harbor. It helped to sharpen the operational efficiency of the *Enterprise* and *Yorktown* carrier personnel, as well as establish the beginnings of the leadership legacy of Nimitz over American naval forces in the Pacific. Though Tokyo radio dismissed the raid as "aerial guerrilla warfare," Yamamoto and his staff could not ignore the power and threat of American carriers roving the seas.[104]

Chapter 3

Rabaul

Apprehend, Attack and Annihilate

On January 29, 1942, COMINCH sent CINCPAC a dispatch revealing the immediate establishment of the ANZAC Force (COMANZAC), commanded by Vice Admiral Herbert F. Leary to maintain operations in the southwest Pacific. On February 2, Task Force 11 "turned south to carry out the remainder of its orders (10–42) to cover Canton. Plans are in the making to employ this force in carrying out COMINCH 311606 (covering convoys)."[1]

On February 6, Nimitz received a dispatch (061513) from COMINCH that the Japanese planned widespread attacks possibly including Midway, Hawaii (Oahu), the New Hebrides, northeast Australia, the Canal Zone, or even the west coast of the United States. A second dispatch (062352) from COMINCH focused attention on an expected enemy offensive in the direction of New Caledonia, the New Hebrides, or other locations in the southwest Pacific. The feeling was that the Japanese would gather at Rabaul, on the volcanic island of New Britain in New Guinea. From there they would launch offensive action against the Allied sites. Admiral King called for "prompt action to check enemy advance" in the southwest areas.[2]

After conferring with his staff, on February 7 Nimitz replied to King's directives in CINCPAC 080239 (Aidac) with the collective view of the situation as they saw it:

> Pacific Fleet markedly inferior in all types to enemy. Cannot conduct aggressive action Pacific except raids of hit-and-run character which are unlikely to relieve pressure Southwest Pacific. Logistic problems far surpass peacetime conception and always precarious due to fueling at sea and dependence upon weather.... Offensive employment battleships does not fit in with hit-and-run operations, and their independence or supporting use precluded by lack of air coverage and antisubmarine protection. Such employment considered inadvisable at present. Continued operations of one or more Pacific Fleet task forces in ANZAC Area will involve dependence upon logistic support from Australia and New Zealand, which support appears limited.... Unless this fleet is strengthened by strong additions, particularly in aircraft, light forces, carriers, and fast fleet tankers, its effectiveness for offensive action is limited....[3]

To remain in compliance with King's directive to guard Hawaii and the shipping line out to Samoa, Nimitz planned to send one of his carrier task forces to the southwest toward Samoa and leave one task force back at Pearl. King's suggestion that battleships be used for raiding was entirely impractical. Battleships could only make 21 knots at top speed and were too slow to screen carriers that cruised at 34 knots. There were not enough cruisers and destroyers in the Pacific Fleet to screen battleships, and the carriers were more effective because they had planes and guns for offensive operations.

A reply to Nimitz's message, received from King on the afternoon of the 9th (COMINCH 092245 (Aidac)) startled the CINCPAC staff: "Pacific Fleet not, repeat *not*, markedly inferior in all types to forces enemy can bring to bear within operating radius of Hawaii while he is committed to extensive operations in Southwest Pacific. Your forces will however be markedly inferior from Australia to Alaska when the enemy has gained objectives in Southwest Pacific unless every effort is continuously made to damage his ships and bases. Action by you towards and in the mandates will of itself cover and protect Midway-Hawaii line while affording badly needed relief of pressure in Southwest Pacific…. Review situation in above northward and eastward or otherwise vary pattern of operations."[4]

Nimitz put together a CINCPAC conference to consider his next steps. The staff could not think of any enemy target that was within range even with refueling that would have any realistic chance of affecting Japanese operations in other areas. Nimitz decided to adjourn overnight to clear their minds and wait for Halsey's attendance the next day. While they worked the problem, Nimitz sent Admiral Pye on a Pan American Clipper to Washington to meet with Admiral King. His mission was to explain to King the situation in the Central Pacific.[5]

While Nimitz was working with Admiral King to resolve the proper level of naval support for the Southwest Pacific area, Vice Admiral Wilson Brown with the *Lexington* and Task Force 11 was already on offensive patrol near the Canton Islands in Southwest Pacific. On February 13 COMINCH in dispatch 122200 (Aidac) directed Vice Admiral Herbert F. Leary (who had planned to establish a command center at Melbourne) to join his flagship and conduct offensive operations with the Anzac Force and TF 11 against the enemy in the Solomons-Bismarck area. Nimitz was directed to furnish logistics support for the operation including ammunition. Three tankers were already assigned and the British had two at Suva. The *Tangier* and the *Curtiss* could also provide bombs and air torpedoes.[6]

The next day, Vice Admiral Brown with Task Force 11 in dispatch 140022 (Aidac) recommended to COMANZAC that the two forces "sweep to bomb Rabaul."[7] COMANZAC's receipt of COMINCH's 122200 was delayed because the Melbourne command center did not have the means to decode the message. When he finally received the dispatch (after CINCPAC had recoded the dispatch), he replied in dispatches 140538 and 140344, in which he asked for reconsidering his rejoining his flagship in order that he would have access to the intelligence and communication channels of the ACNB. In dispatch 140538 Leary also asked Task Force 11 to comply with COMINCH 122200. Meanwhile, the Anzac Squadron commanded by Rear Admiral John Gregory Crace, RN, departed to cover the Noumea-Suva line after he had consulted with the staff aviator of TF 11.[8]

Task Force 11, augmented by cruisers, destroyers, Navy patrol aircraft and Army bombers from other areas, was now tasked to maintain operations in the southwest Pacific under the Commander of ANZAC Forces (COMANZAC). The Task Group consisted of the *Lexington*, heavy cruisers *Minneapolis*, *Indianapolis*, *Pensacola* and *San Francisco*, and destroyers *Phelps*, *Dewey*, *MacDonough*, *Hull*, *Aylwin*, *Dale*, *Bagley*, *Patterson*, *Clark*, and *Drayton*.[9]

Back in March 1941, Rabaul, located on the island of New Britain off the northeastern coast of the New Guinea mainland, had been garrisoned by a force of 1,400 men of the

Australian Army. Commanded by Lieutenant Colonel John Scanlan, this battalion, known as Lark Force, had been deployed as fears of war with Japan were intensifying. The Lark Force was made up of 716 men of the Australian Imperial Force, soldiers from the local militia, the New Guinea Volunteer Rifles, a coastal defense battery, an antiaircraft battery, an antitank battery, and a detachment of the 2/10th Field Ambulance. On the nearby island of New Ireland, a 130-man commando unit 2/1st Independent Company was stationed.

The primary mission of the Australian Army group on Rabaul was to protect Vunakanau, the main Royal Australian Air Force (RAAF) airfield near Rabaul, as well as the flying boat anchorage in Simpson Harbor. From these air base assets, the RAAF was able to maintain surveillance of Japanese movements in the area. Unfortunately, the aircraft available to the RAAF contingent under Squadron Leader John Lerew consisted of only ten CAC Wirraway training aircraft and four Lockheed Hudson light bombers of No. 24 Squadron.[10]

Realizing the tactical importance of Rabaul, and its port and airfield, the commander of the Japanese 4th Fleet (South Seas Force), Vice Admiral Shigeyoshi Inoue, made sure that Rabaul was included in the First Operational Phase of the Japanese invasion plans following Pearl Harbor. Since Rabaul was 700 miles south of Japan's major naval base at Truk in the Caroline Islands, Admiral Inoue felt it was critical to prevent the island from being used as a base for American B-17 bombers to attack Truk. The Japanese also saw Rabaul as a forward base for operations in New Guinea and the Solomon Islands.

Five days after Pearl Harbor, the Australian Chiefs of Staff had advised their War Cabinet that the only options were to reinforce, withdraw, or leave the troops in Rabaul. Despite the fact that the Australian government was aware that there was no hope of holding out against a strong Japanese force should it appear, they decided to leave the Lark Force troops in place, while only evacuating European women and children from Rabaul.

On January 4, 1942, the Japanese had bombed Rabaul with a large number of carrier-based planes from the *Kaga* and *Akagi*. Afterwards, there were nearly daily air raids as the odds of an invasion increased. On January 21, eight RAAF Wirraway training planes attacked a formation of 109 Japanese planes, with three shot down, two crash-landing and one damaged. As a result of the intense Japanese air attacks, the coastal artillery was destroyed, and the Australian infantry was evacuated from Rabaul. That same day an Australian RAAF flying boat found the Japanese invasion fleet and signaled warnings before being shot down.

On January 22, the Japanese landed on New Ireland and took the town of Kavieng with no opposition. That night the Japanese approached Rabaul, and at 0245 the next morning the brigade group of the 55th Division of the Imperial Japanese Army under Major General Tomitaro Horii landed on New Britain. Japanese ships entered the harbor and landed troops at Blanche Bay. Though there was heavy resistance to the Japanese invasion at Vulcan Beach from the Lark Force and militiamen, most of the Japanese forces landed unopposed at locations that were unguarded. Within a few hours, Scanlan ordered "every man for himself"[11] as Australian soldiers and civilians retreated into the jungle. The Japanese loss in the invasion of Rabaul was only 16 men.

The RAAF evacuated by flying boat, but there were no escape plans for the Lark Force. Between March and May 1942 some 450 troops and civilians were rescued at sea by unofficial groups from the mainland. With no food and unprepared for guerrilla warfare, most Australian soldiers were captured or surrendered during the following weeks. Of the 1,050 Australians taken prisoner, 130 were massacred by bayonet on February 4 near Tol Plantation, and 35 were shot at nearby Waitavalo Plantation. Sadly, on July 1, 1942, some eight hundred prisoners of war from Rabaul were lost when the Japanese *Montevideo Maru* was sunk off the north coast of Luzon by the submarine USS *Sturgeon*.[12]

The man to lead the attack on Rabaul was one of the oldest senior U.S. Naval officers in World War II. Wilson Brown was born on April 27, 1882, in Philadelphia. He graduated from the Naval Academy in 1902, ranking 44th in a class of 59. He returned as an instructor at the Academy during 1907–1908. During World War I he served on the staff of Admiral William S. Sims in London and was commander of the destroyer USS *Parker* in 1918. His next assignment was as commander of the destroyer *Blakeley* during 1919–1920. He graduated from the Naval War College in 1921 and was promoted to the rank of commander. That same year he served as the executive officer aboard the battleship *California*.

In 1923 he began serving as aide to Presidents Calvin Coolidge and Herbert Hoover. In 1929 he was appointed as commander of the New London Submarine Base. Brown was promoted to captain in 1932 and took command of the *California*. In 1934 he became chief of staff of the Naval War College. Two years later he was promoted to rear admiral and named as commander of the Training Squadron Scouting Force—Atlantic Fleet. On February 1, 1938, Brown became the superintendent of the U.S. Naval Academy. Three years later he was assigned as the Commander Scouting Force—Pacific Fleet with the brevet rank of vice admiral.[13]

Having conceived of a plan of attack against Rabaul and gained approval from COMANZAC to execute it, Vice Admiral Brown had the responsibility in his hands. The plan called for a coordinated attack against the Japanese base by U.S. Naval forces and the U.S. Army heavy bombers of the Australian command at dawn on February 21, 1942. Brown's movement plan was to pass east of the New Hebrides and the Solomons to come in from the northeast toward Rabaul with an air attack first, followed by a surface bombardment. The *Lexington* would launch her planes at 125 miles from Rabaul at 0400 on February 21.[14]

On February 13, Task Force 11 arrived at the designated rendezvous point 300 miles west of Suva and immediately began fueling from the oiler *Neosho*. The *Lexington* and destroyers were fully fueled, but there was only enough remaining to fuel the cruisers to 75 percent. The lack of fuel would be a serious issue for the upcoming operations. To preserve radio silence, two officers were flown to Suva to transmit messages regarding the need for logistic support, as well as to obtain the latest enemy dispositions and defensive situation at Suva.

The Anzac Squadron, consisting of the heavy cruisers HMAS *Australia* and USS *Chicago*, light cruisers HMNZS *Leander* and HMNZS *Achilles*, with destroyers USS *Lamson* and USS *Perkins*, under the command of Rear Admiral John Gregory Crace, RN, joined TF 11 on the morning of February 15 in heavy seas. Rear Admiral T.C. Kinkaid, commanding the cruisers of TF 11, along with members of his staff, and Admiral Crace and his staff, joined Brown aboard the *Lexington* for a conference. Admiral Crace expressed his delight at joining the task force and indicated he was "most anxious to cooperate and to take an active part in the offensive operations."[15] Unfortunately, with the tanker *Neosho* drained of her fuel, it would only be possible for the *Australia* and *Chicago* to accompany TF 11 on the Rabaul mission. Brown assigned the remaining ships to cover Suva and Noumea against enemy naval attack, as well as to provide safe escort to the second tanker that had been directed to meet TF 11 beyond the range of enemy shore-based patrol planes after the Rabaul attack. After the fueling, TF 11 separated with the Anzac Squadron and sailed to the northwest of the Solomons toward Rabaul.[16]

Leary's intelligence officer reported news of Japanese naval aircraft and shipping at Rabaul. CINCPAC intelligence updated that there was no threat of Japanese carrier aircraft since the carriers were operating from the Dutch East Indies. On February 18 the Australian command estimated that there were 8 vessels in Rabaul's Simpson Harbor and air support of 12 fighters, 12 torpedo planes, and 24 medium bombers at Vunakanau Airfield outside town.

Vice Admiral Inoue made sure the 24th Air Flotilla was well equipped at Rabaul. Ultimately, they would operate two naval air units from there, one for fighters and twin-engine medium bombers, and the other for four-engine flying boats for long-range recon. At Rabaul with the 4th Air Group were 18 land attack bombers and 26 fighters, plus additional Kawanishi flying boats from the Yokohama Air Group.[17]

While Task Force 11 approached Rabaul unseen, the Japanese were getting nervous. On Rabaul the Japanese communicated carrier alerts on February 7, 12, 14, 18 and 19, but no Allied attacks came. The alert sounded on the 19th had been from a shore station on a small island 160 miles southwest of Truk reporting falsely of two enemy destroyers.

On the morning of February 20, Brown's task force was heading northwest and well north of the Solomons, not yet having made the turning point to swing around to the southwest for the attack. At dawn the *Lexington* launched 6 SBDs to search ahead 300 miles. The mission was commanded by Lieutenant Commander Robert E. Dixon of Scouting Two. Ready to assume the CAP when the patrol returned were 5 F4Fs from the 1st Division of VF-3. Captain Frederick C. Sherman's *Lexington* searched 360° with its CXAM radar for unidentified contacts.

At dawn three Japanese four-engine Kawanishi H6K4 Type 97 (code named "Mavis") flying boats out of Rabaul took off on their 500-mile sector searches to the east. At 1030 Lieutenant (JG) Sakai Noboru, pilot of the flying boat covering sector 075 to 090 degrees, reported a large enemy force bearing 075° and 460 miles from Rabaul with a course of 315°. Sakai continued to shadow Task Force 11 in the clouds.[18]

At 1015, while still 460 miles away from the Rabaul harbor, the *Lexington* picked up an unknown aircraft on radar 35 miles from the ship, bearing 180° true. In reaction, a six-plane combat air patrol of F4F Wildcats from VF-3 under the command of Lieutenant Commander John S. "Jimmy" Thach was launched to investigate the contact. Once they were launched, they came under the control of the *Lexington*'s fighter director officer (FDO), Lieutenant Frank F. "Red" Gill. Gill used the CXAM-1 model radar of the *Lexington* to direct the fighters to enemy contacts. Two sections were held in reserve with Lieutenant Edwards H. "Butch" O'Hare and Lieutenant Onia Burt Stanley, Jr., while Lieutenant Gill directed Thach and his wingman, Ensign Edward "Doc" Sellstrom, to the intruder.

At 1056 Thach told Gill there were heavy clouds ahead. Just a few minutes passed as Thach reached a point 205° and 35 miles from the carrier. Thach asked Gill if the bogey was in the rain squall ahead. Gill responded in the affirmative as Thach and Sellstrom disappeared in the murky white clouds. Thach was quickly startled to see the huge flying boat, a Kawanishi Type 97, so close to him in the white haze. At 1100 Thach sent off a quick sighting report as the two VF-3 pilots exited the clouds. Soon the Kawanishi broke out into the clear at 1000 feet altitude.[19]

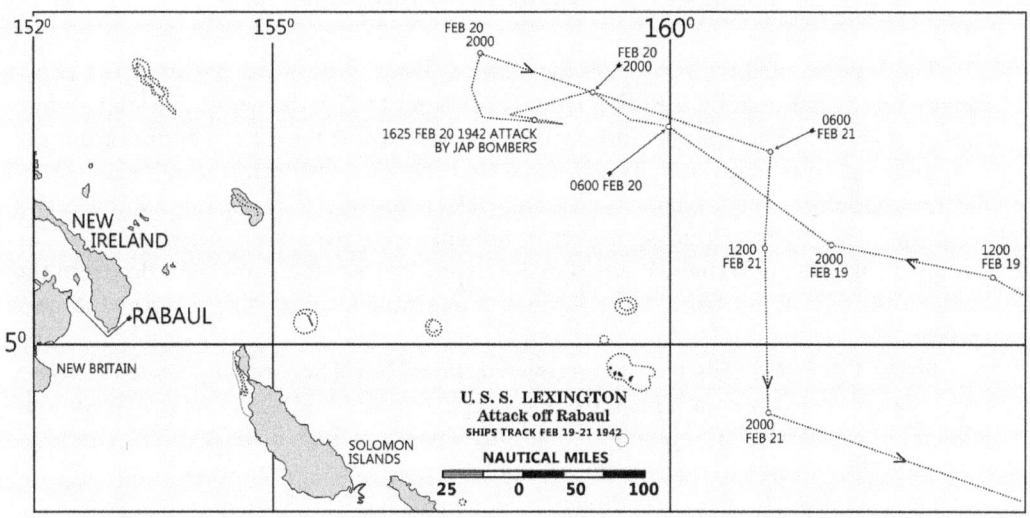

Top: USS *Lexington* attack track—Rabaul raid. Image redrawn based on *Early Carrier Raids in the Pacific Ocean*, 35. *Bottom:* Grumman F4F-3 "Wildcat" fighters of Fighting Squadron Three (VF-3). In flight near Naval Air Station, Kaneohe, Oahu, Hawaii, 10 April 1942. The planes are Bureau # 3976 (marked "F-1"), flown by VF-3 Commanding Officer Lieutenant Commander John S. Thach, and Bureau # 3986, flown by Lieutenant Edward H. O'Hare. Both of these aircraft were lost while assigned to Fighting Squadron Two (VF-2) with USS *Lexington* (CV-2), during the Battle of Coral Sea in May 1942. Photographed by Photographer Second Class H.S. Fawcett (official U.S. Navy photograph #: 80-G-10613, now in the collections of the National Archives).

Thach positioned his fighter on the starboard side behind the enemy flying boat's wings while Sellstrom took the other side. Thach fired and hit the wings, sending a white stream of gasoline spraying behind. Sellstrom had to avoid the 20mm gunfire from the tail gunner as he maneuvered. Thach noted that the Mavis's 20mm cannon shells from the turrets looked "like Roman candles—a black center with a fiery corona." Thach and Sellstrom made their second approach as the enemy's entire wing was in flames. The Kawanishi skidded into the sea with a major explosion. At 1112, some 43 miles from the carrier, the black smoke from the shootdown was visible from the *Lexington* as the crew cheered.

Just as Thach and Sellstrom had recovered aboard *Lexington*, radar detected a second bogey moving into the area. This Kawanishi Type 97 from the Yokohama Air Group was piloted by W.O. Hayashi Kiyoshi. He had, likewise, launched at 0800 to search sector 090° to 105°. Kiyoshi had been radioed to obtain more detail about Task Force 11.[20]

Lieutenant Gill immediately directed Lieutenant (JG) Burt Stanley and his wingman, Ensign Leon W. Haynes, toward the second bogey. The action was recorded in Stanley's diary:

"Orange Section from Romeo [Gill's radio call sign]—Vector 343–Buster [move at top speed]—Angels six" [altitude 6000 feet] came from the fighter control.

I acknowledged and at full speed we started north ahead of the fleet. We had hardly gone twenty miles when Haynes' plane pulled alongside and began to dance energetically. He had sighted our objective. I saw it then, a sleek silver patrol boat, four-engined, tremendous even at a thousand yards.

"Tally-ho from Orange leader," I transmitted gleefully, "A BIG four engine patrol plane."

As we climbed for attack position, I checked my plane; gas switch, prop, gunsight, gun switches—The patrol plane had spotted us. Black spindles of explosives fell from the fuselage to send white geysers a mile below. They had jettisoned their bombs in hopes that the unloaded plane could escape.

As we pulled into position Haynes could see the cannon in the waist sending up its incendiary shells, seeking our range. I was already starting my attack. A half roll and the pull-through. The sights crept up and then held steady—Now. I pressed the trigger and nothing happened. The motor continued its roar and the wind still tugged at my clothing but only the fretful sparkle of the patrol plane's rear machine gun showed that someone was firing. I had missed the Master gun switch. I was flying 3-F-7 and the switch was in a different place.

Haynes had followed me closely and while I snapped on the switch and tested the guns I noticed the tail gun was no longer firing. Good shooting Lee.

From above and behind this time as the broad wing filled the gunsight, the guns responded to the switch. The red trail of the tracers could be seen to end abruptly as they passed from sight into the wing and the pilot compartment. Another burst, longer and more accurate now, and flame burst from the inboard engine on the port side. It disappeared and reappeared as I fired once more before ducking to avoid the tail. I looked back to see it become a solid sheet flowing from the wing to the fuselage. Gray smoke traced the path of the plane as the left wing and nose began to drop. That last burst must have killed the pilots.

"Whee, we got it." I couldn't resist reporting.

Haynes had quickly followed to deliver a last blow. The nose had dipped lower until it was diving out of control—the smoke increasing with the speed. Now, nothing could save it—nothing could stop the dive.

It crashed in a burst of red and black pall quickly covered the spot. The great ball of smoke rose slowly to reveal a circle of flame on the gasoline covered water, but the wreckage was already beneath the surface. Ten men were dead and the plane, efforts of a hundred, was destroyed. But it had to be.[21]

The time of this second kill was 1202.

Admiral Brown knew the Japanese were preparing for an upcoming attack on his task force as every minute passed. The element of surprise had been lost. He had other problems. Because the heavy winds caused Task Force 11 to consume more fuel than expected, he had no reserve for high-speed operations if he had to escape from the attack area. Brown knew his ships would not be able to refuel with the oiler dispatched and en route from Pearl until February 24. By noon on the 20th he made the decision to call off the Rabaul attack. Captain Sherman wanted to continue the raid, but Brown decided he would change course to the southwest directly toward Rabaul as a feint, and then late in the afternoon retired without conducting the raid. At 1337 Brown broke radio silence to inform King and Leary of his decision.

The Japanese commander of the 24th Air Flotilla, Rear Admiral Goto, did expect a dawn attack the next day at Rabaul from the American task force from 200 miles out. To repulse the attack, Goto possessed 18 land attack planes from the 4th Air Group. He also had 16 Mitsubishi A5M4 Type 96 carrier fighters, but none of them could fly to 460 miles away to attack the American carrier and return. Their max range was 250 miles with drop tanks. Goto also had 10 Mitsubishi A6M2 Zero fighters at Rabaul that did not have drop tanks.

At 1310 Goto ordered the 4th Air Group, led by Captain Moritama Kahiro, to sink the American carrier sighted that morning. The Yokohama Air Group was to maintain their contact with the carrier task force using their Type 97 flying boats. At Truk, Vice Admiral Inoue had planned a night surface attack for the evening of the 21st using his available ships (4 heavy cruisers, 2 light cruisers and destroyers).

At 1240 the *Lexington*'s CXAM radar picked up a third bogey 80 miles west of the carrier. The contact closed to 70 miles, but then disappeared at 1317. Thach with the 1st Division on CAP duty aloft stayed until 1330, when they were relieved by Lieutenant Commander Donald A. Lovelace's 2nd Division with 6 F4Fs. Captain Sherman also launched a search patrol of 12 SBDs from Bombing Two out to the west.

At 1400 the Japanese sent airborne a Kawanishi flying boat piloted by Reserve Ensign Makino Motohiro from the seaplane base at Simpson Harbor at Rabaul. His mission was to regain contact with the American carrier. Twenty minutes later, 17 twin-engine Japanese Mitsubishi G4M "Betty" bombers departed Vunakanau Airfield under group leader Lieutenant Commander Ito Takuzo with orders to destroy the American carrier force. Since there were no torpedoes at Rabaul, they were armed with two 250-kilogram bombs each. After the fighter bombers had taken off, the maintenance crews on Rabaul headed to the radio room to hear the action as it progressed.

While the *Lexington* was steaming at 20 knots on a course of 234°T, at 1542 a jagged V-formation of two groups of 9 Betty bombers was detected on *Lexington*'s radar at 76 miles from the ship bearing 270°T at 8,000 feet. The bombers were heading on a course 090° speed 150 knots. At 1600 Lieutenant Gill decided that the CAP should be rotated early to ensure there were fighters on patrol with full tanks as the Japanese approached. The *Lexington* air group commander, Commander Herbert S. Duckworth, agreed and received approval from Captain Sherman.

By 1611, ship's radar showed a large blip bearing 255° at 75 miles heading their way. Four minutes later, Lieutenant Noel A.M. Gayler, directing the 3rd Division with 6 F4Fs, launched. Seven minutes later, the bogeys disappeared off the screen but reappeared at 1625 bearing 276° at 47 miles away. Gill vectored Gayler's fighters to intercept the enemy contacts. The *Lexington*'s bridge ordered flank speed, leaving 4 F4Fs and 11 VS-2 SBD dive bombers on the flight deck.

Nine Bettys with Lieutenant Nakagawa Masayoshi of the 4th Air Group spotted

Task Force 11 and sent their contact report at 1635. They were flying at 11,000 feet at speed 170 knots in a Vee of Vees formation. From 13,000 feet Gayler and his wingman, Ensign Dale W. Peterson, went into steep dives as they attacked the Betty on the edge of the formation. They were engaged by gunfire from all of the 9 bombers, but Gayler and Peterson set the Betty on fire as it fell out of formation.

The next Wildcats to set upon the bombers were Lieutenant (JG) Rolla S. Lemmon and his wingman, Lieutenant (JG) Howard F. "Spud" Clark. They made a perfect attack and shot down another Betty. Gayler's 3rd Section, Ensign Willard E. Eder and Ensign John W. Wilson, arrived after the other sections had started their attacks. For some reason Wilson's F4F was having engine performance problems and could not keep up with Eder as they tried to climb above to get in attack position. Eder came in from below and behind the bombers as he made his attack, but three of his guns would not work. He eventually had to break off his attack to clear his guns. Gayler made his 2nd pass and shot down the third Betty, sharing the downing with Eder.[22]

The first fighter attacks were over at 1641. Now lookouts on the *Lexington* could see the Bettys off 10 miles in light cloud cover. The Japanese tightened their formation and continued toward the carrier. The destroyer *Phelps*'s lookouts saw 6 Bettys heading in as Captain Sherman brought the *Lexington* left into the wind. He wanted to launch all the fueled aircraft on the flight deck. The deck crew worked frantically to clear space to allow the planes to take off. The F4Fs would take off first, then the SBDs. Thach started his roll down the flight deck at 1643, with the 14 remaining planes following aloft. They were all off in 3 minutes.

At the same time, Ensign Peterson shot down the 4th Betty, piloted by Nakagawa. The task force cruisers had begun their antiaircraft firing and later tried to claim they damaged the lead bomber. The bombers on a level run came toward the *Lexington*'s stern on a parallel course. Even as shell bursts surrounded him, Lieutenant (JG) Lemmon shot down the 5th Betty, as it spun away and hit the sea.

Five more F4Fs entered the attack on the remaining 4 enemy bombers as VF-3's 2nd Division climbed to altitude. The pilots were Lieutenant Albert O. "Scoop" Vorse, Lieutenant (JG) Robert J. Morgan, Lieutenant (JG) Howard L. Johnson, Ensign John H. Lackey and Ensign Richard M. Rowell. They swooped in and disrupted the bombing run.

Sailing at 30 knots, Captain Sherman directed his *Lexington* in executing violent turns at the exact moment of the bomb releases and evaded with clean misses. The *Lexington* fired on four incoming Bettys with their starboard 5-inch guns at 10,000 yards, along with antiaircraft guns, inflicting serious damage. One crippled bomber tried to crash into the carrier, but it hit the sea 75 yards astern of *Lexington* with a fiery explosion at 1651. The enemy bombs missed, with the closest bomb short by 3,000 yards.

This first wave attack on the *Lexington* saw 4 fighters and 11 patrol planes launched while landing 5 fighters, even as the carrier maneuvered with 30° rudder changes at 30 knots to avoid bombs. These were excellent air and ship operations during combat, revealing the level of skilled commanders and trained carrier forces of the U.S. Navy in the Pacific in these precarious months after Pearl Harbor.

Lieutenant Commander Lovelace came up on the remaining 3 bombers as they were drawing away from the carrier. He headed in as the bombers split up, accelerating to 200 knots or more. Lovelace was drilling the tail of one Betty with .50 caliber bullets. At this time Lieutenant (JG) Howard Louis Johnson's fighter was hit with 20mm explosive shells. He was hit in the legs but managed to bail out. At 1649 lookouts saw his parachute open, while Lovelace informed the carrier. The destroyer *Patterson* was sent to rescue Johnson.

Thach with 4 F4Fs continued to climb to chase the remaining attackers, while Lieutenant Gill directed Butch O'Hare and wingman Marion Dufilho to stay close by in reserve. Thach and Sellstrom rushed to catch up with the bombers and placed themselves ahead and above of one of the attackers. Thach looked around and saw a newcomer, Jack Wilson, come in from directly behind the target. Before he could alert Wilson of the danger of the Japanese tail gunners' 20mm cannon, a shell exploded on the windshield of Wilson's fighter. As the 2nd F4F pressed its attack, Wilson's plane went into a spin and splashed in the sea six miles off from the onlookers on the carrier. The destroyer *Hull* looked for a survivor, but there was none.

Thach made his run on the bomber that killed Wilson. He put his bullets into the engine and wing and the plane caught fire. Coming out of his run, Thach saw a second bomber beneath him. The bomber dove to escape, and Thach was able to descend to attack, putting bullets in the fuselage. He climbed for a high-side run and engaged the bomber. He placed his bullets accurately up the engine nacelle as the enemy aircraft wing exploded and fell off the plane. Thach had shot down the 7th and 8th Bettys.

A crippled bomber was attacked by an SBD pilot, Lieutenant Edward H. Allen, the executive officer of Scouting Two. He climbed after takeoff from the *Lexington* and engaged a maimed bomber that had somehow avoided the water. With a short burst of his twin .30-caliber nose guns, Allen sent the bomber into the sea. Allen had maneuvered the SBD around to allow his gunner, ARM1c Bruce Rountree, to fire into the belly of the bomber before it crashed, allowing Rountree to share in the downing.

Thach and his 2nd Division were nearly out of fuel, but they could not land until the flight deck was cleared. Though low on fuel, Thach had some difficulty holding his fellow 3rd Division pilots from heading after the 9th bomber. He reigned them back, assuming the last enemy plane had escaped. But the attacker was not so lucky, as Lieutenant Walter F. Henry, the XO of VB-2, was returning from an afternoon search mission. Henry saw the bomber ahead of him and was able to move behind the attacker. In full pursuit, Henry took some time to reach the optimal position. After a short burst of his twin .30s, the bomber caught fire and soon splashed some 80 miles west of the task force. On the return flight, Henry saw a ditched bomber crew abandoning their plane. In an aggressive mood, he dived to strafe the drifting Betty until it exploded and sank.[23]

The second group of 8 Type 1 Bettys under Lieutenant Commander Ito had heard the earlier contact report of Lieutenant Nakagawa at 1635 and adjusted their course to the south to locate the American task force. The scattered clouds served to delay the sighting as they flew along at 15,000 feet, but at 1700 Ito radioed Rabaul that the enemy was in view.

While the first wave attacks were in motion, the *Lexington* had seen Ito's bombers at 1649 bearing 015 degrees at 30 miles. The first visual sighting of the 2nd wave came from lookouts on the destroyer *Patterson* as she had dropped back astern to rescue Howard Johnson. At 1656 they saw a formation of enemy planes circling off 10 miles north. Nine minutes later, sailors had Johnson onboard. One man recalled, "The smile on the pilot's face was a thing to remember."[24] The ship's doctor treated thirty shrapnel cuts on both legs.

The CXAM radar did not provide a continuous 360 degrees display, so all contacts had to be plotted. The plot was so covered with contacts from the 1st wave attack that it was difficult to notice the 2nd wave. At 1700 the radar showed Ito's group at 9 miles away bearing 080. Two minutes later, observers made visual contact with the bombers off the *Lexington*'s starboard quarter. Lieutenant Gill directed the only available VF-3 fighters, O'Hare and Dufilho, to intercept the enemy contacts. At the time, Lovelace's 5 F4Fs from the 2nd Division were low on fuel and were in the pattern to land aboard. Thach was still rounding up his 7 fighters from the 1st wave off to the west.

Ito's group of 8 Bettys was flying in their Vee of Vees formation and in a shallow dive. O'Hare and his wingman were several thousand feet above them and a few miles astern of the task force. As one of the best marksmen in the squadron, O'Hare, with his 50-caliber guns and 450 rounds loaded per gun, had 34 seconds to fire before he ran out of ammunition. O'Hare let the center Vee pass underneath them as they rolled into a high-side run on the right side of the enemy formation. O'Hare singled out his first victim as the right trailing bomber on the right side of the Vee, believed to be flown by Japanese PO2c Baba. O'Hare fired .50-caliber slugs into the starboard engine nacelle and wing. The bomber started smoking, lost power, slowed, and began its dive toward the water.

O'Hare pulled up sharply and saw his next target, piloted by PO1c Mori. His guns hit this 2nd bomber on the left side of the formation, starting a thin trail of raw gasoline as it slowed and fell out of formation to the right and down. O'Hare then crossed over to the left side of the formation. As he looked back, he noticed that Dufilho was not with him. His ammunition belts must have shifted because his guns were jammed and would not fire. Dufilho pulled away to see if he could clear his guns, as events moved quickly ahead.

O'Hare went after the three bombers at the rear of the left echelon. He attacked the rearmost Betty of PO1c Maeda (his 3rd) from his high-side pass and guided his guns on the port engine nacelle. The bomber was set on fire, but later their crew was able to put it out with a fire extinguisher. O'Hare's next target (the 4th) was the Betty behind Ito's left wing, PO1c Uchiyama's. O'Hare hit the engine, causing it to seize, and also hit the wing as the bomber went into a sharp dive to the left as it fell away.

O'Hare was attacking the formation as all the enemy tail gunners focused on him as their only target. He ignored the danger as he continued. Ito's group had overshot their bomb release point over the *Lexington*. Now O'Hare was running through friendly shell busts from their 5-inchers, but again O'Hare paid no attention to them.

Ahead, O'Hare could see 5 Betty bombers (Ito, Ono, Mitani, Kogiku and Maeda) on their run, still in formation. He decided to attack the lead plane to disrupt the master bombardier. Moving in to point-blank range, he fired into Ito's port nacelle. The engine exploded and fell away. The explosion was so violent that the enemy survivors incorrectly reported the plane had been struck by a direct hit of antiaircraft burst. Ito's bomber fell away and down with heavy black smoke trailing. The remaining 4 bombers behind Ito immediately dropped their bomb payloads over the *Lexington*. The closest bomb hit 100 feet astern.

O'Hare took off after his 6th target, but after he fired 10 rounds from each gun, he was out of ammunition. Ito had struggled to stay aloft and change course to direct his plane into the *Lexington*. Antiaircraft fire at 3,000 yards sent waves of tracers at the bomber as Captain Sherman made sharp turns to avoid the attacker. Ito's bomber splashed into the sea at 1712 about 1500, yards ahead of the carrier's port bow.

The 5 Bettys believed to still be aloft included the 4 bombers from Ito's formation and the bomber O'Hare had shot up on his 1st pass. Sellstrom, Thach's wingman, was able to catch up with the separated Betty and shot it down 8 miles ahead of the task force. That left 3 enemy bombers.

Meanwhile, Allen and Rountree of Scouting Two were 30 miles away from Task Force 11 as they spotted the three Bettys (Maeda, Ono and Kogiku) in formation. Allen discovered that his SBD was faster than the Betty G4M1s as he fired on one of them with his .30-caliber gun. The target Betty seemed to endure the wrath of their guns with little impact except possible crew deaths. They chased the 3 bombers out 150 miles before turning back with low fuel. The bomber Allen had fired on, flown by PO1c Ono, did not reach Rabaul.

With the fighters low on fuel, the *Lexington*'s air department worked hard to prepare 4 fighters of the 2nd Division to relieve the CAP. With the flight deck still set for recovery, two SBDs landed. Next, the 2nd Division CAP launched at 1740. They climbed to see a clear sky.

Five minutes after the 2nd Division had launched, 9 F4Fs from the 1st and 3rd Divisions began landing aboard. Their reception was phenomenal and nearly out of control. Observers on the *Lexington* had seen the air battle before them and they had cheered as each fighter shot down a bogey. Admiral Brown reminded the staff that this was overkill and not a "football game."[25] The clear hero was Butch O'Hare, and when he taxied to stop, his plane was mobbed. He was led to the bridge to be congratulated by Brown and Sherman.[26]

Admiral Brown sent off a dispatch to CINCPAC and COMANZAC detailing the preliminary battle summary. He also stated his intension to rendezvous with the oiler *Platte* on February 22. At 1825 the *Lexington* began taking aboard the SBDs from the afternoon search and anti-torpedo patrol. At 1902 the 4 fighters of the CAP and the last of the aircraft were aboard. The *Lexington* changed course to 100°T, speed 22 knots, toward a rendezvous with the fleet oiler *Platte*.[27]

At Rabaul, the headquarters of the 24th Air Flotilla was monitoring the mission of Lieutenant Nakagawa and his contact report. Thirty minutes later they heard the sighting report from Lieutenant Commander Ito. At 1850 the crew of the 1st Division (Chutai) radioed that the attack had ended at 1730 with one enemy warship sunk. They also noted that the defense of the American task force was successful at inflicting the loss of several land-based planes. PO2c Ono ditched his plane at Nugava in the Nugura group east of New Ireland. Twenty-five minutes later, PO1c Maeda and his wingman, PO1c Kogiku, reached Rabaul, landing at Vunakanau. PO2c Mori ditched at 2010 in Simpson Harbor. These happened to be the only survivors who returned. The 4th Air Group lost 3 senior officers with 13 entire flight crews missing in action. The Japanese lost 15 Bettys. The survivors claimed to have sunk one cruiser or destroyer, and set fires to a carrier, as well as shooting down 8 enemy fighters.

The Japanese wanted to track the carrier in hopes of attacking later. The Yokohama Air Group sent out 3 search aircraft, none of which ever returned to Rabaul. At 1430 the Kiyokawa Maru Air Unit sent out an Aichi E13A1 Type 0 reconnaissance floatplane (Jake) to shadow Task Force 11. At 1815, that crew reported the American force bearing 062° some 470 miles from Rabaul. The plane continued to shadow the force until 2000, when it reported that it was returning to base. It was never seen again. Thus, the Japanese air units at Rabaul had lost a total of 19 planes on February 20.[28]

Captain Sherman in his action report covering the Air Attack on February 20, 1942, gave high praise for the performance of his personnel: "The performance of Lieutenant

O'Hare was distinguished from a standpoint of courage, skill and good thinking. His single-handed attack upon nine bombers with the result that only four of the original formation reached the dropping point was of the greatest value in preventing the ship from sustaining serious damage or possible loss." He went on to write:

> Each pilot engaged in this action acquitted himself with honor and in accordance with the best traditions of the Navy. Particular credit is due to Lt. Comdr. J.S. Thach, USN, Commander of Fighting Squadron THREE; Lieutenant N.A.M. Gayler, and Ensign E.R. Sellstrom, each of whom, alone or assisted, shot down three enemy aircraft.... The performance of Lieutenant E.H. Allen, USN, of Scouting Squadron TWO, was outstanding in that he engaged in combat with three enemy bombers in formation while flying a scout-bombing type aircraft. Before this engagement he had already attacked a plane which was badly damaged. He claimed no credit though the plane was seen to fall into the water after his attack. He next attacked another cripple from beneath, and with his free gunner's fire shot the plane down in flames. Finally, he pursued a retiring bomber formation of three remaining planes. During a running fight of 150 miles with one of these planes, in which his estimated speed advantage was only three knots, he managed, with the help of his free gunner, to silence all gunners and damage considerably the enemy plane. He was forced to retire because of low fuel. Rountree, Bruce, RM1c, USN, was his free gunner and did most of the shooting during these attacks.[29]

Sherman also gave praise to Commander Duckworth, the *Lexington* air officer, for the outstanding performance of the entire air department, as well as his work supervising the launching and landing of planes during radical turns of the ship, monitoring enemy planes and giving assistance to the Commanding Officer. The carrier fighter director officer, Lieutenant Gill, was also noted for carrying out his extremely difficult duties during the attack.

Captain Sherman made award recommendations as follows:

Navy Cross: Thach, Allen and O'Hare.
Distinguished Flying Cross: Gayler, Lemmon, Stanley and Sellstrom.
Special Letters of Commendation: Duckworth, Lovelace, Gill, Henry, Vorse, Clark, Morgan, Eder, Lackey, Peterson, Haynes and Rountree.

Rountree was recommended for promotion to Aviation Chief Radioman.

The following *Lexington* Air Group pilots were credited with shooting down Japanese aircraft during the attack:

Lieutenant E.H. O'Hare	5 bombers
Lieutenant Commander Thach	1 bomber, 1 bomber assist, 1 patrol plane assist.
Lieutenant N.A.M. Gayler	1 bomber, 2 bomber assists.
Lieutenant (JG) R.S. Lemmon	1 bomber, 1 bomber assist.
Ensign D.W. Peterson	1 bomber, 1 bomber assist.
Ensign E.R. Sellstrom	1 bomber, 1 patrol plane assist.
Lieutenant E.H. Allen	1 bomber assist, 1 bomber possible.
Lieutenant W.F. Henry	1 bomber.[30]

For destroying five Japanese bombers, Lieutenant O'Hare became the first Navy Ace of World War II, was promoted to lieutenant commander, and received the Medal of Honor from the hands of President Franklin D. Roosevelt on April 21, 1942. The president described the honoree as "modest, inarticulate, humorous, terribly nice and more than a little embarrassed by the whole thing."³¹ In 1945 the U.S. Navy destroyer USS *O'Hare* (DD-889) was named in O'Hare's honor. On September 19, 1949, the Chicago-area Orchard Depot Airport was renamed O'Hare International Airport.³²

Captain Sherman further reported on the Japanese tactics of using the shallow Vee of Vees formations. The first formation had first climbed from 8,500 feet up to the 11,000 feet altitude, while the second group of nine bombers had descended from 14,000 feet. The formations had been approaching "at steady altitude for about 6 miles, flying a steady course and taking no evasive action when approached by fighters. Pilots report that the planes appeared unable to bring much, if any, fire power to bear against an overhead or high-side attack."³³

The *Lexington*'s antiaircraft fire from the starboard 5-inch battery was used as the first enemy bomber attack came in at 10,000 yards range at a 40° angle. The battery fired 105 rounds at the leading plane of the formation and was credited with causing it to shear off. One bomber approached from low altitude from the starboard beam and was engaged by the .50 caliber machine guns and 1.1-inch/75 mounts at 2,500 yards. The firing was right on the mark and the plane crashed at 75 yards on fire in the wake of the ship.

On the second attack, starboard after AA batteries opened up on the bombers coming in at some 30° angle. When the carrier swung to the left, the automatic cut-off cams interrupted the fire. Firing continued using port after and forward batteries, expending 133 rounds. One of the rammers jammed on the port forward battery and no hits were evident. Another bomber came in on the port side at low altitude on a converging course off 3,000 yards at a 30° angle. A 1.1-inch/75 mount and two .50 caliber guns opened fire and shot down the bomber in flames off 1,500 yards on port bow. There was a problem with a 1.1-inch/75 that failed to load in one of its barrels, and a double load found in another barrel. The 5-inch AA guns encountered difficulty distinguishing their bursts from those of the other ships in the formation.³⁴

The following observations were made in Sherman's action report (Paragraph 17):

(a) Japanese planes are equipped with cannon.
(b) Some, possibly all, of the planes encountered had a tall turret.
(c) That bullet-proof windshields are effective. They saved the life of Lieutenant GAYLER when his was struck by a missile during combat.
(d) The guns of the F4F-3 may jam the cartridge belt in a sharp pushover, resulting in guns out of action.
(e) The plane used by the enemy was a twin-engine, midwing, single tail bomber. It had nose gun, waist gun and tail gun. Made bombing run at about 160 knots. Believed to be a new type plane. It appears to be vulnerable from any angle except low and behind. Lieutenant ALLEN's free-gun attack from directly below was not opposed and was instantly effective.
(f) Of the three guns noted, at least one and possibly all three are about 20 mm cannon.
(g) The Japanese ball insignia showed very indistinctly against the brown and green mottled camouflage. The tail had three alternate red and white stripes near the top. These stripes were horizontal. They are nearly duplicates of our own present tail markings.³⁵

Recommendations from the action experienced included (Paragraph 18):

(a) That overhead and high-side fixed-gun approaches be considered as the most effective against Japanese two-engine heavy bombers.
(b) That gunfire be directed upon engines, rear side especially. In this engagement engines were extremely vulnerable and caught fire in almost every case.
(c) That pilots not be sent to operating squadrons without fixed-gun firing practice. Both pilots who were shot down had allowed themselves to be drawn in behind and were hit when in that position. Training under experienced combat-proven pilots would be invaluable.³⁶

In his action report to CINCPAC dated February 24, 1942, Vice Admiral Brown gave his full endorsement to the combat award and commendation recommendations provided by Captain Sherman. He also exercised his authority (Bureau of Navigation Circular Letter No. 1–42) and promoted radioman Bruce Rountree to aviation chief radioman. He also strongly recommended that Captain Sherman be awarded the Navy Cross for the seamanship displayed "in upsetting the aim of the enemy bombers, and the efficient recovery, reservicing and launching of his planes in the midst of the engagement [which] contributed immeasurably to the success of this force." Brown also lauded the "fighting spirit … [and] fighting qualities" of Captain Sherman.[37]

Admiral Brown commented on the analysis of the gunnery experience of the attack. It seems the antiaircraft fire from the Task Force 11 ships in the rear was heavy, but inaccurate. The fighter pilots noted that the bursts were beyond the target by 500 to 1,000 feet on the first attack, and more than 1000 feet short on the second. The fighter pilots also reported that no enemy planes were shot down by AA fire, but observers on deck reported that two to four were hit. As one might expect, the fighter pilots also complained that the AA fire "hampered them in driving home attacks near the bomb release point."[38]

The high density of AA bursts and ineffectiveness of tracers made the problem of spotting fuse range quite difficult, or impossible. Tracers need to burn all the way to the point of burst. The heavy cruiser *Pensacola* suffered battering and rifling scarring damage to the number one five-inch gun some 2.5 feet from the muzzle, requiring replacement. During the enemy bomber's attempt at crashing on the carrier deck, the volume of short-range bursts of AA fire was "excellent," resulting in the plane's crashing on the water close aboard. The action report alerted the range-keeper operators to hold their fire until a good firing solution is obtained. In addition, it was noted AA fire should "be ceased promptly after bombs are released to give fighters, when present, more opportunity to attack."[39]

The power plants of the TF 11 ships generally performed satisfactorily, but there were problems with a few that affected operations. The *Patterson* had a steering gear issue at speeds above 25 knots, the *Aylwin* had one boiler with a leaky superheater limiting her maximum speed to 28 knots, and the *San Francisco* could not reach speeds above 27 knots because of high injection temperatures and length of time out of dock. Fuel supply was also a major problem on this raid attempt, and Brown commented, "Had the raid been made as planned, and even had the Task Force escaped damage during the raid, any subsequence contact with enemy forces prior to rendezvous with the tanker would have been disastrous."[40]

Admiral Brown included some interesting observations about the enemy attacker's tactics, including:

- Damaged planes appear to attempt to crash land on our carriers.
- When a formation leader is shot out of his position, the remaining planes seemed to be unable to execute proper bombing techniques.
- Based on observations of the enemy bombers that were shot down, the majority of the planes had an engine fire in at least one engine. This is likely caused by having unprotected gasoline tanks in the wings between the engine and fuselage.
- The bombers appeared to have orange-striped tail sections that were similar to Honolulu-based U.S. Army planes camouflage that sport red-striped tails.

Recommendations provided were:

(a) Our fighters should endeavor to shoot down the leaders of the enemy groups.
(b) Our fighters should make their point to aim the engine section on enemy bombers instead of the fuselage.
(c) Radar identification of our planes is vitally essential to our force and to our planes.
(d) Scout bombers had difficulty in attaining an attack position on enemy bombers due to lack of speed advantage. The gun-power of our scouts is sufficient to shoot down enemy bombers once the former have attained the proper position from which to start their attacks, but this limitation, due to low speed, should be borne in mind when planning to use scouts to augment fighter protection.[41]

Knowing that CINCPAC Nimitz would be interested in details, Vice Admiral Brown provided a complete explanation of his decision to call off the Rabaul raid in his action report:

> When this force was sighted by enemy scouts during the forenoon of February 20th, I was faced with a difficult decision as to whether or not to continue the scheduled attack on RABAUL. I was quite conscious of the tremendous importance of the issues involved. The destruction of enemy ships previously reported in RABAUL harbor would delay indefinitely any enemy move to the SOUTHWEST PACIFIC. A successful attack there would serve as an important diversion to the threatened attack on TIMOR and JAVA. On the other hand, with twenty hours' warning, the Japanese would have ample time to withdraw all ships from the Harbor of RABAUL to a safe position to the WESTWARD, and to assemble at RABAUL strong air reinforcements from nearby air bases and TRUK, and to be alerted for our attack. Our fuel shortage had required us to plan definite speed limits during the approach, the attack and withdrawal. Any marked deviation from this schedule threatened running out of fuel before we could join up with our tanker. Prevailing calms had already required more speed operations for handling planes than had been hoped for. The approach to the attack launching point at night involved navigational risks because of the presence of coral reefs in the necessary operating area. During the preceding several days, currents had been found strong and variable. The success of the whole operation depended upon an accurate position fix on the night before the attack. (We were unable to obtain star sights on the night of the 20th and would not have had an accurate fix had we gone in). The loss of the carrier or bungled attack would have been still another major calamity to the Allied cause.[42]

Another factor that influenced Brown to cancel the Rabaul raid was that, with the Japanese now alerted to the presence of Task Force 11, Army Air Force bombers would be arriving in "a fully aroused hornets' nest."[43] With his decision made, he made sure that COMANZAC was informed immediately. Later, Brown learned that reconnaissance had confirmed that the Japanese had indeed withdrawn their shipping from Rabaul harbor and were prepared for the attack by TF 11.

Using text underlined for special significance, Brown wrote, "In my opinion, a superiority in carrier strength in the PACIFIC is one of the prime requisites for our final offensive. The loss of a carrier at this time would be a serious blow to our whole carrier development program and delay indefinitely our ability to take the offensive." He also added, "It is my opinion that if we had been attacked by forty planes instead of eighteen, only a miracle could have prevented damage to the LEXINGTON, 3500 miles from the nearest drydock."[44]

Brown closed his action report (in paragraph 10) stating: "I hope that our appearance off RABAUL, the destruction of eighteen of his large aircraft, and our continued radio silence since that appearance may create a diversion of enemy air strength from other areas for a considerable time. The reported diversion of twenty-five long-range bombers from PALAU to RABAUL appears to confirm this hope."[45]

Continuing to retire, on the 21st *Lexington* maintained CAPs from 1030 until darkness.

Radar picked up a bogey at 1545 and 38 miles north of the task force. It was likely a Japanese flying boat on the end leg of his search. On the afternoon of February 22, the *Lexington* rendezvoused with the *Platte* and the ANZAC Squadron. Refueling operations dominated the next three days. In the February 232158 message from COMTASKFOR 11 to CINCPAC, Brown indicated that his TF would send the *Platte* to Pearl Harbor after refueling operations were complete around February 25.[46]

Back home in Japan, the press naturally presented a different view of the engagement. The *Osaka Mainichi* reported that the Japanese "wild eagles" had inflicted "fatal damage" on the U.S. carrier even as they had lost only nine aircraft. The Japanese squadron leader had been lost, Lieutenant Commander Takuzo Ito, as well as two other Japanese Naval Academy grads, Lieutenant Commanders Yogoro Seto and Masayoshi Nakagawa. The press made one man a hero. Lieutenant Noboru Sakai tried to crash into the *Lexington* but failed.[47]

Though the planned attack on Rabaul was canceled, the results were tactically favorable, with the elimination of 19 Japanese aircraft and some key flight leaders. The battle was fought over good seas with clouds from 2,800 to 25,000 feet altitude, with visibility 15 to 20 miles. It showed that a carrier could defend itself against a bombing attack under specific conditions: the enemy planes have no fighter support, the attack is not coordinated with one by torpedo planes, and the number of planes is limited.[48]

On hearing of the engagement, Yamamoto ordered 34 navy shore bombers of the First Air Group from the Netherlands East Indies to head to Truk the following day in relief.[49] From the strategic viewpoint, the *Lexington* sortie toward Rabaul had convinced the IJN command at Truk that their landing operations planned for early March against Port Moresby and Tulagi, after they occupied Lae and Salamaua on New Guinea, was too risky and should be deferred until perhaps the end of April, when Admiral Yamamoto could dispatch more carrier support to the southeast area.[50]

Chapter 4

Wake and Marcus Islands

*...the unhindered escape of the carrier force
leaves the staff frustrated and hopping mad.*

As the *Enterprise* and *Yorktown* task forces were berthed in Pearl Harbor, on February 11 Nimitz issued orders for a Task Force 13 (the combined TF-8 and TF-17) for raids on Wake Island and Eniwetok Island in the northern Marshalls. CINCPAC wanted "as strong an aggressive raid as can be undertaken." Halsey had no objection to leading the raid, but he was furious when he saw the task force designation and the scheduled departure date of Friday, February 13. Halsey sent his fired-up chief of staff, Captain Miles Browning, with his intelligence officer, Marine Colonel Julian P. Brown, to raise hell at CINCPAC headquarters over the incident. Browning blew into the War Plans office and demanded to see Captain Charles H. McMorris as he declared, "What goes on here? Have you got it in for us, or what?" McMorris was not superstitious, but agreed that "no sane sailorman would dare buck such a combination of ill auspices." He agreed to change the task force designation to 16 and told Browning that an overdue oiler would delay Halsey's departure to the 14th.[1]

The specific objectives of the mission were to weaken the enemy and gain intelligence, to divert enemy strength from his offensives in the southwestern Pacific, and to cover U.S. positions and communications in the mid–Pacific. Other guidance directed that any encounter with important enemy combatant forces would be the primary objective. The priority of objectives was as follows: "(1) combatant ships; (2) aircraft, particularly those on ground or water; (3) other ships; (4) aircraft supporting installations, fuel tanks, power and radio installations; (5) troop concentrations and fortifications; (6) storehouses. The groups were specifically ordered to seize any opportunity to destroy important enemy forces."[2]

While this mission was taking shape in the afterglow of the successful Marshall-Gilbert raid, the Japanese forces continued to roll over everything in their path in the southwestern Pacific. The empires of the British and the Dutch were disappearing. Singapore was nearing its end, and the Japanese were moving to take Borneo, Celebes, New Guinea, and the Solomons. Before long, the Japanese thrusts would mean real attacks on Australia.

For the Allied forces, defensive operations seemed like only delaying tactics at best, and there was little hope that the resources were available to stop and then defeat the enemy in this region. The only realistic action for the American naval forces at this point was to create a diversion in the northern and central Pacific. Attacking Wake Island in the direction of the Japanese homeland might give the Japanese military leadership an opportunity to reconsider their advances in the southwest.[3]

On Sunday the 15th, Nimitz received a conciliatory dispatch (151830 Aidac) at noon from COMINCH indicating that he was satisfied with occasional raids by Pacific Fleet forces on Japanese island bases in the Central Pacific. King also agreed that ships should be held back in reserve, as well as suggesting that one carrier be positioned in the Canton Islands area. These refreshing words from Admiral King were direct evidence of the success of Admiral Pye's mission to explain what was happening in the Pacific.[4]

The plans were to have the U.S. submarines clear the area of Wake and Eniwetok islands by the time Task Force 16 arrived in the area for the attacks. All intelligence information about Wake Island forces was provided to the task force, including updated photography that was taken from an Army plane and delivered to Oahu for film developing. Information about Eniwetok Island and Marcus Island, a Japanese island 600 miles northwest of Wake Island, was still limited. The Eniwetok attack was assigned to the *Enterprise* group, to commence 10 minutes before sunrise on February 24. The *Yorktown* group was directed to simultaneously attack Wake Island. Halsey was given the authority to substitute Marcus Island for Eniwetok if he deemed it more useful to the mission.[5]

The *Enterprise* Task Group with Halsey departed Pearl Harbor at 1215 on Valentine's Day, February 14, 1942, in company with the familiar cruisers *Northampton* and *Salt Lake City*, with the screening destroyers *Maury, Balch, Dunlap, Blue, Ralph Talbot* and *Craven*. *Craven* was new to the post–Marshall-Gilbert task force, as well as the oiler *Sabine* that replaced the *Platte*.[6] Halsey announced the mission to the crew that day to cheers. The spirits of the men had been generally good since the successful Marshall attack, but nothing to compare with the delight they all felt in attacking Wake Island. The memories of delivering marines to the island and having the F4Fs flying off the *Enterprise* to support the friendly forces trying to resist the Japanese invasion were still fresh. Any revenge they could take would be satisfying.[7]

While in port, VF-6 had replaced the boilerplate with factory-designed armor, but only 4 of the 17 F4Fs had self-sealing fuel tanks installed. On the afternoon of the 14th, Lieutenant Commander Wade McClusky led his fighters out to land on the *Enterprise*.[8]

The *Yorktown* with Rear Admiral Frank J. Fletcher sailed out of Pearl on the morning of February 16 with the cruisers *Louisville* and *Astoria*, oiler *Guadalupe*, and four destroyers—*Sims, Anderson, Hammann* and *Walke*. At noon of the departure day, Nimitz received a message from Admiral King disagreeing with the use of two carrier task forces for the Wake and Marcus Raid. COMINCH felt that "occasional raids on the Mandates are sufficient"[9] and suggested that either the *Enterprise* or the *Yorktown* task force should be deployed to Canton Island. On February 24, Nimitz ordered the *Yorktown* Task Force 17 to join with the *Lexington* Task Force 11 to raid Rabaul. Halsey's Task Force 8 would carry on with the planned raid on Wake Island.[10]

The *Enterprise* Task Force headed to the northwest as the shipboard personnel prepared for the Wake attack. On the 17th, target practice was held with the 5-inch guns on the *Enterprise*. The cruisers and destroyers also began their drills. The next day they fired 1.1 and 20mm machine guns at a target towed by a plane.

The 18th also saw two Marine Catalina PBYs fly in at low altitude from the northwest as one of the planes dropped a package on the *Enterprise*'s flight deck. The high-priority package contained the intelligence and photos from the Army plane reconnaissance over

Wake Island. It was not a good day for Lieutenant (JG) Thomas Eversole of Torpedo Squadron Six as he returned from an afternoon patrol. He had been launched with a second TBD earlier. In his Devastator, Eversole became disoriented in poor visibility and ditched at sea 60 miles from the ship. The next morning Eversole was found with his two crewmembers exercising their oars in their bright yellow life raft. The other TBD was able to locate the carrier just before dark. That night the Task Force crossed the International Date Line.[11]

Halsey issued his operational orders for an air attack on Wake on February 21. He modified the orders the next day as he directed Rear Admiral Raymond A. Spruance, commanding the surface forces, to take the two cruisers and the destroyers *Balch* and *Maury* and bombard Peale Island (adjoining Wake Island) and the north end of Wake Island. The air group would bomb the airfield on Wake, as well as the neighboring Wilkes Island. Spruance would sail in from the west in a synchronized attack with the air group commencing 10 minutes before sunrise.[12]

In the "rainy and dreary looking" weather of the 21st, Ensign Norm Hodson of VF-6 rolled down the flight deck at 0620 in his F4F-3A, scheduled for an inner patrol. He was unable to maintain proper takeoff speed and he went over the bow and crashed in the sea 75 yards off the *Enterprise*. His plane sank in less than a minute, but he was able to escape. He was picked up by the destroyer *Blue* and returned to the carrier the following day.[13]

On Sunday the 22nd, the Task Force was 675 miles from Wake Island as it began refueling operations. In his wartime diary, Clarence W. Olive recorded the following: "Still steaming north of Wake. Started fueling destroyers this morning.... The *Blue* came along first. The fighter pilot came aboard via breeches buoy. The *Dunlap* came next and the three torpedo plane men came aboard in the same manner. The *Balch* was next and G.Q. sounded, enemy plane sighted, supposedly. Was one of our carrier planes. G.Q. sounded at 1250 and lasted about 17 minutes. The *Sabine*, oil tanker, came alongside next. The weather was rainy and dreary looking. I had 12–4 watch. Injection dropped to 67 deg. during the day. Is cool enough to sleep under a blanket."[14]

On the 23rd the *Enterprise* was steaming toward Wake at 20–22 knots as the air patrols searched for contacts within 160 miles of Wake Island. No contacts were encountered. The crew began to have their meals on the flight deck, so they would not have to leave their stations. Late in the afternoon at 1735 the bombardment group broke off from the *Enterprise* and "began working its way to the westward."[15]

The original attack plan for the *Enterprise* Air Group called for a divebombing attack by Scouting Squadron Six and two divisions from Bombing Squadron Six on the airfield and facilities on the southern portion of Wake Island. This attack was to be coordinated with a horizontal bombing attack on Wilkes Island by nine planes from Torpedo Squadron Six, as well as bombardment of Peale Island and the northwest portion of Wake Island by CruDiv-5. The third division of VB-6 was to provide mopping-up operations on the landing field area if enemy planes were found. One division of F4F fighters from Fighting Squadron Six was tasked to provide fighter protection for the attack group.

Three planes from VS-6 were equipped with mapping cameras and directed to establish a composite bombing group with the second section of VT-6 to make a mapping run across the entire island. In addition, there were three radioman-gunners and bombers equipped with small hand-held cameras.

If "suitable targets"[16] for a torpedo attack were located, the carrier planned to launch the second division of VT-6 armed with torpedoes. There were no additional attacks anticipated unless opportunities presented themselves. A combat air patrol of four fighters would be maintained over the carrier during the daylight hours.[17]

The general plan for the bombardment of Wake Island was as follows:

(a) To approach from the west, in column, distance 1,500 yards, order of ships *Maury, Northampton, Salt Lake City, Balch*, remaining out of sight of the island until the carrier air group had attacked, and then to proceed as expeditiously as possible to initial point for commencing bombardment, in order to coordinate bombardment with air attack as far as practicable.

(b) To commence bombardment as a point 16,000 yards, 295° from Peale Island, in order to permit maximum fire down the length of that island, the western part of which is too narrow in width to present a good bombardment target.

(c) To close range to make destroyer fire effective, and also cruiser five inch, if practicable.[18]

Enterprise Air Group Action at Wake Island

At 0430 on Tuesday, February 24, general quarters was sounded aboard the *Enterprise*. The aviators rushed to their ready rooms. At 0505 an RDF (radio direction finding) bearing was taken of a Japanese voice transmission on frequency 340kcs from a suspected patrol plane. The bearing to Wake Island at that time was 157° at 37 miles. The contact may have been a patrol craft too small to be picked up by radar, reporting contact with the task force.

At 0517, some 120 miles north of Wake Island, the *Enterprise*, in company with the *Dunlap, Blue, Ralph Talbot*, and *Craven*, turned into the wind to the east at 25 knots and prepared to launch her planes. It was a rainy, dark morning with overcast conditions when the planes rolled down the flight deck. A strange halo effect was seen in the propeller wash of the planes because the spinning propellers condensed the moisture in the heavy air, creating spirals from the blade tips.[19]

The first planes that were spotted on the flight deck were the 4 F4Fs of Jim Gray's 3rd Division of VF-6 set for CAP duty. Keith Wheeler, a war correspondent, witnessed Gray's takeoff into the damp sky: "A shadowy fighter skittered up the deck.... For eternal seconds the shadowy plane down there crabbed sideways. It slid across the port row of deck lights ... the pilot wrenched it back and drummed over the bow. It dipped and the blue spots of exhaust flame vanished under the carrier's bow.... The twin blue spots came into view again and climbed away, swinging off to the right."[20]

At 0540 the CAP was launched with 4 F4Fs. Utilizing all the pilots of the squadron, these combat air patrols of 4 to 10 planes were maintained all day. The last fighter would land that day at 1835.[21] The next planes spotted for takeoff were the SBDs from VS-6. The XO of Scouting Six, Lieutenant Commander Earl Gallagher, began his takeoff with his 18 SBD scout bombers around 0600. The morning's first incident occurred with the second SBD to launch: an experienced pilot rolled off the port bow into the sea after his Dauntless dropped the left wheel into the catwalk and its left wing hit a 5-inch gun mount. The badly injured pilot, Lieutenant (JG) Peary Teaff, was rescued by the destroyer *Blue*, but not before hearing radioman-gunner 3c E.P. Jinks calling out from the darkness.

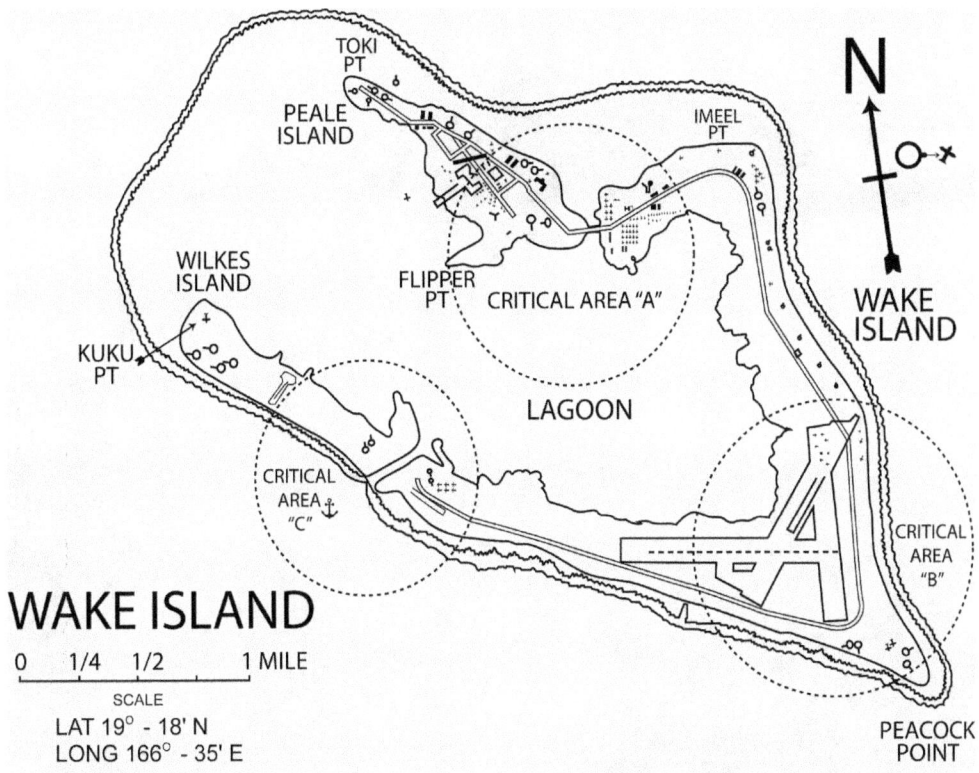

Wake Island map. Image redrawn based on *Early Carrier Raids in the Pacific Ocean*, 52.

Jinks vanished and the plane guard destroyer was unable to locate him. Teaff lost his left eye in the accident.[22]

Due to the accident and the poor weather conditions, the remaining takeoffs were delayed until 0650, thirty minutes later than planned. The attack group continued their takeoffs with Lieutenant Commander Bill Hollinsworth's 18 Bombing Six SBD bombers. Next to launch at 0630 was an escort of 6 F4F fighters with Lieutenant Commander Wade McClusky. The last plane with Lieutenant Commander Gene Lindsey's 9 TBD torpedo planes took off at 0647, followed three minutes later when the air group commander, Commander Howard L. Young, launched. His attack group of 52 planes and 106 men was now 30 minutes late. Each bomber was armed with one 500-pound and two 100-pound bombs using instantaneous fuses. Each torpedo plane was loaded with twelve 100-pound fragmentation bombs.[23]

After rendezvous, Young's attack group took a heading of 180 degrees toward Wake, 110 miles away. At 0750, as the *Enterprise* air attack group reached their attack position 10 miles west of Wake Island, the weather improved to scattered clouds between 3000 and 5000 feet, with a sea level breeze from the east at 24 knots. The bomber and fighter planes climbed to between 14,000- and 18,000-feet altitude, and the horizontal torpedo bombers moved to 12,000 feet.

As the surface bombardment group completed the shelling operations on Peale and the northern area of Wake, Commander Young ordered the air attack group to action. The primary mission of the VF-6 fighters was to protect the 9 horizontal bombers of VT-6.

Wake Island raid, 24 February 1942. A Douglas TBD-1 torpedo plane from USS *Enterprise* (CV-6) flies over Wake during the raid. Note fires burning in the lower center. View looks about WNW, with Wilkes Island in the center and the western end of Wake Island in bottom center. Peale Island is at right (photograph #: 80-CF-1071-1, Department of the Navy collections in the U.S. National Archives).

The fighters patrolled at 15,000 feet during the entire bombing and strafing attack. No enemy aircraft were encountered at Wake Island.[24]

Bombing Six had flown in formation in line astern and above Torpedo Six, which was in the lead. At 0725 an AA barrage was seen ahead some twenty to thirty miles, just before sighting Wake. The primary objective of VB-6 planes was to destroy any enemy land planes located on Wake Island. Their secondary objectives were to destroy underground hangars, revetments, magazines, antiaircraft batteries, and gasoline storage located in the area around the airfield on Wake Island.

Lieutenant Commander Hollingsworth took his first division of six planes of Bombing Squadron Six down first in near-vertical dives from 12,000 feet in staggered tandem formation to attack the Wake Island airfield from the west. They pulled out up sun (about 110°T). When the flash of bombs was seen, Gallagher pushed over his 1st Division of Scouting Six SBDs to their attack from 12,000 feet. In an easterly direction, the divebombing attack released their bombs on the landing field and retired to the east. The second division of VS-6 divebombed from 11,000 feet heading in a northerly direction and released their bombs on the installation to the east of the field, retiring to the east at high speed and low altitude. The third division of VS-6 conducted their divebombing attack from 11,000 feet heading northeast on installations on the south and east side of the landing field. The bomb releases were made from 1,500 to 2,500 feet for 500-pound bombs and 800 to 1,500 feet for the 100-pound bombs.

After Scouting Six had completed their three bombing runs, the second and third divisions of Bombing Six commenced their divebombing attacks. Their specific target objectives were to mop up operations on the airfield. The second division led by Lieutenant R.H. Best came in from the east and bombed from 11,000 feet on the installations to the east of the field. They retired to the south. The third division led by Lieutenant J.D. Blitch executed their divebombing attack from 11,000 feet slightly to the north of the field, pulled out to the north, and retired to the east. The bomb releases were by ripple drop between 4,000 and 2,000 feet, pulling out at 1,000 feet. Each divebombing attack was made using one 500-pound bomb and two 100-pound bombs with instantaneous fuses. The attackers used .50 caliber and flexible .30 caliber machine guns on strafing runs on the surface vessel. The enemy had used .30 and .50 caliber bullets and fired bursts up to as high as 19,000 feet with 3-inch and 5-inch guns.

Douglas SBD-2 Dauntless scout bombers, of Scouting Squadron Six (VS-6). Composite photograph of 9 planes in flight, with USS *Enterprise* (CV-6) and a plane guard destroyer below. The original photograph is dated 27 October 1941. Note differences in ocean surface wave patterns between the upper and lower images, skillfully blended to combine the two photographs (official U.S. Navy photograph, now in the collections of the National Archives, Catalog #: 80-G-6678).

While retiring some 10 to 15 miles east of Wake Island just before the attack group rendezvous, the second and third divisions of VS-6 encountered a 175-ton Japanese patrol type vessel of from 120 to 150 feet in length. Two strafing runs were made by all planes. The damaged vessel was left abandoned and turning in "aimless circles," leaving a large oil slick in its wake. A destroyer from the bombardment group opened fire on the vessel and made two direct hits.[25]

At 0802 on course 076°T the three photographic mapping planes from Scouting Six joined with the second section of Torpedo Squadron Six with CEAG Commander Young for a composite bombing attack with each plane dropping one 500-pound and two 100-pound bombs in salvo on the gasoline storage at the southwest end of the island. Seven of the ten gasoline storage tanks exploded in orange flame and black smoke. After the attack, Scouting Six made a mapping run across the island as planned.[26]

Torpedo Squadron Six sighted Wake Island bearing 240°T at 10 miles. At 0755 the attack signal was given as each section broke from formation to work independently. The first section of VT-6 at 0808 divebombed from 12,000 feet at 100 knots on a course of 330°T and dropped ten bombs on a four-engine seaplane moored near the Pan American pier on the beach at the southwest end of Pearle Island. It was a direct hit. Seven minutes later they dropped 9 bombs alongside buildings on Wilkes Island northwest of the new channel under construction. They scored near misses.

At 0835 the first section continued by dropping 15 bombs on AA batteries on the southwest side of Wilkes Island with unknown results, then five minutes later they dropped two bombs on the runway of the landing field. The third section of VT-6 entered the attack at 0803, dropping six bombs on AA gun positions in the center of Wilkes Island, and silencing them. At 0807 heading on a course 000°T, they dropped 12 bombs on the Pan American Airways gas tanks on the eastern end of Wilkes, leaving them in flames. Six minutes later they left the Marine camp buildings on fire west of the airfield using 11 bombs. In another run they dropped 7 more bombs in the same area.

As the designated "mopping up" bombers, the first section of VT-6 made its first run on a four-engine patrol seaplane on the water 300 yards south of the Pan American Airways pier, two runs on AA batteries on the south of Wilkes Island, and the last run on the intersection of the N-S, NE-SW runways. The bombs were released in salvo and ripple drops.

During the VT-6 attacks, the enemy AA fire had been "sporadic and ineffective." The runs were so fast that they had been completed before the AA bursts had come close to the planes. VT-6 sections two and three retired to the east some ten miles away from the island, joined up and departed for the carrier at 0834. The first section joined the group en route. Lindsey's squadron began landing aboard at 1000.[27]

At 0815, after the VS-6 planes had completed their divebombing, they proceeded to execute their glide-bombing attacks with light bombs at about 0825, preparing to retire to the east to rendezvous. At about 0830, Ensign Delbert W. Halsey (not related to the Admiral) found another four-engine Kawanishi Type 97 seaplane in the air five miles off the eastern shore of Wake and attacked from behind and below the enemy. Halsey alerted the F4F Wildcats circling overhead as he called out on his radio, "This is Halsey. This is Halsey. I got a Kawanishi five miles east of the island heading straight east and can't catch him."[28]

Lieutenant Commander McClusky was patrolling at 15,000 feet when he heard Halsey. Before Halsey had completed his radio alert, fighters were descending to attack the seaplane. The fighters first turned toward the cruisers bombarding the island, and they naturally turned away when the antiaircraft fire was opening up. The fighters descended to 1,000 feet and leveled off to find they were behind the seaplane in the slot to the right, ready to pounce on the Japanese plane.

McClusky took the first turn; he silenced the plane's gunners and hit the left outboard engine. Pilot and Gunner B.H. Bayers were next as McClusky raked the fuselage and started the second engine burning. Then Lieutenant Roger Mehle headed in to attack with repeated gun bursts, which caused the seaplane to suddenly explode in pieces and fall into the sea. Later inspection on the leading edge of Mehle's right wing found an embedded hinge fitting from the enemy plane. On the fitting was stamped "1938." The spectacular visual event in front of the Bombardment Group ship crews brought cheers from the sailors. Hearing of McClusky's jubilant report, at 0835 Commander Young radioed, "You win a cigar."[29]

The Japanese antiaircraft fire from 3- and 5-inch batteries was totally ineffective, although they were able to fire to a height of 19,000 feet. Machine gun fire "from pits along the beach was erratic and showed no evidence of director control."[30] All the attack squadrons rendezvoused independently east of Wake Island and departed for the carrier to gather over the carrier an hour later to land. Between 0948 and 1014, all the strike planes recovered aboard the *Enterprise*.[31]

Bombardment Group Action at Wake Island

Earlier, Spruance's bombardment group had moved as planned in a column with 1,500 yards separation toward the southwest at 20 knots. The *Maury* was in the lead spot followed by *Northampton*, *Salt Lake City*, and *Balch*. Arriving at a point 30 miles from Wake Island, at 0641 the column changed course to 090°T with speed 21.2 knots and maintained an easterly and northeasterly course throughout the Wake bombardment operation, keeping the targets on their starboard.

Knowing the *Enterprise* Air Group was due over Wake at 0708 (10 minutes before sunrise), the cruisers held up catapulting their planes off their stern decks as long as they could to prevent shore detection of the resulting flashes. Their delay turned out to be of no value since the planes launched from the *Enterprise* were some 30 minutes late due to bad weather.[32]

At 0710 the *Northampton* launched four Curtiss SOC planes piloted by Lieutenant Commander E.A. Junghans (spotter two for *Northampton*), Lieutenant M.C. Reeves (spotter one for *Northampton*), Ensign C.A. Shipman (spotter for *Balch*), and Ensign F.H. Covington (spotter for *Maury*). The *Salt Lake City*, likewise, launched their 2 SOC planes starting at 0710 for reconnaissance and spotting work. The two groups of observation planes rendezvoused and then climbed to 5,000 feet en route to their spotting point located north of Peale and Wake islands.[33]

As it turned out, the bombardment group first sighted 3 Japanese Nakajima E8N2 Type 95 seaplanes at 0707 as they planned to execute divebombing attacks on the *Maury* and *Northampton* when they were 18 miles off Wake. The planes circled and were lost in the clouds. The *Maury* sighted an enemy seaplane coming in ahead to make a divebombing attack and opened fire on the intruder at 0727. The seaplane dropped a bomb that landed about 30 yards abeam of the stack, but it did not explode. Three minutes later, a second seaplane attacked from ahead as the *Maury* engaged gunfire. The bomb exploded 50 yards off the starboard beam.

At 0733 the *Maury* sighted Wake Island off 9 miles bearing 170°T. Two minutes later another enemy seaplane came in on the starboard bow, sheared off from the *Maury* and dropped a bomb off the starboard beam of the *Northampton*, landing 150 yards away. Then, at 0740 another seaplane conducted a divebombing attack that exploded 300 yards on the port bow. If the air attack group had been on time, these threats would have been eliminated.[34]

When their range to Peale Island reached 16,000 yards, Spruance's bombardment group opened fire at 0742 bearing 115°T to the island. The group had favorable weather, but a mist covered the island. Another problem was created by coming in from the west, since the sun was now in the eyes of the targeting operators. At the same time, the Japanese shore batteries opened fire on the bombardment group. Cruising at 15 knots, the *Northampton* had fired its main battery on target number 3, bearing 115°T range at 16,700 yards, then at 0745 the ship changed to fire on target number 2, bearing 140°T at 16,200 yards. Ten minutes later, the shells from the shore batteries were landing 500 yards to the starboard as the *Northampton* changed course to 070°T and shifted to target number 5,

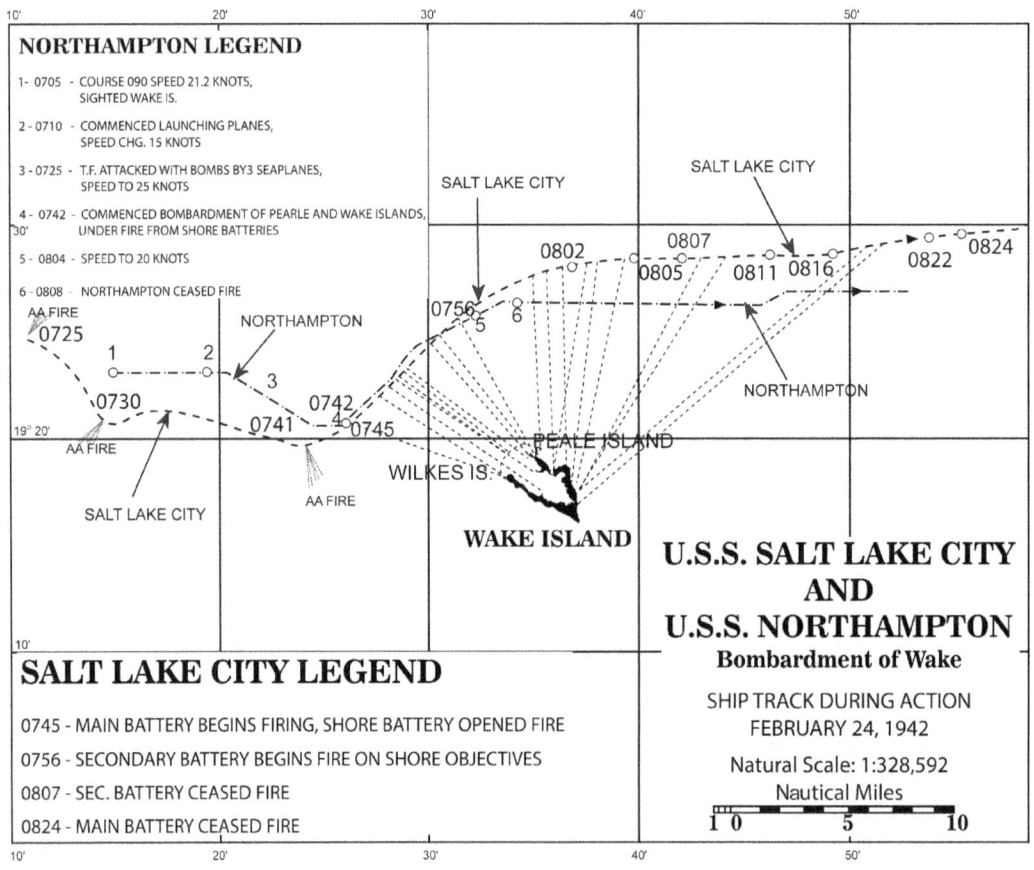

USS *Salt Lake City* and USS *Northampton* attack track—Wake Island raid. Image redrawn based on *Early Carrier Raids in the Pacific Ocean*, 55.

bearing 137°T at 16,600 yards. The final salvos from the cruiser's turrets 1, 2, and 3 fired at 0808 on target 5, bearing 174°T range at 14,650 yards. Three fires were raging on the island.[35]

The *Salt Lake City* had observed the first bombing attacks by *Enterprise* planes at 0736. Three minutes later they spotted a four-engine patrol seaplane coming in on their port bow. Their AA battery fired two or three rounds at the enemy plane at about 12,000 yards. The plane did not close on the cruiser.

At 0743 the *Salt Lake City* received the "Commence Firing"[36] signal, but the ship had difficulty resolving the target settings because the sun and visibility problems gave the director pointer and trainer trouble. After trying multiple filters, the spotter was able to see the target using the light neutral filter. The rangefinders were not working well either, but radar was providing a reasonable estimate of range to Peale Island. Splashes from shells fired by the shore batteries were falling short. At 0745 the cruiser commenced firing single-gun salvos using radar ranging set at 14,900 yards targeted at the water tank on the island. The plane spotter was directed to strafe the shore batteries. The first salvo was not seen by the ship or the plane spotter. The second salvo was seen by the spotter landing left of the target. Finally, the third salvo landed near the target.

The cruiser changed course to 030°T (changing courses every minute or so) at 0747 and began rapid-fire ten-gun salvos "to take advantage of opportunity for good enfiladed fire."[37] Communication with the spotter plane was now excellent. At 0752 the firing was slowed with full salvos targeted to the seaplane shore installations. Four minutes later, the secondary battery commenced firing at shore targets on Peale Island with ranging about 13,500 yards. They started first using two or three salvos, until accurate ranging was obtained, and then shifted to rapid continuous fire. Fire from five-inch guns was most effective. As the cruiser moved out of range, firing ceased from the main battery at 0812. One shore battery at the northeastern corner of Wake Island continued to fire. The *Salt Lake City* fired two salvos from turret 2 and one from turret 3 at the enemy battery, ending their bombardment at 0824.[38]

At 0830 the SOC planes from the *Northampton* and *Salt Lake City* divebombed buildings on the northwest tip of Wake Island, each dropping eleven 100-pound bombs. One of those pilots later remarked, "Dropping our little, puny bombs with our obsolete aircraft was more a gesture than anything else."[39]

During the bombardment, the destroyers *Maury* and *Balch* conducted bombardment of Peale Island and the northern end of Wake Island. At 0746 the *Balch* opened fire on three shore batteries that were firing from the northwest end of Peale Island, bearing 135°T at opening range of 13,700 yards. After firing 200 rounds of ammunition, the three batteries ceased firing and a fire was spotted among several cranes and steam shovel installations to the southeast of the initial point of aim. The *Balch* then shifted to fire at the next two shore batteries down the island bearing 210° at 14,600 yards. At 0820 the shore batteries were seen to be silenced. The destroyer moved the targeting to two more batteries at the north beach of Peale Island (bearing 225° at 15,500 yards). After opening fire, two explosions were observed behind the point of aim believed to be oil tanks, near the Pan American Airways seaplane hangar. No enemy fire was observed from the area.

The *Balch* then shifted its fire to a single gun battery on the northwest tip of Wake Island at some 16,000 yards. After splashes were seen between Wake and Peale islands, the spotter had redirected the fire at tanks and buildings in this section of Wake. The *Balch* ceased firing at 0835, believing it had silenced from 5 to 7 enemy shore batteries with its gunfire. Their total expenditure of ammunition was 1269 rounds.

At 0840 the *Balch* sighted a 100-foot-long (175-ton) enemy patrol boat coming in bearing 071° off 16,000 yards. The *Maury* was ordered to close and sink it, which it did at 0850. At 1050 a second patrol boat was sighted, bearing 000°T at range 16,000 yards. At 1105 the *Balch* opened fire and sank the vessel at 1114. Just after the patrol boat sank, there was an underwater explosion believed to be made by depth charges that had not been set to "safe." At 1130 the *Balch* picked up four Japanese survivors. Three of the four had superficial injuries and were treated by the pharmacy mate. These prisoners of war were placed under guard. They could not speak, write, or understand English. Their white life preservers were marked with the word "Pioneer."[40]

When the *Balch* later returned to Pearl Harbor and was moored, an armed Marine guard took custody of the four Japanese prisoners. Just as the first prisoner was brought topside, "a pneumatic riveter cut loose on an adjacent ship, and ... the three Japs still below decks tried to scream the bulkheads down: they thought their comrade was being welcomed with a machine gun."[41]

The *Maury* had expended 348 rounds of 5-inch AA common at shore batteries, buildings, a power house (at the northwest end of Wake Island), and tanks. The ship used less ammunition than expected on shore batteries because of the necessity to alert gun batteries to fire at enemy patrol seaplanes conducting divebombing attacks on ships of the bombardment group. *Maury*'s 5-inch gun number one was out of commission with a bulge in the gun barrel after firing 84 rounds. Four divebombing attacks were made on the ship.[42]

After completing the bombardment, the *Northampton* proceeded to the plane rendezvous about 20 miles northeast of Wake Island. Between 0910 and 0947, the six SOC planes were recovered by their parent cruisers. No casualties were suffered by the air personnel during the engagement. Then the *Northampton* steamed at 20 knots on course 040° in company with the *Salt Lake City*, *Balch*, and *Maury*. The *Northampton* had expended her allotment of 264 main battery 8-inch shells. The *Salt Lake City* had expended her 261 8-inch shells.

At 1600, while retiring from the area, the *Salt Lake City* picked up a radar contact bearing 230°T at 34,000 yards. The "shadowing" planes were seen at various times until 1800, when two enemy twin monoplanes made a high-altitude bombing attack from 13,000 feet. The cruiser fired 26 rounds from their starboard AA guns and executed sharp turns to hamper the bombers' aim. Bombs landed 150 yards from the starboard quarter of the *Salt Lake City* and on each side of the *Northampton*, which had its radar out of commission.[43]

Admiral Spruance wrote of the "shadowing" incident as follows:

> At the time of the attack cruisers were in line of bearing approximately normal to the sun, to best cope with an attack from that direction. It is interesting to note, however, that in this case the planes made their approach along the line of bearing, in which direction the least effective antiaircraft fire could be developed. The fact that the sun was low (45 minutes before sunset) may have convinced the enemy of the advantages of approach from a direction where least concentration of fire might be expected, rather than from the direction of the sun. Also, both cruisers could be bombed on the same run. The inoperative status of *Northampton* radar was sorely felt at this time. The approach of these planes undetected may have been caused by too much attention being concentrated on the tracking patrol plane, which was in plain sight. This emphasizes the serious consequence of lookouts and others being distracted from their assigned sectors by such a diversion.[44]

The commanding officer of the *Salt Lake City*, Captain E.M. Zacharias, also wrote of this serious situation encountered while retiring after the bombardment attack:

The carrier fighter planes left the scene before all enemy planes (particularly four-engined patrol planes) had been destroyed. This left the heavy ships vulnerable to shadowing and later bombing, which should have been prevented. It is, therefore, recommended that the carrier be sufficiently close to the heavy ships to send fighters to destroy shadowers when notified of their existence. It is noted that as a result of this shadowing, in addition to the bombing attack made near dark, the persistence of the enemy enabled them to fix the position at dark and provide for a systematic search from that point the next day. The radius of search was just short of finding us. There appears to be a special technique used by the shadower after his bombing planes have arrived in the area. In this case, the shadower, after remaining on the horizon all day and at times invisible, suddenly started an approach as if to attack. This had the effect of centering attention on himself. Meanwhile the bombers at very high altitude approached the release point unobserved until just as they were about to release. Observed at this time proper avoiding action was taken and heavy bombs fell where the ship would have been. It is therefore recommended that in the presence of a shadower a special overhead 'release point' lookout be established in a reclining chair on the bridge, particularly when cloud formations exist as in this case.[45]

Though the action reports from the various bombardment group ships revealed differing opinions as to the results, there was definite damage to Peale Island's facilities from the attack. A gasoline storage tank exploded and sent flames 100 feet into the air. A dredge in the lagoon at the seaplane ramp was set on fire. There were other small fires, but unfortunately some of the shore batteries on the north shores of Peale and Wake Islands were not silenced. There were no casualties suffered or attack damage during the bombardment, but at 0828 the *Northampton*'s radar antenna array collapsed from the vibrations from the main guns.

All commanding officers and executive officers reported conduct of personnel as having been excellent throughout the engagement. Rear Admiral Spruance wrote of the bombardment, declaring, "The conduct of the Commanding Officers of the *Northampton*, *Salt Lake City*, *Balch* and *Maury*, and of Commander Destroyer Squadron Six, during the bombardment and subsequent enemy actions detailed herein was very satisfactory."[46]

The ships continued to sail away with occasional visits from the shadowing enemy plane. At 1043 Spruance radioed Halsey requesting air support. At 1125 the *Enterprise* launched 5 F4Fs-2 for CAP and 3 of Mehle's search-and-destroy fighters. Lieutenant R.W. Mehle was joined by Ensign Ralph M. Rich and a new pilot, Ensign Joseph R. Daly. They soon ran into bad weather with thick clouds and a rain squall. The cruisers were believed to be 100 miles to the southwest of the carrier at launch time. Unfortunately, the planes, crisscrossing the area for 90 minutes, were unable to locate the intruder or Spruance's ships in the rain and constant wind changes.

The returning aircraft had difficulty getting back to the carrier due to the weather and the fact that the *Enterprise* had changed course 25 degrees to port and increased speed to 3 knots without notifying the fighters. Daly ran out of gas and was forced to make a down-wind water landing at 1548 some 300 yards ahead of the destroyer *Ralph Talbot*. Daly cut his head on the gunsight mount on landing. His plane sank quickly, but he floated in his life jacket until he was picked up by the destroyer. Daly had endured a flight of 5 hours and 20 minutes. Mehle and Rich were lost too, but Mehle managed to tune in the ship's YE signal on his Zed Baker homing receiver.[47]

At 1743 another patrol plane was spotted approaching closer than usual. While the flotilla was focused on the shadowing patrol plane, at 1800 two twin-engine landplanes came from a different direction and released bombs from 13,000 feet. The antiaircraft fire was slow to engage, and three bombs landed close by the *Salt Lake City* and one near the

Northampton. There was no damage to the cruisers and the Japanese bombers departed out of sight.

The attacks on Wake Island had resulted in no enemy damage or casualties to Spruance's bombardment force. The *Maury* reported that one of the 5-inch guns was out of action. Two planes from the *Salt Lake City* that had not been launched for any attacks were damaged due to the shock of the intense gunfire.[48]

From the time the *Enterprise* recovered the attack group at 1014 on February 24, she retired, making course changes between 020°T to 045°T running between 19 and 25 knots. Flight operations were continued with launching and recovering of the combat air patrols maintained during daylight hours. Zigzagging was first commenced during the retirement at 1807 on the 25th and periodically ceased as ordered. At 0623 on Thursday, February 26, the *Enterprise* joined with the fleet oiler *Sabine* and the destroyer *McCall*. The carrier sighted the *Northampton* off 11.5 miles, bearing 159°T at 0744, and soon the full bombardment group of ships rendezvoused with the carrier northwest of Midway Island. The ships of the task force were refueled, with the *Enterprise* finally having her turn at the *Sabine* at 1234 on March 1.[49]

The *Enterprise* air attack had been textbook and successful. They had destroyed two Japanese patrol seaplanes and caused extensive damage or destruction to a fuel barge, a pier, numerous ammunition magazines, AA batteries, numerous buildings, gasoline storage tanks, an underground gasoline system, fuel oil storage, and runways. A few high-value targets that were not assigned to the air group and appeared to be undamaged were the high-frequency radio direction finder station, power plant, bridge, fuel and gasoline tanks at the inboard end of the ramp at Peale Island, the seaplane ramp, the contractor's camp storage tanks and water tower, and the shore battery at the NW point of Peale Island.

The air attack had resulted in the loss of one pilot and two aircrewmen. The last time Ensign Percy W. Foreman and his radioman-gunner, AMM2c J.E. Winchester, from Scouting Squadron Six were seen was about 0810, retiring eastward at low altitude with their engine smoking. It was thought that they had made a water landing and were picked up by the Japanese.

The plane lost on takeoff over the port bow severely injured pilot Lieutenant (JG) P.L. Teaff. The plane guard destroyer rescued the pilot within five minutes but failed to locate RM3c E.P. Jinks. Ensign L.R. Daly of VT-6 suffered minor facial injuries when he made a down-wind water landing while preparing to land aboard the *Enterprise*.[50]

Damage to aircraft during the battle included 6 SBD-2 and 3 scout bombers hit by antiaircraft fire, as well as one F4F-3 hit by fragments from the exploding Japanese patrol plane. Damage to aircraft was light and the aircraft were repaired in short order.

An officer from the *Enterprise* Air Group recalled: "It was just a matter of going in and unloading your bombs. We found no surface ships at all and no airplanes except three 4-engined big boats, and one of the Japanese destroyers which were probably damaged in their attack on Wake and which they had beached. Also, they had removed the guns and installed them on the island. The only difference that we noticed in Wake from the photographs taken before it was captured by the enemy was that they had dug a trench all the way around the three islands. It appeared that they had planned to put their guns in there and use it as a trench to defend themselves against any attack that we might try to make."[51]

Another officer from the air group gave his critical observation of the attack: "We made our attack and, in my opinion, made a mistake in not staying there to repeatedly attack them. We have found that you only do real damage when you make a second and third attack. But we knew that an air group was flying up to take possession of the air field that day around 12 o'clock, and also the Japs made a statement that they had 300 American war prisoners still in the construction camp area."[52]

CEAG Commander Young made the following comments and recommendations relative to the Wake Island attack:

- (a) Delay arriving at the attack position nullified the element of surprise for the air group. The absence of diversion of enemy fire by aerial attack exposed the surface bombardment group to concentrated fire of the shore batteries. Fortunately, there were no Japanese bombers or fighters based at Wake I. Fighter escort is considered essential for protection of an attack group. It is strongly recommended that flights launched for attacks on shore objectives be provided with a fighter escort of at least one division (6 planes) of VF when one carrier only is involved and the distance to objective permits.

- (b) All bombs were armed with "instantaneous" fuses. Photographic evidence and pilot reports indicate that the 500# bomb armed with Mk. XIX nose fuse and Mk. XXIII tail fuse in several instances failed to detonate properly. 500# bomb craters on the coral surfaced runways and the area emitted brilliant orange flames for a period of two or three minutes after the explosion and then died out suddenly. In other instances, the bomb impacts on the runway set off an explosion which was accompanied by a column of flame reaching heights of two or three hundred feet. It is requested that the Bureau of Ordnance disseminate information by dispatch as to the proper fuses to be used against land objectives that will be normally encountered.

- (c) Only eight VSB and four VF planes were equipped with leak-proof tanks. The balance of the air group's planes are especially vulnerable. A hit in an unprotected tank introduces the grave danger of fire. Also, any appreciable loss of gasoline will be accompanied by loss of the crew and plane on the return to the rapidly retiring carrier.

- (d) Identification of our returning aircraft was accomplished by flight leaders broadcasting, "Signal affirm, altitude and bearing (followed by number of planes in flight)," when sighting the carrier. On this occasion no confusion resulted. However, immediate procurement and installation of simple and reliable "IFF" equipment is recommended. The security of the carrier may be endangered by a number of planes broadcasting their bearing after sighting the carrier, as these bearings will be generally on the line of retirement from the objective.

- (e) Again it is recommended that the number of VSB planes in operation be reduced to permit operation of 27 VF. Fighter protection for VTB's, surface bombardment groups, as well as the carrier is mandatory. The present eighteen-plane VF squadron can not supply adequate patrols and escorts during offensive carrier operations.

- (f) At *least* fifty-percent spare qualified pilots are necessary for any prolonged operations lasting longer than one day. As a whole, the *Enterprise* Air Group, with few exceptions, is considered a thoroughly trained and experienced outfit. With the influx of new pilots and replacements reasonably anticipated in the near future, losses in action, in deck landings, and minor casualties will abruptly increase. Fighter squadrons will require a greater percentage of replacement and relief pilots than the other squadrons due to constant combat patrols which must be maintained in addition to other missions assigned VF in action.[53]

Commander Young added these remarks to his action report: "The Enterprise Air Group accomplished the mission assigned it in a most satisfactory manner. Launching delays could not be foreseen. The bombing was accurate, and the attacks well executed. The promptness in which the one enemy plane encountered in the air was destroyed by the three planes of Fighting Squadron Six is commendatory."[54]

Captain George D. Murray, the commanding officer of the *Enterprise*, concurred with all of CEAG Young's recommendations, but made specific recommendations (for increasing VF plane complements to 27 from the present 18) regarding flexibility in aircraft type and number to be utilized in particular Task Force missions:

> A principle is involved here that merits consideration. In the opinion of the Commanding Officer, during the period of rapid expansion of the Aeronautical Organization, less confusion will occur if the present administrative organization of four 18-plane squadrons per carrier is maintained on paper for purposes of planning and distribution of planes, personnel and material. To meet operating requirements, however, the composition of the air group within a carrier should be left to the discretion of the Commander Aircraft, Battle Force or the Commander-in-Chief. In effect, this would apply the same principle of the Task Force organization to the air groups of carriers that now is in effect with respect to ships in the Fleet. Depending upon the mission and the composition of the Task Force (surface), it is quite conceivable that a carrier air group might be composed of any one of the following combinations, for example:

	VF	VS	VB	VT	Total
CVA	18	18	18	18	72 plus CAG
CVB	24	15	15	18	72 plus CAG
CVC	27	15	15	15	72 plus CAG
CVD	30	15	15	12	72 plus CAG[55]

Murray added additional comments to the action report:

> (a) In co-ordinated attacks between surface and aircraft out of visual touch, timing becomes the most important factor in the operation. Therefore, there must be sufficient flexibility in the plan for operation to permit wide variation in aircraft launching interval, time required to rendezvous, and time to reach the objective that will be required under extremely dark and unfavorable weather conditions and variable winds.
>
> (b) Fighters (F4F type) in service should be provided as expeditiously as possible with auxiliary droppable tanks attached to the wing racks. These tanks are urgently needed for fighter escort and combat air patrol missions.
>
> (c) The development of incendiary ammunition should be pressed for use in aerial combat. It is now apparent that the Japanese fighters are hesitant to attack in the face of machine gun fire and it is, therefore, believed the use of such ammunition would have a salutary effect on the psychology of Japanese aviator. In this connection, it is considered that this ammunition would increase the protection free guns afford when VSB and VTB aircraft are attacked by fighter.[56]

Murray also lauded the work of the Air Group:

> [T]he attack was carried out by the Air Group boldly and with the highest degree of efficiency, in spite of extremely unfavorable weather conditions at the ship at the time of launching, en route to the objective, and at the target. It is believed that the resolute manner in which all personnel engaged in the attack successfully accomplished their mission was in keeping with the highest traditions of the Naval Service. It is recommended that letters of commendation from the Secretary of the Navy be awarded

[to] the Air Group Commander and each Squadron Commander in recognition of the leadership each displayed in making this operation a success.⁵⁷

The XO of the *Enterprise*, Commander T.P. Jeter, added his comment on the performance of the ship's company and the air group: "The officers and men of the ship conducted themselves in a routinely efficient manner without special incident. On completion of the operations the Task Force Commander sent to the officers and men of the Enterprise and Enterprise Air Group a 'Well Done.'"⁵⁸

Task Force 16 Commander Admiral Halsey wrote of the attack: "The lateness of the air group in arriving at the objective, incident to launching delays, was a matter of deep concern, and might well have proved costly had appreciable enemy air opposition existed. Otherwise the attack plan was well executed." He also concurred with the need for VF droppable tanks, increasing VF squadron strength to 27 planes, the urgency of installing IFF gear and leak-proof fuel tanks, increasing the number of flight crews to 150 percent of the number of deployed planes, and with the urgent need to develop and supply incendiary ammunition to combat aircraft. On March 21, 1942, Nimitz concurred with Halsey's recommendations from the Wake Island attack.⁵⁹

On February 24, 1942, Yamamoto's Chief of Staff Ugaki wrote the following regarding the Wake Island attack: "Around 5 o'clock this morning a dawn patrol aircraft reported sighting 1 carrier, 2 heavy and light cruisers, fire on our shore batteries; this was followed by attacks by some 50 carrier planes. Shortly thereafter the enemy began to withdraw to the northeast at high speed. Our Naval shore-based bombers from Kwajalein attacked, claiming a hit on the stern of a cruiser. Once again our counterattack did not achieve any worthwhile results.... This and the unhindered escape of the carrier force leaves the staff frustrated and hopping mad."⁶⁰

Raid on Marcus Island

Halsey wrote in his autobiography:

We were retiring to the northeast to pick up TG 16.7 and our tanker, the *Sabine*, with her escort, the destroyer *McCall*, for the return to Pearl when, the following evening, a dispatch from CINCPAC caught us: Desirable to strike Marcus if you think it feasible. Three mileages have always stuck in my head—Wellington, New Zealand, is 1,234 miles from Sydney; Espiritu Santo is 555 miles from Guadalcanal; and Marcus Island is 999 miles from Tokyo. That figure comprised our knowledge of Marcus, except that it was within easy range of planes from Iwo Jima and was supposed to be well-defended. This would be another morale raid. By venturing so near the home islands of the Empire, we would presumably disconcert the Japs and stimulate the Allies more than ever.⁶¹

Marcus Island (also called Minami Tori Shima by the Japanese) was 650 miles to the northwest of Wake Island in a line leading directly toward southern Japan. Not only was it only 1,000 miles from Tokyo, it was only 600 miles from large Japanese air bases in the Bonins and Marianas. The Japanese had claimed the island for many years, and at the time of the attack order, it was being used as an administrative center with radio and weather reporting facilities.

Halsey informed the task force of the Marcus tasking on the morning of February 26, then fueled the destroyers, and headed on the new course of 275°T. He was hoping to complete fueling on the 27th, but the weather was "overcast, low visibility, high wind, and heavy seas." Since the forecast called for these conditions in the area to continue, the

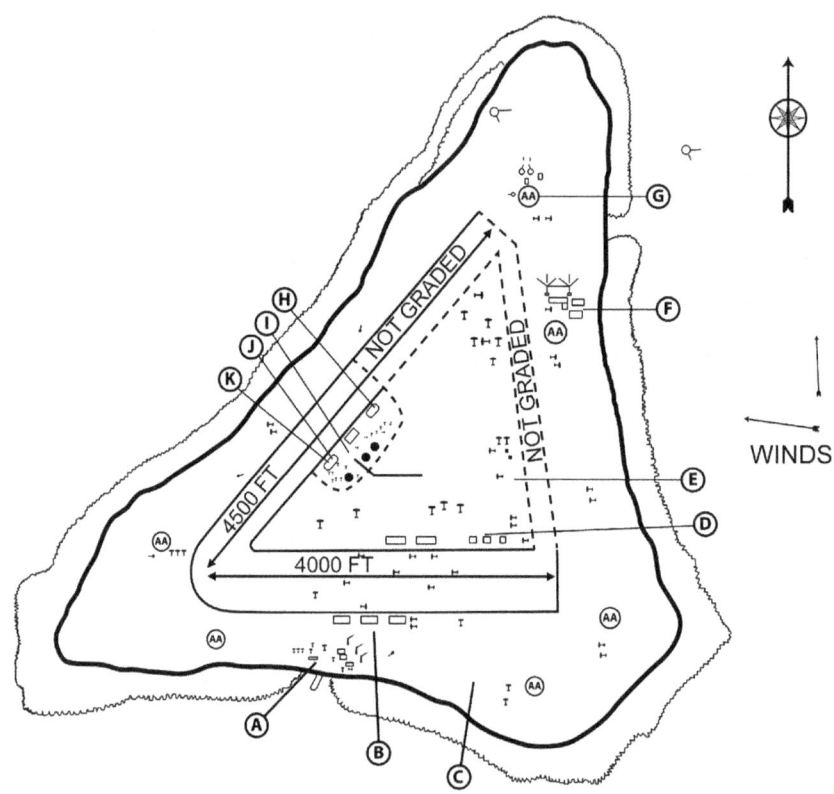

4 MARCH 1942

MARCUS ISLAND

AN AIRFIELD SURROUNDED BY WATER

SUMMARY OF ESTIMATED DAMAGE

Ⓐ FOUR SHACKS FIRED
Ⓑ LARGE SQUARE BLDG. HIT AND FIRED BRIEFLY
Ⓒ OIL TANK AFIRE
Ⓓ SMALL BLDG. AFIRE
Ⓔ LONG RECTANGLE BLDG. AFIRE
Ⓕ "L" SHAPED BLDG. AFIRE BRIEFLY
Ⓖ AA BATTERY SILENCED: SHACK DESTROYED
Ⓗ HANGAR HIT AND FIRED
Ⓘ MAGAZINE OR GAS STORAGE BLOWN UP
Ⓙ HANGAR AFIRE
Ⓚ GAS TANK FARM AFIRE

LEGEND

AA = ANTI-AIRCRAFT MOUNT

Marcus Island map. Image redrawn based on *Early Carrier Raids in the Pacific Ocean*, 53.

task force changed course to the south in the hope of finding better weather the next day. Halsey recorded in his war diary: "The situation was more anxious than it may sound. The *Sabine* could supply enough fuel to take us to Marcus and back only if we shoved off by March 1. Here is the entry for the twenty-eighth: 'Weather and sea conditions this morning preclude possibility of fueling.' We steamed at our most economical speed all night, watching the skies. Just before daybreak we saw the stars; the wind moderated... Completed fueling about 1700. *Enterprise*, *Northampton*, and *Salt Lake City* commencing run in for air attack."[62]

Expecting heavy weather all the way to Marcus and knowing the task force would have to progress at high speed, on February 28 Halsey made a courageous decision. He wrote of the situation: "The destroyers were too light to match our speed through the heavy seas, and I was afraid they might delay both the attack and the retirement, so I ordered them to stay behind with the tanker."[63] He was taking only his two cruisers with him to Marcus. The mission orders were to have the *Enterprise* and Cruiser Division Five (the *Northampton* and *Salt Lake City*) head to a point 175 miles northeast of Marcus by March 3 and to launch an air attack before sunrise around 0630 on March 4 (zone minus 11 time). With a full moon there was an expectation that there would be sufficient light to launch and rendezvous for the attack.[64]

The plan of attack on Marcus directed:

> VB-6 to strafe and bomb the airfield, planes on ground if found, hangars, fuel tanks and other suitable objectives nearby that might present themselves. VS-6 to follow VB-6, strafing and bombing the radio station, any remaining military buildings, storage tanks and buildings in the settlement at the south edge of the island. The Group Commander accompanied by three photographic planes had as a primary objective any ships that might be encountered, followed by taking photographs if conditions permitted. One division of VF-6 to act as protective escort and for offensive action against any enemy planes attempting to take off after the dive bombing had been completed. Only one attack was contemplated followed by a high speed retirement to the southeast.[65]

On March 2, radio silence was broken to recover search planes in bad weather. Two submarines had been sighted and planes dropped bombs on their positions. Unfortunately, both attacks were made on the USS *Gudgeon* on the outward leg of her 2nd combat patrol. Thankfully, the planes had inflicted no damage. By now, there was some doubt that the three gray ships plowing through the rough waters would arrive at Marcus Island undetected.

On March 3, everyone was on alert with guns manned and pilots sitting in their planes. That day intelligence indicated that Marcus had an airfield since land-based planes had been sighted near the island. Halsey changed his attack plans to close to 125 miles of the island to accommodate the shorter-range F4Fs.

On the early morning of March 4, the *Enterprise*, in company with the *Northampton* and *Salt Lake City*, was near the new launch point running at 24 knots, course 235°T. At 0438 the *Enterprise* turned into the wind and launched her first birds. The order of launch for the air attack group was the CEAG Commander Young in his SBD, the 14 SBD scout bombers from Scouting Six, the 17 SBD bombers from Bombing Six, and lastly the 6 F4F escort fighters. For the CAP, VF-6 would have 9 F4Fs available, with the first CAP of 4 F4Fs led by Frank Corbin launching later at 0643. The SBDs were all armed with one 500-pound bomb and two 100-pound bombs each. Torpedo Squadron Six was held in readiness aboard the carrier to attack any major enemy ships that might be encountered, but none were found.

At 0504 the air attack group was airborne, and the *Enterprise* slowed to await their return as they changed course to 070°, speed 25 knots. Young signaled his departure of the air group toward Marcus at 0525, bearing 251°. Only one plane, the fighter of Lieutenant (JG) John C. "Jack" Kelly, did not make the rest of the group on time. He did not risk returning to the *Enterprise* until dawn, since he could not use his radio without breaking radio silence. He resigned himself to circling out of range until dawn.[66]

The moon was full (moonset at 0717), but there were strong southerly winds with heavy cumulus clouds from 4,000 to 8,000 feet. The planes had their running lights dimmed until they reached the objective. Since Marcus was such a small target to find from 128 miles away and the weather was overcast, the *Enterprise* used the new technique of tracking the planes on radar and radioing the air group commander of necessary deviations. On the *Enterprise* the radar officer, Lieutenant John Baumeister, watched the blips on the scope and determined the distance off the direct track to Marcus. Course directions were sent on the "Yoke Easy" high frequency, with coded radio transmissions to the attacking planes. Commander Young's radioman/gunner used his knee pad to record the letters and numbers as he passed them on the intercom to the pilot. The new approach worked well, and at 0630 the island was sighted through a break in the clouds. The island's white runways were displayed prominently in spite of the darkness. Dawn was still 40 minutes away, but Young gave the signal to attack.[67]

The attack came as a complete surprise to the Japanese. There were no enemy aircraft present, either in the air or on the ground, and no ships were seen. The VB-6 bombers had been climbing steadily to 16,000 feet until they spotted their objective. The squadron split into their three divisions on top. The first division was led by Lieutenant Commander W.R. Hollingsworth, with the second division with Lieutenant R.H. Best, and the third division with Lieutenant J.D. Blitch. These divisions began their divebombing approaches from 16,000 feet from the south and west. The dives used steep angles of up to 070° from 8,000 to 10,000 feet to release their bombs in ripple drops from 3,000 to 2,000 feet, pulling up at 1,000 feet with a "continued power glide retirement." Several parachute flares were deployed to illuminate the targets. One plane in the 1st section was tasked to reconnoiter the island for planes on the ground or other objectives. Lieutenant Jack Blitch's attack on the L-shaped building next to two radio towers resulted in destruction of the transmitter, as confirmed by ending the Japanese commentator in midsentence. The bomber retirements were made to the southeast, making "frequent, irregular, and radical changes in course and altitude" until out of sight. The bombing attacks were made between 0640 and 0645. The bombers returned in small groups to the carrier, landing at 0845.[68]

Limited strafing was conducted during the dives and on retirement using the fixed .50 caliber and flexible .30 caliber machine guns. There was almost no enemy large-caliber AA fire from 3-inch guns. There was a large volume of rapid AA fire from 20mm and 30mm or 1.1-inch guns. The smaller caliber fire was very accurate and came close in. On retiring, some planes saw tracers close by from targets some five miles away. The plane doing the spotting saw a hit on a storage tank and some fire coming from it. Several buildings or hangars on both sides of the field were burning at 0705. The field appeared to be under construction.[69]

The Scouting Squadron Six planes from the second division, led by Lieutenant R. Rutherford, attacked about 0650, following the attacks from the bombing group. The attacks varied with the cloud conditions over the island at the time of the attack. Some of the planes used conventional divebombing attacks, approaching from 15,000 feet, and entering the dives from 10,000 feet, while other attackers dived through the cloud cover to conduct glide-bombing run-ins. The first division from VS-6, led by Lieutenant W.E. Gallagher, was delayed until 0700 by not being able to see the target. The last group to bomb used a high-speed approach in the bottom of the cloud layer at about 4,500 feet altitude and conducted a glide-bombing attack over the objective. The release altitudes varied from 1,500 to 2,500 feet with bombs dropped in the ripple salvo. The pullouts were made at around 1,000 feet followed by a high-speed and low-altitude retirement toward the southeast. As with VB-6, the Scout Bombing planes departed in small groups and landed aboard the carrier at 0845.[70]

The three-plane Photographic Section of Scouting Six, led by CEAG Commander Young with section leader Ensign C.J. Dobson, was unable to get photographs due to insufficient light at the time of the attack. In most cases the pilots were unable to assess the impact of their bombing attacks due to heavy AA fire forcing them to make high-speed retirements. Early in the attack, as Commander Young had pulled out of his successful 6,000-foot divebombing attack, he thought he saw some fighters taking off and yelled out on the radio, "Get those fighters taking off!"[71] Lieutenant James S. Gray, Jr., heard Young's call, dropped to low altitude, and buzzed the field without seeing any such attackers.[72]

As the Japanese reacted to the surprise attack with heavy antiaircraft fire, at 0705 Lieutenant (JG) Hart Dale Hilton, with his gunner ARM2c Jack Leaming, reported that his plane was on fire and he was making a water landing. Lieutenant Richard H. Best from Bombing Six saw Hilton's plane land at sea about 10 miles east of Marcus. The downed crew was in their rubber boat waving thumbs up as Best departed the area. They were taken prisoner by the Japanese. The Commander of Scouting Squadron Six, Lieutenant Wilmer E. Gallagher, stated, "It is believed that 6-S-7 [Hilton's plane] would not have been lost had it been equipped with leak-proof tanks. Otherwise no deficiencies in our aircraft armament or equipment were noted."[73]

After the water landing, Hilton and Leaming were able to climb aboard their rubber raft. With Hilton injured, Leaming rowed westward toward Marcus Island, only to find they were going in circles. Hilton told Leaming, "Jack, keep that cloud behind us steady behind us and you will row in a straight line." As they neared, they noticed the waves were breaking too strong on the east side. In addition, there was a sentry pacing on shore. They decided to try landing on the southern shore, where they hoped the coral was less. As Leaming rowed around the southeastern tip of the island, other men joined the sentry as they followed along the shoreline. As the tide took control of the raft, the American aviators heard a motor crank up and saw a boat coming out to them. Leaming noted:

> Ye Gods, what a boat they had! It was about thirty foot long with a small wheelhouse amidships and a small funnel aft of the wheelhouse that belched smoke rings into the air. With its chug-chug motor, it pulled alongside our rubber boat as we were forced to throw up our hands in surrender.... Would they shoot us now? Or wait? What could we expect? What did they want to know? What could we tell them or should we tell them? What tortures would be inflicted upon us? In quick succession these thoughts passed and could not be answered except by the passage of time. The transition from being a free aggressor, and free, to the loss of freedom and subjected to those you had rained death upon moments before is a very, very, unenviable position.

The Japanese boat came next to their raft as they were taken aboard. They were now prisoners.[74]

There were no Japanese aircraft encountered in the air attack on Marcus, but the antiaircraft fire from 3-inch guns proved to be heavy enough to prevent close damage assessment. The spotter plane saw a hit and resulting fire on the fuel storage tank. Some buildings and hangars on both ends of the field were on fire. Two major fires and some smaller ones were visible from 20 to 30 miles at 0705. Unfortunately for the attacking aircraft, there were fewer high-value targets than anticipated at Marcus.

At 0650 McClusky gathered three of his VF-6 pilots and followed the last SBDs in. They then circled at 5,000 feet to the southeast of Marcus to be ready to cover the withdrawal later. McClusky's group departed Marcus twenty minutes earlier than they were scheduled to attack (having arrived over the island ahead of schedule). Lieutenant Jim Gray had been separated during his last run and was lost in overcast and struggling to find the carrier. His Zed Baker receiver was acting up. Before dawn the carrier detected a bogey, though it was likely a strike plane that did not join with others.

Between 0837 and 0907 the *Enterprise* recovered 35 aircraft, leaving only the one SBD and one fighter that had failed to return. Halsey's task force of the *Enterprise*, *Northampton* and *Salt Lake City*, then changed course to 050°, speed at 25 knots to exit the area. At 0940 the speed was increased to 30 knots. After searching for the *Enterprise* for a few hours, Lieutenant Gray was now down to 20 gallons of fuel and fearing he would soon be in the water with little chance of surviving in the cold. As radar officer, Lieutenant Baumeister tracked the bogey, and decided it might be Gray. He received approval from Captain Murray to send a short radio message to him with the correct course to the carrier. Gray landed aboard the *Enterprise* at 0956 with only 9 gallons of fuel left, thankful for the support from his Annapolis classmate.[75]

VF-6 maintained a CAP until 30 minutes after sunset. The next morning of March 5, Task Force 16 was again in a "delightfully ugly" storm. No flights were possible in that weather. Late in the afternoon, the task force joined with the destroyers as Tokyo radio reported that the American attack on Marcus had "killed eight people and wrecked a shanty."[76] On the 6th, Task Force 16 fueled from the oiler *Sabine* under the umbrella of VF-6s fighters. The next three days, with the weather so poor, there were few CAPs.[77]

The CEAG Young reported that there were fewer objectives than had been anticipated. Though the island was totally blacked out, "the white coral or gravel runways of the field stood out plainly." At 30 minutes before sunrise, the targets could not be seen from 16,000 feet. He noted that although the overcast had provided excellent concealment, it did slow up the attacks. Young called out again the need to obtain incendiary bullets that would have aided the ability of the planes to attack the land targets. He also emphasized the need to complete the installation of leak-proof fuel tanks for the VSB and VF planes. The requirement for reserve pilots was of major importance because after his crews completed their attack missions, which lasted four hours or more, they were often called upon to be "available for search and patrol, reserve combat patrol or anti-torpedo plane patrol for the rest of the daylight period, and possibly at night under moonlight conditions when attack by enemy planes is threatened."

Commander Young deemed the attack to be highly successful and noted his squadrons carried out their missions in a commendable manner, but "regretted that more valuable targets could not be found."[78]

Captain Murray, as *Enterprise* commanding officer, concurred with most of the comments and recommendations reported by Commander Young. Regarding the issue of the attack group arriving at the objective in the darkness, Murray added his thoughts:

Wind, sea and light (moonlight) conditions were favorable and there resulted in accelerated take-off and rendezvous of the Air Group approximating in time that required for normal day operations. It now appears that the attack group could have remained in the vicinity of the ship for twenty minutes to one-half hour before taking departure for the objective. That this was not done was due to the uncertainty of immediately locating a small, distant and isolated objective and the necessity of making ample allowance for navigational errors and adverse winds. Radar detected the Air Group five miles to the south of the line from the ship to Marcus Island prior to contact and so informed the Air Group Commander. Radar was also able to inform him his distance from the island. This proved to be positive and of great value. In similar circumstances in the future, this accurate navigational assistance can be counted upon to eliminate one uncertainty. It should be used in timing the attack of a single group to coincide with most favorable conditions, or in co-ordinating two or more groups in an attack.[79]

Murray called for the complement of a normal 18-plane VSB squadron to be approximately 27 and noted that "the need is additional pilots in the squadrons in order to distribute among a greater number the extreme and concentrated load imposed by intensive operations extending over considerable periods of time. On recent occasions, it has been necessary to make demands upon pilots that, if continued, will unquestionably become injurious to health. Unless these conditions are ameliorated there is real danger of prematurely losing the service of some pilots because of incipient breakdown." He also recommended, in regard to war operations involving carriers and their Air Groups, that serious consideration be given to operating two carriers in mutual support. His reasoning was that, with two carriers, the loss of one carrier would not necessarily mean the loss of its Air Group. With two carriers there was always an "alternative airport" that could accommodate two Air Groups in an emergency.[80]

Murray noted the Marcus Island attack was "executed smoothly, efficiently and according to plan," and that since no unusual demands were made of any individual, "no especially meritorious conduct was observed and no individual commendations are recommended." He also recommended that "the Department authorize a suitable campaign ribbon for all personnel attached to this Force on March 4, 1942 (Zone Minus Eleven) to commemorate the action against Marcus Island. It is further recommended that individual campaign ribbons be authorized for the operations against the Marshalls on February 1, 1942 (Zone Minus Twelve) and Wake, on February 24, 1942 (Zone Minus Twelve), respectively."[81]

In Admiral Halsey's action report endorsement, as Task Force 16 commander, he acknowledged the early morning attack situation. He also noted the value of the use of radar to assist in aerial navigation to the targets, and the use of YE equipment, indicating that other carriers and the Commander Aircraft, Atlantic Fleet were being informed of their use in the Wake and Marcus attacks. He agreed with the advantages of using two carriers in mutual support when availability permitted such a move and concurred with comments about the need for reserve pilots, incendiary ammunition and leak-proof fuel tank deployment. Halsey did not concur with the use of separate campaign ribbons for the Marshall, Wake and Marcus raids. His reasoning was that "the war is young and such a precedent should not be established. It is recommended, however, that an appropriate campaign medal be struck now with provision for attachment of a clasp, or other suitable emblem, to denote participation in important raids or actions, past and future. Senior officers should have the medals available and full authority to make presentations on the spot."[82]

Admiral Nimitz later reported, "The raid against Marcus caused some concern as to the defenses of the Japanese homeland but the exact amount of diversion from Japanese effort in the southwest cannot be measured at this time." The attack was completely successful, but he recounted that this was the third action by the *Enterprise* Air Group, and yet after three months at war, they were still (a) lacking reserve pilots, (b) leak-proof tanks and (c) incendiary bullets, noting these three problems "severely circumscribe the action of a single carrier against an island base."[83]

On March 4, Chief of Staff Ugaki wrote, "Learned late today of an enemy carrier's dawn attack on Marcus Island this morning. At this pace the enemy carriers are likely to appear next off Tokyo Bay. The delay in receiving the report from Marcus Island was because the radio transmission station was destroyed in the beginning of the attack.... Marcus's aviation gasoline storage was also set afire and destroyed."[84]

On Tuesday, March 10, Halsey's air squadrons flew ahead to Ford Island. The *Enterprise* entered Pearl Harbor later in the morning and tied up at the Navy Yard. Liberty for the 4th section left the ship at 1300.[85] The pilots were off to the Royal Hawaiian Hotel, a near tradition. For the aviators heading to liberty, Halsey furnished five bottles of what had become a rare item, good whiskey. In defiance of Navy regulations, Halsey had a liberal policy towards alcohol for his men under strain. In his memoirs Halsey wrote that after Pearl Harbor, "I took the law into my own hands." He recorded further: "As Commander Aircraft Battle Force, I directed my representative ashore, Rear Adm. Aubrey W. Fitch, to requisition 100 gallons of bourbon for our flight surgeons to issue to our pilots. This eventually became standard practice. I don't remember if it was officially approved, but I do remember that 'Jake' Fitch accused me of inaugurating highly unorthodox procedure and leaving him to hold the bag."[86]

Chapter 5

Lae and Salamaua

*It is extremely regrettable that again
the enemy was able to escape unharmed.*
—Admiral Ugaki

After having provided his updated action details in two messages to COMANZAC and CINCPAC concerning the aborted Rabaul raid of February 20 with its Japanese bomber attack on his TF 11, on February 23 Vice Admiral Brown (COMTASKFOR 11) sent COMANZAC an Aidac message (232214) containing just one short sentence: "Need for support by another carrier." Through this dispatch and Brown's formal *Report of Action of Task Force Eleven with Japanese Aircraft on February 20, 1942*, dated February 24, 1942, it was clear to all that any renewed plan to attack Rabaul must include two carrier task forces. But even Brown was surprised by how quickly his message had gotten through to his superiors. On February 25, COMANZACFOR Leary sent Nimitz his thoughts (message 250100): "In view of latest intelligence suggest consideration be given early attack Rabaul area by Task Force 11 and 17." This was followed up with the COMANZAC to CINCPAC (message 250430) stating: "Concur Brown's remarks regarding further attacks Rabaul outlined in his 232214. See my 250100."[1]

Nimitz immediately sent off his 251209 Aidac to COMINCH: "Recommendations concerned employment two task forces against Rabaul." Events had moved so swiftly that Brown sent off a cautionary comment to Nimitz (message 260458) on the 26th declaring, "Comanzac 250100 my 232214 not intended to recommend two carrier attack on Rabaul. I do not recommend it under present conditions." But Vice Admiral Brown's message, with the last comment, "under present conditions" was received too late. His original recommendations were taken for action, and Fletcher's Task Force 17 was on its way to join with Brown's Task Force 11 to attack Rabaul. The formal orders were received via COMINCH Aidac 021615 directing Task Force 11 and Task Force 17 to make an attack in the New Britain–Solomon Area about March 10.[2]

On February 16, Fletcher's Task Force 17 with the *Yorktown* had sailed out of Pearl Harbor to take up position in the Canton Island area. TF 17 was originally set to join Halsey's TF 16 to take part in the Wake Island raid, but COMINCH had objected to having two carrier task forces engaged there. Now Fletcher was sent to take up station, so he could provide support either to Halsey's Task Force 16 then en route to attack Wake Island, or move south to support Brown's Task Force 11 in the Southwest Pacific. Five days later, north of Canton Island, Fletcher lost an SBD from Bombing Five during landing. Three days after that accident, another SBD hit the water on takeoff. For several days the task force marked time sailing along the equator, until receiving orders on the 28th from CINCPAC (message 280417) stating, "Task Force 17 join COMTASKFOR 11 now assumed to be in area westward of New Hebrides."[3] To join with Admiral Brown TF 11, Fletcher would have to pour on the coal to make the designated rendezvous point 300 miles north of Noumea, New Caledonia, by noon on March 6.[4]

On March 2, 1942 (Aidac message 021615), Admiral King issued orders to Brown's *Lexington* Task Force 11, Fletcher's *Yorktown* Task Force 17, and the ANZAC squadron "to attack enemy ships and air bases in the Bismarck Archipelago–Solomon Islands area about March 10, in order to check enemy advance and cover arrival of troops in New Caledonia."[5] Vice Admiral Wilson Brown had the task to plan and direct the operations of the three naval forces under the combined Task Force 11 designation.[6]

The two primary strategic objectives of the operation were to stop the southward movement of the Japanese and to ensure the safe transit of United States Army troops from Australia to New Caledonia planned to occur between March 7 and 12. The Japanese had already advanced into the New Guinea and New Britain area with occupation of Rabaul, Gasmata, Kavieng in New Ireland, Massau Island, Buka Island, Kieta on Bougainville Island in the Solomons, and Rossel Island in the Louisiades. The Japanese had already conducted bombing attacks at their anticipated next invasion targets in New Guinea at Salamaua, Port Moresby, and Buna, and on Tulagi and Gizo Islands in the lower Solomons.

There was reasonably good intelligence about the Japanese fleet movements and resource strength in the area. Reconnaissance had confirmed that the Japanese had in the Rabaul area at least 3 heavy cruisers, 5 light cruisers, 8 destroyers, 15 transports, a submarine tender, a submarine squadron, a division of gunboats, and 50 land-based aircraft with fighters and bombers. These Japanese assets, plus other units nearby including seaplane tenders and pontoon planes, were expected to be on the offensive into New Guinea and other southwest Pacific islands by March 5. The Japanese were expected to launch planes from two airfields on Rabaul and one near Gasmata.

On retiring, Task Force 11 was joined on March 3 by the ANZAC Squadron at the designated rendezvous point. That same day the oiler *Kaskaskia* arrived to begin refueling operations. On the morning of March 6, Task Force 11 and the ANZAC Squadron were still refueling from the *Kaskaskia*. At noon, as planned, Fletcher's Task Force 17 joined up in company with its heavy cruisers *Astoria* and *Louisville*, six destroyers and fleet oiler *Guadalupe*. Now Admiral Brown had a significant array of naval forces for the next attack including Task Force 11 built around the *Lexington*, Task Force 17 centered on the *Yorktown*, and the ANZAC Squadron. Besides the two carriers, the combined force included a strong array of warships and other naval support ships:

Australia,
  Capt. H. P. Farncomb, R.A.N.
Astoria,
  Capt. Francis W. Scanland.
Chicago,
  Capt. Howard D. Bode.
Indianapolis,
  Capt. Edward W. Hanson.

MacDonough,
  Lt. Comdr. John M. McIsaac.
Hull,
  Lt. Comdr. Richard F. Stout
Clark,
  Comdr. Myron T. Richardson.
Bagley,
  Lt. Comdr. George A. Sinclair.

Louisville,
  Capt. Elliott B. Nixon.
Minneapolis,
  Capt. Frank J. Lowry.
Pensacola,
  Capt. Frank L. Lowe.
San Francisco,
  Capt. Daniel J. Callaghan.
Phelps,
  Lt. Comdr. Edward L. Beck.
Dewey,
  Lt. Comdr. Charles F. Chillingworth, Jr.
Dale,
  Lt. Comdr. Anthony L. Rorschach.[7]

Russell,
  Lt. Comdr Glenn R. Hartwig.
Walke,
  Lt. Comdr. Thomas E. Fraser.
Anderson,
  Lt. Comdr. John K. B. Ginder.
Hammann,
  Comdr. Arnold E. True.
Hughes,
  Lt. Comdr. Donald J. Ramsey.
Sims,
  Lt. Comdr. Wilford M. Hyman.

The two task forces and the Anzac Squadron had been able to avoid a typhoon that passed just a few hundred miles from them. Fletcher's TF 17 had been fortunate to follow just behind the storms' center and far enough away to dodge any severe weather. Through the excellent work of their aerologist, TF 11 had moved to the north just in time to complete its refueling in moderate seas.

Now joined, Admiral Fletcher with his staff and air personnel from the *Yorktown* came aboard the *Lexington* for a conference to discuss the upcoming attack plan. In selecting specific targets, Admiral Brown reported that there were only three Japanese locations that had air bases with shipping; Rabaul and Gasmata in New Guinea, and Kavieng in New Ireland. Since Kavieng was the least important in terms of air and shipping traffic, the other locations were selected for attack. Though COMINCH had recommended that the forces should attack from the east or northeast, Admiral Brown felt it was tactically better to approach with all his forces from the south. In his post-attack action report Admiral Brown explained his decision:

1. Experience of February 20th had shown that the enemy was maintaining an extensive search to the eastward of Rabaul.
2. Greater mutual protection would be afforded by keeping all units together, and better control of movement and timing of attack effected.
3. Advance from the south offered a shorter route to the selected objectives, involving less expenditure of fuel and consequently affording more fuel for high speed.
4. There was more likelihood of encountering a southeast wind, which would facilitate retirement after the attack.[8]

Admiral Brown felt, based on his previous experience, that it was unlikely that they would be able to approach Rabaul or Gasmata within 125 miles without being detected. Thus, he recommended that they "make a moonlight attack rather than to make the stereotyped attack at dawn—believing that an enterprising enemy would attack us at dawn or late moonlight before we could launch our planes to attack him." The officers from the *Yorktown* responded that many of their aviators were inexperienced in night flying, and therefore strongly recommended against a moonlight attack. They explained that not only was there more chance of launching casualties, but it was probable that bombing under moonlight conditions would be ineffective. Brown agreed to go forward with a dawn attack from a position 125 miles from Gasmata and Rabaul.

The attack plan called for the attack groups of cruisers and destroyers "to bombard both bases as a means of inflicting maximum damage and of diverting some enemy air attack away from the carriers." The cruisers would be placed at risk, but it appeared to be necessary under the specific mission Brown had been given. Admiral Crace visited the *Lexington* for his second time to urge Brown to utilize the ships of the ANZAC Squadron in the upcoming operation. His ships had essentially been used in reserve in the first attack on Rabaul. Crace revealed that the morale of his men was low. Brown had already decided to assign the ANZAC Squadron as the attack group against Gasmata, which pleased Crace.[9]

On March 7, after Admiral Brown had already transmitted the attack plans in his message COMTASKFOR Eleven Secret Operation Order 5-42 (Serial 0105) of March 6, 1942, information from COMANZAC reported that a Japanese convoy with one cruiser, destroyers, and transports was sighted off Buna, New Guinea. On the following day, more intelligence from COMANZAC revealed that enemy forces were landing in the early morning at Salamaua. At 0830 local time, 11 Japanese ships, including 4 cruisers or destroyers, had begun to shell both Salamaua and Lae, and by noon both ports were in enemy hands. In addition, RAAF air reconnaissance reported that day that there were no warships and only 3 transports at Rabaul, and no shipping at all at Gasmata. The obvious conclusion was that the Japanese were intent on taking New Guinea.

After conferring with Fletcher's staff and his own, Admiral Brown replaced the targets from Rabaul and Gasmata to Salamaua and Lae to disrupt the Japanese before they became entrenched at these two ports, and to reduce the immediate threat to the Allied base at Port Moresby. A big question for Brown was from which direction his forces should attack the enemy targets. There were only two options available: attack from the east on the northern side of the Papuan Peninsula, or from the south below the peninsula in the Gulf of Papua. Later in his action report he documented the points in making his decision. On the favorable side of attacking from the south, there was a better chance to surprise the enemy, while attacking from the east involved moving through seas patrolled by the Japanese. There was less risk that the enemy would be able to launch repeated air attacks from Rabaul and Gasmata in the southern approach. Also, there was a better chance that the planes could approach and retire at slower speeds, and thereby conserve fuel if unfavorable weather was encountered on a given day.

On the other side of the risk ledger, attacking from the south involved flying over 100 miles of unknown and mountainous terrain that was often obscured by clouds. The advantages outweighed the disadvantages in Admiral Brown's mind, and late in the afternoon of March 8, the final decision was reached to attack from the Gulf of Papua on March 10. Admiral Brown issued his modified orders with COMTASKFOR 11 dispatch 080555, dated March 8, 1942. Captain Sherman issued his revised orders to the air group via message Commander Air Operations Order No. 3-42, dated March 9, 1942.[10]

To reduce the risk that enemy surface forces might move southward to attack Port Moresby, to be in a position to cover the arrival of American troops in New Caledonia, and to cover carrier operations in the Gulf of Papua, Rear Admiral Crace was given command of a surface group that included the cruisers *Australia*, *Chicago*, *Astoria*, and *Louisville*, and destroyers *Anderson*, *Hammann*, *Hughes*, and *Sims*. The special detachment of warships would take up a position southeast of Rossel Island in the Louisiades, "at a distance not less than 600 miles south of Rabaul" at "point pig." Crace was in tactical command of the two fleet oilers, *Neosho* and *Kaskaskia*, that were tasked to position themselves a few miles apart off "point pig" to rendezvous with the main body on March 14 at 0100 GCT.[11]

Brown's task forces moved quietly up the Gulf of Papua off Australia toward the northwest. As they approached the launch position, concern grew over the planned flight path over the Papuan Peninsula using the Owen Stanley Range. The peaks were known to be some 15,000 feet high and the interior was generally unexplored jungle. The fleet's charts were inadequate and did not reveal any interior details. Since the fleet had to be positioned closer to the shore than usual to reduce the range to the target for the planes, the carriers had to be in waters full of coral reefs that were not necessarily charted accurately.

As the senior aviator present, Captain Frederick C. Sherman was designated to command the two air strike groups. To gain better navigation, terrain and weather information, Cdr. Walton W. Smith on Admiral Brown's staff took a plane to Townsville, Australia, while Cdr. William B. Ault from the *Lexington* Air Group flew to Port Moresby. Commander Ault had landed at Port Moresby between two Japanese air bombings. His visit was shortened somewhat in order to depart before the second attack arrived. These two officers returned with enhanced data that would prove to be of great benefit to the upcoming mission. They learned that pilots flying to the gold fields used a pass through the mountains at 7,500 feet between Mounts Chapman and Lawson. The pass was in a direct line from the planned launch point and Salamaua, and it was usually clear of clouds between 0700 and 1000. Based on this information, Sherman planned the course and speed around hitting the launch point at 0800 on the 10th.[12]

On March 9, COMANZAC message 091300 to TF 11, TF17 and the cruiser *Chicago* alerted them that 8 B-17s would be taking off at 0900 on the 10th from Horn Island to attack the Japanese in the Salamaua-Lae area at noon with priority of targets to be (1) aircraft carrier or seaplane, (2) transports and (3) warships.[13]

Task Forces 11 and 17 had maintained radio silence since the Rabaul attack on February 20, but that ended on March 8 when there were two violations. The first one occurred on the warning net when Brown authorized communications to avoid possible collision of the two task forces caught in a blinding rainstorm before flag signals could be utilized. This event was a sure demonstration of the need for TBS (talk between ships) on all ships. The second violation of radio silence was made when a cruiser plane became lost and could not locate its home cruiser. Another five cruiser planes were also lost while serving with Admiral Crace; they drifted to Rossel Island, where they were later rescued. These events clearly showed the need for Model YE radio equipment on cruisers and Model ZB radio equipment in cruiser aircraft as homing equipment. These unfortunate radio violations would have had a serious impact on operations if the Gasmata and Rabaul attack had been scheduled, but it would fortunately be an advantage for the Salamaua-Lae mission by holding enemy air at Rabaul and Gasmata.[14]

The planned attack required the absolute maximum range of the torpedo and fighter planes. Brown was most anxious to send at least one of the torpedo squadrons to test the performance of the planes and the torpedoes. It was decided that the *Lexington*'s VT-2 planes would be armed with torpedoes and the *Yorktown*'s VT-5 planes would be armed with two 500-pound bombs each. To ensure the fighters were available to coordinate the attack and be on-scene during the action, they would lead the forces after launch and then return and land to top-off with fuel. Using their high speed, the Wildcats would catch up with the other squadrons to be on-scene over Salamaua and Lae.

The plan called for the *Lexington* Air Group to attack by squadron at ten-minute intervals, followed by the same interval scheme by the *Yorktown* Air Group. To ensure close timing of launches and landings, the navigation of the force was under the control of the *Lexington*. This was required because of the location near land and shoals, the uncertain wind conditions, and the need to maintain the distance of 125 miles from Salamaua.[15]

Salamaua-Lae Air Strike Group

Lexington Air Group

Commander, *Lexington* Air Group	1 SBD-3	Cdr. William B. Ault
VF-3	8 F4F-3	Lt. Cdr. John S. Thach
VS-2	18 SBD-2 & 3	Lt. Cdr. Robert E. Dixon
VB-2	12 SBD-2	Lt. Cdr. Weldon L. Hamilton
VT-2	13 TBD-1	Lt. Cdr. James H. Brett, Jr.
52 aircraft		

Yorktown Air Group

VF-42	10 F4F-3	Lt. Cdr. Oscar Pederson
VS-5	13 SBD-3	Lt. Cdr. William O. Burch
VB-5	17 SBD-3	Lt. Cdr. Robert G. Armstrong
VT-5	12 TBD-1	Lt. Cdr. Joe Taylor
52 aircraft[16]		

At 0545 on the 10th, the *Yorktown* went to general quarters, as *Associated Press* war correspondent William H. Hipple reported: "You would have seen a stirring and unforgettable table sample of the spirit of our Navy at war." He felt a "spirit of determination ... everywhere" on the carrier and "an air of excitement." At 0636, lookouts on the *Yorktown* spotted "the jagged verdant spine of New Guinea" out 50 miles away.[17]

At 0704 the *Yorktown* launched the first CAP of 4 F4Fs under the command of VF-42's XO, Lieutenant Commander Fenton. Onboard the *Yorktown* the deck plane handlers were busy spotting the planes. Correspondent Hipple noted that the strike aircraft had the names of their crewmembers' wives and girlfriends in chalk on the sides of their planes, along with catchy phrases. It raised a laugh with Hipple to see witty ones such as "Heads Up Below," "Another Cloud for the Rising Sun," "Don't Laugh—This is Over Your Head," and "All this and Heaven, too." The bombs were also chalked with winners like "Get a Load of This" and "A Present from F.D.R."[18]

The carriers reached their planned positions 45 miles west of the Gulf of Papua shoreline at the mouth of Freshwater Bay on New Guinea. The first strike group planes were sent down the *Lexington*'s flight decks at 0749 as the carrier made 25 knots on a course of 088.5°. The *Lexington* cleared her decks by 0822. The *Yorktown* launched her aircraft 20 minutes after the *Lexington* and had cleared her decks by 0840. The combined air attack force under Commander Ault, consisting of 104 planes, was now airborne. These aircraft carried 38 tons of bombs and torpedoes, six 1,000-pound bombs, seventy-nine 500-pound bombs, one-hundred-ten 100-pounders, sixteen 30-pounders and 13 torpedoes.

The *Lexington* fighters landed back aboard at 0825, refueled, relaunched at 0834, and raced ahead to catch up with the attack group en route. To confirm the weather conditions were satisfactory, Commander Ault flew his scout bomber to a position midway across the peninsula at the highest point that was to be transited by the attack group. Remaining on station between Mount Chapman and Mount Lawson, Ault broadcasted weather and operational information to planes and surface units until all planes had

5. Lae and Salamaua

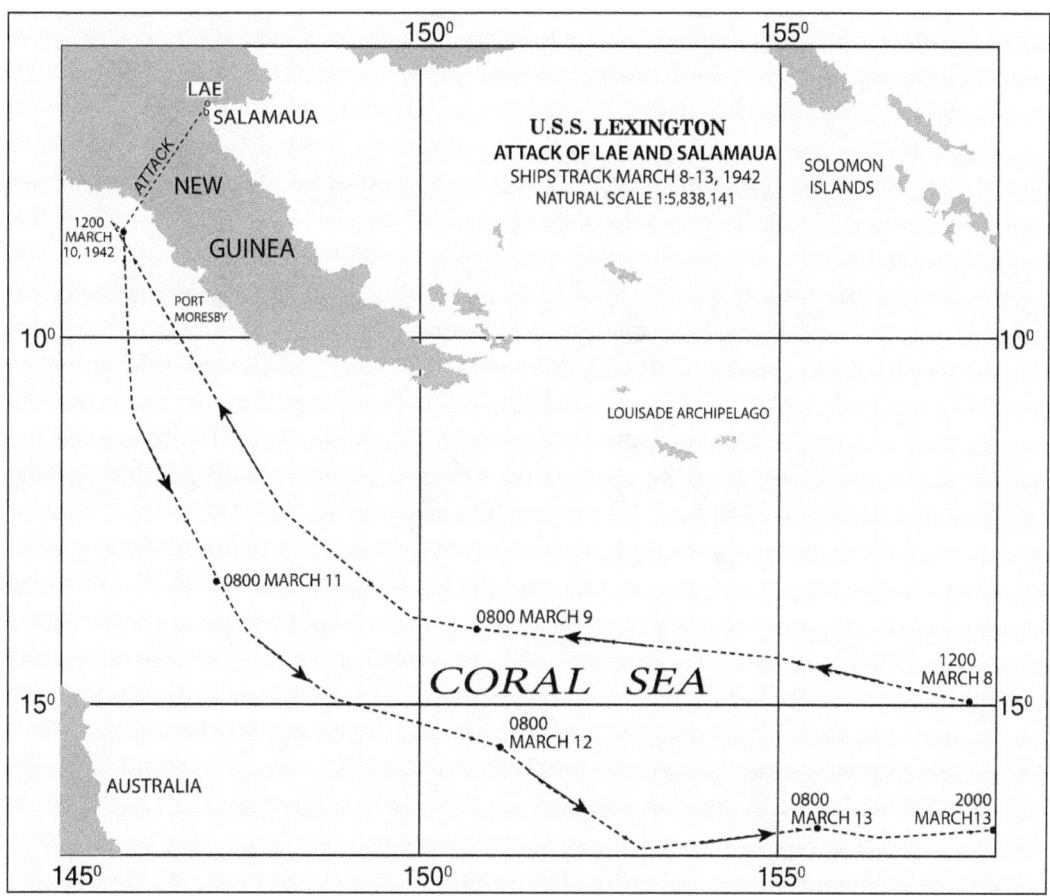

USS *Lexington* attack track—Lae and Salamaua raid. Image redrawn based on *Early Carrier Raids in the Pacific Ocean*, 57.

returned to their carrier. Thankfully, seas were calm, and the skies were good, with ceiling unlimited and winds at 9 knots.

The air cover for protection of the task force consisted of 6 fighters from each carrier, 5 bombers from the *Lexington*, and 4 bombers from the *Yorktown*. Fighting Three overtook the slower attack planes and proceeded ahead to cover the arrival of the strike force. The Japanese were taken totally by surprise as their invasion convoy lay off the Lae beaches without any air cover. The Japanese ships included two Army transports, *Yokohama Maru* and *China Maru*; two Navy transports, *Tenyo Maru* and *Kongo Maru*; the armed merchant vessel *Kokai Maru*; and two destroyer escorts, *Mutsuki* and *Yayoi*. In Huon Gulf was the light cruiser *Yubari* flying the flag of RADM Kajioka Sadamichi, as well as the minesweeper *Tsugaru* and three destroyers, *Yunagi*, *Oite* and *Asanagi*.[19]

As planned, the *Lexington* Air Group attacked first at 0922 as planes from Scouting Two moved to a position overhead Lae at 16,000 feet. Lieutenant Commander Robert E. Dixon picked out 3 transports. There were three divisions of VS-2 SBD-3s each loaded with one 500-pound bomb and two 100-pound bombs attacking the transports. They divebombed one large Japanese transport unloading at the dock and two more anchored a half mile offshore. These planes also strafed the transports with their .50 caliber machine

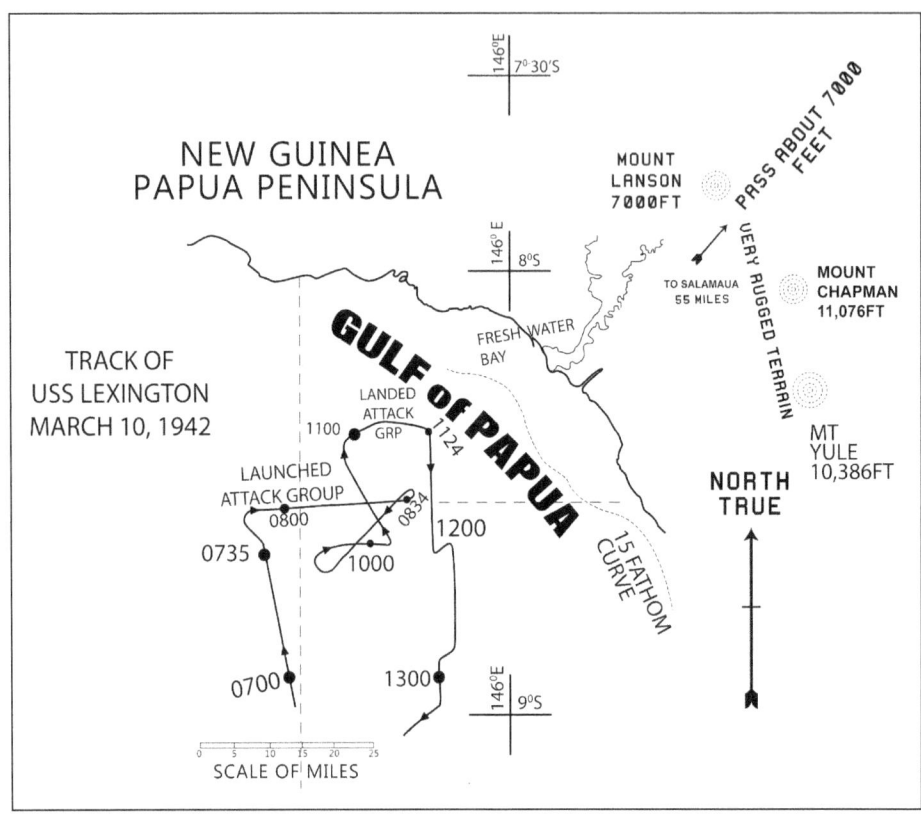

Photostat of track of USS *Lexington* in Gulf of Papua during the Salamaua-Lae raid, March 10, 1942, Enclosure E. Image redrawn based on *Report of Bombing Attack on Enemy Shipping and Shore Establishments in Salamaua-Lae Area*, March 10, 1942, Commander TG 11.5, CO USS *Lexington*, Serial 008, dated March 15, 1942.

guns. The *Kongo Maru* and the *Tenyo Maru* went to the bottom and the *Kokai Maru* caught fire and was beached east of Lae.

Pilots ran into difficulty with fogged windshields and sighting telescopes when they came out of their dives. Two planes took on the light cruiser *Yubari* with their 500-pound bombs. While the cruiser was underway, one bomb scored a hit aft of the second stack, causing a major explosion as the ship headed toward the beach in flames. Photos from a *Yorktown* plane 30 minutes later revealed no ships in the area, a clear indication of the ship's sinking.

Other action from these scout planes included hitting a possible minesweeper with a 100-pound bomb. The ship lost headway and caught fire. The enemy naval base troops onshore, firing four 8cm high-angle antiaircraft guns, claimed the shootdown of VS-2 SBD pilot Ensign Joseph Philip Johnson and radioman 3rd class James Buford Jewell, as they flew at 200 feet altitude. The plane was seen on fire and immediately crashed just offshore east of Lae with both air crewmen aboard.

With no Japanese aircraft encountered, Lieutenant Commander Thach's VF-3 fighters had split his group into two four-plane attack groups. One division of fighters flew with the scouting bombers to Lae and attacked an antiaircraft gun, resulting in the cessation of fire by the enemy. This division also attacked with small 30-pound fragmentation

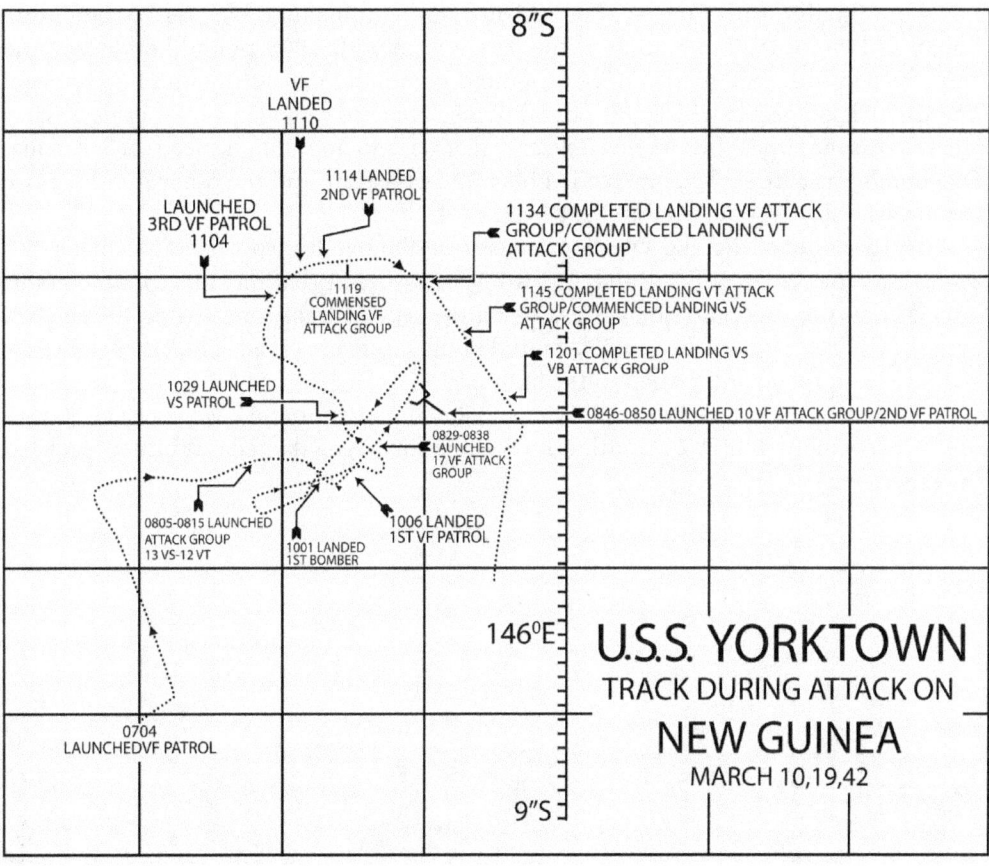

Track of USS *Yorktown* in the Gulf of Papua during the Salamaua-Lae raid of March 10, 1942. Image redrawn based on *Attack made by Yorktown Air Group against Enemy Forces at Salamaua and at Lae, New Guinea*, CO USS *Yorktown* (Serial 022), dated March 12, 1942.

bombs and .50 caliber machine gun fire at a cruiser, one destroyer and a small auxiliary underway off Salamaua. Small fires were seen on the destroyer and auxiliary with some crewmen killed. Lieutenant Noel A. Gayler shot down a Japanese single-float biplane seaplane trying to intercept the torpedo planes.

Thach's second fighter division that operated off Salamaua dropped seven 30-pound fragmentation bombs on the buildings at the airfield, and then strafed one small auxiliary vessel, resulting in at least 12 casualties. The squadron covered the later rendezvous of the attack squadrons and returned to the carrier. Reports from VF-3 crews estimated that they had killed between 45 and 50 Japanese.[20]

Three planes from Lieutenant Commander James H. Brett, Jr.'s Torpedo Squadron Two from the *Lexington* began their TBD-1 Devastator attacks at 0938 against two transports anchored near shore at Samoa Bay off Salamaua. One torpedo hit the *Yokohama Maru* and sank her, while two others ran too deep and exploded against the shore. Five planes dropped bombs on two transports off Lae at the beach that had been attacked previously. Two torpedoes were believed to have hit, as the third one exploded at the beach. Another plane dropped a torpedo at a Japanese light cruiser sailing off Salamaua, but the resulting damage was undetermined.

Coordinating with Torpedo Two, Lieutenant Commander Weldon L. Hamilton's Bombing Two loaded the 6 SBDs of the 1st Division with 1,000-pound bombs and the 2nd Division of six SBDs with one 500-pound bomb and two 100-pound bombs each. The 1st Division planes with 1,000-pound bombs attacked a Mogami-class cruiser (later identified as the large minesweeper *Tsugaru*) that was moving at high speed off Salamaua. One bomb was a direct hit, one landed only 20 feet astern, and the other four hit close to port. The ship was believed to have been sunk.

The 6 planes of the 2nd Division focused on the two transports off Salamaua, the same ships attacked by VT-2. Bombing Two planes scored two direct hits with their 500-pound bombs on the port side amidships on the second transport, setting the ship on fire as it was beached. No hits by 100-pound bombs were observed. The other transport was hit by a torpedo and settled to the bottom.[21]

Lieutenant (JG) Mark Twain Whittier and Radioman/gunner ARM2 Forest G. Stanley of VB-2 flew in their SBD-2 Dauntless on the mission over Salamaua. Whittier recorded his experiences:

USS *Lexington* (CV-2) leaving San Diego, California, 14 October 1941. Planes parked on her flight deck include F2A-1 fighters (parked forward), SBD scout-bombers (amidships) and TBD-1 torpedo planes (aft). Note the false bow wave painted on her hull, forward, and badly chalked condition of the hull's camouflage paint (official U.S. Navy photograph, now in the collections of the National Archives, Catalog #: 80-G-416362).

The flight across New Guinea and the 16,000 foot Owen Stanley Mountains to our targets (heavy and light cruisers, destroyers, cargo and transport ships) was at the most 150 miles and 2B2 sang like a mechanical bird as she lifted the 1000# bomb up to 19,000 feet over the mountains which, at halfway, seemed to just slide away in a sloping blanket of green to the distant, quiet harbor, shortly to become the "object of our affections." The SBD cockpit from the outset was found to be a place of comfort with everything at an easy glance to see and a comfortable reach to operate. (There was even a small ashtray—heaven forbid!) A new sense of security accompanied the wartime installation of the heavy armor seat and the thick bulletproof windshield glass giving me the feeling that I was safe as I'd ever be this far away from my old hometown. The accompanying TBD-2s [actually TBD-1s] torpedo planes of VT-2 with great effort scraped over the 16,000-foot tops of the mountains and immediately began their long glide to sea level and the Harbor of Huon Gulf. The ships became visible as mere specks in the water 30–40 miles distant. I was flying #2 on the Skipper [LCDR Weldon Hamilton, CO of VB-2] with Clem Connally #3 and excitement was taking control as the realization came over me that 2-B-2 and I were going to make that first dive. It had to be perfect. My throat and mouth were very dry probably from oxygen, certainly not fear, as it was too late for that. The silence in my helmet earphones was broken by my gunner saying, "Mr. Whittier, would you like some peanuts?" I couldn't have swallowed them at best, but it did boost my morale to hear how confident my "passenger" was in the "ride" we were taking. He was as relaxed as I was in #2106 [Navy aircraft BuNo 2106].

All of a sudden as we neared the target, I couldn't find my leader in front of me. The Skipper—he had just disappeared. I could imagine many things, but there was no time for that. The other 16 planes of Bombing Two were right behind me in a formation of which I had suddenly become the leader. Doctrine went to work as I signaled Clem to close in on my wing. I then arm pumped to visually order all planes into a long echelon, and I began a gentle turn toward the Gulf with a gradual loss of altitude. All of a sudden up popped the Skipper out of nowhere and he again took his position ahead of me in the glide. (I later learned his engine quit as he let a tank run dry—an oversight not uncommon with grogginess coming from low oxygen.)

For more than four years I had been practicing for this one dive, so it had to be perfect. Gliding down in a very gradual turn the airspeed indicator began to wind up 240–260–280 knots as my target began to slide under the nose cowl of my plane. To compensate, my mental checklist began. "Nose over a little more, set props, reduce throttle slightly, adjust gas mixture for lower altitude, carburetor heat, electric bomb releases 'on' and safety 'off,' adjust seat for best comfort with eye up to the bombing telescope, check rear seat man—ready, altimeter now at 12,000 feet—2,000 feet to go to pushover for the vertical part of the dive. There it was, 10,000', dive breaks open, goggles down, hood open, push it straight down and even so the airspeed braked back by 120 knots to 250; target now clearly in my telescope sight—making a tight circle and leaving a white wake; 2B2 felt perfect in the dive, trimmed for almost hands off flight as though flying at a level cruise but instead straight up and down; eye to the scope, cross-hairs on the ship (cruiser or large destroyer), estimate ship's speed, allow for the turn, catch a glimpse of the altimeter; see any AA? The stinging bite of high altitude, cold air now became hot and tropically humid; I'd better release—punch 'the pickle' on the stick, 1000 pounds drop off, and I heave back, tighten gut muscles, yell to keep blood in the head, no blackout on this ride; close the dive flaps—close—close!" They wouldn't! Windshield, goggles, and hood all steamed over from the rapid temperature change. Close those flaps! No, something is wrong! Instead of enjoying a nice 200–250 knots for a hasty retreat I was having to apply more and more power just to maintain 100 knots! Altitude 500 feet and just able to hold it. What's wrong? AA? Run out of fuel? Cannibals? Water landing? All flashed through my mind. Then I began to simmer down. "Don't let this plane fly you, Whittier," I'd said many times. "Now what could be wrong? The dive brakes open hydraulically, so do the wheels and engine flaps; maybe system pressure from the prolonged dive airlocked the plumbing; try lowering the gear. Here I am over enemy territory with wheels down, dive flaps open at 100 knots! Wheels up again. Try the flaps once more." AND THEY CLOSED! The speed shot up, and I began to climb. Again, Lucky Whittier! With the urgency of my pullout predicament, I'd no time to turn and look back to see where my thousand pound bomb had gone. The dive felt good all the way down, and I didn't see how we could miss. Planes were all over the sky but way ahead of me, and I didn't try to race for a rendezvous with my own. Instead I picked out two TBDs lumbering along starting their trip back over "the hill," and I joined them as they might need my help. The return and landing on the carrier were uneventful, and the scene in the ready room was anything but ordinary. Elation was at an all time high as damage assessments added up from the crew debriefings. The pilots who had followed me in the dive said my bomb hit in the afterpart of the ship, that the explosion raised the stern out of the water, propellers in the air, only to settle back on her side in the immediate throes of sinking. Our score that day was: 12 ships sunk, one plane shot down. So it was. Our first offensive strike against the Japanese—only the beginning of an atonement that could be claimed, over the next three and one-half years, by many SBD victories. Cdr. Duckworth, the air officer of the ship and later to become a three-star admiral, collared me in the wardroom a few days later to say that "...We are recommending you for the Navy Cross, Whittier." My reply was to the effect that I couldn't see why. It was nothing more than I had been trained to do for three years, and it came natural for 2B2, #2106.

Whittier did receive that Navy Cross.[22]

The *Yorktown* Air Group attacked just after the *Lexington* group. Lieutenant Commander Armstrong's Bombing Five split into three divisions of SBD-3s as it pushed over for attack at 0950. The first division of six planes with Armstrong attacked the convoy commander's flagship, the light cruiser *Yubari*, underway in Salamaua Roads. They released six 500-pound bombs and twelve 100-pound bombs with no direct hits, claiming only near misses. The planes followed by strafing a PG type gunboat.

At nearly the same time, the second division under Lieutenant Sam Adams attacked the same cruiser with six 500-pound and six 100-pound bombs, claiming 3 direct hits and 3 probable hits. The third division under Lieutenant William S. Guest with 5 planes also made attacks on the cruiser as they released five 500-pound and four 100-pound bombs, but scored three near misses. The cruiser was believed to have sunk. The third division continued on and attacked the enemy destroyer *Yunagi* and her sister destroyer *Asanagi* as they maneuvered in the same area. They scored two direct hits with 100-pound bombs on the *Yunagi* and one on her sister ship. This group also strafed a PG type gunboat and set it afire.

As Lieutenant Commander Bill Burch's VS-5 entered the attack at 1005, they split into two divisions. The first division of 7 planes with Burch took on two auxiliaries near the beach, dropping seven 500-pound and fourteen 100-pound bombs. The auxiliaries had previously been attacked by *Lexington* planes, and the *Yorktown* VS-5 division scored at least 2 direct hits on each auxiliary as they received returning antiaircraft fire. The six planes in the second division under squadron XO Wally Short dropped their six 500-pound and twelve 100-pound bombs on one of the auxiliaries off the beach at Lae with undetermined results. Reports revealed that both ships were beached and on fire. As VS-5 departed the area, the armed merchant cruiser *Kongo Maru* and transports *Tenyo Maru* and *Kokai Maru* were "beached and burning."[23]

Armed with two 500-pound bombs each, Torpedo Squadron Five with 12 TBD-1 Devastators commanded by Lieutenant Commander Joe Taylor attacked a Japanese seaplane tender, later identified by photo interpretation as the *Kamoi*, some 25 miles east of Salamaua at 1020 using level bombing. This ship was part of a second enemy force coming in from the east with at least one cruiser, four destroyers and six transports. VT-5 attacked with bombs in level flight at 13,000 feet. The first division scored a direct hit, stopping the tender and damaging 4 seaplanes on her deck (3 Mitsubishi F1M2 Type 0 reconnaissance floatplanes and 1 Nakajima E8N2 Type 95 reconnaissance floatplane). With a limited number of fully qualified bombsight operators, the squadron only placed one bomb on a target of 24 bombs dropped.

During the attack run, three VT-5 planes were attacked by one Japanese Type 95

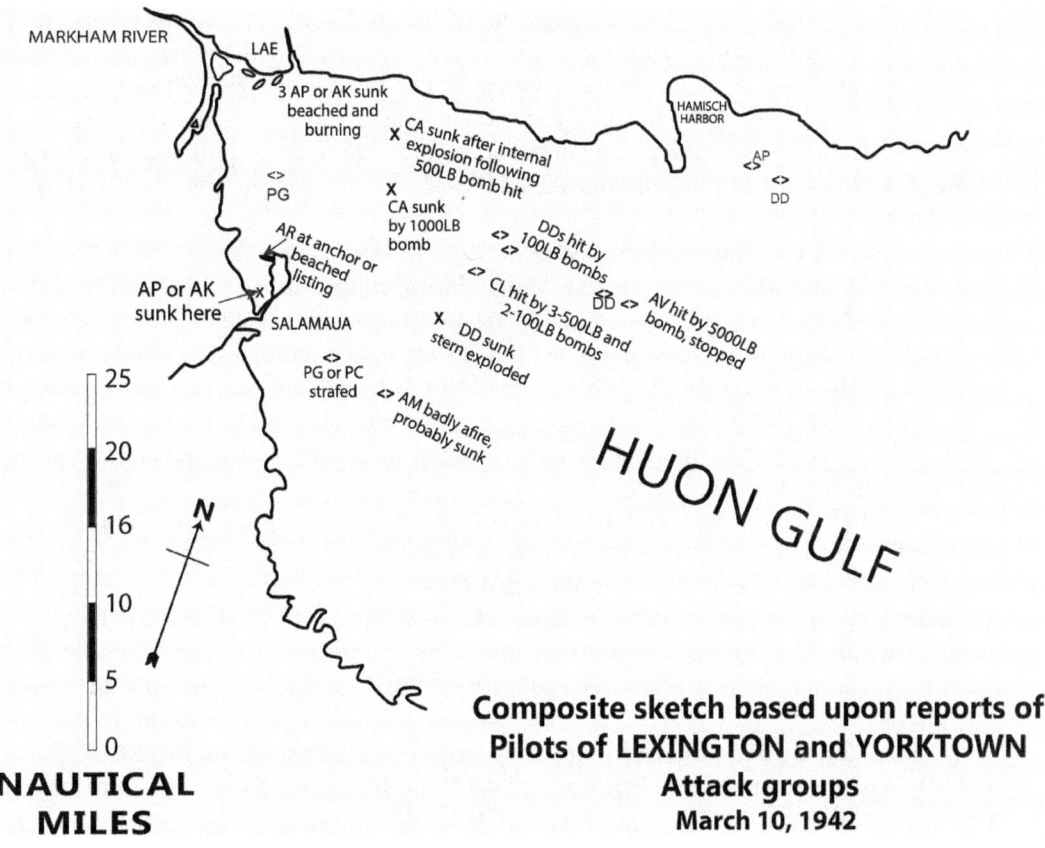

Composite sketch of operations in Salamaua-Lae area, based on reports from pilots of the *Lexington* and *Yorktown* during the Salamaua-Lae Raid in Huon Gulf, March 10, 1942, Enclosure D. Image redrawn based on *Report of Bombing Attack on Enemy Shipping and Shore Establishments in Salamaua-Lae Area.*

reconnaissance floatplane firing two fixed guns, which inflicted bullet holes in their tail sections. Only the return fire from the rear seat gunners caused the attacker to break off his attack. The floatplane fired his antiaircraft barrage with little effect.

Lieutenant Commander Oscar Pederson's ten F4F-3s from Fighting Forty-Two provided combat air patrol over Salamaua-Lae deployed in two 5-plane sections. With no enemy air opposition, they strafed surface targets on shore and small Japanese boats trying to rescue men in the water. Ensign Bassatt had a good run on his birthday by "blowing up two motor launches and raking enemy barges."[24] The only trouble they encountered was when Pederson suffered a bent strut mount on his F4F, which caused serious engine vibrations all the way back to the carrier.[25]

AP war correspondent Bill Hipple had listened to the radio chatter during the attack. He commented that "the planes were certainly having great success." As the planes landed aboard the *Yorktown*, he noted, "They came near the carrier and flew around. The planes had personality—they seemed to fly jubilantly now, their motors seemed to purr happily ... one by one, the planes came down, coming to a jaunty halt on the flight deck." The pilots and aircrews exited their planes "as calm as if they'd just returned from a routine patrol flight."[26]

While the strike force was attacking, the surface task force operations in the Gulf of Papua were fairly routine. Continuous CAPs were maintained by the *Yorktown*, relieved by the *Lexington* fighter units. Visibility was good out to 50 miles from altitude. At 1015 the task force spotted 8 B-17s heading to Lae-Salamaua. At 1050 the *Lexington* began to land its strike planes. The last plane landed aboard the *Yorktown* at 1201 and Task Force 11 retired to the southeast at 20 knots until darkness came, when the speed was reduced to 15 knots.

Late on that morning, the Japanese 24th Air Flotilla sent a search group of 3 Kawanishi Type 97 flying boats to the waters south of Port Moresby. Just before dusk, the *Yorktown*'s radar detected a bogey 26 miles away. As both carriers prepared to launch fighters, the contact disappeared from the scope. At 1720 the bogey radioed to Rabaul a report that they had located an American carrier task force with one Saratoga-carrier, two heavy cruisers, and five destroyers bearing 250 degrees and 90 miles from Port Moresby. Fortunately for Task Force 11, the weather was closing in and it was too late to launch a Japanese daylight strike.[27]

On March 11, both the carrier task forces were withdrawing into the Coral Sea to the southeast. The *Lexington* sent two SBDs to Townsville to deliver dispatches for land transmission, while the *Yorktown* maintained CAP duty. Enemy contacts appeared on the radar scopes, but they soon disappeared. The next day in CINCPAC 120335, the *Yorktown* Task Force was ordered to continue operations in the ANZAC area. Also, Brown was directed to comply with COMINCH 071820 to "Fill Task Force Seventeen with Stores and Spares."[28]

March 13 was a quiet day with routine operations when the task force sighted a Curtiss SOC floatplane in the sea. This was a plane from the cruiser *San Francisco* that had been lost five days earlier. During the debrief, the pilot indicated that he planned to drift toward Australia using the southeasterly trade winds until he was close enough to shore to use the last of his gasoline to reach land.

The next day as planned, Task Forces 11 and 17 joined with Rear Admiral Crace's cruisers, destroyers, and the valuable fleet oilers *Neosho* and *Kaskaskia* at the designated rendezvous, point pig.

The bad news was shared of the loss of five of the cruiser SOCs two days earlier. Brown sent out SBDs on a search, but there was no trace of the planes.

Once the orders came in specifying that *Lexington*'s TF 11 was heading back to Pearl while *Yorktown*'s TF 17 was remaining in the ANZAC area for continued operations, Fletcher and Buckmaster reviewed their respective aircraft status. The object of the exercise was to consider transferring as many aircraft as needed to make Fletcher's aircraft air group as combat ready as possible. The focus of the attention went to VF-42's situation. Though they had 17 F4F-3s, three of them had developed leaks in their self-sealing fuel tanks. VF-42's engineer officer, Lieutenant (JG) Arthur J. Brassfield worked with his chiefs to determine why the tanks were leaking. They submitted a preliminary report on March 14 indicating that the leaking tanks were the "cemented" versions that used glue to hold the seams together rather than the vulcanized type. The *Yorktown* officers proposed to trade two of these fighters for "fresh" F4F-3s from *Lexington*'s VF-3 plus additional SBDs and TBDs. Captain Sherman agreed to "sell" 12 aircraft (6 fighters, 5 dive bombers, and 1 torpedo plane) to the *Yorktown* Air Group.

At 1314 that day, the *Lexington* landed aboard two aged F4Fs, plus 5 TBDs carrying ten pilots to fly the trade planes back to the *Yorktown*. While the 12 "fresh" aircraft were being spotted on the flight deck, the VF-42 pilots were hosted by Thach in the ready room. After 90 minutes passed, the pilots headed to the designated planes to fly home to the *Yorktown*. After takeoff of his assigned Grumman SBD dive bomber, Walter Haas's engine cut out on him. He assumed the main fuel tank was empty, so he switched to the reserve tank to no avail. The plane, traveling at 400 feet a mile from the *Lexington*, made an "excellent water landing." Though Haas was stunned after suffering a head injury from hitting his gunsight mount, he managed to exit the cockpit and broke out the life raft. He was soon picked up by the destroyer *Dale*. Unfortunately, this was the second such ditching for Haas, who had experienced one two months earlier. Bill Leonard later recorded the event: "This contretemps rather chilled any warm regard held for VF-3 in this swap." Later it was determined that there were particles in the fuel line, absolving Haas of any blame.[29]

On March 15, TF 11 refueled with the *Neosho*, while Fletcher's ships drained the *Kaskaskia*. Admiral Crace departed the group that evening on a course to Suva. Refueling was finally completed the morning of the 16th, as Fletcher's Task Force 17 steamed northwest toward the New Hebrides to take up the continued mission to guard the lines of communication between the U.S. and Australia. In the afternoon, Brown's Task Force 11 got underway on a course to the northeast toward Pearl Harbor.

On the 22nd, the *Lexington* conducted a series of training exercises for the air group. With the task force nearing Oahu, at 0730 on Thursday, March 26, the *Lexington* launched her air group to airfields around the island. The senior pilots headed for briefings at headquarters with the admirals. The pilots were granted a week's leave at the Royal Hawaiian Hotel. The *Lexington* entered Pearl Harbor at 0920 and was secured at the dock at 1130 at the Repair Basin for a short overhaul. The Lae-Salamaua Raid was ended.[30]

Though there were conflicting reports from the air groups, first analysis of the overall damage against Japanese forces from the Lae-Salamaua Raid were the sinking of 5 transports, 2 heavy cruisers, 1 light cruiser, and 1 destroyer, and the probable sinking of 1 minelayer, 2 destroyers and 1 gunboat. One seaplane and one gunboat were also seriously damaged. Actually, the task forces sank 3 transports (*Kongo Maru*, *Tenyo Maru*, and *Yokohama Maru*), caused "medium damage" to the transport *Kokai Maru* and the seaplane tender *Kiyokawa Maru*, and shot holes in the *Yubari*, the minesweeper *Tsugaru*, and the destroyers *Asanagi* and *Yunagi*. Japanese losses were 130 killed and 245 wounded.[31]

Captain Takashi Miyazaki, the commanding officer of the Fourth Air Group at Rabaul, indicated in his postwar interrogation that in the reaction to the Allied raid on Lae-Salamaua, six fighters from the "Fourth Air Group came from Rabaul, staged at Gasmata and attempted to land at the Lae Field; but due to bad weather only one or two were able to land. The rest returned to Gasmata. The idea was to stage at Gasmata, go to Lae and engage in defense of the field and the transports in the area." For background he noted: "From February to April 1942, the Fourth Air Group had 36 bombers and 36 fighters attached to it. Also at Rabaul was the Yokohama Air Group which had a strength of 18 flying boats. In April 1942 the Fourth Air Group was reduced in size and lost its 36 fighters to the Tinian Air Group. These three forces, the Fourth Air Group, the YOKOHAMA Flying Group and the TINIAN Flying Group were organized into the 25th Air Flotilla."[32]

The sole American loss was one scout bomber shot down by shore-based antiaircraft fire off Lae. Eight scout and three torpedo planes were slightly damaged by antiaircraft shell fragments and bullets.

On May 12, Captain Buckmaster wrote in his Action Report of the Attack made by *Yorktown* Air Group against Enemy Forces at Salamaua and Lae, New Guinea:

The performance of all personnel involved in the action was of the highest order. It is not considered that any individual performance was sufficiently outstanding to warrant special mention. Weather and visibility conditions were excellent. It is considered that the time of the attack set achieved the same element of surprise as would the usual, standard, dawn arrival at objective points. The high altitude of the sun permitted bombing runs down the sun path. Lack of qualified and experienced bomb sight operators considerably handicapped VT-5 and results attained are directly attributable to this factor. Dissemination of information by squadron and divisional leaders was handicapped by radio failures possibly caused by prolonged periods of disuse during radio silence. It was noted with interest that cruisers and destroyers, when attack was being launched, made complete turns 360 degrees at high speeds. The tactical diameter of the destroyer turning circle was noticeably small.[33]

Buckmaster also exalted the use of delayed action fuses on bombs used against surface ships. He noted that his scout bombers were handicapped by the fogging of windshields and sights in a dive, and recommended immediate attention be given to installing satisfactory heating elements to alleviate the problem. Failed solenoid bomb-releases in SBDs was mentioned as a problem which was the subject of special report from the squadrons involved.[34]

The commanding officer of the *Lexington*, Captain Frederick Sherman, in his Action Report declared, "The performance of all personnel taking part in this attack was of the highest order. The skill, initiative, determination, and personal courage demonstrated by all members of the air groups were in accordance with the best traditions of the service."[35]

The report noted the TBDs loaded with torpedoes were able to negotiate the mountain pass at 8,000 feet altitude and above. They had carried the torpedoes for 1 hour and 25 minutes going to the target of the total mission flight time of three hours' duration. The TBDs were averaging some 47 gallons per hour, which was considered excellent. Sherman mentioned that the fuel supply for the F4F-3s was sufficient for this operation since there was no protracted duration for combat fighting, but he recommended that fighters should have detachable fuel tanks available to them if the mission dictated their use.

The bombs and fuses worked as designed with no duds reported. The *Yorktown* Air Group bombers used instantaneous fuses, while the *Lexington* Air Group used two fuse settings: one-third of the planes used instantaneous, and two-thirds used $1/100$th second delays. The 100-pound bombs were used primarily to attack aircraft on the ground at the two airfields—one located a mile off Lae and the other a mile off Salamaua. Since there were no Japanese aircraft at the airfields, the bombs were used on minor targets as encountered. The 30-pound fragmentation bombs were used by fighters on airport buildings, though they had already been damaged by Japanese or Australian bombardment.

Machine guns of both .30 and .50 calibers operated satisfactorily. Several electric solenoid bomb releases failed for the *Yorktown* bombers, but like the *Lexington* planes, they switched to manual release operation. Sherman, like Buckmaster, noted the dive bomber problems with fogged windshields, but his primary focus in the section of his report on material performance covered the situation with the torpedoes. The torpedoes were set to run at 15 feet. Of the 12 that were launched at the Japanese ships, running straight and normal, 9 should have been "sure hits." Five were seen to have passed underneath the enemy ship, and 3 of them ran up to the beach to explode. Of the remaining 4, 3 of the torpedoes hit their targets. The results were quite disappointing. These torpedoes were launched at ranges between 1,000 to 1,500 yards. The cause of the poor performance was unknown. It could have been depth setting set too deep, but the weather was not a factor—clear skies with windless conditions. Further study was necessary, but it was recommended that all torpedoes be set to 10 feet unless the target was known to be a deep-draft ship. It was likewise recommended that a method be developed to allow the depth settings to be changed while the plane was in the air.

Captain Sherman wrote that the *Lexington* and *Yorktown* air squadrons had initially encountered and attacked 11 enemy vessels: 2 cruisers, 4 destroyers, 5 transports and cargo ships, yet only a few planes became aware of another Japanese surface force approaching from the east about 25 miles away. This second force was believed to consist of 1 cruiser, 4 destroyers, 1 seaplane tender (*Kamio*), and 6 transports. The cruiser and destroyers of the second group sailed into the Salamaua area to defend and rescue personnel already under attack by the American force. *Yorktown* dive bombers attacked the cruiser and destroyers, and the seaplane tender was attacked by Torpedo Squadron Five. The U.S. Army Air Corps B-17 bombers later attacked the transports.

Sherman was correct in noting that carrier planes had flown over difficult mountains through a pass that even in good weather days was only available for four hours between 0700 to 1100. He explained that if the weather had "closed in behind these planes, the loss of both carrier groups might have occurred due to shortage of gasoline and inability to climb to the altitude necessary to get over the mountains." The captain stated, "I do not recommend that this kind of an operation for carrier planes be repeated very often."[36]

Vice Admiral Brown weighed in that he considered "that the attack was highly successful and inflicted severe damage on the enemy," and that the "planning and execution of the attack by the Air Group Commander and the two air groups was of the highest order." He also reported that the "performance and conduct of all personnel taking part in the attack was in accordance with the best traditions of the service." He also recommended that urgent attention be given (1) to provide detachable fuel tanks to increase their radius of action for the fighters, (2) to devise means of prevent fogging of the sight telescopes and windshields of carrier aircraft, and (3) to develop means to prevent initial deep dive of aircraft torpedoes.[37]

Brown provided a worthy account and analysis of the Salamaua-Lae raid in his report on the *Cruise of Task Force Eleven from January 31 to March 26, 1942*. He commended the commanding officers of the fleet oilers *Neosho*, *Platte*, *Guadalupe*, and *Kaskaskia* for "their intelligent execution of orders, as well as their good seamanship in fueling at sea." He covered in detail the situation with obtaining not just oil but provisions for the men. The long voyage for his Task Force 11 had required that nearly all his ships go on reduced rations until March 15. The *Lexington* had 90 days of dry stores rather than the prescribed 42 days' allowance and was able to share their dry provisions with the cruisers and destroyers. The transfer of goods at sea running at 15 knots in moderate seas was in his mind:

> the finest exhibition of resourcefulness and seamanship I have witnessed in my entire naval experience. The fact that Task Force Eleven has been able to operate at sea under war conditions for a period of nearly two months, away from any port, is a tribute to the intelligence, skill and seamanship of every officer and man in the force. The engineering performance alone is an accomplishment that few experienced officers would have believed possible. Some minor engineering breakdowns occurred, but they were all repaired by the forces afloat while underway. I doubt if any similar force of any navy since the days of steam has made as long a cruise. It would have been an outstanding accomplishment if all the ships had come fresh from the navy yard; but coming as it does after previous almost continuous operations at sea since December 7th, it sets a record of cruising endurance.[38]

Admiral Brown continued:

This fine performance is all the more remarkable when one considers the many changes in personnel in the fleet during the past year, and the many important stations that are now held by officers and men with very limited sea experience. It certainly is a reassuring indication of the intelligence and capabilities of the youth of our nation. Operations close to the equator have added to the general discomfort. The temperature in sleeping quarters rarely gets below 92°, and is most of the time closer to 100°. Notwithstanding the severity of the duty and the trying conditions, I have heard no word of complaint by a single officer or man. As a matter of record, I recommend that all reporting officers see that proper notations of this cruise be entered on the records of all hands.[39]

Brown's report also noted:

During the cruise, the health of the men has been from good to excellent. There were some heat related problems reported. One ship indicated that the weight loss aboard was from 10 to 15 pounds per man due to heat and reduced rations. Though the task force suffered, there was useful information about logistics, defense, air approach procedures, and communications gained while operating in the ANZAC area. Based on these experiences, the need for a secondary naval base in the area is most critical. Trying to maintain radio silence, while having limited ability to coordinate activities with the OTC while at sea is a real issue. A base would enable the OTC "to hold conferences, to assemble complete information and to issue definite instructions immediately before commencing offensive operations." The requirements for a secondary base are:

(a) A sufficient anchorage area, secure from submarine attack.
(b) Local air fields and barracks, where carrier planes can be established temporarily and a break afforded in exacting routine of sea operations.
(c) Logistic support.
(d) Anti-aircraft defense.[40]

Brown indicated that his staff had studied the strategic problems of the Southwest Pacific back in December and had come to the conclusion that Suva had the best natural facilities for an advanced naval base. Rear Admiral Crace had the opinion that Noumea would provide the better base because it was closer to the coast of Australia and had good anchorage facilities. Brown felt either Noumea or Suva would be ideal.

The admiral indicated that based on his experiences in the ANZAC area and the strategic studies, he was of the opinion that unless the Japanese moved a very large portion of their fleet to the Southwest Pacific, it was possible to hold off the enemy by taking the following actions:

(a) Daily bombing of enemy shipping and bases by about 40 or 50 Army bombers out of Australia.
(b) Constant and determined attacks on enemy shipping by a division of submarines, based at either Townsville or Noumea.
(c) Maintaining a squadron or more of fighters at Port Moresby.
(d) Maintaining a Task Force with a carrier, cruisers and destroyers in the vicinity of Townsville or Noumea kept in readiness to attack enemy amphibious forces that might attempt to capture Port Moresby from seaward, or to extend their holdings in the Solomons or New Hebrides.[41]

Brown provided another substantive analysis of what he had learned from the operation: "It appears to me important that Admiral Halsey's outstandingly successful attack on the Marshalls on January 31, and our successful attack on the enemy in the Salamaua-Lae area, while fully demonstrating the very great value of offensive action, in contrast with only passive defense, should not mislead us to wrong conclusions. I respectfully submit:

(a) "That in general, the most effective use of carriers is against enemy naval forces and against enemy shipping.
(b) That since carrier planes have shorter radii than shore-based planes, carrier attacks on enemy shipping in defended ports will be successful only when the attack arrives as a complete sur-

prise to the enemy, and that even then, when surprise is successful the carrier will run serious risks of heavy attacks by surviving enemy planes. In other words, the ever-growing importance and effectiveness of aircraft has not changed the old truism that ships are at a disadvantage in attacking strongly defended shore positions.
(c) That although both of our major attacks have been carried out on a time schedule prescribed by higher authority remote from the scene of operations, such timing cannot always be expected. Weather conditions and the action of the enemy may make it necessary for the OTC to set his own time schedule—having due regard to the general operation of which his action may be only a part.
(d) That owing to the favorable sea conditions usually found in the Southwest Pacific, our success in fueling at sea and transferring stores is no indication that similar performances can be expected or hoped for in stormier seas.
(e) That whenever possible, the option to attack or not to attack, and what to attack, should be left to the OTC—particularly as the strategic situation may change with great rapidity."[42]

Vice Admiral Brown called his Lae-Salamaua raid a success and defended both his exploits, noting, "It seems probable that our appearance off Rabaul on February 20 and our overwhelming attack at Salamaua on March 10 caused them to proceed with caution quite apart from the losses they have suffered in ships."[43] In his endorsement, Admiral Nimitz said the raid was "well planned and very well executed," and stated, "It is probable that the attack had an important effect in checking enemy operations in the New Guinea area."[44] But, in fact, it did not dissuade the Japanese from taking New Guinea. In CINC-PAC's Graybook was recorded, "[I]t is doubtful that the enemy will be greatly retarded."[45] President Franklin D. Roosevelt communicated to Prime Minister Winston Churchill that the raid was "the best day's work we've had."[46]

Nimitz had hoped for more from the raid, but not nearly as much as Admiral King. This seemed to be an unfortunate judgment for such a determined effort by a valuable task force leader. But after Admiral Brown had been 54 days at sea and completed only one raid, Nimitz detached Brown from his command of the *Lexington* Task Force and named him as commander of the new Amphibious Force headquartered at San Diego. Brown's replacement was an experienced carrier flag officer, Rear Admiral Aubrey W. "Jakey" Fitch.

In effect, Vice Admiral Wilson Brown had been "kicked upstairs." His transfer was truly a promotion, as he was now responsible for training forces to capture bases in support of the coming advance on Japan. Regardless of King's evaluation that he was not aggressive enough, Brown was one of the best men who could have taken on this new role. He was known as an expert organizer, and a skilled trainer and educator, as he had demonstrated in a recent assignment as superintendent of the Naval Academy at Annapolis.[47]

The major operational disappointment from the Lae-Salamaua Raid was the poor performance of the torpedoes. Of 13 torpedoes dropped, only 3 were confirmed as hits. According to CINCPAC, there should have been 9 hits if operating optimally. There was more disappointment as later evidence deemed the reported sinking of two enemy heavy cruisers was inaccurate. From the standpoint of operational advancement for carriers, there was one shining accomplishment. The Lae-Salamaua Raid was the first time in history that two United States carrier groups operated together in a totally coordinated attack.[48]

On March 10, Rear Admiral Matome Ugaki wrote of the attack: "At about 0730 this morning our ships off Lae and Salamaua, which we had occupied on the 8th, received a

2-hour surprise attack from carrier fighters, dive bombers, torpedo planes and allied shore-based aircraft. The light cruisers *Yubari* and Destroyer Squadron 6 received light damage, but heavy damage was suffered by our converted naval vessels. Around 2 P.M. an enemy carrier force composed of the carrier *Saratoga*, 2 heavy cruisers and 5 destroyers was sighted south of Port Moresby. It is extremely regrettable again that the enemy was able to escape unharmed."[49]

Chapter 6

Tokyo

OK, fellas, this is it. Let's go!
—Admiral Marc A. Mitscher

Back on Sunday, December 21, 1941, exactly two weeks after the attack on Pearl Harbor, staff cars arrived at the White House with the military leadership of the United States to brief the president. After warm greetings, President Roosevelt sat down in his study with the Joint Chiefs, Admiral Ernest J. King, Commander-in-Chief U.S. Fleet and Chief of Naval Operations; Lieutenant General Henry "Hap" Arnold, the Chief of the Army Air Forces (AAF); and General George C. Marshall, Army Chief of Staff. Also in attendance were Harry Hopkins, Roosevelt's special advisor; Admiral Harold R. Stark; Secretary of War Henry Stimson; and Secretary of the Navy Frank Knox. These were the men who were tasked to take the war to the enemy.

General Marshall briefed the president on the global military situation. As the briefing continued, Roosevelt made a clear and emphatic request that he wanted Japan bombed as soon as possible to boost morale. The request was not to be ignored. Each of the Joint Chiefs took Roosevelt's directive back to their respective staffs for action.

During one of the Arcadia Conference meetings on January 4, 1942, the planning for an invasion of French North Africa was discussed. Admiral King suggested that three U.S. carriers should be used to transport needed aircraft to the area. The idea was that one carrier would carry 75 to 80 Navy fighters, the second carrier would carry 80 to 100 Army fighters, and the third carrier would carry Army bombers, cargo planes, gasoline, bombs, and ammunition. King later wrote, "By transporting these army bombers on a carrier, it will be necessary for us to take off from the carrier, which brings up the question of what kind of plane—B-18 bomber and DC-3 for cargo? We will have to try bomber take-offs from carriers. It has never been done before but we must try out and check on how long it takes."[1] This was the seed of an idea that would take shape in the most daring raid yet attempted in the Pacific war.

After a meeting with the president on January 10, Admiral King motored to the Washington Navy Yard to meet with his key staff aboard his temporary flagship and former German yacht, *Vixen*. After briefing his staff about the meeting with the president, King retired to his cabin. Later, there was a knock on his door by Navy Captain Francis S. Low, King's assistant chief of staff for antisubmarine warfare.

King invited Captain Low inside and asked, "Yes, Low, what's on your mind?"

Low responded, "Sir, I've got an idea for bombing Japan I'd like to discuss with you."

King was interested as Low continued, "I flew to Norfolk today to check on the readiness of our new carrier, the *Hornet*, and saw something that started me thinking. The enemy knows that the radius of action of our carrier airplanes is limited to about three hundred miles. Today, as we were taking off from Norfolk, I saw the outline of a carrier deck painted on an airfield which is used to give pilots practice taking off from a short distance...."[2]

King responded, "I don't understand what you're getting at, Low."

"Well, sir, I saw some army twin-engine planes making bombing passes at this simulated carrier deck at the same time. If the army has some planes with longer range than our carrier planes, and if they could take off in the length of a carrier deck, then it seems to me a few of them could be loaded on a carrier and used to bomb Japan."

Admiral King thought a second and then said, "Low, you may have something there. Talk with Duncan about it in the morning." As Low was leaving, King added, "One thing, Low. Don't tell anyone else about this." Low then phoned Captain Donald B. "Wu" Duncan at home and asked to meet with him first thing in the morning. Duncan was the air operations officer on King's staff and a solid expert on carrier aviation.[3]

Low and Duncan met and discussed the various issues with Low's idea. To solve the issue of which bomber was the best suited to take on this mission, Duncan made discreet inquiries of the Army regarding the specifications and capabilities of the two candidate bombers. He also researched Navy data about deck space requirements, loaded takeoffs and weather patterns. The range of 2,400 miles was set as a minimum requirement, and a bomb load of 2,000 pounds was considered essential to the mission.

Duncan explained that the two newest bombers were the North American B-25 Mitchell and the Martin B-26 Marauder. The B-18 was considered obsolete, and the B-23 (an upgraded B-18) had a wing span that was too large. The B-26 was untried and, although it met the range and bombload requirements, it took more takeoff run than was available on a carrier deck. That left the B-25 as the only real bomber option. But there was still another problem. The B-25 (as well as the B-26) could not land on a carrier because the tail was too high for a landing hook to work, and the rear structure was too weak to take the shock of carrier landing to a quick stop. There would be no carrier landing for the selected bomber.

On January 16, Low and Duncan met with King to present Duncan's 30-page handwritten analysis. They told King the recommended aircraft was the B-25. It could carry two 1000-pound bombs and make a 2000-mile flight with extra fuel tanks installed. King read the report and said, "Go see General Arnold about this and if he agrees with you, ask him to get in touch with me. But don't mention this to another soul.... Duncan, if this plan gets the green light from Arnold, I want you to handle the navy end of it."[4]

The next day Low and Duncan presented the information to Hap Arnold, and as Low recalled, Arnold "was most enthusiastic" about the idea.[5] He did not reveal that his staff was already working on the idea of having bombers fly off carriers, as covered in the North African discussion during the Arcadia Conference meeting back on January 4. Arnold contacted King and indicated his agreement with the plan. King told Arnold that Captain Duncan would coordinate the Navy side of planning and he should choose the man to lead the Army Air Force side of the operation. His choice would have to manage the modifications of the bombers, the training, and the transfer of the planes to the West Coast to be loaded aboard the carrier.

General Arnold did not have to go far to find his man for the mission. He was just down the hall, and his name was Lieutenant Colonel James H. "Jimmy" Doolittle. Arnold later wrote in his memoirs, "The selection of Doolittle to lead this nearly suicidal mission was a natural one. He was fearless, technically brilliant, a leader who not only could be counted on to do a task himself if it were humanly possible, but could impart that spirit to others."[6]

Jimmy Doolittle was an exceptional man with an incredible background of achievement. He was born at Alameda, California, on December 14, 1896. His youth was spent in Nome, Alaska, where his father was a gold prospector. In 1910 Doolittle was in Los Angeles attending school when his class attended the Los Angeles International Air Meet at Dominguez Field. It was there that Doolittle saw his first airplane. After graduating from high school, he attended Los Angeles City College before being admitted to the University of California at Berkeley. In October 1917, Doolittle took a leave of absence to join the Signal Corps Reserve as a flying cadet. He was trained at the University of California School of Military Aeronautics at Rockwell Field, California, and was commissioned in March of 1918 as a second lieutenant in the Signal Corps' Aviation Section.

In World War I, Doolittle served stateside as a flight instructor at six different airfields. When World War I ended, he avoided the reduction in force effort and received a Regular Army commission with a promotion to 1st lieutenant on July 1, 1920. Then he attended the Air Service Mechanical School at Kelly Field, Texas, and the Aeronautical Engineering Course at McCook Field in Ohio. He returned to finish his college education and graduated with a bachelor of arts degree from UC Berkeley in 1922.

Doolittle was soon to gain significant public fame with his aviation exploits. In September 1922 he flew the pioneer flight in a de Havilland DH-4, which was equipped with early navigational instruments, from Pablo Beach, Florida, to Rockwell Field at San Diego, California, in 21 hours and 19 minutes with only one refueling stop. The Army awarded him the Distinguished Flying Cross.

He entered MIT in July 1923 while serving as a test pilot and aeronautical engineer at McCook Field. In March 1924, Doolittle earned his second Distinguished Flying Cross based on his master's thesis derived from his work conducting aircraft acceleration tests at McCook Field. In record speed, he earned his master's degree in aeronautics from MIT in June 1924 and his doctorate in aeronautics one year later.

After graduation, Doolittle took special high-speed seaplane training at Anacostia Naval Air Station in Washington, D.C. He was a member of the Naval Test Board at Mitchell Field, Long Island, New York. He was active in air speed racing, and in 1925 he won the Schneider Marine Cup race in a Curtiss R3C with an average speed of 232 mph. He won the Mackay Trophy in 1926 and took a leave of absence in April of that year to perform aerial demonstration flights in South America in his P-1 Hawk. In Chile, he broke both his ankles, yet was able to conduct maneuvers using ankle casts. Returning to the United States, he was confined to Walter Reed Army Hospital for his injuries until April 1927.

Doolittle served as a test pilot for the Army at McCook Field in Dayton, Ohio, and for the Navy at Mitchell Field in New York. It was during this time that he was the first to perform an outside loop. His major technical contribution to aviation was his work in developing instrument flying. He was the first to understand that a pilot could be trained to fly through fog, clouds, rain and darkness by using his instruments and avoiding his own confused perception of motion senses that are so prevalent in fast-moving aircraft.

In 1929 Doolittle was the first pilot in history to take off, fly, and land an airplane using only instruments, without a view outside the cockpit. He assisted in the development in fog flying equipment and was the first to test the artificial horizon and directional gyroscope. He received wide media acclaim for his "blind flying"[7] and later received the Harmon Trophy for his experiments.

In February 1930, Doolittle resigned his commission and was commissioned as a major in the Specialist Reserve Corps. He joined the Shell Oil Company as manager of the Aviation Department because he could no longer afford to support his wife, his mother-in-law and two sons on lieutenant's pay. In this role he conducted numerous aviation tests. He was influential in pushing Shell to develop 100 octane aviation gasoline for high-performance planes that were coming along in the 1930s.

His air racing continued with a win in the 1931 Bendix Trophy Race from Burbank, California, to Cleveland, Ohio, in a Laird Super Stallion biplane. In 1932 he set the world high-speed record for land planes at 296 mph in a Shell Speed Dash. He also won the Thompson Trophy Race at Cleveland in the notorious Gee Bee R-1 racer with a speed averaging 252 mph. After having won the Schneider, Bendix, and Thompson races, Doolittle retired from air racing, having stated, "I have yet to hear anyone engaged in this work dying of old age."[8]

When war broke out in Europe in September 1939, Doolittle was sure that the United States would be involved at some point. He returned to active duty on July 1, 1940, as a major and assistant district supervisor of the Central Air Corps Procurement District at Indianapolis and Detroit. In this role he worked with large auto manufacturers in converting their plants for production of planes. On December 24, 1941, Hap Arnold phoned him and asked, "Jim, I'd like to have you on my staff here in Washington. How soon can you come?" Doolittle responded immediately, "I can be there in four hours." On January 2, he was officially transferred to Washington and promoted to lieutenant colonel.[9]

After Duncan and Low departed from the meeting, General Arnold brought Doolittle into his office to discuss the best bomber aircraft to carry out a mission to take off in 500 feet, with "a two-thousand-pound bomb load and fly two thousand miles." Doolittle came back the next day and told Arnold that the North American B-25 was the best choice. Arnold then covered the challenging mission to hit Japan in detail. Doolittle was impressed and volunteered to head up the project. It was just the kind of challenge he liked. Doolittle later recalled, "I was given the greatest gift you can be given in the service to get a job done—top priority. I had top priority on everything right from Hap. I could have anything I wanted."[10]

Doolittle began immediately on his tasks as Captain Duncan started moving ahead with the Navy tasks. Duncan put in a request for a submarine to be ordered to collect weather data from the waters off Japan. The assignment went to the *Thresher*, skippered by Lieutenant Commander William L. Anderson. The orders were to proceed off Midway Island and make frequent weather observations while noting enemy shipping traffic and attacking worthy targets.[11]

At noon on February 1, 1942, the new carrier *Hornet*, under the command of Captain Marc A. Mitscher, was anchored in Hampton Roads at the entrance to Norfolk harbor. A meeting between Mitscher and his visitor, Captain Donald Duncan, began with a question to Mitscher: "Can you put a loaded B-25 in the air on a normal deck run?"

Mitscher asked, "How many B-25s on deck?"

"Fifteen," answered Duncan.

Mitscher did some calculations and used his scale model layout of the *Hornet*'s flight deck to formulate a reply. He told Duncan, "Yes, it can be done."

Duncan responded, "Good. I'm putting two aboard for a test launching tomorrow."[12]

Doolittle had already selected three Army Air Force crews to assist in confirming that a loaded B-25 could actually fly off a carrier. An experienced B-25 officer, Lieutenant John E. Fitzgerald, received orders to report to Norfolk along with his crew and two other crews. The three crews made 30 practice short takeoff runs at a nearby Navy auxiliary field. One of the B-25 planes had engine problems and was not used in the actual test.

At 0536 on February 2, the fires were lit in Boiler No. 6 in the engineering spaces aboard the *Hornet* for the experimental test mission at sea. Two hours later, the two B-25 bombers were hoisted aboard the carrier. At 0900, with light snow falling, the *Hornet* moved away from the pier and began to steam to a designated location some 100 miles off the coast. The two B-25s were spotted on the flight deck: one aft (to represent the takeoff position of the 15th bomber) and the other forward with the right wingtip only six feet from the island (representing the initial bomber launch point).

At sea the *Hornet* turned into the wind as the two crews manned their planes. Fitzgerald and one of the other pilots, Lieutenant James F. McCarthy, would make the takeoffs. Mitscher and Duncan stood together thirty feet off the deck on the port bridge wing, shivering in the foul weather as they watched the operation. Fitzgerald's lightly loaded plane in the forward launch position started his engine.[13]

Fitzgerald recalled the 1300 takeoff event:

> I was surprised to see that we had almost five hundred feet of usable deck space and that the plane's airspeed indicator showed about forty-five miles per hour just sitting there. That meant that we had to accelerate only about twenty-three miles per hour. When I got the "go" signal, I let the brakes off and was almost immediately airborne—well ahead of my estimate. One thing that worried me though was the "island" out over the flight deck on which the skipper stood so that he could have a clear view of the deck operations. The wing of my plane rose so rapidly that I thought we were going to strike this projection. I pushed the control column forward and the wings just barely passed underneath. I climbed and circled back to watch Lieutenant McCarthy take off.[14]

Just as the first B-25 was airborne, the *Hornet* received a semaphore signal (ship-to-ship communications using blinkers) from the escort destroyers *Jones* and *Ludlow* about seeing a submarine periscope. The carrier went to general quarters and the two destroyers raced in rough seas toward the contact. Lieutenant James F. McCarthy, in the second Mitchell bomber, turned off the engines and climbed down from the bomber. The destroyers dropped depth charges at will until the sea was churned, yet the periscope remained. Within a few minutes the destroyers' skippers sent messages that the "periscope" was actually the mast of a sunken merchant ship.

The second Mitchell bomber with McCarthy piloting finally took off 2½ hours after the first one, as easily as Fitzgerald's had. The two B-25s joined up and flew over the horizon to a landing field. Duncan was happy with the test results. The recorded wind was 20 knots down the deck, with the *Hornet*'s speed at ten knots. With a B-25 takeoff speed of 25 knots, he was sure this loaded bomber could successfully take off from a carrier. The *Hornet* promptly returned to the Norfolk pier, where Duncan disembarked and headed to Washington. It was only hours before Mitscher received orders to prepare to sail March 1.[15]

While Captain Duncan was coordinating the carrier test, Doolittle was already busy.

Back on January 22, he had ordered 18 Mitchell B-25B bombers to be made available to Mid-Continental Airlines at Minneapolis, "for alteration as required." Ultimately there were a total of 24 planes ordered, which allowed for 6 spares. He flew to see Brigadier General George C. Kenney at Wright Field, Ohio, to discuss assistance he needed for his "B-25B Special Project." From his office at 4414 in the Munitions Building on January 31, Doolittle had begun to document his thoughts on the mission in what he called the "B-25 Special Project." In it he covered his blueprint for the operation.[16]

Doolittle's bombers needed new gas tanks, new bomb shackles, removal of the bottom gun turret, de-icing boots in the leading wings and tail surfaces, and replacement of the $10,000 top secret Norden bombsights with a simple "twenty-cent" bombsight that was more accurate at 1,500 feet altitude. A 500-pound demolition bomb was selected, which would "contain 50% TNT and 50% Amatol, with a $1/10$-second nose and $1/40$-second [fuse that] required extreme low-level bombing. A 500-pound cluster, containing 128 incendiary bombs, was also to be carried."[17]

To determine the best targets to bomb in Japan, Doolittle called on Arnold's intelligence staff. On the last day in January, Brig. General Carl Spaatz presented him with the list of industrial targets including Tokyo, Kobe, Nagoya, Yokohama, and six other major cities. The plan called for the planes to be spread over a 50-mile front for "greater coverage, to create the impression of a larger force than existed, and to dilute the ground fire."[18]

Based on the B-25B aircraft selected, the logical choice was to select the flight crews from three squadrons, the 34th, 37th and 95th, and from the 17th Bombardment Group and the 89th Reconnaissance Squadron from Pendleton, Oregon. These squadrons had qualified crews because of their extensive antisubmarine patrol missions off the coasts of Oregon and Washington.

The commanding officer of the 17th Bombardment Group, Lieutenant Colonel William C. Mills, received orders on February 3 to transfer the group to the Columbia Army Air Base in Columbia, South Carolina. Before the crews moved, Mills passed the word that there was a need for volunteers for an extremely hazardous mission. The volunteer response was universally positive. Mills recommended to Doolittle the commanding officer of the 89th, Major John A. Hilger, to lead the volunteer flight crews. Doolittle agreed and Hilger became his deputy.

Doolittle directed Hilger to take 24 qualified crews and ground personnel to Eglin Field, Florida, to start the training program. Hilger assigned the task of selecting the best crews and ground staff to three squadron commanders. These volunteers arrived for special training at their new base between February 27 and March 3.

At Hilger's suggestion, Doolittle asked the Navy to provide a flight instructor for the flight training. Orders were sent to Lieutenant Henry L. Miller, USN, and he transferred from Pensacola to Eglin. Miller later wrote of his adventure: "When I arrived, I met Capts. 'Ski' York, Davey Jones, and Ross Greening. I told them why I was reporting aboard. They seemed surprised. After we chatted a while they asked me if I had flown a B-25 before. I had to be honest. I had never even seen a B-25 before."[19]

Doolittle's special unit was organized along standard Army Air Force lines with Major Jack Hilger as executive officer, Major Harry Johnson as adjutant, Captain Edward J. "Ski" York over operations, Captain David M. Jones heading up the navigation and intelligence departments, Captain Ross Greening with gunnery and bombing, 1st Lieutenant William M. Bower as engineering officer, and 1st Lieutenant Travis Hoover in supply.

He revealed this mission to these unit leaders, but not to the rest of the squadron. Doolittle called all the men together at Eglin on March 3 to welcome the men to the training. He did not reveal any information about the actual mission, but he did emphasize the absolute requirement for total secrecy and said, "The lives of many men are going to depend on how well you keep this project to yourself."[20]

Though the flight crews learned quickly, it was trying for them. Army pilots were never trained to take off in short distances, and having the tails of their medium bombers almost touching the runway was strange. The training program planned for 50 hours divided among day and night navigation, gunnery, bombing, and formation flying. In fact, the crews received only about 25 hours due to maintenance problems with the aircraft. There were continual leaky gas tanks and other issues.

Doolittle maintained offices in Washington and Eglin and flew back and forth, but was able to get in on some of the Eglin training. He flew with Captain Vernon L. Stinzi's B-24B crew, and when Stinzi became ill, Doolittle filled in as pilot. He said, "Naturally, I wanted to fly the mission as first pilot, but I wanted to go only on the basis that I could do as well as or better than the other pilots who had already started on the training program."[21]

In his second week at Eglin, Doolittle flew to Washington to try to talk Hap Arnold into letting him lead the mission to Japan. Arnold's first response was, "I'm sorry Jim, I need you right here on my staff. I can't afford to let you fly every combat mission you might help plan." But as Doolittle recalled, "I launched into my sales pitch, and finally Hap shrugged his shoulders and said, 'OK, Jim, it will be all right with me if it's all right with Miff Harman.'" Doolittle got his approval and was set to lead the Japanese strike.[22]

On February 20, Captain Mitscher received information that the *Hornet* would be sailing to the Pacific accompanied by the heavy cruiser *Vincennes*, the light cruiser *Nashville*, the fleet oiler *Cimarron*, and several destroyers. On March 4, the *Hornet* task force sailed from Norfolk en route to the West Coast via the Panama Canal. By March 11, the *Hornet* had transited Gaillard (Culebra) Cut at the Continental Divide of the Panama Canal. They stopped overnight at Balboa on the Pacific side to allow the crew to purchase personal items, including Havana cigars.[23]

As the *Hornet* was sailing north from Panama and Doolittle was completing the second week of training at Eglin, Hap Arnold invited Admiral King to his office to tell him that Doolittle was ready. King asked Arnold to have Doolittle come to Washington for a full briefing. Arnold spun around and called out to a subordinate, "Get Doolittle up here right away, tonight!"[24]

After a rough flight from Florida through bad weather, Doolittle met at the Navy Department. Captain Duncan gave Doolittle the single copy of his plan. Duncan recalled that Doolittle read it once and said, "That's fine." Doolittle and Duncan agreed that the Army group would leave Eglin as soon as possible for McClellan Field at Sacramento, where the B-25s would await final instructions before joining the *Hornet*. Duncan would fly to Pearl to brief Nimitz and Vice Admiral Halsey. As Duncan was about to leave, Admiral King took him aside and told him to tell Nimitz that the raid against Japan was "not a proposal made for [Nimitz] to consider but a plan to be carried out by him."[25]

Duncan flew to Honolulu and met at CINCPAC Headquarters with Admiral Nimitz on March 19. Captain Duncan briefed Nimitz on his plan. Nimitz liked it, and since it involved carriers, he called in Halsey. Halsey later recalled the session:

Wu Duncan told us that something big was in the air, something top secret; Lt. Col. James H. Doolittle, with Navy cooperation, had trained sixteen Army crews to take B-25s off a carrier's deck, and the Navy had promised to launch them for Tokyo. They might not inflict much damage, Wu said, "but they would certainly give Hirohito plenty to think about."

Nimitz asked me, "Do you believe it would work, Bill?"

I said, "They'll need a lot of luck."

"Are you willing to take them out there?"

"Yes, I am."

"Good," he said. "It's all yours!"

I suggested that the operation would run more smoothly if Miles and I could discuss it man-to-man with Doolittle, whom I had never met. Chester agreed and gave us orders to proceed to San Francisco.[26]

Duncan worked with the CINCPAC planning staff on the details for a 16-ship task force. Seven ships would accompany the *Hornet* from Alameda and they would sail westward and rendezvous with Halsey's eight-ship task force near the 180th meridian. Duncan cabled Admiral King to "tell Jimmy to get on his horse."[27] King called Hap Arnold, who delivered the message to Doolittle on the morning of March 23.

On Friday morning of March 20, people could see the silhouette of the *Hornet* on

USS *Hornet* (CV-8) photographed circa late 1941, soon after completion, probably at a U.S. east coast port. A ferry boat and Eagle Boat (PE) are in the background (U.S. Naval History and Heritage Command photograph. Catalog #NH 81313).

the horizon off Point Loma at San Diego, California. In an hour the carrier was entering the narrow shipping channel, sailing to its berthing pier at North Island Naval Air Station across from downtown. The *Hornet*'s flight deck was bare as its Air Group 8 had already flown into the air base. At North Island they received nineteen new F4F-4 fighters sporting self-sealing fuel tanks, hand-activated folding wings, increased firepower of six-gun batteries to replace the four-gun batteries, and heavier armor plate. Bombing Squadron 8 and Scouting Squadron 8 replaced their Curtiss biplanes with brand-new Douglas SBD-3 Dauntless bombers. The planes were tougher, faster, and able to cruise at 250 knots carrying a bombload of 1,200 pounds. The pilots of the new aircraft were required to engage in carrier requalifications training, which they completed on Friday, March 27. Mitscher was now waiting for his next orders.[28]

Duncan flew back from Pearl Harbor to San Francisco on a Pan American Clipper and then down to San Diego to meet with Mitscher. When he arrived, the *Hornet* was tied up at the pier and the men were on liberty weekend. The two men met in Mitscher's cabin as Duncan covered the final plans, which included a mid-ocean rendezvous with Halsey's *Enterprise* and Task Force 16, which would provide air cover for the mission. After the meeting, Duncan flew to San Francisco to await the arrival of Doolittle and Halsey.[29]

At 0300 in the early morning of March 25, Doolittle woke up his men and told them they would be heading to Sacramento within 8 hours. Only the crews for 22 planes would make the trip because one plane had crashed on takeoff and the second was damaged in a landing gear accident. The route chosen for the trip took the planes through San Antonio and Phoenix to March Field in southern California, and on to the Sacramento Air Depot at McClellan Field. Doolittle's planes arrived on March 27.[30]

At McClellan, Doolittle met with the depot commander and his staff to discuss some modifications he required of the aircraft. He also insisted that the depot technicians were not to tamper with any of the equipment or remove anything. Aside from the requested modifications, the planes were there to be inspected only. The modifications included the installation of a new 60-gallon rubber fuel tank in the rear compartments, new propellers, replacement of Plexiglas navigational windows with glass ones, removal of the heavy 230-pound liaison radios, and new hydraulic valves for the gun turrets. The parachutes had to be changed from the seat-type to the back-type chute.

Doolittle was disappointed to hear that some of the material they needed had not yet arrived. There was no sense of urgency with the civilian workers at the base. Doolittle told his men to keep an eye on their planes and note all the work being done. Soon there were complaints coming from every corner. Doolittle was upset with the work and called Hap Arnold on two occasions to get his B-25B Special Project placed as the top priority. Doolittle was never satisfied with the urgency or quality of the work at McClellan, but once he cleared his crews from the base, he ordered them to fly to a small airfield north of Sacramento near Willows. There, for the last time, Lieutenant Hank Miller drilled the crews in short takeoffs.[31]

On Monday morning of March 30, the *Hornet* sailed from North Island down the San Diego shipping channel past Point Loma, and then turned northward. Late on the afternoon of the next day, with her 80 planes stored below on the hangar deck, Mitscher's carrier tracked under the Golden Gate Bridge and carefully steamed into Alameda Naval Air Station through a muddy, partially dredged channel to moor at the pier.[32]

In the evening of that same day, April 1, Doolittle and Duncan met with Halsey and

Captain Miles Browning, his chief of staff, in the bar at San Francisco's Fairmont Hotel. To avoid running into one of Jimmy's friends while they were discussing top-secret plans, the group retired upstairs to Halsey's room.[33]

The meeting covered all of the detailed plans for the mission. Duncan explained that Mitscher's *Hornet* would be accompanied by the cruisers *Nashville* and *Vincennes*, the oiler *Cimarron* and DESDIV 22 destroyers *Gwin*, *Meredith*, *Monssen* and *Grayson*, using their current designation as Task Force 18, and would leave San Francisco on April 2. Task Force 16.1 with Halsey's carrier *Enterprise*, with cruisers *Northampton* and *Salt Lake City*, the oiler *Sabine* and destroyers *Balch*, *Benham*, *Ellet* and *Fanning* would sail from Hawaii on April 7. Both task forces would rendezvous on Sunday, April 12, at latitude 38° north and 180° longitude. At this point Mitscher's TF 18 would then become TF 16.2.

Halsey was impressed with the incredible risks that Doolittle and his airmen were undertaking. Doolittle came to understand the risk that Halsey's task force was taking by moving so close to the shores of Japan where the Navy could lose half their Pacific carrier fleet, 14 other ships and some 2000 men.

Doolittle agreed with Halsey that if the task force was discovered before they reached their takeoff point at around 500 miles from the coast of Japan, the bombers would be launched if they had a chance to reach either Tokyo or Midway. If the bombers were not in range of either location, the B-25s would be pushed overboard so the *Hornet* could use her own planes to defend the task force. The meeting lasted for two hours, after which they all shook hands and parted company.

After the meeting with Halsey, Doolittle called Jack Hilger and told him to get the planes to Alameda the next day for loading aboard the *Hornet*. Doolittle said, "When we get to Alameda, we'll want to know if there's anything wrong with our ships. Give them a good test flight and put at least an hour's time on them."[34]

The next morning, April 1, when the flight crews approached the *Hornet* over San Francisco Bay, they were fascinated. One of the crewmen on Lieutenant Lawson's plane remarked, "Damn! Ain't she small?" As the bombers landed at Alameda, they were met by Doolittle and "Ski" York, who asked each pilot, "Anything wrong with your ship?" If the pilot admitted there was a malfunction, the plane was directed to a hangar instead of the wharf. When Doolittle completed talking with each of the 22 B-25 pilots about the condition of his aircraft, he had received positive responses from 16 planes that were ready to be loaded. He told York, "These planes will go. Tell all the crews to get aboard the carrier whether or not their plane is on the dock."[35]

The Navy personnel surrounded the planes as soon as the pilots turned off the engines. They promptly drained the fuel from the B-25s' tanks, and then hooked the "donkey" with a tow bar to the nose of the planes and towed it down to the pier as the crews followed. Then a large crane on the dock reached down and hauled the bombers aboard the flight deck to be tied down.

Doolittle was talking with Captain Mitscher as the bombers were being loaded. When the 15th plane was tied down, Doolittle remarked, "I think we'll take one more. Since none of the lads have made a carrier takeoff or even seen one, it would give them a lot of confidence to see it done. About a hundred miles out, we could send that sixteenth plane back. Hank Miller could be the co-pilot." Mitscher rubbed his head, turned to Doolittle and said, "All right, Jimmy, it's your show."[36]

Lieutenant Lawson stood on the dock admiring the *Hornet* and recalled, "She was a great sight. I can't describe the feeling I got, standing there, looking up at her sides."

Miller came up and warned him not to tell the "Navy boys" anything about the mission. Miller later recalled, "I was proud of those fellows that day. As each man came aboard, he saluted the National Ensign and then the Officer of the Deck...." Miller reported aboard for duty like any other sailor.[37]

At 1500 that day, the *Hornet* backed away from Alameda Pier, moved to Berth Nine in the middle of the Bay, and anchored for the night. With his Army Air Force unit of 70 officers and 130 enlisted men now assigned bunks and settled aboard, a restricted liberty was granted. Several pilots headed to the Hopkins Hotel to see the sights and drink a few.

Doolittle spent his last evening with his wife, Joe, in a San Francisco hotel and was back on the *Hornet* the morning of April 2 talking with Mitscher in his cabin. Doolittle received messages from the intelligence officer. One was from General Stilwell in China confirming that the stored gas and airports were ready for their arrival. There were two other messages:

> May good luck and success be with you and each member of your command on the mission you are about to undertake. [signed] Arnold
>
> As you embark on your expedition please give each member of your command my deepest appreciation of their services and complete confidence in their ability and courage under your leadership to strike a mighty blow. You will be constantly in my mind and may the good Lord watch over you. [signed] Marshall"[38]

At 1000, as Doolittle and Mitscher talked, the other seven ships of Task Force 18 (later to become TF 16.2) sailed out of San Francisco Bay in a fog with visibility at about 1000 yards and formed up, waiting for the *Hornet* to follow. At the last minute, Doolittle was ordered to go ashore for an urgent phone call from Washington. He took the captain's gig. Doolittle heard General Marshall on the line as he said, "I just called to personally wish you the best of luck. Our thoughts and prayers will be with you. Good-bye, good luck, and come home safely."[39]

At 1148 the *Hornet* entered the channel and passed under the Golden Gate Bridge with the deck loaded with 16 B-25B Mitchell bombers in full view of the hundreds of onlookers. Once the *Hornet* cleared into the open sea, a course was set to the northwest. Because the *Hornet*'s planes were stowed in the hangar deck below and unavailable, the commander of the Western Sea Frontier provided air patrol protection until late afternoon, when the PBY Catalina seaplanes took over the patrol. Soon the Navy Blimp L-6 floated across the horizon to a point aft of the flight deck. Two backordered boxes of navigators' windows for the B-25s were winched down to the deck. After dropping off the load, the blimp departed.

The news went out about the mission using semaphore message to all the ships of Task Force 18 late in the afternoon. The ships then used loudspeakers to inform the crews. Mitscher used the loudspeaker on the *Hornet* to broadcast, "This ship will carry the army bombers to the shores of Japan for the bombing of Tokyo."[40] Exultant cheers went up as each section learned that they were heading to bomb Japan. Morale was now high and it remained so until they cleared the combat area.

After the meeting with Doolittle and Duncan, Admiral Halsey and Captain Browning had expected to be back at Pearl Harbor on April 2, but strong westerly winds prevented the flights from leaving for Honolulu. With no naval or commercial flights to Hawaii, Halsey was a restless man. He soon developed an itchy rash that was the beginnings of dermatitis. On the morning of the 6th, Halsey was ill with what he diagnosed as the flu. Browning was able to find a Navy doctor who "dosed me with dynamic pills,"[41] as Halsey recalled. That evening they learned that there were one of three planes available to him for the flight. He and Browning rushed to the airport and took a Pan American Clipper. There were nine other passengers as Halsey continued to take more pills. Before long he piled into his bunk and fell fast asleep. The next morning of the 7th, as the plane descended for landing, Halsey woke up with a bloody nose, but he was feeling better. Only his dermatitis remained.

On landing, they briefed Nimitz on the meeting and spent the rest of the day with the CINCPAC staff. The day ended with an approved CINCPAC Operational Plan 20-42 which stated, "This force will conduct a bombing raid against the enemy objective specified in Annex 'C' which is being furnished Commander Task Force Sixteen only."[42] Halsey had also tasked the submarines USS *Trout* and USS *Thresher* to maintain patrol stations off Japan and report any enemy forces that could harm his fleet. All American submarines would be routed south of the equator.

Meanwhile, the *Hornet* and ships of TF 18 sailed westward. On the carrier, the situation began to cause some uneasy emotions among the men. They were now at sea, steaming in the open Pacific, where the enemy could hit them at any time. Both Army and Navy personnel knew they were on a ship full of ordnance and gasoline, with thin armor plating that could not withstand a torpedo hit. To make the sleeping arrangements more comfortable, Doolittle's sergeants and corporals were given the ship's enlisted bunks, while the remaining men slept in hammocks or big mesh nets. The *Hornet* seemed to be a large ship until the crewmen faced the cramped conditions caused by the presence of the Army contingent.[43]

On April 6, a strange numeral code was heard as a strong signal on frequency 3095kcs. Japanese broadcast stations sent out continuous signals that were monitored by American forces to detect any change from the ordinary, which could be construed as a possible danger warning. Throughout the voyage across the Pacific the weather was foul, with high winds and heavy seas. Much of the time the available cruiser aircraft that could provide some air reconnaissance were unable to fly due to the poor weather conditions.

Because of the delay with Halsey getting back to Pearl Harbor, on April 9 CINCPAC radioed the *Hornet* with instructions to defer their scheduled rendezvous with the *Enterprise* for 24 hours to join on the 13th. Mitscher recorded his activities with the delay: "Reversed course and slowed to comply. Attempted to fuel *Hornet* from *Cimarron* but had to defer the operation because of heavy seas. *Cimarron* lost two men overboard in the attempt; one was recovered by life ring and heaving line, the other by *Meredith*. A man previously lost overboard from *Vincennes* was also recovered by *Meredith* in a prompt and efficient manner."[44]

Since April 1 the *Enterprise* had been based at Pearl Harbor. At 1232 on April 8, 1942, the *Enterprise* got underway from berth F-2, with Halsey accompanied by the *Northampton*, *Salt Lake City*, oiler *Sabine* and destroyers *Balch*, *Benham*, *Ellet* and *Fanning*. Several hours later south of Oahu, the *Enterprise* Air Group landed aboard as the course was changed westerly and then northwest to 310°T, which would take the task force 30 miles southwest of Nihoa Island.[45]

An inner air patrol of 4 VS bombers and an intermediate air patrol of 5 VS bombers were established on the 8th to cover the TF 16.1 sortie, plus an additional 4-plane inner air patrol to cover for the oiler *Sabine*. Just before the last VS patrols landed, VF-6 fighters were launched to patrol until dark. The next day, April 9, an inner air patrol at forenoon and afternoon was launched with 4 F4F-4s each. In the afternoon, VS scouting flights using 13 Dauntless planes conducted sectors searches between 255° and 015° out to 175 miles. Two extra planes accompanied the flights to provide new pilots with scouting experience.

On April 10 the dawn inner air patrol used 6 Wildcats, while 13 Dauntless bombers flew the scouting flights searching sector 250° to 050° for 200 miles. Two new pilots accompanied the flight for their first-long distance scouting patrol. Bad weather was encountered by two scout bombers and they joined the inner patrol. Six Wildcats handled the inner air patrol and took turns towing a sleeve and firing. The next inner patrol was conducted by 4 Wildcats and was maintained all day. In addition to the standard patrols, 8 cruiser planes took over the scouting flight in the afternoon, covering the sector 120° search to 150 miles out. There were no reports of sightings. One torpedo plane was launched during the afternoon to make simulated high-altitude runs for an AA director training period. All day fighter planes tested their guns on the flight deck.

The air operations for April 11 consisted of the usual inner air and scouting flights. Sector search 250° to 010° out 150 miles was conducted in the morning and afternoon. The inner patrol conducted gunnery exercises with the conjunction with their patrol. The gun firing runs were conducted ahead of the task force formation with 4 Wildcats maintaining control. The next day's inner air patrol (April 12) was scheduled for the forenoon and afternoon, while the scouting flights of sector 250° to 010° out 200 miles was conducted by the cruiser planes. The Wildcats and Dauntless aircraft held gunnery and bombing practice during the day. In the afternoon 9 torpedo planes from VT-6 made high-altitude bombing runs on a sled towed by the *Salt Lake City*.[46]

Unknown to the Americans, back on April 10 at 0630 a Japanese Combined Fleet Radio Intelligence unit intercepted messages between Halsey's and Mitscher's task forces. The Japanese Imperial Naval headquarters under Vice Admiral Matome Ugaki, chief of staff of the Combined Fleet, calculated that if the enemy continued westward, they would be able to attack Tokyo about April 14. They figured that even if the Americans steamed at full speed, they would have to approach within 300 miles of the home islands in order to fly the carrier planes. As a Japanese historian noted, "[O]ur surveillance net was 700 nautical miles off-shore and the enemy, in order to break through this net and penetrate 300 nautical miles inward, would require 15 or 16 hours, so it would be possible for us to attack the enemy at our leisure the day before he launched his planes."[47]

U.S. Naval Intelligence was not aware that a line of approximately 50 Japanese radio-equipped fishing boats formed an early warning surveillance network. Though the U.S. submarines had covered the area from time to time, they had never noticed a hundred 300-ton fishing vessels that acted as part of an early warning system.

Admiral Ugaki knew a large force with four of the most experienced Japanese carrier—*Akagi, Kaga, Soryu* and *Hiryu*—was returning from the Indian Ocean on the 18th, but that was too late to engage the U.S. force should they attack. But the 26th Air Flotilla was available and could provide home defense with 69 bombing and scouting planes. Ugaki worked with Vice Admiral Seigo Yamagata, the commanding officer of the 26th, to approve a plan to handle an American attack. If the carriers came within 600 miles of land, they would launch the first wave of torpedo bombers within hours. The carriers would be destroyed. But April 14 came and went with no more radio intercepts. They decided to keep the alert in effect even as they felt the U.S. carriers had gone to some other area.[48]

The two submarines patrolling the task force area were active just before the carriers arrived. On the 9th, the *Trout* had fired two torpedoes at two small enemy cargo vessels, but they both missed. On the 10th, they attacked a steamer with no success. But finally, on the 11th, one of two torpedoes fired from the *Trout* at a large freighter hit. Unfortunately, the freighter survived the attack.

The *Thresher* had also fired at several targets on the 10th, including a 10,000-ton freighter, but it escaped undamaged. On the 11th the *Thresher* was patrolling off Inubo Saki, gathering weather information. Off Yokohama in Tokyo Bay, the submarine finally had success, sinking a 5,000-ton freighter in just 3 minutes. A Japanese subchaser attacked the *Thresher* with depth charges, causing some damage, but the subs continued to patrol. The *Trout* and *Thresher* reported that there were no large naval ships in the vicinity of the launch area.[49]

Meanwhile, with Task Force 18, on the 10th the *Cimarron* fueled both the cruisers, and the next day the course for Mitscher's Task Force 18 was set to 255°T to rendezvous with Halsey's force. The *Hornet* was fueled on the 12th and the cruisers and destroyers were topped off. At 1630 that day, radar transmissions were detected from 230°T at a distance of 130 miles. It was the *Enterprise* task force. At 0610 on April 13, the *Hornet* Task Force 18 was sighted, with the two task forces rendezvousing at 0713. The *Hornet* TF 18 under Captain Mitscher was now redesignated Task Group 16.2.[50]

As the crew of the *Enterprise* stared at the *Hornet*, there was tremendous speculation about the B-25 bombers on her flight deck. Though Mitscher had already revealed the mission to his task force crews, Halsey decided that now was the time to pass the word to *Enterprise* task force personnel. On the "squawk box" on the *Enterprise*, Halsey told the men, "This force is bound for Tokyo!" Halsey recalled, "In all my experience in the navy, I have never heard such a resounding cheer as came from the ship's company."[51]

At 0949 on the 13th, with the full Task Force 16 joined, a course 270°T, speed 12 knots, was set as the ships lined up in cruising disposition 7V formation. In the center of the course axis was the *Hornet* followed by *Sabine, Cimarron, Enterprise* in column astern, *Northampton, Vincennes* in column, *Nashville, Salt Lake City* in column, destroyer *Batch*, and other destroyers screening the heavy ships. The day's air operations consisted as usual of the inner air patrol and the scouting flights during the forenoon. The scouting flights searched sector 220° to 340° out to 200 miles. The morning scouting flight encountered carburetor icing problems. The inner air patrol was launched in the afternoon, but the afternoon scouting flight was canceled due to weather conditions.[52]

Having crossed the International Date Line at midnight, the task force went from the 13th to April 15. Until the weather became too bad, Halsey sent out air patrols during daylight hours in a 60° arc in the westerly heading to 200 miles. On the 15th, Halsey sent semaphore messages to the ships of the task force that the refueling operations would occur 1,000 miles off Japan. That morning the task force was 1,400 miles east of Tokyo. He also directed the destroyers and tankers to remain in the vicinity of the fueling point and rejoin with the rest of the task force when they were retiring after launching the B-25s to Japan.

The air operations for April 15 called for the inner air patrol during the afternoon, after all morning flights had been canceled by rain, haze, overcast and strong southerly winds. In the afternoon one scout was launched to tow a sleeve for gunnery practice, and also to drop guard mail on the *Hornet*. Another scout flight was sent out during the afternoon to search sector 204° to 324° out 100 miles.[53]

As they sailed into ever rougher weather, Halsey was concerned on the 16th by a propaganda broadcast from Radio Tokyo: "Reuters, British news agency, has announced that three American bombers have dropped bombs on Tokyo. This is a most laughable story. They know it is absolutely impossible for enemy bombers to be within five hundred miles of Tokyo. Instead of worrying about such foolish things, the Japanese people are enjoying the fine spring sunshine and the fragrance of the cherry blossoms."[54] There was never an explanation for the false information.

On that day aboard the *Hornet*, the B-25Bs were fueled and spotted for their final takeoff position on the flight deck. The leading B-25 was 467 feet from the front of the flight deck and the last plane hung out over the stern to conserve takeoff space. Two lines were painted on the deck in front of the planes. The first line was for the left wheel and the second for the nose wheel. If the pilots kept their wheels on these lines, they could be confident that the right wing would not hit the superstructure of the carrier island on takeoff.[55]

The inner air patrol for April 16 launched at 0501 with 6 fighters, followed by patrols the entire day of 5, 4, and 6 fighters each. No contacts were sighted. The first scouting

Doolittle Raid on Japan. USAAF B-25B bomber lines up for takeoff from USS *Hornet* (CV-8), on the morning of 18 April 1942. Note white lines painted on the flight deck, below the plane's nose and port side wheels, to guide the pilot during his takeoff run. This is the 3rd or 4th plane to be launched (U.S. Naval History and Heritage Command photograph. Catalog #NH 53420).

flight of 13 scout bombers searched sector 204° to 324° to 200 miles in the morning. The afternoon scout flight consisted of 8 torpedo planes searching the same sector out to 150 miles with no contacts.[56]

Aboard the *Hornet* there were continual problems keeping the bombers ready for action. The high winds caused vibrations in all the control surfaces and there were generator failures, spark plug changes, leaky fuel tanks, brake problems, and engine trouble. Constant inspections were required to make sure the planes were secured on the flight deck. The *Hornet*'s carrier aviation mechanics developed a feeling that the Army's enlisted men were lazy. Aviation Machinist's Mate 2nd Class Eugene Blackmer and his peers became disgusted with the Army sergeants' and corporals' lack of knowledge of the "mechanical structure" of their B-25s. They left all the repairs of their planes to the navy. Doolittle was about to make a decision to throw one the bombers overboard because of its persistent engine malfunctions. The *Hornet*'s mechanics removed the engine on the deck, took it below, took it apart, and soon discovered that the only problem was with a single broken washer. The machinist's mate quickly made another washer, and the team put the engine back together and reinstalled the engine on the B-25. Doolittle had a bomber pilot's sleep interrupted and sent him to the flight deck. The engine was started, and it ran flawlessly. Doolittle appeared on the deck and thanked the machinists and mechanics for a "job well done."[57]

During the entire Pacific transit of the *Hornet* to the launch point, Doolittle made sure his men were engaged in various training activities. There were classes on navigation, carrier operations, first aid and sanitation, gunnery, meteorology, Chinese customs, escape and evasion, and more. Actual gunnery and turret practice was carried out using kites flown off the *Hornet* for targets. They were briefed on the target cities of Tokyo, Yokohama, Nagoya, Osaka and Kobe, as well as the specific military and industrial places to drop their bombs on. There were also sites to avoid, like hospitals, schools and the Imperial Palace.[58]

At dawn, 0537 on the 17th, the *Enterprise* launched 18 scout bombers to patrol, 12 to search sector 180° to 360°, and six to search sector 000° to 180°, both out to 75 miles. No contacts were reported. At 0845 the first inner air patrol and morning scout flights landed aboard the *Enterprise*. During the event the 20,000th landing aboard was accomplished by pilot H.M. Sumrall ACMM (NAP), USN, in plane number 6-F-24. With the task force at about 1000 miles east of Tokyo, fueling of the two carriers and the four cruisers was completed by 1414. The operation had just completed when the winds increased to gale force from the south in rough seas, cutting visibility to 1 to 2 miles. Captain Murray canceled all flights at 1222 as the storm coming from the southeast hit 41 knots in heavy seas.[59]

The *Enterprise*'s assistant landing signal officer, Robin Lindsey, wrote of the furious weather: "God damnest weather I've ever seen. For days the waves were so high the deck was pitching so much that I had to have a person stand behind me to hold me on the landing signal platform so I wouldn't fall down. Several times I did, and you can imagine the amazement of the pilot's face as he passed over with no signal officer there."[60]

At 1445, the *Hornet*, the *Enterprise*, and cruisers *Northampton*, *Salt Lake City*, *Vincennes*, and *Nashville* steamed independently, leaving the destroyers and oilers behind. The course was set westerly at 20 knots. If all worked as planned, the task force would be 500 miles from Tokyo at 1400 on the 18th to launch Doolittle's bomber to arrive over Tokyo at dusk to drop incendiary bombs. At sunset the remaining 15 B-25Bs would launch to bomb Tokyo or their designated Japanese city. After bombing one of the Japanese cities in darkness, the bombers would fly over the East China Sea to China and land at Chuchow or one of the other four friendly-held airfields for refueling.[61]

At dusk on the 17th, Task Force 16 ships were enduring gale force winds and rain as the carriers took waves over their flight decks, sixty feet above their waterlines. Planes were double lashed on the flight and hangar decks.

Next morning on the 18th, Ensign Robert R. Boettcher was the *Hornet*'s watch officer of the deck as the task force sailed on a course 267°T at 20 knots. At 0310 Boettcher reported to Mitscher in his sea cabin that radar operators were picking up unidentified objects on their screens. The *Enterprise*'s radar revealed that two enemy surface craft contacts were bearing 255°T at 21,000 yards. Two minutes later a light was seen from that same bearing. The ships went to general quarters setting Material Condition "AFIRM" as the task force changed course to 350°T using a high-frequency, short-range radio broadcast. At 0341 the two enemy contacts faded from the radar screen at bearing 201°T at distance 26,400 yards. Since apparently the task force was unnoticed by the enemy, a westerly course of 270°T toward Japan was resumed at 0415. The task force secured from general quarters and set condition BAKER and Condition of Readiness 11.[62]

At 0508 the *Enterprise* sent out 8 F4F Wildcats from Fighting Six for inner air patrol, and 3 SBDs from Bombing Three for engine run-in and a combat air patrol. Also 3 SBDs, piloted by Lieutenant (JG) O.B. Wiseman USN, Ensign C.F. Lane A/VN(N) USNR, and Ensign A.W. Hanson A-V(N) USNR, were launched at 0515 to sector search 260° to 280°T ahead, out 200 miles. The weather turned worse now as rain squalls and high waves hammered the ships with winds of 28 to 30 knots. At 0558 Wiseman saw a small fishing vessel (patrol craft) and recorded on his knee pad the message, "Enemy surface ship—latitude 36–04N, Long. 153–10E, bearing 276 degrees true—42 miles from *Enterprise*. Believe seen by enemy."[63] He handed the paper to his gunner in the rear seat as he made a throwing motion with his hand. The gunner took out a small beanbag from his pocket and crammed the message into it. As Wiseman flew over the *Enterprise*, the gunner threw the beanbag onto the deck. A sailor grabbed the beanbag and took it to Halsey on the bridge. Halsey immediately ordered the task force to change course to 220°T. Wiseman then augmented the inner patrol until he landed at 0855. Had Wiseman's plane been seen?[64]

In fact, the IJN was indeed being alerted to the presence of Task Force 16. The converted fishing sampan, *No. 23 Nitto Maru*, part of IJN's 5th Fleet and armed with machine guns and a cannon, was on its standard patrol. Japanese sailor S2c Nakamura Suekichi, on the picket vessel, later recalled, "The waves were high that day and I could not help worrying that our 70-ton *Nitto Maru* would capsize at any moment."[65] On watch he had seen planes and went below to tell the skipper, CPO Gisaku Maeda. Maeda assumed the patrol planes were Japanese and stayed below, snug in his bunk.

A short while later Suekichi came below again and said, "Sir, there are two of our beautiful carriers now dead ahead." Maeda leaped from the bunk and climbed the ladder to the deck. There were no Japanese carriers expected in the area as the skipper studied the gray hulks through his binoculars. He then replied, "Yes, Suekichi, they are beautiful but they are not ours." Maeda then gave the sailor his binoculars, went below, opened his sea bag, took out his revolver and shot himself in the head. Suekichi said, "At that time [0630] we radioed the *Kiso*, the flagship of the Fifth Fleet, that the enemy had been sighted."[66]

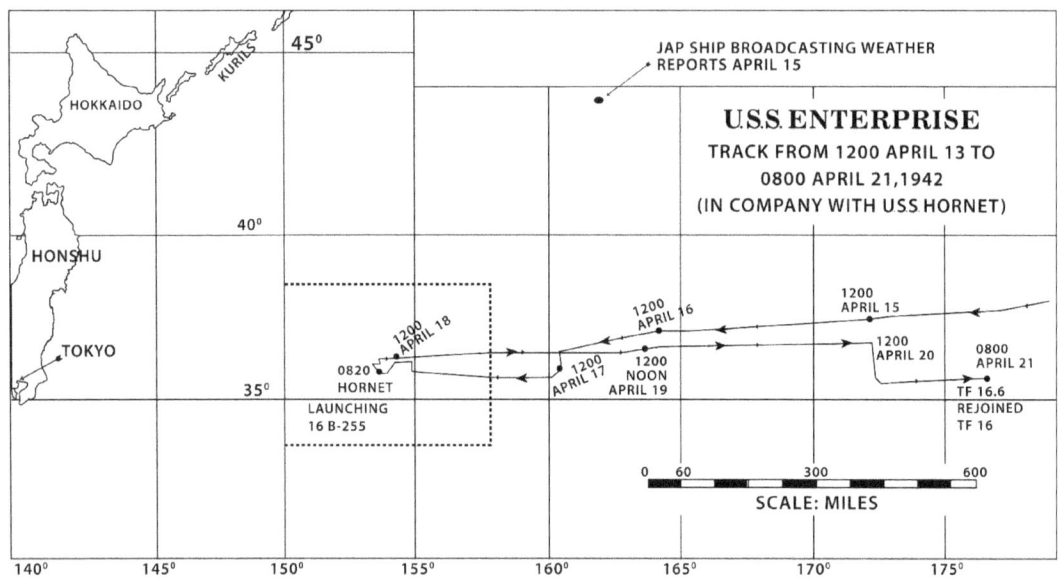

Attack track map for USS *Enterprise*, Tokyo raid, April 18, 1942, Halsey-Doolittle raid: Bombing of Tokyo. Image redrawn based on *Action Report: USS Enterprise (CV-6)*, Captain G.D. Murray to Admiral Chester W. Nimitz, April 23, 1942, ibiblio.org/hyperwar/USN/ships/logs/CV/cv6-Tokyo.html.

The IJN staff received the alert message: "Three enemy carriers sighted. Position 650 nautical miles east of Inubo Saki." The Combined Fleet headquarters transmitted immediately: "Tactical Method Number 3 against the United States Fleet," an order to engage the Task Force 16. Ships of the 1st and 2nd Fleets sortied out of Yokosuka and Hiroshima to search for the enemy carriers. Vice Admiral Nagumo Chuichi's carrier fleet from the Indian Ocean changed direction toward the reported position of the U.S. carriers. The IJN also notified General Prince Higashikuni's Eastern Army Command and they ordered a preliminary air-raid warning to alert all air defense units. The next day at 0630, Yamagata, commander of the 26th Air Flotilla, would launch his G4M Mitsubishi Betty patrol planes out to 700 miles to find and hit the enemy hard.[67]

Ensign J.Q. Roberts, A-V(N), USNR, had earlier been launched from the *Enterprise* for a combination of engine run in and inner air patrol to the west. At 0745 Roberts sighted one patrol vessel sized at 125 feet long of metal construction and painted dark gray at Lat. 35–40N, Long. 153–25E, bearing 160° T, distance 20 miles from the *Enterprise*. At 0800 he conducted a "glide bombing attack up wind and dropped one 500-lb. AF fuze bomb which hit about 100 feet over the target. He also fired a short burst of .50 caliber ammunition from one gun during the dive. No noticeable damage resulted except that which may have been caused during the strafing. The enemy did not fire or execute any radical maneuvers." Ensign Roberts landed aboard at 0855 with the group.[68]

At 0744 the *Hornet* lookouts sighted a Japanese picket ship bearing 221°T at 10,000 yards. Halsey ordered all ships to general quarters after the *Nitto Maru* sighting as the *Enterprise* Wildcats F4F-4 fighters on combat air patrol strafed the picket ship, trying unsuccessfully to sink her. At 0750 the commander of the *Nashville*, Captain F.S. Craven, asked for permission by flag hoist to attack the Japanese craft. Halsey approved the request two minutes later. At 0753 the *Nashville* began firing with six-inch shells from its main battery at range 9,000 yards. The *Nashville* checked firing at times to allow the fighters to engage. Incredibly, the cruiser expended 938 rounds of six-inch ammunition and finally sank the *Nitto Maru* at 0823. Craven explained the poor performance in his action report: "During this engagement 938 rounds of 6" ammunition were expended due to the difficulty of hitting the small target with the heavy swells that were running and the long range at which fire was opened. This range was used in order to silence the enemy's radio as soon as possible. The ship sunk was a Japanese patrol boat and was equipped with radio and anti-aircraft machine guns.... When the *Nashville* rejoined the formation [at 1153] the ships had reversed course and were steaming on course 092°T at 25 knots."[69]

Radiomen aboard the task force heard the operator on the *Nitto Maru* tapping out the garbled message to the IJN. Halsey's staff officer responsible for monitoring enemy communications, Lieutenant Gilven Slonim, advised launching the B25s immediately. At 0800 Halsey flashed a message to Mitscher: "LAUNCH PLANES X TO COL DOOLITTLE AND GALLANT COMMAND GOOD LUCK AND GOD BLESS YOU." Doolittle was on the *Hornet*'s bridge with Mitscher when the message came in. He shook hands with Mitscher and then jumped down the ladder, shouting to everyone he ran into, "OK fellas, this is it. Let's go!" The klaxon horn sounded, followed by an announcement, "Army pilots, man your planes!"[70]

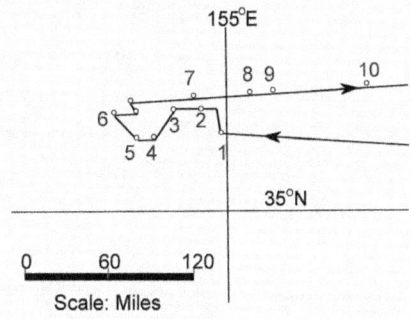

Detailed view of USS *Enterprise* ship track during the Tokyo raid, April 18, 1942. Redrawn image based on *Action Report: USS Enterprise (CV-6)*.

At 0803 Halsey ordered the fleet to change course to 310°T into the wind, steaming at 22 knots to launch the B-25s. There was a mad scramble as the B-25 crews packed their last possessions and ran to their aircraft. Doc White handed out two pints of rye to each crewmember who passed by. Lieutenant Dick Knobloch ran to each plane with bags of sandwiches from the galley. The flight deck crews handed out ten extra 5-gallon tin cans of fuel, took off the engine covers, unfastened the tie-down ropes to each crew, and pulled the wheel chocks away. The Navy "donkey" attached the tow bar to the nose wheel and moved the planes into position in two lines for takeoff.[71]

The launching order and times of all B-25s is shown below[72]:

1.	Lt. Col. Doolittle	0820–8:20 a.m.
2.	1st Lt. Hoover	0825–8:25 a.m.
3.	1st Lt. Gray	0830–8:30 a.m.
4.	1st Lt. Holstrom	0833–8:33 a.m.
5.	Captain Jones	0837–8:37 a.m.
6.	2nd Lt. Hallmark	0840–8:40 a.m.
7.	1st Lt. Lawson	0843–8:43 a.m.
8.	Captain York	0846–8:46 a.m.
9.	1st Lt. Watson	0850–8:50 a.m.
10.	1st Lt. Joyce	0853–8:53 a.m.
11.	Captain Greening	0856–8:56 a.m.
12.	1st Lt. Bower	0859–8:59 a.m.
13.	1st Lt. McElroy	0901–9:01 a.m.
14.	Major Hilger	0907–9:07 a.m.
15.	1st Lt. Smith	0915–9:15 a.m.
16.	1st Lt. Farrow	0919–9:19 a.m.

Doolittle in the lead plane started his engines and let them warm up. Near the bow on the left side, the signal officer, Lieutenant Edgar G. Osborne, held his checkered flag. When Doolittle had his instruments ready for takeoff, he gave Osborne the thumbs-up signal. Osborne then made faster and faster circular motions with the flag as the signal to throttle his engines forward to reach max takeoff speed. When the deck was beginning an upward movement, the chocks were removed from the wheels and Osborne gave the "go" signal. Doolittle released his brakes and slowly moved down the deck with speed increasing. As he passed the carrier island, the nose wheel lifted off, then the main wheels, and with deck to spare the B-25 was airborne at 0825. Doolittle retracted his gear and flaps, circled around to the left, and flew over the *Hornet*'s deck to set his compass against the carrier's course. The Japanese raid was on its way, and Doolittle was 620 miles east of the lighthouse at Inubosaki, the easternmost point of Japan.

Next came Lieutenant Travis Hoover's B-25 as he moved into position, revved his engines, and took off seven minutes after Doolittle. Lieutenant Hank Miller noticed the first three planes had their stabilizers at the "full back position," which was keeping their nose up too long, causing then to almost stall out. He wrote in big letters on a blackboard that each of the pilots could see: "STABILIZER IN NEUTRAL," but few pilots obeyed.[73]

The rest of the planes took off without serious problems other than one major accident on the flight deck. As Lieutenant Bill Farrow's plane was being maneuvered for takeoff on the pitching, rain-soaked deck, Aviation Chief Machinist's Mate Tom Respess and a small detail were fighting to keep the nose wheel down by hand on the deck. As Farrow taxied forward and revved his engine, suddenly, in horror, they saw Aviation Machinist's Mate Robert W. Wall lose his footing, to be sucked into the left propeller. One blade chewed up his arm and another hit Wall in the rear and threw him clear. His deck mates rushed Wall to sick bay and his arm was amputated in a short time.

Farrow was the 16th and last B-25B to take off. He was so rattled by seeing Wall's injury that he set his flaps incorrectly, retracting them versus putting them in a neutral position. His plane almost hit the waves, but Farrow recovered and flew away. It was 0920 and Farrow was 600 miles from Inubosaki.

Eight minutes after the last B-25 was airborne, Halsey turned Task Force 16 on a reverse course eastward at 090°T, speed 25 knots, with the *Enterprise* in the guide position. On the hangar deck of the *Hornet*, the wings were being re-bolted to the torpedo, scout and bomber planes as they were sent up the three centerline elevators to the flight deck. The F4F-4 fighters were unlashed and sent up. By 1100 the *Hornet*'s flight deck was full of aircraft, fueled and ready for action. Fifteen minutes later, the *Hornet* launched 8 fighters to join the *Enterprise* combat air patrol, which had relieved the 1st CAP at 0827. The 1st CAP landed at 0900.[74]

At 1130 the *Enterprise* launched 3 VB-3 Dauntless bombers for a 200-mile search to the southwest piloted by Ensign R.M. Elder, A-V(N), USNR, Ensign R.K. Campbell, A/V(N), USNR, and Ensign J.C. Butler, A-V(N), USNR. Lieutenant R.W. Arndt was launched to lead a 3-plane section from VB-3 on a special mission to attack enemy surface vessels reported bearing 120° at distance 58 miles. At 1150 Ensign Campbell attacked a 150-foot Japanese metal auxiliary vessel sporting a radio mast on bearing 233° out 63 miles, Lat. 35–22N, Long. 153–00E from the *Enterprise*. Campbell made a glide-bombing attack upwind, releasing his 500-pound bomb on the first attack and two 100-pound bombs simultaneously on the second run. All bombs landed over the target approximately 100 feet. He strafed using both of his .50 caliber fixed and .30 caliber free guns. The vessel did not return fire, but maneuvered radically to avoid the bombs. No damage was apparent to the enemy except for a small amount caused from the strafing fire.

At 1226 the section led by Arndt attacked one 75-foot metal motor patrol boat painted gray with radio mast at Lat. 36–15N, Long. 153–58E. Each plane dropped one 500-pound bomb, and five 100-pound bombs were utilized in divebombing action. There was no apparent damage except for the near miss of a 100-pound bomb which silenced a small caliber AA gun located aft. The divebombing runs included strafing with .50 caliber and .30 caliber MG guns, which forced radical maneuvers and returning AA fire from a 1-inch gun.

At Lat. 33–30N, Long. 152–33E, Ensign Butler attacked one small 125-foot gray-painted metal vessel at 1245. Small guns were seen amidships, and the vessel was towing a small white boat. Butler made three separate glide-bombing runs, dropping 100-pound bombs on the first two dives and one 500-pound bomb on the third run. The 100-pound bombs missed and were duds because they were not armed. The 500-pound bomb landed close aboard on the port side, causing fragmentary damage to the ship, which turned in a small circle during the attack and fired a small .25 caliber gun. After bombing, Butler strafed both the larger and small boats. He reported that the smaller boat was sunk and that the larger one received some damage. After he landed at 1500, there were three holes discovered in the plane and one small caliber bullet was recovered, having been lodged in the leak-proof substance of the gasoline tank. Ensign Elder landed with the group and reported no contacts encountered.[75]

Thirty minutes into the flight, Doolittle was joined by Lieutenant Hoover, the second to take off from *Hornet*. As they both flew 200 feet above the sea, at an hour from takeoff, they sighted a "Japanese camouflaged naval surface vessel of about 6,000 tons" that they thought might be a light cruiser. An hour later they spotted a twin-engine plane overhead "flying at about 3,000 ft.—2 miles away" toward the launch point, but apparently it did not see the B-25s. Doolittle later reported that they passed "innumerable Japanese patrol and fishing boats from some 300 miles off-shore until crossing the Japanese Coast, the Japanese were apparently entirely unprepared for our arrival."

The 16 B-25B planes had been organized in flights of 3 planes each to hit the planned targets. Doolittle had joined the first flight of three B-25s under Hoover, and they bombed northern Tokyo. The second flight, led by Captain Jones, bombed central Tokyo, while Captain York's third flight hit southern Tokyo and the north central part of Tokyo Bay. The fourth flight, with Captain Greening, bombed the southern part of Kanagawa, Yokohama and the Yokosuka Navy Yard. The fifth flight of three bombers split up, one taking on Nagoya, one covering Osaka and the other hitting Kobe.[76]

The list of industrial and military targets hit in the raid was impressive. In Tokyo they hit Nippon Electric Corporation, Tokyo Gas and Electric Company, and an army arsenal. At Yokohama they bombed the Ogura Oil Company, the Kawasaki Dockyard Company Aircraft Works, and the Kawasaki Aircraft Company. In Nagoya they bombed the 3rd Division Military Headquarters, a Matsushige Oil storage site, the factory of the munitions firm Atsuta, and Mitsubishi Aircraft Works.[77]

The Army Air Force Action Intelligence Summary for the Tokyo Raid recorded the following combat details observed by each B-25 aircraft flight crew:

Plane 40-2242 (Capt. Edward J. York). This airplane, carrying 3 demolition and 1 incendiary bomb, had Tokyo as its target. Due to high gasoline consumption, it proceeded to Siberia, landing some 40 miles north of Vladivostok. The crews were interned and therefore no reliable reports are available. The turret of this plane was not operating when it started.

Plane 40-2247 (Lt. Edgar E. McElroy). Dropped 3 demolition and 1 incendiary bomb from 1,300 feet at 200 mph on the Yokosuka Navy Yard, the dock, and a partially completed boat. Destroyed everything on the dock and enveloped the boat in flames. A large crane was seen blown up and thirty miles away huge billows of black smoke could be seen rising from the target. Heavy A.A. of fair accuracy was encountered, but there was no pursuit.

Plane 40-2249 (Capt. Charles Ross Greening). Four incendiaries were dropped in train from 600 feet on a large oil refinery near Sakura, east of Tokyo. Primary target (Yokohama) not reached. A large explosion followed with several successive explosions which were felt by the crew. A large column of smoke was visible fifty miles away from the target. On the approach, four enemy fighters with in-line engines were encountered. They mounted six machine guns in the wings and appeared to have a ground speed of 260 mph. Two were reported shot down.

Plane 40-2250 (Lt. Richard Outcalt Joyce). To Tokyo—dropping from 2,400 feet and at 210 mph 2 demolition bombs on the Japanese Steel Company. One bomb fell in the center of the plant and one between two buildings. The third bomb was dropped on a thick industrial area in Shiba Ward, one-quarter mile in shore. The incendiary bomb was placed in the dense residential section near the primary target. A.A. was heavy and nine Zero fighters were evaded by increasing the plane speed to 330 mph in a dive.

Plane 40-2261 (Lt. Ted W. Lawson). At 1,400 feet, dropped 3 demolition bombs on factories in the Tokyo area. One hit was observed with smoke and flying debris. The incendiary was released over the densely settled residential area near the Palace. A.A. fire was intense while running over the targets. It appeared to be light flak with black bursts about the size of weather balloons. Six pursuit ships were observed but they did not close. Large fires and smoke were seen in the northeast part of the city—presumably in the area attacked by the Doolittle plane.

Plane 40-2267 (Lt. Donald G. Smith). Before reaching the coast of Japan picked up a radio station broadcasting a musical program. It continued over an hour and then suddenly went off the air. After ringing an alarm for forty-five seconds, a voice shouted three words. This took place about ten times before the station became silent. Made a landfall north of its course at 1350. Swung south across Tokyo and Nagoya Bays, which were observed filled with small fishing craft. Proceeded to Kobe where 4 incendiary clusters were dropped along the waterfront. The first fell in the area west of the Uyenoshita Steel Works; No. 2 on the Kawasaki Dock Yard; No. 3 in an area of small factories, machine shops and residences and the fourth on the Kawasaki Aircraft Factory. A.A. was light and two planes sighted (97's) were soon outdistanced. A large aircraft carrier was seen nearing completion and several new factories were observed east of Kobe.

Plane 40-2268 (Lt. William G. Farrow). No reliable report received.

Plane 40-2270 (Lt. Robert Manning Gray). Bombed Tokyo at 1,450 feet. The first bomb hit not observed. The second hit the gas works; the third, a chemical plant; the fourth, an incendiary, not seen. Machine-gunned barracks and men. On the approach, a burning oil tank was seen just west of the Ara Waterway. A.A. was of right altitude, but wrong deflection.

Plane 40-2278 (Lt. William M. Bower). To Yokohama at 1,100 feet and 200 mph. Dropped 1 demolition bomb on Ogura Refinery and the other two on nearby factories and warehouses. The incendiary was dropped on another factory area. Machine-gunned a power house. Several pursuits tailed the ship but did not attempt to close. A.A. from 37 or 40 mm was reported intense—of good altitude but a little late. A large fire was observed east of Tokyo. The original target was the Yokohama Dock Yards, but a balloon barrage prevented the attack being made as planned.

Plane 40-2282 (Lt. Everett W. Holstrom). Pilot decided to approach Tokyo from the south on the theory that the three preceding planes had stirred up enemy interceptors further north. As a result, pursuit planes were encountered heading in his direction, two of these attacked while still off the coast and tracer bullets were seen going over the pilot's compartment. Later, two more cut across the bow and appeared ready to peel off for an attack. At this point the bombs were salvoed from 75 feet and the plane turned down the coast. The guns were not operating.

Plane 40-2283 (Capt. David M. Jones). Flew up Tokyo Bay and dropped 1 demolition bomb from 1,200 feet on an oil tank south of the Palace. Another bomb hit a power plant or foundry, and the third, an incendiary, covered a large factory roughly two blocks long. It had a saw-toothed roof and resembled the North American Plant. The last target was overrun at 260 to 270 mph. Primary targets were not attacked because the approach had not been made as expected. No pursuit but intense A.A. was encountered after the first bomb was dropped.

Plane 40-2292 (Lt. Travis Hoover). Followed Doolittle's plane into Tokyo. Dropped 3 demolition bombs and 1 incendiary from 900 feet on the Army Arsenal. There is no information available as to whether this plant was used as a producer of munitions or merely for storage. Results of the bombing were not observed although debris flew higher than the plane. Training planes were seen in the distance but there was no near A.A.

Plane 40-2297 (Major John A. Hilger). To Nagoya. Dropped 4 incendiaries from 1,500 feet on four targets: Barracks adjacent to Nagoya Castle, Matsuhigecho Oil Storage, Atsuta Factory, which is reported capable of producing 500 planes a year, and the Mitsubishi Aircraft Works, which produces the "Zero" fighter. Hits were observed on all targets and a column of smoke was seen when 20 miles away. A.A. was heavy but poor, and only one plane was seen. Cities were drab and targets did not appear as expected.

Plane 40-2298 (Lt. Dean Edward Hallmark). No reliable report.

Plane 40-2303 (Lt. Harold Francis Watson). Target was the Tokyo Gas & Electric Company, which was bombed with 3 demolition and 1 incendiary dropped in train from 2,500 feet at 220 to 230 mph. (The target has also been reported as a Tank and Truck Factory.) One hit was observed. On the way in, about twenty 2-engined bombers were seen dispersed on a field and 15 or 20 pursuits were soon warming up on a ramp. One pursuit attacked from below but made only one pass. A.A. was intense. Fires were observed near the Electric Light Plant, radio station, the Japanese Steel Company's plant, and in the Doolittle target area.

Plane 40-2344 (Brigadier General James Harold Doolittle). On the approach to Japan, passed a camouflaged Naval vessel and saw a multi-motored land plane. Arrived north of Tokyo and turned south. Saw flying fields and many small biplanes in the air—apparently trainers. Ten miles north of Tokyo encountered 9 fighters in three flights of three. They maneuvered for attack but did not close. Proceeded to Tokyo and dropped 4 incendiaries in the congested areas northeast and southwest of the Armory. Then lowered to housetops and slid over the western outskirts into a low haze. A.A. was heavy and of good elevation but to the right and left. Rivers, canals, and railroads "stood out" but the highways did not.[78]

Tokyo Area Targets Hit:
1. Plane 40-2344—Armory Area
2. Plane 40-2292—Army Arsenal
3. Plane 40-2270—Steel, Gas, Chemical Works
4. Plane 40-2283—Oil Tank, Large Factory
5. Plane 40-2261—Factories, Residential Area
6. Plane 40-2303—Tokyo Gas & Electric Company
7. Plane 40-2250—Steel Works, Residential Area
8. Plane 40-2249—Sakaru Refinery & Tanks
9. Plane 40-2278—Ogura Refinery, Factories
10. Plane 40-2247—Dock Yard, Ship, Crane[79]

The overall Japanese defense as observed and experienced by the B-25 aircrews was totally inadequate. They were "entirely unprepared for the attack ... either their dissemination of information was faulty or the communication system had broken down completely."[80] The IJN had been already alerted back on April 10 by the radio intercept of a message sent between Halsey and Mitscher, as well as by the April 18 early morning contact with Task Force 16 initiated by the *No. 23 Nitto Maru*.

When the planes flew over the countryside, "farmers in the field looked up and went back to work undisturbed; villagers waved from the streets; a baseball game continued its play; and in the distance training planes took off and landed apparently unaware of any danger present." Some 20 Japanese twin-engine bombers were seen on airfields and a like number of fighters on the ramps warming up, but only a few actually attempted to intercept, and the ones that did were not "inclined to press home the attack." It seemed the pilots were inexperienced and inaccurate in their gunfire.[81]

The AA defense fire came from mostly 37mm or 40mm weapons, although the absence of tracers in some explosions indicated that larger caliber guns were firing. No AA fire was observed below 1,500 feet. Though it appeared the AA fire was at the proper altitude, it was always behind the bombers, which may have been caused by underestimating the speed of the B-25. Over Tokyo there were a few barrage balloon clusters of 5 or 6. It was obvious that any camouflage was inadequate to hide choice targets.

It seems incredible that an important city like Tokyo would have been so poorly defended. The air defense warning system essentially did not function. The fighter pilots were too cautious and lacking trained sufficiency. The AA fire was slow to respond and the lacked intensity.[82]

Doolittle's personal report from Chungking, China, on May 4, 1942, detailed the highlights of his flight to Tokyo and on to China:

> Take off at 8:20 A.M. ship time.
> Take-off was easy. Night take-off would have been possible and practicable.
> Circled carrier to get exact heading and check compass. Wind was from around 300°.
> About a half hour after take-off was joined by AC 40-2292, Lt. Hoover, pilot, the second plane to take off.
> About an hour out passed a Japanese camouflaged naval surface vessel of about 6,000 tons. Took it to be a light cruiser.
> About two hours out passed a multi-motored land plane headed directly for our flotilla and flying at about 3,000 ft.—2 miles away.

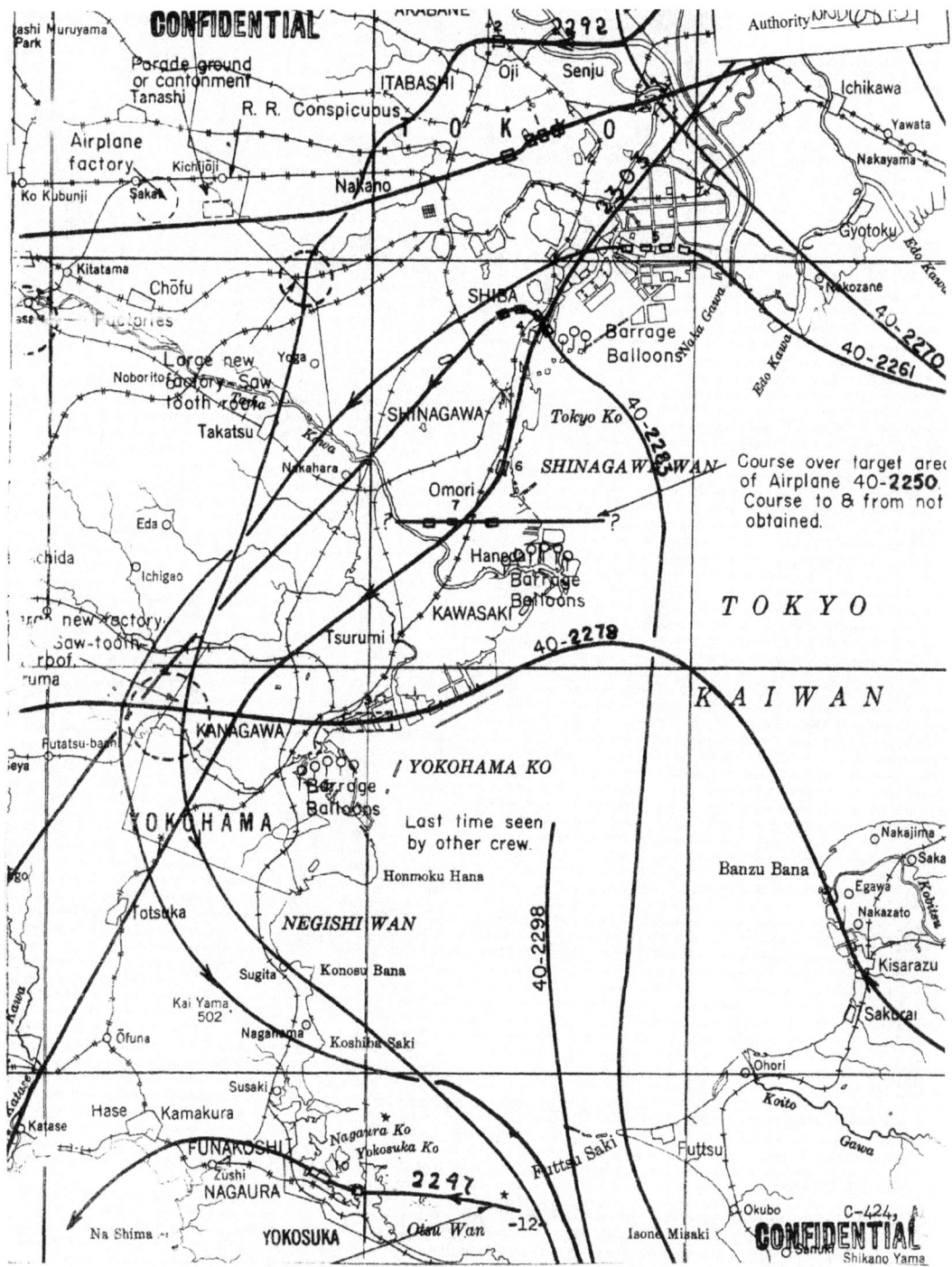

B-25 track map 12, Tokyo raid. U.S. Army Air Forces, Director of Intelligence Service, Informational Intelligence Summary (Special) No. 20, October 25, 1942. NARA College Park, Maryland.

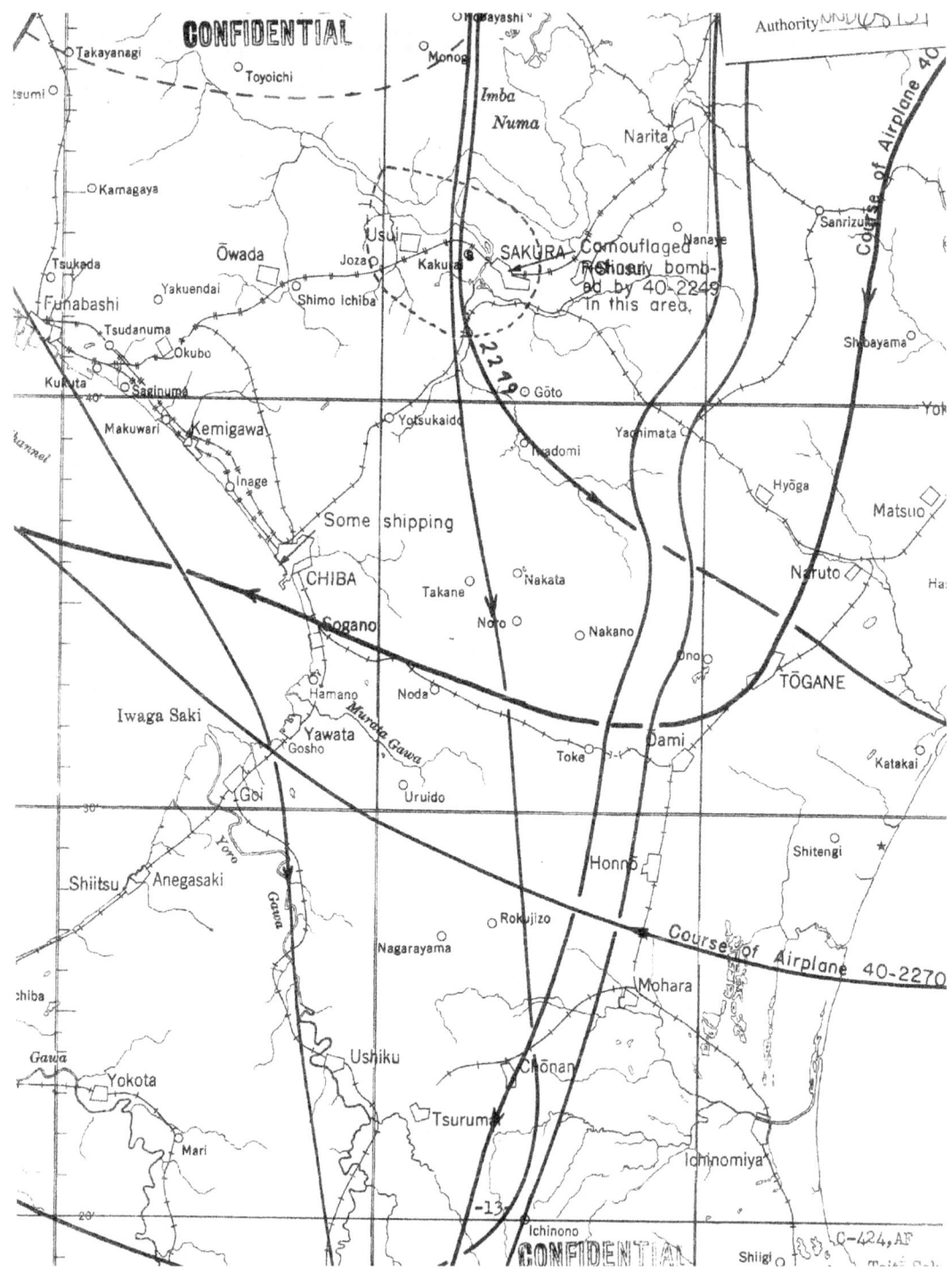

B-25 track map 13, Tokyo raid. U.S. Army Air Forces, Director of Intelligence Service, Informational Intelligence Summary (Special) No. 20, October 25, 1942. NARA College Park, Maryland.

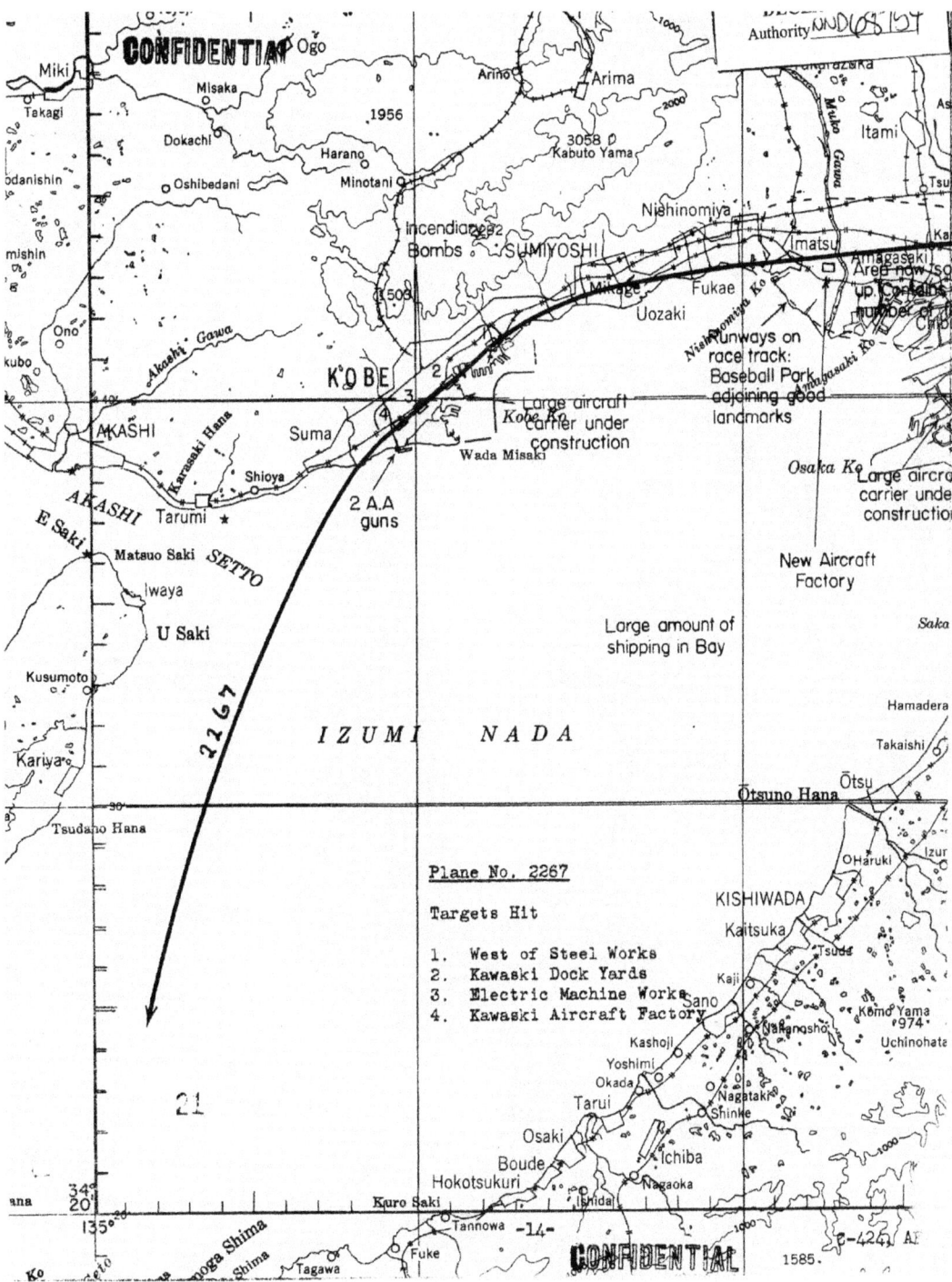

B-25 track map 14, Tokyo raid. U.S. Army Air Forces, Director of Intelligence Service, Informational Intelligence Summary (Special) No. 20, October 25, 1942. NARA College Park, Maryland.

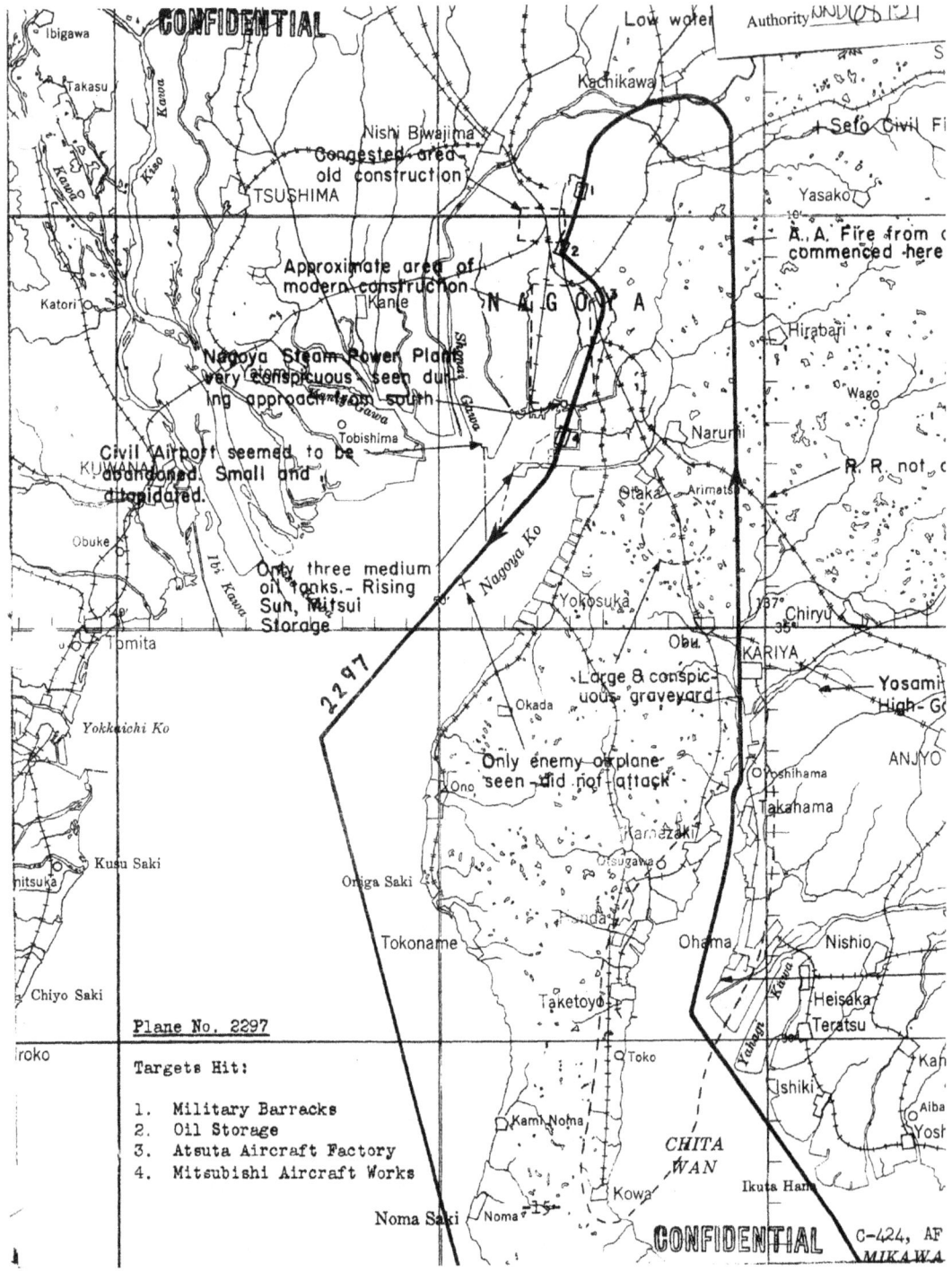

B-25 track map 15, Tokyo raid. U.S. Army Air Forces, Director of Intelligence Service, Informational Intelligence Summary (Special) No. 20, October 25, 1942. NARA College Park, Maryland.

Passed and endeavored to avoid various civil and naval craft until land fall was made north of Inubo Shuma. Was somewhat north of desired course but decided to take advantage of error and approach from a northerly direction, thus avoiding anticipated strong opposition to the west. Many flying fields and the air full of planes north of Tokyo. Mostly small biplanes apparently primary or basic trainers.

Encountered nine fighters in three flights of three. This was about ten miles north of the outskirts of Tokyo proper. All this time had been flying as low as the terrain would permit. Continued low flying due south over the outskirts of and toward the east center of Tokyo.

Pulled up to 1,200 ft., changed course to the southwest and incendiary-bombed highly inflammable section. Dropped first bomb at 1:30 (ship time).

Anti-aircraft very active but only one near hit. Lowered away to housetops and slid over western outskirts into low haze and smoke.

Turned south and out to sea. Fewer airports on west side but many army posts.... Passed over small aircraft factory with a dozen or more newly completed planes on the line. No bombs left. Decided not to machine gun for reasons of personal security. Had seen five barrage balloons over east central Tokyo and what appeared to be more in the distance.

Passed on out to sea flying low. Was soon joined again by Hoover who followed us to the Chinese coast. Navigator plotted perfect course to pass north of Yaki Shima.

Saw three large naval vessels just before passing west end of Japan. One was flatter than the others and may have been a converted carrier. Passed innumerable fishing and small patrol boats.

Made land fall somewhat north of course on China coast. Tried to reach Chuchow on 4495 but couldn't raise. It had been clear over Tokyo but became overcast before reaching Yaki Shima.

Ceiling lowered on coast until low islands and hills were in it at about 600'. Just getting dark and couldn't live under overcast so pulled up to 6,000 and then 8,000 ft. in it. On instruments from then on though occasionally saw dim lights on ground through almost solid overcast. These lights seemed more often on our right and pulled us still farther off course.

Directed rear gunner to go aft and secure films from camera (unfortunately they were jerked out of his shirt front where he had put them, when his chute opened.)

Decided to abandon ship. Sgt. Braemer, Lt. Potter, Sgt. Leonard and Lt. Cole jumped in order. Left ship on A.F.C.E., shut off both gas cocks and I left. Should have put flaps down. This would have slowed down landing speed, reduced impact and shortened glide.

All hands collected and ship located by late afternoon of 19th.

Requested General Ho Yang Ling, Director of the Branch Government of Western Chekiang Province to have a lookout kept along the seacoast from Hang Chow bay to Wen Chow bay and also have all sampans and junks along the coast keep a lookout for planes that went down at sea, or just reached shore.

Early morning of 20th four planes and crews, in addition to ours, had been located and I wired General Arnold, through the Embassy at Chungking, "Tokyo successfully bombed. Due bad weather on China Coast believe all airplanes wrecked. Five crews found safe in China so far." Wired again on the 27th giving more details.

Bad luck:
(1) Early take-off due to naval contact with surface and aircraft.
(2) Clear over Tokyo.
(3) Foul over China.
Good luck:
(1) A 25 m/h tail wind over most of the last 1,200 miles.

Take-off should have been made three hours before daylight, but we didn't know how easy it would be and the Navy didn't want to light up.

Dawn take-off, closer in, would have been better as things turned out. However, due to the bad weather it is questionable if even daylight landing could have been made at Chuchow without radio aid.

Still feel that original plan of having one plane take off three hours before dusk and others just at dusk was best all-around plan for average conditions.

Should have kept accurate chronological record.

Should have all crew members instructed in exact method of leaving ship under various conditions.

J.H. DOOLITTLE
Airplane AC 40-2344-B-25B[83]

Doolittle's flight had lasted 13 hours, covering 2,250 miles.

Of the sixteen flight crews, fifteen made China with the unexpected tail wind. Four of the China flight crews ditched in the East China Sea in Chekiang Province and the other eleven crews bailed out in the interior of China in the darkness when their fuel ran out.

There were casualties from the raid. Corporal Leland D. Faktor was found dead from a secondary fall on his parachute landing from Lieutenant Gray's plane. Crewmembers from Lieutenant Hallmark's and Lieutenant Farrow's B-25s were captured by the Japanese, having bailed out over occupied China. Two of the crewmembers had drowned, and the other eight were taken to occupied Shanghai, and later to Tokyo. They were interrogated and tortured to gain their confessions that they had attacked civilian targets. On June 18 they were transferred back to Shanghai to Kiangwan Prison to await trial.

The Japanese trial began on August 28. The Americans, who were never told their charges, were not allowed to speak in their defense and their signed confessions were all it took to get them all death sentences. In fact, only Hallmark, Farrow, and Sergeant Harold Spatz were executed at 1630 on October 15, 1942. They were taken by truck to Public Cemetery Number 1 outside of Shanghai. The Americans were marched by prison guards to three small wooden crosses placed twenty feet apart. They were forced to kneel with their backs against the crosses as the guards removed the handcuffs and tied the prisoners' wrists to the cross-pieces. "They wrapped the upper portions of the men's faces with white cloth, marking black 'X's just above the noses. A six-man firing squad took positions twenty feet in front of the Americans. At the count, they pulled the triggers." The next day the other five crewmembers were given life imprisonment. In April 1943 they were moved to Nanking, where 2nd Lieutenant Robert J. Meder died of malnutrition on that December 1. The remaining four men survived the three years of brutal treatment at the hands of the Japanese.[84]

With early fuel problems during the attack and unable to make China, Captain Edward "Ski" York's crew flew north and landed at a location in the Primorsky Province, 25 miles north of Vladivostok in the USSR. Twelve Soviets dressed in long black coats inspected the plane on landing, and as soon as they learned the crew were Americans, treated them well. The crew did not disclose their mission, but later it was discovered. American diplomats were unable to gain the release of the crew, even though the U.S. and USSR were allies, because Stalin wanted to remain neutral with Japan. So York's crew was interned at a cost charged to the U.S. of 30,000 rubles per month. They were moved to Okuna, 300 miles south of Moscow, then to Okhansk on the western edge of Siberia. In late May they were moved to Ashkhabad in central Asia, where York bribed a guard for $250, who smuggled them across the Iranian border. The crew was able to find a British consulate and they were offered sanctuary.[85]

The final death toll from Doolittle's raid was 7 dead, but 73 crewmembers ultimately returned home. Sadly, the real tragedy and loss was with those Chinese people who assisted the Doolittle raiders. The Japanese military began the Zhejiang-Jiangxi Campaign to intimidate the Chinese from helping downed American airmen. The Japanese killed an incredible number of civilians while searching for Doolittle's men. General Claire Chennault reported, "Entire villages through which the raiders had passed were slaughtered to the last child.... A quarter million Chinese soldiers and civilians were killed in the three-month campaign."[86]

Having lost all 16 of his aircraft in the raid on Japan, Doolittle expected to be court-martialed. Instead, he was awarded the Medal of Honor by President Roosevelt and was promoted two grades to brigadier general. During the following 3 years, Doolittle was to command the 12th Air Force in North Africa, the 15th Air Force in the Mediterranean, and the 8th Air Force in England.

All the 80 raider flight crewmembers were awarded the Distinguished Flying Cross, and those killed, wounded, or injured also received the Purple Heart. Corporal David J. Thatcher, the flight engineer/gunner on Lawson's crew, and 1st Lieutenant Thomas R. White, who was the flight surgeon/gunner with Lieutenant Smith, received the Silver Star for helping the wounded crewmembers of Lawson's crew evade Japanese troops in China. On May 1, 1942, in Chungking, Doolittle and the men present were awarded the Chinese Medal of Honor for Meritorious Service by Madame Chiang Kai-shek.[87]

Halsey's Task Force 16 continued to retire eastward on April 18, passing through the line of picket vessels of the IJN 5th Fleet, and avoiding the enemy ships and patrol planes tasked to find them. At 1214 the radar from the *Enterprise* picked up an unidentified plane at bearing 020°T, distance 70,000 yards. It came within 64,000 yards but passed off the screen at 1228. At 1347 an unidentified aircraft was reported by radar closing at bearing 020°, distance 60,000 yards. Fighters picked up the plane and it was identified as friendly.

At 1400 two Japanese patrol vessels bearing 031° from the *Enterprise* were sighted by Dauntless bombers returning home from patrol. The planes sank one of the ships but caused only minor damage to the other. The enemy ship was sighted by the *Nashville* bearing 350° range 10,700 yards. At 1413 the *Nashville* was ordered to sink her. The ship's crew was thought to have displayed a white flag, but the report was incorrect. At 1422 the *Nashville* opened fire on the 90-foot wooden vessel from its main battery, and then with the 5-inch battery. At 1440 they prepared to take on five survivors. "All but one was uninjured and suffered only from shock and immersion."[88] The *Nashville* sank the Japanese patrol craft at 1446 after firing an incredible 167 rounds.

During a divebombing attack at 1503, Lieutenant L.A. Smith from Bombing Six crashed into the sea from engine failure caused by machine-gun fire from the patrol vessel also being engaged by the *Nashville*. At 1517 the flight crew was recovered by the *Nashville*, and the cruiser maneuvered to rejoin the formation.[89]

Back at 1425 the *Enterprise* changed course to 315°T, and five minutes later the fourth inner air patrol and *Hornet* transfer group were launched. The *Hornet* transfer group of 6 scout bombers (located on the *Enterprise*) were directed to attack the patrol vessel that was being engaged by the *Nashville*, and then land aboard the *Hornet*, but once the vessel was sunk, the mission was canceled. The third inner patrol, the combat patrol with special search, and regular search groups were landed at 1444 aboard the *Enterprise*. At 1739 all Task Force 16 aircraft had been recovered aboard the two carriers. That day had seen the IJN lose 5 picket patrol boats, having traded for one American SBD.[90]

The first news of the Tokyo raid was picked up by the task force at 1445 on English-language radio: "Enemy bombers appeared over Tokyo today shortly after noon for the first time in the current East Asia War. Heavy and telling damage was inflicted on schools and hospitals, and the population shows indignation." Curiously, the Japanese language newscast of the raid gave more detail: "A large fleet of heavy bombers appeared over Tokyo this noon and caused much damage to non-military objectives and some damage to factories. The known death toll is between three and four thousand so far. No planes were reported shot down over Tokyo. Osaka was also bombed. Tokyo reports several large fires burning." The news of the Tokyo raid brought cheers throughout the task force ships as they sailed to Pearl Harbor.[91]

The next morning, Saturday, April 19, the task force was steaming on course 090° speed 25 knots, located some 1,350 miles east of Tokyo and 1,000 miles north of Wake Island. The guide ship was the *Enterprise*, followed by the *Hornet* in column astern, with the cruisers screening the carriers. It was to be a "rough, rainy, and cold day." At 0526 the inner air patrol was launched with 6 fighters; all day followed other patrols, each with 6 fighters. The scouting flight of 13 scout bombers was launched to search sector 195° to 330° out to 200 miles. The afternoon scout search consisted of 10 scout bombers on sector search 225° to 280° to 100 miles and another search sector 135° to 225° out 175 miles.

The lookouts on the *Enterprise* saw the tops of the masts of their destroyers on the horizon at 0558 bearing 043°T out 25,000 yards. With them were the two oilers, less the destroyer *Monssen*, which had been designated to escort Task Group 16.4 (Desron Six). This was a welcome sight that reduced the submarine threat somewhat. At 0607 formation set with *Hornet* as guide ship in the center axis, course 090°T, speed 20 knots. "The seas were so heavy that 3 planes were seriously damaged during the landing operations." At 1434 as the third inner air patrol was landing on the deck of the *Enterprise*, the pitching deck dropped out from underneath Walter Hiebert's F4F-3 and his plane floated into the barrier with nose up and landed hard on the deck. The fighter required a major overhaul. At dusk there was more trouble as Frank Quady's F4F came in low as the deck rose up, causing him to swerve and end up with his left wheel in the port catwalk. AMM1c Howard Packard's F4F caught the last wire but was slammed into the barrier, damaging his propeller. Packard had more landing trouble that day. His F4F "got a little high at the ramp and ducked too hard," as he nosed downed steeply after the LSO gave his cut signal. Packard overreacted by pulling down his tail, landing hard and crumpling his left landing gear. The last inner air patrol and afternoon scouting flights landed at 1815.[92]

Back at 1400 the officers and men on the signal bridge of the *Enterprise* sighted what appeared to be a periscope. Flag Lieutenant Ashford signaled the task force of the location of the object, as a cruiser headed toward the object at full speed. *Enterprise* Captain Miles Browning leaped out of his cabin bunk and came to the bridge in a tirade. He ordered a cease fire to the cruiser and chewed out Lieutenant Ashford, which did not end until Halsey entered the bridge. Ashford defended what he saw and recommended that the scheduled fueling operation to be delayed until after nightfall after changing course 90 degrees. Halsey directed Ashford to execute his recommendation over Captain Browning's objections. The captain stormed off below to sulk. Browning's tirade was not unusual, as he was described by the historian Samuel Eliot Morrison as "one of the most irascible and unstable officers ever to earn a fourth stripe, but a man with a slide-rule brain."[93]

The fueling had gone off well that evening. The next day, April 20, a sailor brought Ashford a photograph of the controversial object, taken from the flight deck the previous day. It was indeed a periscope. Ashford showed it to Halsey. Later that day Ashford recalled that Browning appeared at his cabin door and said that Halsey had asked him to apologize for things he had said. Browning said "he had never apologized to anyone in his life and proceeded to talk for about twenty minutes, giving reasons why he should not apologize." Ashford finally shut off the conversation by saying, "I accept your apology." That ended it.[94]

That morning at 0540 the first inner patrol was launched with 6 fighters, followed six minutes later by the launch of 12 scout bombers to search sector 135° to 225° to 200 miles, and sector 243° to 280° to 100 miles. No contacts reported. At dusk the task force was 700 miles northwest of Midway.

On April 21 the task force was steaming course 090° T speed 14 knots. At 0633 the *Enterprise* sighted 3 ships in formation on the horizon bearing 129°T, distance 15 miles. They were identified as the fleet oilers *Cimarron* and *Sabine* and the destroyer *Monssen*. The three ships fell into their slots in Task Force 16's 7V cruising formation at 0758.

The *Enterprise* was the duty carrier that day at 0848 when all planes had completed their landings, except a VB-8 SBD plane 6-B-2 that was missing. *Hornet* pilot Lieutenant G.D. Randall with crewman RM2c T.A. Gallagher were lost as the *Enterprise* attempted to direct the pilot to various courses back to the task force. The plane did not close the formation until 1100. The destroyer *Meredith* was directed to meet the plane, but the plane was out of gasoline and ditched in the sea at 1110 some 100 yards from the destroyer. Unfortunately, the SBD-3 sank in 30 seconds and both the crewmembers were lost.[95]

The task force crossed the International Date Line at 2000 and moved from Monday, April 20, to Tuesday, April 21, located 470 miles northeast of Midway and 1,200 miles from Oahu. The task force continued on course toward Pearl Harbor. Finally, at dawn on Saturday, April 25, Halsey's Task Force 16 neared Pearl Harbor in clear weather. A little while later the carrier planes flew to their assigned Oahu airfields. Air Group 8 flew to Ewa Air Station near Barber's Point. Around 1100 the task force ships entered the anchorage with little fanfare. The *Enterprise* moored off Ford Island at 1118 at berth F-2 and the *Hornet* moored at F-9. This time there were no cheers as no one knew of the carriers' role in the Doolittle Raid over Japan. Doolittle was America's first real hero of the new war. For Halsey, there was only the suffering from dermatitis that had now spread to his entire body. The oatmeal baths gave him only temporary relief. Halsey was looking forward to some time off to recover, as were his men. As it turned out, Task Force 16 was given only five days before heading off to the Coral Sea.[96]

Halsey sent the following dispatch to all the ships of Task Force 16: "Recent operation well done by all hands. Ships of former Task Force 18 took their places and carried on smoothly and efficiently. They are a welcome and valuable addition."[97]

The purpose of the raid on Japan, as stated in the Army Air Forces Intelligence Summary (Special) No. 20 of October 5, 1942, had been to "inflict both material and psychological damage on the enemy." The report went on to explain that "it was expected that material damage and the retarding of production could be obtained by the destruction of specific targets in the industrial centers of Japan. It was hoped also that it would result in the recalling for home defense of combat equipment from areas then under pressure. It was anticipated that a fear complex among the Japanese people would follow a successful bombing attack ... that it would improve relations with our Allies and create a favorable reaction on the American public."[98]

The U.S. Army Air Force conclusions regarding the Tokyo Raid were reported in October 1942 as follows:

> Sixteen B-25's made the flight to Japan. From the pilots or crew members of thirteen of these planes have come reports from which a reasonable estimation of the execution and success of the mission may be made.
>
>   The preparation was thorough. The flight was well executed and, in most cases, primary targets were reached, hits were made at low altitudes, and explosions, followed by smoke and fires, were observed by several ships as they passed over the area.

The magnitude of the destruction and the effect on Japanese morale may not be evaluated from the few rumors that have come out of the enemy's country. Had it been known beforehand how complete was going to be the surprise and how weak the resistance, it would have been possible to concentrate all planes on such a target as the Mitsubishi Aircraft Factory.

The reaction on our Allies and the American public was essentially favorable. Any encouragement, however, accruing to the Chinese must have been tempered by the fact that immediately following the raid the Japanese initiated a severe attack on those areas in China which they suspected had been used in the project.

The important lesson of this raid may be that no country should be without home defenses and an adequate system of communication and detection always on the alert.[99]

The Doolittle Raid had caused limited material damage to Japan, but the morale of the American people now soared with Roosevelt's press announcement back on April 21 that the attack had come from "our new secret base at Shangri-La." The newspapers gave the raid extra-edition status with headlines like that of the *Los Angeles Times*, "Doolittle Did It." The *New York Times* reported, "Japan Reports Tokyo, Yokohama Bombed by 'Enemy Planes' in Daylight." The *Columbus Evening Dispatch* declared, "U.S. Warplanes Rain Bombs on Leading Cities of Jap Empire." In Nome, Alaska, where young Doolittle had once delivered papers, the headline in large typeface read, "Nome Town Boy Makes Good."[100]

America's honor had been restored from the effects of Pearl Harbor. Halsey declared the raid to be "one of the most courageous deeds in all military history," and certainly the public opinion agreed with him. A French journalist in Tokyo recalled that he had rushed outside: "I heard a rugged, powerful sound of airplane engines. A raid at high noon! Explosions. I spotted a dark airplane traveling very fast, at rooftop level. So they've come!" Halsey also noted in his endorsement of the *Hornet*'s report of the raid the following: "The Task Force Commander considers that the successful transportation and launching of the Army bombers under the continuous adverse weather conditions which prevailed reflects great credit to the Commanding Officer, *Hornet*, Lt. Col. Doolittle, and the Army personnel involved."[101]

The CINCPAC report dated May 4, 1942, of the action in connection with the bombing of Tokyo on April 18, 1942, reported these excerpts:

> It is with a satisfaction to know that from actual experience 16 planes can be flown from the deck of a Hornet plane carrier, and further that these planes can be carried in addition to 65 of the regular allowance of 72 planes.
>
> The presence of so many small craft in a relatively small area of operations considerably distant from shore must be borne in mind in planning future operations against important enemy objectives. In addition to the Radar contact with two craft at 0310, actual contact show one submarine, 14 PY's and 3 AK's concentrated in an area about 130 miles by 180 miles. A similar concentration was reported by a submarine just returned from patrol in the east China sea which stated that 65 sampans had been sighted on the 18th day of patrol in an area just about same size as that mentioned above. These are indications of the degree to which the Japanese are using small craft for patrols and screens around their vital area. There is no indication that these sampans are equipped with Radar. They do, however, carry radio and in spite of their vulnerability, can be considered as useful distance screens, which fact must be weighed carefully in considering any future operations in that area....
>
> The excessive expenditure of ammunition by the NASHVILLE to sink two patrol craft has been taken up direct with the CO of that ship.
>
> The Commander in Chief, U.S. Pacific Fleet, commends the COMTASKFOR 16 (Vice-Admiral W.F. Halsey, USN), and the Commander Army Group (Lt. Col. James Doolittle, USA), and the participating officers and men of the Army and Navy on the successful accomplishment of the mission.[102]

In the diary of the U.S. Ambassador to Japan, Joseph C. Grew, for April 18, he wrote of that day while he was under loose restriction in Tokyo: "The Swiss Minister came again, and just as he was leaving before lunch we heard a lot of planes overhead and saw five or six large fires in different directions with great volumes of smoke. At first we thought it was only maneuvers but soon became aware that it was the first big raid on Japan by American bombers.... We saw one of them, apparently losing altitude and flying very low, just over the tops of the buildings to the west.... All this was exciting.... We were all very happy and proud in the Embassy, and the British told us they drank toasts all day to the American flyers."[103]

For the Japanese it was a severe psychological blow. A commercial attaché, Ramon M. Lavelle, at the Argentine Embassy in Tokyo had observed the raid from the roof and said, "That raid by Doolittle was one of the greatest psychological tricks ever used. It caught the Japs by surprise. Their unbounded confidence began to crack. The day after the raid, the Tokyo newspapers said nine American planes had been shot down.... The people knew it was a lie. The officer in charge of the Japanese antiaircraft defenses was compelled to commit suicide."[104]

The confidence in their leaders had been shattered. Toshiko Matsumura, who was age 13 at the time of the bombing and living outside Tokyo, recalled her parents speaking in hushed voices after the raid. She explained, "My people had always placed emphasis on spiritual strength and the medieval belief that Japan would never be attacked. As children we had been taught to believe what the emperor and his advisors told us. It was a severe psychological shock ... when it was announced that we had been attacked.... We then began to doubt that we were invincible."[105]

The Japanese leadership tried to counter the impact of the bombing by describing the act in inhuman terms. Though there may have been some collateral damage to civilian targets, the Japanese government listed the civilian targets as "six wards of the Nagoya Second Temporary Army Hospital, six elementary or secondary schools, and innumerable nonmilitary residences." Such a story was published on April 19 in the *Ashi Shimbun* about a 14-year old boy, Hinosuke Ishibe, who was entering his school classroom as the enemy bomber fired ten rounds into the schoolyard. One of the rounds entered the corridor window and hit the young man in the right thigh. "At 2:00 P.M. the same day he breathed his last in the arms of his teacher."[106]

For the Japanese military leaders, the raid was a shameful embarrassment. Vice Admiral Matome Ugaki, the Chief of Staff of the Combined Fleet headquarters in Tokyo, began to receive reports at lunch on April 18 of an enemy attack. Ugaki recalled his actions that day:

> I repeatedly ordered the Third Submarine Fleet, which was located two hundred miles west of the enemy aircraft carriers, to attack but no units came in contact with the enemy, and in spite of the fact that our primary purpose was to catch the enemy, the enemy's position was unknown. I did not know what was happening, and all I could do was order a pursuit to the east. Today I was very irritated when the sun went down at 1700; at 1600 I received a message from the Kirarazu unit that had departed to attack. It stated that the unit had gone several hundred nautical miles without finding a trace of the enemy. According to later reports the attack planes were twin-engine long distance bombers, which took off from aircraft carriers, bombed nine places in Tokyo, and dropped incendiary bombs. Casualties were twelve dead and more than one hundred wounded. Fifty houses were burned down, fifty were half destroyed. Kobe, Wakayama, and Nagoya were bombed and it is reported that one plane bombed the Nitsu oil wells in Niigata. The bow of a large whaling vessel that was at anchor at Yokosuka sustained come damage. Apparently, there were more than a few planes, and it is not clear whether they returned

to their mother ship, headed toward Siberia or China, or contacted a Soviet vessel that was sailing twenty nautical miles south of Ashizurizaki. However, the enemy aircraft carrier seems to have pulled back to the east, and it is regrettable that I missed my chance three or four times. It had always been my motto not to allow Tokyo or the homeland to be attacked from the air, but today my pride has been deeply hurt and my spirits are low as today I gave the enemy his glory.[107]

On the 19th Ugaki received additional news about 13 American bombers reaching China in Chung-shui. He was concerned that these aircraft might return to hit Japan again, but acknowledged that "sufficient measures had to be taken ... after lunch I ordered my staff to solve the riddle of the American planes." He ordered the Second and Fifth Fleets and all the available planes to chase the American task force, but soon declared, "I am at the end of my resources. The enemy casts an eye of contempt at the clamoring Japanese. Thus we were invaded, but missed our chance to fight back; this is most regrettable."[108]

The Japanese military was forced to divert resources to provide better defense of the homeland. The IJN increased reconnaissance patrols while the Japanese Army Air Force moved four fighter air groups with their 250 planes to defend Japan against bomber attack. Captain Toshikazu Ohmae of the IJN Bureau of Military Affairs disclosed in his postwar interrogation that the Tokyo Raid, "though in itself not very destructive, caused considerable discussion and confirmed the need for eastward expansion to acquire bases to protect the home island, the mainland."[109]

The Tokyo Raid was unquestionably an incredible strategic victory that fascinated and invigorated the American people, giving them reason to believe that there was real hope for a victory over the Japanese. Over the years many have called the results of the surprise attack a strategic victory, but the key fact is that the event did not prevent, or even slow up, the planned Japanese strategic advances to take more territory in Asia and in the western Pacific. The Japanese aim was "subjugation of the Philippines and the capture of the immense natural resources of the Netherlands East Indies and Malaya ... and to capture other strategic areas where they could establish advance posts and raise an outer barrier [including the Aleutians, Midway, Fiji and Samoa, New Britain, eastern New Guinea, points in the Australian area, and the Andaman Islands] against an Allied counteroffensive."[110]

The Tokyo Raid did have a direct impact on what would be the strategic turning point in the Pacific War at Midway. With the success at Pearl Harbor, on December 9, 1941, Admiral Yamamoto ordered his chief of staff, Rear Admiral Matome Ugaki, to draw up a plan for an invasion of Hawaii. According to Yamamoto's operations officer, Captain Kameto Kuroshima, Yamamoto proposed to use the capture of Hawaii as a bargaining chip to draw the United States into peace talks. The plan was that Midway Atoll was to be a staging point, and after seizing Midway Atoll and destroying the carriers of the U.S. Pacific Fleet, they would capture Johnston Island, then use Japanese land-based bombers to attack and ultimately seize Pearl Harbor.

Between April 2 and 5, the Midway/Hawaii Plan was reviewed by the Operational Section of Japan's Navy General Staff. It was opposed by two officers of the Operations' Plans Division, Captain Sadatoshi Tomioka and his air expert, Commander Tatsukichi Miyo. These two officers argued that the proposed "decisive action" between the Japanese and American fleets should occur in the Southwest Pacific, where their warships could by supported by land-based bombers, while the American ships would be far from their base at Pearl Harbor. Commander Yasuji Watanabe, Admiral Yamamoto's operations officer during the first half of 1942 and the man who had submitted the plan to the Navy General Staff, engaged in a significant confrontation with Commander Miyo. That argument led to the famous threat by Yamamoto to resign if his Midway/Hawaii plan was not accepted. Reluctantly, the Chief of the Navy General Staff, Admiral Nagano, accepted the plan on April 5.[111]

On April 12 an edited version of the Midway/Hawaii Plan was submitted by Captain Sadatoshi Tomioka, chief of the Plans Division of the Navy General Staff, to the Japanese Army general staff, Major General Shin'ichi Tanaka. Tanaka had shown consistent opposition to any further extension of Japan's eastern defensive perimeter, and specifically opposed the plan on the grounds that the logistical and operational problems were overwhelming, and the army could not spare the three divisions deemed necessary to capture Hawaii.

Despite Major General Tanaka's opposition, Captain Tomioka prepared a report titled "Imperial Navy Operational Plans for Stage Two of the Greater East Asia War." The report called for the Pacific to be given the highest priority and that "Midway should be seized and the U.S. Pacific Fleet destroyed; Midway would be captured and garrisoned by Imperial Navy marines. Achievement of these objectives would signal the end of revised Stage Two. In Stage Three, Johnston and Palmyra Islands would be occupied. The invasion of Hawaii would take place in Stage Four."[112]

On April 16, 1942, the Midway/Hawaii plan was submitted to Emperor Hirohito by Admiral Osami Nagano. The expectation was that the chief of Army General Staff, General Sugiyama, would object vehemently to the report. But the resistance never came as a result of the Tokyo Raid on April 18. Once Doolittle's pilots disclosed that the carrier-launched attack originated from Hawaii, the Imperial Army changed its attitude. On April 19 Major General Tanaka informed Captain Tomioka that the Imperial Army had changed its mind about expanding the Pacific perimeters. The army would provide troops for the Midway and Aleutian offensives.[113]

On May 5 the Imperial General Headquarters issued Navy Order Number 18 allowing Yamamoto to "carry out the occupation of Midway Island and key points in the western Aleutians in corporation with the Army."[114] Code named Operation MI, Yamamoto's plan forced the delay in moving aggressively south to Australia until the threat of American carriers could be eliminated in the central Pacific.

The Army also took specific actions to provide training for certain army units for an assault on the Hawaiian Islands (Imperial General Headquarters order issued May 23), and on June 3, 1942, Major General Tanaka instructed his subordinates in the Operations Section of Army General Staff to prepare a feasibility study for an assault on Oahu. The June 5 Japanese disaster at Midway, with the loss of four front-line carriers, put an end to the Eastern Operation, and on June 8, 1942, all training for the proposed Hawaii invasion was canceled.[115]

The Battle of Midway was to become the turning point in the Pacific War, and the beginning of the end for the Japanese threat. Thus, as fate would have it, the Tokyo Raid did remove all opposition to the Midway attack, yielding a most dramatic strategic impact upon the Pacific War.

Richard E. "Dick" Cole, the last surviving member of Doolittle's Raiders and copilot to Jimmy Doolittle, died April 9, 2019, at Brooke Army Medical Center in San Antonio at age 103.

Chapter 7

Aftermath

"...we left our mark on a cruel and treacherous enemy."
—Admiral William F. Halsey

The U.S. Navy Pacific carrier raids in early 1942 represented a transitional period from peaceful operations to an all-out war. With limited war resources available to the fleet because the major rearmament program had not begun until 1939, in addition to the imposed British-American policy of Germany first, the only realistic offensive option was to conduct carrier raids in an effort to slow the advance of the Japanese in the Pacific.

Nimitz had been given three strategic directives from Admiral King on December 31, 1941, as he assumed his duties as CINCPAC. They were (1) to defend vital military areas, (2) to halt the Japanese advances, and (3) to keep the lines of communication with Australia open. As for defending vital military areas, the carrier raids generally kept the action to the west and away from Hawaii and the West coast of the U.S. The five carrier raids unfortunately had quite limited effect on halting the Japanese advances. The collective effect of the raids did manage to keep the lines of communications open to Australia.

The carrier raid with the most strategic impact was the unorthodox Doolittle Raid on Japan. That raid, without question, altered the course of the war in the Pacific. The day after the Tokyo Raid, all opposition from the Chief of Army General Staff, General Sugiyama, and from others in the Imperial Japanese Army and Navy to Yamamoto's Midway/Hawaii Plan to aggressively seize central Pacific U.S. possessions had quickly disappeared. Two weeks after the Doolittle Raid on May 5, 1942, Nagamo approved the attack on Midway Island with Navy Order Number 18, authorizing Yamamoto to "carry out the occupation of Midway Island...."[1] Aided by cryptanalysis of the Japanese JN-25 code from Commander Joseph J. Rochefort and his team at Station Hypo, Nimitz knew the date, location and complete IJN order of battle of the planned Japanese attack on Midway. CINCPAC sent his *Yorktown* and *Enterprise* carrier task forces to ambush the Japanese.

The Battle of Midway on June 4–7, 1942, was the most important naval battle of the Pacific War and was called "the most stunning and decisive blow in the history of naval warfare."[2] The Japanese losses were four front-line strike carriers, one cruiser, 248 carrier planes, and 3,057 men. The American losses were the *Yorktown*, one destroyer, 150 planes, and 307 men killed. After Midway, the Japanese Navy was unable to keep pace with pilot training and shipbuilding programs to replace their losses, even as the U.S. steadily increased output.[3] Clearly, the Battle of Midway was the turning point in the Pacific War, and the beginning of the end for the Japanese threat.

Though the Japanese carrier attack on Pearl Harbor had ironically proven the case for the carrier task force from the outset, the early U.S. Pacific carrier raids continued to enhance the status of the aircraft carrier as the center of naval power. Nimitz, through his carrier admirals, had proven that carriers could indeed successfully project power against fixed land-based air forces. Halsey's Marshalls Raid with Task Force 8 was the first offensive combat operation by U.S. carriers ever. The Rabaul Raid, which turned into a defensive operation to protect the carrier *Lexington*, saw the American carrier aircraft shoot down 19 of the 20 attacking Japanese planes. The carrier was certainly not invincible, but it had proven its case.

Without question the Pacific carrier raids yielded numerous and valuable operational lessons for the U.S. Navy carrier forces. The Marshall and Gilbert Islands Raid had proved that having two carrier task forces working in proximity could spell success. Further refining the practice, the Lae-Salamaua Raid was the first time in history that two U.S. carrier groups operated together in a totally coordinated attack. As the war progressed, the U.S Navy would adopt this multi-carrier tactic as standard doctrine.[4]

With advanced CXAM radar and improved techniques using the Combat Information Center (CIC), the carrier was able to enhance the management of its combat environment. New fighter tactics were identified during the early raids, including the use of radar to guide pilots to their designated targets, especially in poor weather conditions. This practice was developed with the guidance of the new role of a fighter director officer (FDO) aboard carriers. Combat experience refined all manner of fighter and bomber tactics. Successful combat attack maneuvers were shared with fellow pilots and reported up the chain in action reports to other like commands.

In the realm of detailed carrier operations during of the early carrier raids, the most serious issues that were raised and specified in the action report recommendations of senior naval officers centered on aircraft and their associated equipment. These issues were:

(a) Lack of installed IFF (Identification Friend or Foe) gear.
(b) Lack of installed self-sealing fuel tanks.
(c) Lack of armored pilot seats.
(d) Inadequate number of F4F fighter aircraft aboard carriers to handle all the various required missions.
(e) Insufficient number of qualified VF pilots in reserve to conduct missions.
(f) Fogging up of windshields and sight telescopes during SBD dive-bombing attacks.
(g) Need to expand the range of F4F fighters by providing auxiliary droppable tanks attached to the wing racks.
(h) Need to increase significantly the reliability of the MX 13 torpedo.
(i) Need to increase the damage resulting from strafing and air-to-air combat by developing and deploying incendiary bullets for carrier aircraft.

Over time these aircraft-related combat deficiencies were corrected. By May of 1942, incendiary bullets became available and were used by F4Fs. The IFF equipment installation was being continually deployed in 1942. The F4F-4s were introduced with self-sealing fuel tanks and some of the older F3F-3s had them retrofitted. The new fighters also had armored seats and engines, and available drop tanks under the fixed parts of the wings. By August 1942 all F4F-3s had been replaced aboard carriers.[5]

The SBD Dauntless made up half of the carrier-deployed plane types during 1942. In terms of both numbers and impact, the Douglas SBD Dauntless was America's most important naval aircraft during the first critical year of the war. Unfortunately, some

SBD-2s were still in the mix of aircraft carrier VS and VB squadrons, and they had no self-sealing tanks or armored seats. Full deployment of the SBD-3s, with their more powerful engines, slightly higher speed, and critical improvements in armor, armament, and self-sealing fuel tanks, was completed after Coral Sea. In May of 1943, with the introduction of the new SBD-5 with reflector bombing sights for the pilot (and one for the gunner), the old telescope sights that fogged up in humid climates were gone.[6]

As the war progressed, the compositions of the carrier air groups changed drastically. When the scouting squadrons were disestablished in early 1943, the number of fighter planes increased. The typical Essex class carrier in 1943 had 36 fighters, 36 bombers, and 18 torpedo planes.[7]

A constant plague for the carrier flight crews in the early carrier raids was the unreliable ammunition they used, especially the MX 13 torpedo. This torpedo was most renowned for its poor performance. In the Lae-Salamaua Raid, 13 torpedoes were dropped, but only 3 yielded confirmed hits. Finally, over a year after the Battle of Midway, the Bureau of Ordnance tested 100 of these MK 13 air-launched torpedoes, and only 31 percent had satisfactory runs. Sadly, the performance of torpedoes was not improved until later in the war.[8]

The poor bombing accuracy of the flight crews during the attack raids was a constant problem. Nimitz confirmed this phenomenon in many of his action report endorsements to King. Certainly, the pressure on the aircrew to deliver a weapon on a target while in combat was intense, but the results of many of these attacks were below established Navy operational standards. Nimitz pointed out "how much proficiency drops off in wartime and the necessity for target practices at every opportunity in order to keep pilots completely trained in all phases of aerial warfare."[9] Though poor bombing accuracy was only one factor, practically all action reports from flight crews overstated the damage inflicted on the enemy. It was a universal problem for all military actions, because it was impossible to accurately report damage inflicted in the heat of a rapidly changing combat environment.

Like all the carrier aviation forces in the Pacific, the pilots of the fighter squadrons honed their skills and gained their experience in the unforgiving environment of aerial combat. They prevailed against the Japanese fighters like the Zero even as they flew less than optimal planes. The controversy surrounding the Grumman F4F-4 Wildcat fighters' poor climb rates and maneuverability drove the skipper of the *Enterprise*, Captain George Murray, to note in a letter to the Bureau of Aeronautics in April 1942, "Under no circumstances should our fighter pilots in F4F-4s permit themselves to engage in tactics involving 'dog fights' with enemy fighters."[10] This was a major indictment for an aircraft designed for dogfights.

Even burdened with these aircraft limitations, between February and June 1942 the Navy fighter squadrons shot down 17 Japanese carrier fighter aircraft (3 Mitsubishi A5M4 Type 96 fighters and 14 Zero fighters, killing 16 pilots), while the U.S. Navy lost only 10 Wildcats in combat with the loss of 7 pilots. The first seven months of carrier air combat in 1942 taught Navy fighter pilots how to maintain air superiority over the Pacific theater for the remainder of the war.[11] Total losses in the carrier raids were 54 killed, 46 wounded and loss of 36 aircraft (including the 7 killed and 16 aircraft lost in the Tokyo Raid). Considering the impact of the raids, it was considered a sad but understandable loss of brave men and aircraft.

The results of refining the equipment and flight crew tactics after the five raids served to increase the efficiency and effectiveness of the U.S. carrier task forces as the Pacific War continued to victory. As for the operational and strategic impacts of the five early U.S. Pacific carrier raids, the most significant result was in the positive influence on morale, both for the American public and for the men of the U.S. Navy. These raids showed there could be real naval victories after Pearl Harbor. It made heroes of men like Halsey, Nimitz, and O'Hare. It restored the faith that there could be an American victory in the Pacific War.

The contribution of Admiral King and Admiral Nimitz in defining the ultimate strategy and directing the U.S. forces that defeated the Japanese in the Pacific cannot be overstated. From the beginning, King essentially defied the official Rainbow War Plan for the Pacific in deviating from the defensive mandate (specified until the European enemies were defeated) by ordering Nimitz to take his limited carrier task force resources and attack the Japanese using island raids. He was not willing to wait for opportunities to attack the enemy; he was interested in creating those opportunities. Although King was certainly influenced by political, not just military, motives, the strategy turned out to be successful.

In the first months of the Pacific War, Nimitz was understandably concerned over the lack of resources in men, ships and aircraft for the Pacific Fleet, and an appreciation for the risks associated with the carrier raids. The success of Halsey in the first raid against the Marshalls and Gilberts gave him more confidence and influenced his transition to a more aggressive offensive approach. King was initially reluctant to give up his direct control of the Pacific to Nimitz because he felt he was an "unproven fleet commander." But because of the geographic distance and corresponding communications challenge, as well as acknowledging Nimitz's successful Pacific raids, King finally gave operational control to Nimitz. From daily message communications, letters, periodic face-to-face meetings, and the exchange of representatives, King was always up-to-date on the status of the Pacific situation. Both admirals knew their role. King handled the political parties in Washington and saw the view of the entire global war status, while Nimitz directed the fleet tactics of the war in the Pacific. With this excellent information flow (by the standards of the early 1940s) between these two leaders, the war moved forward rapidly in the Pacific from defensive to offensive.

When King directed Nimitz to send carriers to the South Pacific, Nimitz and his senior staff were not in agreement because they did not want to split their limited fast carrier forces away from the Central Pacific. What helped Nimitz to become more confident in supporting the South Pacific were his successful intelligence operations at intercepting the Japanese radio traffic and breaking the IJN encryption codes.

Later, when the *Lexington* was sunk in the Battle of the Coral Sea, King and his Washington planners became more defensive, while Nimitz became the aggressor. Without approval from King, Nimitz moved the Pacific Fleet to Hawaii in preparation for the upcoming Midway attack based on the confirmed intelligence. Nimitz was ultimately able to convince King of the strategy for Midway, thereby changing the course of the Pacific War. The actual strategy of the Pacific War was therefore defined by the King-Nimitz team, and it was these two men who showed courage and perseverance to defeat the Japanese by the end of July 1945, when the IJN was incapable of conducting operations, just three months after V-E Day of May 8, 1945.[12]

For all the strategic brilliance of King and Nimitz, there is no question that the real success of the early carrier raids in the Pacific was due to the outstanding tactical leadership of the carrier task force commanders, and to the bravery of their carrier air crews. These admirals, Vice Admiral William Halsey, Vice Admiral Wilson Brown and Rear Adm. Frank Jack Fletcher, were willing to leave Pearl Harbor with their carriers and venture out with yet unproven naval aviators on raids against the Japanese, who were still feeling the afterglow of their victories. The flight crews took on the direct risk with life-or-death combat missions over unfamiliar island locations to destroy the Japanese enemy, while they overcame any skill deficiencies and dealt with equipment disadvantages. Without the actions of Pacific task force commanders and carrier flight crews during the period from February through April of 1942, there would have been little optimism in the mind of Nimitz or the American people in mid–1942 that the war in the Pacific could be won.

As Americans learned their 1st Marine Division had stormed the beaches of Tulagi and Guadalcanal in the Solomon Islands on August 7, 1942, in the first U.S. amphibious landings of the Pacific War, they knew their forces were finally ready to take the offensive and, before long, victory would be complete. Three years later, at 1300 on August 15, 1945, Admiral Halsey stood on the deck of his flagship, the USS *Missouri*, off the coast of Japan. There he spoke to the gathered audience of his crew and, via microphone, to his fleet. He recalled his 1942 early carrier raids against enemy-held islands, when "with nothing but indomitable courage and hope to support us, we left our mark on a cruel and treacherous enemy. We paved the way—we blazed the trail—for the overwhelming victories that have followed." He continued with words to the men: "You shall always occupy a special and honored space in my mind and heart. We have been through this trying time together. We have shared the good, we have shared the bad. We are brothers—blooded by our active participation in combat operations in an unprecedented naval war."[13]

Appendix A

Marshall and Gilbert Islands Raid, U.S. Navy Task Forces 8 and 17, February 1, 1942

Task Force 8, Vice Admiral William F. Halsey commanding (*Enterprise* flag).

CARRIER GROUP

CV-6 USS *Enterprise*, Capt. George D. Murray, Yorktown class Fleet Carrier

CVG-6	1 SBD-3	Cdr. Howard L. Young
VF-6	18 F4F-3 & 3A	Lt. Cdr. C. Wade McClusky
VS-6	18 SBD-2 & 3	Lt. Cdr. Halsted L. Hopping
VB-6	18 SBD-2 & 3	Lt. Cdr. William R. Hollingsworth
VT-6	18 TBD-1	Lt. Cdr. Eugene E. Lindsay

Ref: Lundstrom, John B., *The First Team: Pacific Naval Air Combat from Pearl Harbor to Midway* (Annapolis: Naval Institute Press, 2005), 64.

SUPPORT GROUP

DD-390 USS *Ralph Talbot*, Commander Ralph Earle, Jr., Gridley class Destroyer
DD-387 USS *Blue*, Commander Harold N. Williams, Gridley class Destroyer
DD-400 USS *McCall*, Commander Frederick Moosbrugger, Gridley class Destroyer

FUELING GROUP

AO-24 USS *Platte*, Capt. Ralph H. Henkle, Cimarron class Fleet Oiler
DD-382 USS *Craven*, Lt. Comdr. Allen P. Calvert, Gridley class Destroyer

Task Force 17, Admiral Fletcher commanding (Yorktown flag)

CARRIER GROUP

CV-5 USS *Yorktown*, Capt. Elliott C. Buckmaster, Yorktown class Carrier

CVG-5	1 SBD-3	Cdr. Curtis S. Smiley
VF-42	18 F4F-3	Lt. Cdr. Oscar Perderson
VS-5	19 SBD-3	Lt. Cdr. William O. Burch, Jr.
VB-5	19 SBD-3	Lt. Cdr. Robert G. Armstrong
VT-5	12 TBD-1	Lt. Cdr. Joe Taylor

Ref: Lundstrom, 56.

Support Group

DD-410 USS *Hughes*, Lt. Comdr. Donald J. Ramsey, Sims class Destroyer
DD-409 USS *Sims*, Lt. Comdr. Willford M. Hyman, Sims class Destroyer
DD-414 USS *Russell*, Lt. Comdr. Glenn R. Hartwig, Sims class Destroyer
DD-416 USS *Walke*, Lt. Comdr. Thomas E. Fraser, Sims class Destroyer
CL-49 USS *St. Louis*, Capt. George A. Rood, St. Louis class Light Cruiser
CA-28 USS *Louisville*, Capt. Elliott B. Nixon, Northampton class Heavy Cruiser

Fueling Group

AO-25 USS *Sabine*, Commander Houston L. Maples, Cimarron class Fleet Oiler
DD-364 USS *Mahan*, Lt. Comdr. Rodger W. Simpson, Mahan class Destroyer

Wotje Bombardment Group

Rear Admiral Raymond A. Spruance commanding (*Northampton* flag):

CA-26 USS *Northampton*, Capt. William D. Chandler, Northampton class Heavy Cruiser
CA-25 USS *Salt Lake City*, Capt. Ellis M. Zachanas, Pensacola class Heavy Cruiser
DD-384 USS *Dunlap*, Lt. Comdr. Virginius R. Roane, Fanning class Destroyer

Maleolap Bombardment Group

Capt. Thomas M. Shock (*Chester* flag):

CA-27 USS *Chester*, Captain Shock, Northampton class Heavy Cruiser
DD-363 USS *Balch*, Commander Charles J. Rend, Porter class Destroyer
DD-401 USS *Maury*, Lt. Comdr. Elmer D. Snare, Gridley class Destroyer

Ref: www.ibiblio.org/hyperwar/USN/ships/, Compiled and formatted by Patrick Clancey, HyperWar Foundation, Ships of the U.S. Navy, 1940–1945.

Appendix B

Rabaul Raid, U.S. Navy Task Force 11, February 20, 1942

Task Force 11, Vice Admiral Wilson Brown (*Lexington* flag).

Carrier Group

CV-2 USS *Lexington*, Capt. Frederick C. Sherman, Lexington class Aircraft Carrier

CVG-2	1 SBD-3	Cdr. William B. Ault
VF-3	18 F4F-3	Lt. Cdr. John S. Thach
VS-2	18 SBD-2 & 3	Lt. Cdr. Robert E. Dixon
VB-2	18 SBD-2	Lt. Cdr. Weldon L. Hamilton
VT-2	23 TBD-1	Lt. Cdr. James H. Brett, Jr.

Ref: Lundstrom, 127.

Support Group

CA-36 USS *Minneapolis*, Capt. Frank J. Lowry, New Orleans class Heavy Cruiser
CA-35 USS *Indianapolis*, Capt. Edward W. Hanson, Portland class Heavy Cruiser
CA-24 USS *Pensacola*, Capt. Frank L. Lowe, Pensacola class Heavy Cruiser
CA-38 USS *San Francisco*, Capt. Daniel J. Callaghan, New Orleans class Heavy Cruiser
DD-360 USS *Phelps*, Lt. Comdr. Edward L. Beck, Porter class Destroyer
DD-349 USS *Dewey*, Lt. Comdr. Charles F. Chillingworth, Jr., Farragut class Destroyer
DD-351 USS *MacDonough*, Lt. Comdr. John M. McIsaac, Farragut class Destroyer
DD-350 USS *Hull*, Lt. Comdr. Richard F. Stout, Farragut class Destroyer
DD-355 USS *Aylwin*, Lt. Comdr. Robert H. Rogers, Farragut class Destroyer
DD-353 USS *Dale*, Lt. Comdr. Anthony L. Rorschach, Farragut class Destroyer
DD-366 USS *Drayton*, Lt. Comdr. Laurence A. Abercrombie, Mahan class Destroyer
DD-386 USS *Bagley*, Lt. Comdr. George A. Sinclair, Gridley class Destroyer
DD-392 USS *Patterson*, Comdr. Frank R. Walker, Gridley class Destroyer
DD-361 USS *Clark*, Comdr. Myron T. Richardson, Porter class Destroyer

Ref: www.ibiblio.org/hyperwar/USN/USN-ships.html, HyperWar: Ships of the U.S. Navy, 1940–1945; *Early Raids in the Pacific Ocean, February 1 to March 10, 1942, Publication Section, Combat Intelligence Branch,* Office of Naval Intelligence, United States Navy, 1943, 35–36.

Appendix C

Wake and Marcus Island Raid, U.S. Navy Task Force 16, February 24, 1942

Task Force Task Force 16, Vice Admiral William F. Halsey commanding (*Enterprise* flag)

Carrier Group

CV-6 USS *Enterprise*, Capt. George D. Murray, Yorktown class Fleet Carrier

CVG-6	SBD-3	Cdr. Howard L. Young
VF-6	18 F4F-3 & 4	Lt. Cdr. C. Wade McClusky
VS-6	18 SBD-3	Lt. Cdr. Halsted L. Hopping
VB-6	18 SBD-2 & 3	Lt. Cdr. William R. Hollingsworth
VT-6	18 TBD-1	Lt. Cdr. Eugene E. Lindsay

Ref: Lundstrom, 64; Brown, David, *Carrier Operations in World War II,* vol. 2: *The Pacific Navies Dec 1941–Feb 1943* (London: Ian Allan, 1974), 38.

Rear Admiral Raymond A. Spruance, commander Cruiser Division FIVE (*Northampton,* commanding)

CA-26 USS *Northampton*, Capt. William D. Chandler, Northampton class Heavy Cruiser
CA-25 USS *Salt Lake City*, Capt. Ellis M. Zacharias, Pensacola class Heavy Cruiser

Capt. Richard L. Conolly, commander Destroyer Squadron SIX (*Balch*, commanding)

DD-401 USS *Maury*, Lt. Comdr. Elmer D. Snare, Gridley class Destroyer
DD-363 USS *Balch,* Commander Charles J. Rend, Porter class Destroyer
DD-384 USS *Dunlap*, Lt. Comdr. Virginius R. Roane, Fanning class Destroyer
DD-387 USS *Blue*, Commander Harold N. Williams, Gridley class Destroyer
DD-390 USS *Ralph Talbot*, Commander Ralph Earle, Jr., Gridley class Destroyer
DD-382 USS *Craven*, Lt. Comdr. Allen P. Calvert, Gridley class Destroyer
AO-25 USS *Sabine*, Commander Houston L. Maples, Cimarron class Fleet Oiler

Ref: www.ibiblio.org/hyperwar/USN/USN-ships.html, HyperWar: Ships of the U.S. Navy, 1940–1945; *Early Raids in the Pacific Ocean*, 42–43.

Appendix D

Lae-Salamaua Raid, Allied Task Force 11 (TF 11, TF 17 and ANZAC Squadron), March 10, 1942

Task Force 11, Vice Admiral Wilson Brown, commanding (*Lexington* flag)

RAdm F.J Fletcher commanding (*Yorktown* flag)

CARRIER GROUP

CV-5 USS *Yorktown*, Capt. Elliott Buckmaster, Yorktown class Aircraft Carrier

CVG-5		
VF-42	10 F4F-3	Lt. Cdr. Oscar Pederson
VS-5	13 SBD-3	Lt. Cdr. William O. Burch
VB-5	17 SBD-3	Lt. Cdr. Robert G. Armstrong
VT-5	12 TBD-1	Lt. Cdr. Joe Taylor

CV-2 USS *Lexington*, Captain Frederick Carl Sherman, Lexington class Aircraft Carrier

CVG-2	1 SBD-3	Cdr. William B. Ault
VF-3	8 F4F-3	Lt. Cdr. John S. Thach
VS-2	18 SBD-2 & 3	Lt. Cdr. Robert E. Dixon
VB-2	12 SBD-2	Lt. Cdr. Weldon L. Hamilton
VT-2	13 TBD-1	Lt. Cdr. James H. Brett, Jr.

Ref: Lundstrom, 127.

ANZAC SQUADRON, SURFACE GROUP

Rear Admiral Crace, RN, commanding (*Astoria*)

(*Australia*, *Chicago*, *Astoria*, *Louisville*, and the *Anderson*, *Hammann*, *Hughes*, and *Sims*)

D-84 HMAS *Australia*, Capt. H.P. Farncomb, RAN, County class Heavy Cruiser, Royal Australian Navy (RAN)
CA-34 USS *Astoria*, Capt. Francis W. Scanland, New Orleans class Heavy Cruiser
CA-29 USS *Chicago*, Capt. Howard D. Bode, Northampton class Heavy Cruiser
CA-35 USS *Indianapolis*, Capt. Edward W. Hanson, Portland class Heavy Cruiser
CA-28 USS *Louisville*, Capt. Elliott B. Nixon, Northampton class Heavy Cruiser
CA-36 USS *Minneapolis*, Capt. Frank J. Lowry, New Orleans class Heavy Cruiser
CA-24 USS *Pensacola*, Capt. Frank L. Lowe, Pensacola class Heavy Cruiser
CA-38 USS *San Francisco*, Capt. Daniel J. Callaghan, New Orleans class Heavy Cruiser
DD-360 USS *Phelps*, Lt. Comdr. Edward L. Beck, Porter class Destroyer
DD-349 USS *Dewey*, Lt. Comdr. Charles F. Chillingworth, Jr., Farragut class Destroyer
DD-353 USS *Dale*, Lt. Comdr. Anthony L. Rorschach, Farragut class Destroyer
DD-351 USS *MacDonough*, Lt. Comdr. John M. McIsaac, Farragut class Destroyer
DD-350 USS *Hull*, Lt. Comdr. Richard F. Stout, Farragut class Destroyer
DD-361 USS *Clark*, Comdr. Myron T. Richardson, Porter class Destroyer
DD-386 USS *Bagley*, Lt. Comdr. George A. Sinclair, Gridley class Destroyer
DD-414 USS *Russell*, Lt. Comdr Glenn R. Hartwig, Sims class Destroyer
DD-416 USS *Walke*, Lt. Comdr. Thomas E. Fraser, Sims class Destroyer
DD-411 USS *Anderson*, Lt. Cdr. John Kenneth Burkholder Ginder, Sims class Destroyer
DD-412 USS *Hammann*, Comdr. Arnold E. True, Sims class Destroyer
DD-410 USS *Hughes*, Lt. Comdr. Donald J. Ramsey, Sims class Destroyer
DD-409 USS *Sims*, Lt. Comdr. Wilford M. Hyman, Sims class Destroyer

Ref: *Early Raids in the Pacific Ocean*, 58; Brown, 38.

Appendix E

Tokyo Raid, U.S. Navy Task Force 16, April 18, 1942

Task Force 16, Vice Admiral William F. Halsey, Jr., commanding (*Enterprise* flag).

Task Group 16.1, CV-6 USS *Enterprise*, Capt. George D. Murray, Yorktown class Fleet Carrier

CVG-6		Lt. Cdr. C. Wade McClusky
VF-6	27 F4F-3 & 4	Lt. Cdr. James Seton Gray, Jr.
VS-6	18 SBD-3	Lt. Cdr. Wilmer Earl Gallaher
VB-3	18 SBD-2 & 3	Lt. Cdr. Maxwell Franklin Leslie
VT-6	18 TBD-1	Lt. Cdr. Eugene Elbert Lindsey

Ref: Lundstrom, 127; Chun, Clayton, *The Doolittle Raid 1942* (New York: Osprey, 2006), 20–21; Horan, Mark E., co-author of *A Glorious Page in our History: The Battle of Midway, 4–6 June 1942*, Appendix Four: U.S. Carrier Air Groups.

CA-26 USS *Northampton*, Capt. William D. Chandler, Northampton class Heavy Cruiser
CA-25 USS *Salt Lake City*, Capt. Ellis M. Zacharias, Pensacola class Heavy Cruiser

AO-25 USS *Sabine*, Commander Houston L. Maples, Cimarron class Fleet Oiler
DD-363 USS *Balch,* Commander Charles J. Rend, Porter class Destroyer
DD-397 USS *Benham*, Lieutenant Commander T. F. Darden, Benham class Destroyer
DD-398 USS *Ellet*, Benham class Destroyer
DD-385 USS *Fanning,* Lieutenant Commander E. H. Geiselman, Mahan class Destroyer

Task Group 16.2, CV-8 USS *Hornet*, Captain Marc A. Mitscher, Yorktown class Aircraft Carrier

CVG-8		Lt. Cdr. Stanhope C. Ring
VF-8	27 F4F-4	Lt. Cdr. Samuel G. Mitchell
VS-8	16 SBD-3	Lt. Cdr. Walter F. Rodee
VB-8	19 SBD-3	Lt. Cdr. Robert R. Johnson
VT-8	15 TBD-1	Lt. Cdr. John C. Waldron
17 Bomb Group, USAAF		Lieut. Colonel Doolittle
	16 B-25B Mitchell	

Ref: Lundstrom, 330.

CL-42 USS *Nashville*, Capt. William W. Wilson, Brooklyn class Light Cruiser
CA-44 USS *Vincennes*, Capt. Frederick Lois Riefkohl, New Orleans class Heavy Cruiser
AO-22 USS *Cimarron*, Cimarron class Fleet Oiler
DD-433 USS *Gwin*, Lt. Cdr. James S. Roberts, Gleaves class Destroyer
DD-434 USS *Meredith*, Lt. Cdr. Harry Ensor Hubbard, Gleaves class Destroyer
DD-436 USS *Monssen*, Cdr. Roland Nesbit Smoot, Gleaves class Destroyer
DD-435 USS *Grayson*, Cdr. Thomas Murray Stokes, Gleaves class Destroyer

Ref: *Doolittle Raid on Japan, 18 April 1942—Ships of the Doolittle Raid Task Force*, Department of the Navy–Naval Historical Center.

Chapter Notes

Introduction

1. *Evolution of Aircraft Carriers*, Department of the Navy, Naval Historical Center, Washington, D.C.
2. Reynolds, Clark J., *The Fast Carriers: The Forging of an Air Navy* (New York: McGraw Hill, 1968), 17.
3. Micallef, Joseph V., *The First Attack: Pearl Harbor, February 7, 1932*, Military.com.
4. *Ibid.*
5. Reynolds, 18.
6. Astor, Gerald, *Wings of Gold: The U.S. Naval Air Campaign in World War II* (New York: Ballantine Books, 2004), 18–19.
7. Bernstein, Marc D., "The Early Carrier Raids: Proving Japanese Vulnerability," *Naval Aviation News* (March–April 1992).

Chapter 1

1. Potter, E.B., *Nimitz* (Annapolis: Naval Institute Press, 1979), 16.
2. *Ibid.*
3. Cressman, Robert J., *A Magnificent Fight: Marines in the Battle for Wake Island* (Washington, D.C.: History and Museums Division, Headquarters, U.S. Marine Corps); Rickard, J., *Battle of Wake Island, 8–23 December 1941*, historyofwar.org; Heinl, Lieutenant Colonel R.D., Jr., USMC, *Marines in World War II. Historical Monograph: The Defense of Wake*. Chapter 4: "The Fall of Wake" (Washington, D.C.: Headquarters USMC, 1947).
4. Potter, *Nimitz*, 16.
5. *Ibid.*, 17.
6. *Attack at Pearl Harbor, 1941*, eyewitnesstohistory.com.
7. Prange, Gordon W., *At Dawn We Slept* (New York: McGraw-Hill, 1981), 490–492.
8. Parillo, Mark, "The United States in the Pacific," Chapter 10 of Robin Higham and Stephen Harris, *Why Air Forces Fail: The Anatomy of Defeat* (Lexington: University Press of Kentucky, 2006), 288.
9. *A Pearl Harbor Fact Sheet—Census*, U.S. Department of Commerce, U.S. Census Bureau, census.gov/history/pdf/pearl-harbor-fact-sheet-1.pdf; *Damage to United States Naval Forces and Installations as a Result of the Attack, Report of the Joint Committee on the Investigation of the Pearl Harbor Attack* (Washington D.C.: United States Government Printing Office, 1946); Wallin, Vice Admiral Homer N., USN, *Pearl Harbor: Why, How, Fleet Salvage and Final Appraisal* (Department of the Navy, Naval History Division, 1969), 94, 100–103, 108.
10. Hoyt, Edwin P., *How They Won the War in the Pacific: Nimitz and His Admirals* (Guilford, CT: The Lyons Press, 2002), 13.
11. Potter, *Nimitz*, 8–9.
12. *Ibid.*, 9.
13. Hoyt, 28–34.
14. *Ibid.*, 34.
15. Potter, *Nimitz*, 56.
16. *Ibid.*, 57–62.
17. Hoyt, 40–45.
18. Potter, *Nimitz*, 8–15; Hoyt, 28, 46–47; Barnes, Major Gary I., USAF, *Great Warriors of World War II: Admiral Ernest J. King–Admiral Chester W. Nimitz* (Maxwell AFB, AL: Air Command and Staff College, Air University DTIC), March 1984, 18–19.
19. *Command Summary of Fleet Admiral Chester W. Nimitz, USN*, Nimitz "Graybook," vol. 1, 86.
20. Potter, *Nimitz*, 18.
21. Nimitz "Graybook," vol. 1, 09–110.
22. Hoyt, 50–51.
23. *Ibid.*, 51.
24. *Ibid.*, 51.
25. Potter, *Nimitz*, 19.
26. Potter, *Nimitz*, 16–21; Hoyt, 45–53.
27. Wallin, 119.
28. Morton, Louis, *Strategy and Command: The First Two Years, US Army in World War II, The War in the Pacific*, Chapter 6: "The First Weeks of War, 7–26 December" (Center of Military History, 1960), 133–142; Bowen, James, *The Pacific War 1942, The United States Strategy*, Pacific War History, kokodatreks.com/history/thepacificwar1942, *Admiral Ernest J. King (1878–1956)*, PBS American Experience, PBS, pbs.org/wgbh/amex/macarthur.
29. Nimitz "Graybook," vol. 1, 122.
30. *Ibid.*, 123–135.
31. Buell, Thomas, *Master of Sea Power: A Biography of Fleet Admiral Ernest J. King* (Annapolis: Naval Institute Press, 1980), inside cover flap.
32. Borneman, Walter R., *The Admirals* (2012), 207.
33. *Admiral Ernest J. King (1878–1956)*, PBS American Experience, PBS, www.pbs.org/wgbh/amex/macarthur/peopleevents/pandeAMEX86.html
34. Buell, 11.
35. Skates, John Ray, *The Invasion of Japan: Alternative to the Bomb* (University of South Carolina Press, 2000); Buell, 223.

36. Lundstrom, John B., *The First Team: Pacific Naval Air Combat from Pearl Harbor to Midway* (Annapolis: Naval Institute Press, 2005), 47.
37. *Early Raids in the Pacific Ocean, February 1 to March 10, 1942*, Publication Section, Combat Intelligence Branch, Office of Naval Intelligence, United States Navy, 1943, 1–2.
38. Potter, *Nimitz*, 33.
39. Ibid., 34.
40. Ibid., 33–35.
41. Nimitz "Graybook," vol. 1, 142.
42. Potter, *Nimitz*, 31–35; Halsey, Fleet Admiral William F., and Lieutenant Commander Joseph Bryan III, *Admiral Halsey's Story* (New York: McGraw-Hill, 1947), 87.

Chapter 2

1. *Early Raids in the Pacific Ocean*, 3.
2. *Fleet Admiral William Frederick Halsey, Jr.* (Washington, D.C.: Department of the Navy, Naval Historical Center); Tillman, Barrett, "William Bull Halsey: Legendary World War II Admiral," *World War II Magazine* (July/August 2007).
3. Potter, E.B., *Bull Halsey* (Annapolis, MD: Naval Institute Press, 1985), 39.
4. Lundstrom, *First Team*, 50–51.
5. USS *Enterprise* CV-6, "Marshall Islands Raid, February 1, 1942," cv6.org/1942/marshalls.
6. Cressman, Robert J., *That Gallant Ship: USS Yorktown (CV-5)* (Missoula, MT: Pictorial Histories Publishing Company, 1989), 53–55.
7. Lundstrom, John B., *Black Shoe Carrier Admiral: Frank Jack Fletcher at Coral Sea, Midway, and Guadalcanal* (Annapolis, MD: Naval Institute Press, 2006), Chapter 1; Bauer, James L., *Fletcher, Task Force Commander: The Early Years of the Pacific War and a Former Sailor* (Marshalltown, IA: Manorborn Press, 2010), 1, 5, 8.
8. Lundstrom, *Black Shoe Carrier Admiral*, 45.
9. Ibid., 45; Bauer, 36.
10. Lundstrom, *Black Shoe Carrier Admiral*, 44–46.
11. Ibid., 46–49.
12. Ibid., Chapter 2.
13. Stafford, Edward P., *The Big E: The Story of the USS Enterprise* (Annapolis: Bluejacket Books, Naval Institute Press, 1962), 44–45.
14. Cressman, *That Gallant Ship*, 55–56.
15. Lundstrom, *The First Team*, 61–63.
16. *Early Raids in the Pacific Ocean*, 4–7.
17. Blair Jr., Clay, *Silent Victory: The U.S. Submarine War against Japan* (Annapolis: Naval Institute Press, 2001), 116.
18. *Dolphin First War Patrol*, COMSUBPAC, February 5, 1942; Blair, 115–116.
19. *USS Tautog Patrol Report, 26 December 1941–4 February 1942*, Commanding Officer, USS *Tautog*, February 4, 1942; Blair, 116.
20. Lundstrom, *The First Team*, 60–61.
21. *Early Raids in the Pacific Ocean*, 4, Stafford, 45–46.
22. USS *Enterprise* CV-6, cv6.org/1942/marshalls.
23. Lundstrom, *The First Team*, 6–7.
24. *Report on Attacks Made by Enterprise Air Group on Northern Marshall Islands*, Commander *Enterprise* Air Group (Serial 01), February 4, 1942.
25. Lundstrom, *The First Team*, 63.
26. Ibid., 63.
27. Halsey and Bryan III, 90.
28. *Report of Attack on the Marshall Islands, February 1, 1942*, Commander, Scouting Squadron Six (serial 08-c), dated February 3, 1942, 1–2.
29. Ibid., 2–3.
30. *Flight Leader's Report of Dawn Attack on Kwajalein Atoll, 1 February 1942*, Enclosure C, *Attacks on Marshall Islands, 1 February 1942*, Commander Bombing Squadron Six (serial 06), dated February 2, 1942.
31. *Flight Leader's Report of Dawn Attack on Kwajalein Atoll*.
32. *Report After Battle*, Commander Torpedo Squadron Six (serial 02), February 2, 1942.
33. *Narrative of Torpedo Attack on Vessels Anchored in Lagoon Adjacent to Island of Kwajalein in Kwajalein Atoll*, XO Lieutenant Commander Massey, Enclosure D, *Report After Battle*, Commander Torpedo Squadron Six (serial 02), February 2, 1942.
34. Ibid.
35. *Report After Battle*.
36. *Battle Engagement—1 February 1942*, Commander Fighting Squadron Six (serial 001), dated February 2, 1942; Lundstrom, *First Team*, 67–69.
37. *Report After Battle*; *Early Raids in the Pacific Ocean*, 7–11.
38. *Battle Engagement—1 February 1942*.
39. *Early Raids in the Pacific Ocean*, 7–11.
40. Ibid., 20.
41. Ibid., 17–21.
42. Moore, Stephen L., *Pacific Payback: The Carrier Aviators Who Avenged Pearl Harbor at the Battle of Midway* (New York: NAL Caliber-Penguin Group, 2014), 101; *Report After Battle*.
43. *Report of Attack on the Marshall Islands, February 1, 1942*.
44. *Early Raids in the Pacific Ocean*, 6–7.
45. Ibid., 21–23.
46. Ibid., 22–23.
47. *Report of Action on February 1, 1942*, Commanding Officer USS *Enterprise* (serial 026), dated February 7, 1942; Lundstrom, *The First Team*, 72–74.
48. Ibid., 75.
49. *Report of Action on February 1, 1942*; Lundstrom, *The First Team*, 74–75.
50. *Report of Action on February 1, 1942*; Lundstrom, *The First Team*, 75–76.
51. *Early Raids in the Pacific Ocean*, 23–26.
52. *Action in the Marshall Islands, 1 February 1942*, Commander Task Force Eight (serial 006), dated 9 February 1942; *Report of Action on February 1, 1942*.
53. *Report of Action on February 1, 1942*.
54. Ibid.
55. Ibid.
56. *Report on Attacks Made by Enterprise Air Group on Northern Marshall Islands*.
57. Ibid.
58. *Early Raids in the Pacific Ocean*, 4–7.
59. *Operation Order No. 2-42, Task Organization, Task Force 17*, Commanding Officer, serial 0014(Y), dated January 25, 1942.
60. *Early Raids in the Pacific Ocean*, 27.
61. Ensign B.G. Preston, *Air Action at Jaluit 31 January 1942*, Enclosure A, *Report of Attack of Yorktown Air Group on Jaluit, Milli and Makin in Marshall and Gilbert Islands*, Commanding Officer USS *Yorktown* (serial 07), dated February 5, 1942.
62. Lieutenant W.S. Guest, *Air Action at Jaluit 31 January 1942*, Enclosure A, *Report of Attack of Yorktown Air Group*.

63. Ensign J.T. Cranford, *Air Action at Jaluit 31 January 1942*, Enclosure A, *Report of Attack of Yorktown Air Group.*
64. Ensign G.E. Bottjer, *Air Action at Jaluit 31 January 1942*, Enclosure A, *Report of Attack of Yorktown Air Group.*
65. *Report of Attack of Yorktown Air Group*, 5.
66. Lieutenant A.H. Furer, *Air Action at Jaluit 31 January 1942*, Enclosure A, *Report of Attack of Yorktown Air Group.*
67. *Ibid.*
68. *Ibid.*
69. *Ibid.*
70. Ensign A.J. Schultheis, Aviation Ordnanceman 3c H.N. Sybrant, *Air Action at Jaluit 31 January 1942*, Enclosure A, *Report of Attack of Yorktown Air Group.*
71. Radioman 3c F.J. Chantiny, *Air Action at Jaluit 31 January 1942*, Enclosure A, *Report of Attack of Yorktown Air Group.*
72. *Air Action at Jaluit 31 January 1942*, Enclosure A, *Report of Attack of Yorktown Air Group.*
73. *Report of Air Group Commander-USS Yorktown, Air Attacks on Marshall-Gilbert Islands, 31 January 1942*, Enclosure D, 1-2.
74. *Ibid.*, 3.
75. *Ibid.*, 4.
76. Lieutenant Commander W.C. Burch, Lieutenant T.F. Caldwell, *Report of Air Action at Makin*, Enclosure B, *Report of Attack of Yorktown Air Group.*
77. Lieutenant R.B. Woodhull, *Report of Air Action at Makin*, Enclosure B, *Report of Attack of Yorktown Air Group.*
78. *Report of Air Group Commander-USS Yorktown.*
79. Lieutenant (JG) A.L. Downing, *Report of Air Action at Milli*, Enclosure C, *Report of Attack of Yorktown Air Group.*
80. Ensign H.W. Nicholson, *Report of Air Action at Milli*, Enclosure C, *Report of Attack of Yorktown Air Group.*
81. *Report of Air Action at Milli*, Enclosure C, *Report of Attack of Yorktown Air Group.*
82. *Report of Air Group Commander-USS Yorktown.*
83. *Ibid.*
84. *Engagement Report*, Task Force 17.1.1 Striking Group, Commanding Officer, USS *Louisville* (serial 001), dated February 6, 1942, *Report of Action*, Commanding Officer, Commander Destroyer Division Three (serial 07), dated February 7, 1942; *Action Report*, Commanding Officer USS *Hughes* (serial 06), dated February 6, 1942; *Report of Action 31 January 1942*, Commanding Officer USS *Walke* (serial 02), dated February 5, 1942.
85. Lundstrom, *The First Team*, 78-79.
86. Cressman, *That Gallant Ship*, 61.
87. *Report of Engagement, January 31, 1942*, Commander Task Force 17 (serial 0018(Y), dated February 9, 1942.
88. *Report of Action*, Commanding Officer, Commander Destroyer Division Three (serial 07), dated February 7, 1942.
89. *Engagement Report*, Task Force 17.1.1 Striking Group.
90. *Ibid.*
91. *Report of Attack of Yorktown Air Group.*
92. *Early Raids in the Pacific Ocean*, 35; *Cruise of Task Force Eleven, from January 31 to March 26, 1942*, Commander TF 11, serial 0123, March 23, 1942, 1-3.
93. Lundstrom, *The First Team*, 81-82.
94. Halsey and Bryan III, 96.
95. *Ibid.*, 96.
96. Potter, *Nimitz*, 39-40.
97. Stafford, 72-73; Potter, *Bull Halsey*, 51-52.
98. *Early Raids in the Pacific Ocean*, 33-34.
99. Halsey and Bryan III, 97.
100. Edwin, Layton T., *Earlier Carrier Raids during World War II*, Naval History, The Sixth Symposium of the U.S. Naval Academy (Wilmington, DE: Scholarly Resources, 1987), 263-264.
101. *Ibid.*, 263-264.
102. Willmot, H.P., *Empires in the Balance: Japanese and Allied Pacific Strategies to April 1942* (Annapolis: Naval Institute Press, 1982), 285-286.
103. Belote, James H., and William M. Belote, *Titans of the Seas: The Development and Operations of Japanese and American Carrier Task Forces During World War II* (New York: Harper & Row, 1975), 54-55.
104. Belote, 54-55.

Chapter 3

1. Nimitz "Graybook," vol. 1, 207.
2. *Ibid.*, 209; Potter, *Nimitz*, 41.
3. Nimitz "Graybook," vol. 1, 210; Potter, *Nimitz*, 40-41.
4. Nimitz "Graybook," vol. 1, 211; Potter, *Nimitz*, 41.
5. Potter, *Nimitz*, 42.
6. Nimitz "Graybook," vol. 1, 214.
7. *Ibid.*, 215.
8. *Ibid.*, 215.
9. *Early Raids in the Pacific Ocean*, 36.
10. *2/22nd Battalion, Second World War, 1939-1945 units*, Australian War Memorial, retrieved April 20, 2013; *1st Independent Company, Second World War, 1939-1945 units*, Australian War Memorial, retrieved April 20, 2013; Wigmore, Lionel, *The Japanese Thrust: Australia in the War of 1939-1945*, vol. 4, 1st ed. (Canberra: Australian War Memorial, 1957), "Chapter 18: Rabaul and the Forward Observation Line."
11. *Ibid.*, 410.
12. *Fall of Rabaul*, Australian Government, Department of Veterans' Affairs, ww2australia.gov.au/japadvance/rabaul; Brooks, Brenton, "The Carnival of Blood in Australian Mandated Territory." *Sabretache: Military Historical Society of Australia* 54 (4) (December 2013): 22; Moremon, John, *Rabaul, 1942, Campaign history*, Australian War Memorial, 2003, archived from the original on 31 August 2008; Wigmore, 408, 668-669, 674; Stanley, Peter, *The Defence of the 'Malay barrier': Rabaul and Ambon, January 1942*, Remembering 1942, Australian War Memorial; Hodges, Ian, *The Sinking of Montevideo Maru, 1 July 1942*, Remembering 1942, Australian War Memorial.
13. Budge, Kent G., "Brown, Wilson, Jr.," *The Pacific War Online Encyclopedia*, retrieved August 4, 2010; Tucker, Spencer C., "Brown, Wilson, Jr. (1882-1957)," *World War II at Sea: An Encyclopedia*, vol. 1 (ABC-CLIO LLC, 2012), 130-131.
14. *Early Raids in the Pacific Ocean*, 35-36.
15. *Cruise of Task Force Eleven*, 1-3.
16. *Ibid.*, 1-3.
17. Lundstrom, *The First Team*, 86-88.
18. *Ibid.*, 88-89, 91.
19. *Ibid.*, 89-93.
20. *Report of Air Attack on Lexington on February*

20, 1942, Enclosure A, Commanding Officer *Lexington*, February 23, 1942 (College Park, MD: NARA); Lundstrom, *The First Team*, 92–93,

21. Lundstrom, *The First Team*, 93–94.
22. Ibid., 94–98.
23. Ibid., 94–101.
24. Ibid., 101.
25. Ibid., 106.
26. Ibid., 101–106.
27. Ibid., 104–109.
28. Ibid., 106–107.
29. *Report of Air Attack on Lexington*.
30. Ibid.
31. *Aviation History Magazine*, November 1995.
32. Offner, Larry, "The Butch O'Hare Story," *St. Louis Magazine* (July 29, 2006).
33. *Report of Air Attack on Lexington*, 4.
34. Ibid., 4–5.
35. Ibid., 6.
36. Ibid., 6.
37. *Report of Action of Task Force Eleven with Japanese Aircraft on February 20, 1942*, Commanding Officer TF 11 dated February 24, 1942 (College Park, MD: NARA), 1–2, 6.
38. Ibid., 2–3.
39. Ibid., 3–4.
40. Ibid., 4.
41. Ibid., 4–5.
42. Ibid., 6.
43. Ibid., 7.
44. Ibid., 6.
45. Ibid., 8; *Early Raids in the Pacific Ocean*, 39–40.
46. Lundstrom, *The First Team*, 108–109; Nimitz "Graybook," vol. 1, 254.
47. Belote, 61–62.
48. *Early Raids in the Pacific Ocean*, 40.
49. Edwin, 264.
50. Belote, 62.

Chapter 4

1. Nimitz "Graybook," vol. 1, 217; Halsey and Bryan III, 98.
2. *Early Raids in the Pacific Ocean*, 41, 43.
3. Ibid., 41.
4. Potter, *Nimitz*, 42–43; Nimitz "Graybook," vol. 1, 220.
5. *Early Raids in the Pacific Ocean*, 40–55.
6. Stafford, 62.
7. Ibid., 62–63.
8. Lundstrom, *The First Team*, 111.
9. Cressman, *That Gallant Ship*, 62.
10. Ibid., 62.
11. Newton, David, *Journal of the Pacific War: From the Wartime Diary of Clarence W. Olive, M Division, USS Enterprise*, bookemon.com; Stafford, 63.
12. *Early Raids in the Pacific Ocean*, 44.
13. Lundstrom, 112.
14. Newton.
15. Newton; *Early Raids in the Pacific Ocean*, 44.
16. *Report on Attacks Made by Enterprise Air Group on Wake Island*, Commander *Enterprise* Air Group (Serial 07), dated February 26, 1942, 1.
17. Ibid., 1.
18. *Report of Bombardment of Wake Island on 24 February 1942*, Commander Task Group 16.7 (serial 025), dated March 3, 1942, 1.
19. *Early Raids in the Pacific Ocean*, 45–48.
20. Lundstrom, *The First Team*, 113–114.
21. *Narrative–Action 24 February 1942 (Wake Island)*, Enclosure (C), Commander Fighting Squadron Six (Serial 08), dated 26 February 1942.
22. Stafford, 64.
23. *Early Raids in the Pacific Ocean*, 48–49; *Report on Attacks Made by Enterprise Air Group on Wake Island*.
24. Ibid.; *Narrative–Action 24 February 1942*.
25. *Report of Attack on Wake Island*, Enclosure C, Commander Scouting Squadron Six (serial 016-c), dated February 25, 1942; *Attack on Wake Island, February 24, 1942*, Enclosure C, Commander Bombing Squadron Six (Serial 08), dated February 25, 1942; *Report on Attacks Made by Enterprise Air Group on Wake Island*.
26. *Report of Attack on Wake Island*; *Report of Attack on Wake Island*; *Report on Attacks Made by Enterprise Air Group on Wake Island*.
27. *Report of Attack on Wake Island*; *Report on Attacks Made by Enterprise Air Group on Wake Island*.
28. *Report on Attacks Made by Enterprise Air Group on Wake Island*, 3; Stafford, 67.
29. Lundstrom, *The First Team*, 115.
30. *Early Raids in the Pacific Ocean*, 50.
31. Lundstrom, *The First Team*, 115.
32. *Early Raids in the Pacific Ocean*, 44; *Report of Bombardment of Wake Island on 24 February 1942*.
33. *Air Observations and Operations during Bombardment of Wake Island*, Enclosure B, *Report of Action with Enemy–Bombardment of Wake Island*, Commanding Officer USS *Northampton* (serial 021), dated February 25, 1942; *Bombardment of Wake and Withdrawal Therefrom*, Commanding Officer USS *Salt Lake City* (serial 020), dated March 9, 1942.
34. *Report on Raid on Wake Island, USS Maury*, Commanding Officer USS *Maury* (Serial 05), dated March 3, 1942.
35. *Report of Action with Enemy–Bombardment of Wake Island*.
36. *Bombardment of Wake and Withdrawal Therefrom*.
37. Ibid.
38. Ibid.
39. *Early Raids in the Pacific Ocean*, 46.
40. *Report of Attack on Wake and Peale Islands of Wake Islands*, Enclosure D, Commanding Officer USS *Balch* (serial 040), CO Narrative of Events.
41. Halsey and Bryan III, 100.
42. *Ship Bombardment of Wake Island*, Commander Destroyer Squadron Six (Serial 030), dated March 8, 1942.
43. *Report of Action with Enemy–Bombardment of Wake Island*, Commanding Officer USS *Northampton* (serial 021), dated February 25, 1942, 1–3.
44. *Early Raids in the Pacific Ocean*, 47.
45. *Bombardment of Wake and Withdrawal Therefrom*, 2–3.
46. *Report of Bombardment of Wake Island on 24 February 1942*, Commander Task Group 16.7 (serial 025), dated March 3, 1942, 5.
47. *Narrative–Action 24 February 1942 (Wake Island)*; *Report on Attacks Made by Enterprise Air Group on Wake Island*.
48. *Early Raids in the Pacific Ocean*, 47–48.
49. Enclosure A, *Report of Action on February 24, 1942 (Zone Minus Twelve) against Wake Island*, Commanding Officer USS *Enterprise* (Serial 054), dated March 8, 1942.

50. *Report on Attacks Made by Enterprise Air Group on Wake Island.*
51. *Early Raids in the Pacific Ocean,* 51–52.
52. *Ibid.,* 52.
53. *Report on Attacks Made by Enterprise Air Group on Wake Island.*
54. *Ibid.*
55. Enclosure A, *Report of Action on February 24, 1942.*
56. *Ibid.*
57. *Ibid.*
58. *Conduct of Ship's Company in Action Incident to Participation of Enterprise in Operations Against Wake Island on Tuesday, 24 February, 1942 (Zone Minus Twelve),* Enclosure D, Executive Officer USS *Enterprise*; Enclosure A, *Report of Action on February 24, 1942.*
59. 1st Endorsement, Commander Task Force Sixteen (Serial 037), dated March 9, 1942, *Report of Action on February 24,1942 (Zone Minus Twelve), against Wake Island,* Commanding Officer, USS *Enterprise* (Serial 054), dated March 8, 1942; 2nd Endorsement, Commander-in-Chief, U.S. Pacific Fleet (Serial 0890), dated March 21, 1942, *Report of Action on February 24, 1942 (Zone Minus Twelve) against Wake Island,* Commanding Officer USS *Enterprise* (Serial 054), dated March 8, 1942.
60. Edwin, 265.
61. Halsey and Bryan III, 99.
62. *Ibid.,* 99–100.
63. *Ibid.,* 100.
64. *Early Raids in the Pacific Ocean,* 53.
65. *Report of Attack Made by Enterprise Air Group on Marcus Island,* Commander Enterprise Air Group (Serial 018), dated March 6, 1942, 1.
66. Lundstrom, *The First Team,* 117–118, Stafford, 68–69.
67. *Report of Attack Made by Enterprise Air Group on Marcus Island,* 1–2; Stafford, 69–70.
68. *Attack on Marcus Island, March 4, 1942,* Enclosure C (Commander Bombing Squadron Six), *Report of Attack Made by Enterprise Air Group on Marcus Island,* Commander Enterprise Air Group (Serial 018), dated March 6, 1942.
69. *Ibid.*
70. *Ibid.,* 1–2.
71. Stafford, 69–70.
72. *Report of Attack on Marcus Island,* Enclosure C (Commander Scouting Squadron Six); *Report of Attack Made by Enterprise Air Group on Marcus Island;* Stafford, 70.
73. *Report of Attack on Marcus Island,* 3.
74. USS *Enterprise* CV-6 Association, *Account of Jack Leaming, RM 2/c: Prisoner of War,* www.cv6.org/company/accounts/jleaming/default.htm; *Report of Attack on Marcus Island.*
75. Lundstrom, *The First Team,* 118–119.
76. *Ibid.,* 121.
77. *Ibid.,* 121.
78. *Report of Attack Made by Enterprise Air Group on Marcus Island.*
79. *Report of Action on March 4, 1942 (Zone Minus Eleven) against Marcus Island,* Commanding Officer, USS *Enterprise* (Serial 055), dated March 9, 1942.
80. *Ibid.*
81. *Ibid.*
82. 1st Endorsement (Commander Task Force Sixteen), *Report of Action on March 4, 1942 (Zone Minus Eleven) against Marcus Island,* Commanding Officer, USS *Enterprise* (Serial 055), dated March 9, 1942.
83. 2nd Endorsement, Commander-in-Chief, U.S. Pacific Fleet (Serial 0854), dated March 17, 1942, *Report of Action on March 4, 1942 (Zone Minus Eleven) against Marcus Island,* Commanding Officer, USS *Enterprise* (Serial 055), dated March 9, 1942.
84. Edwin, 265.
85. Newton.
86. Lundstrom, *The First Team,* 119–121.

Chapter 5

1. Nimitz "Graybook," vol. 1, 254–260.
2. *Ibid.,* 254–260.
3. *Ibid.,* 257.
4. Lundstrom, *The First Team,* 122–123; Nimitz "Graybook," vol. 1, 257.
5. *Report of Attack on Enemy Forces in Salamaua-Lae Area, March 10, 1942,* Commander Task Force 11 (Serial 0125), March 25, 1942, 1.
6. Nimitz "Graybook," vol. 1, 260.
7. *Early Raids in the Pacific Ocean,* 57–58.
8. *Report of Attack on Enemy Forces in Salamaua-Lae Area,* 1–2.
9. *Early Raids in the Pacific Ocean,* 58–59; *Cruise of Task Force Eleven,* 5–6.
10. *Report of Attack on Enemy Forces in Salamaua-Lae Area,* 1–4; *Report of Bombing Attack on Enemy Shipping and Shore Establishments in Salamaua-Lae Area, March 10, 1942,* Commander TG 11.5 (Commanding Officer USS *Lexington*) (Serial 008), 1.
11. *Early Raids in the Pacific Ocean,* 60–61.
12. *Ibid.,* 61–62; *Report of Attack on Enemy Forces in Salamaua-Lae Area,* 4; *Report of Bombing Attack on Enemy Shipping and Shore Establishments in Salamaua-Lae Area,* 1–2.
13. Nimitz "Graybook," vol. 1, 282.
14. *Cruise of Task Force Eleven,* 6–7.
15. *Report of Bombing Attack on Enemy Shipping and Shore Establishments in Salamaua-Lae Area,* 2–3.
16. Lundstrom, *The First Team,* 127.
17. Cressman, *That Gallant Ship,* 66.
18. *Ibid.,* 67.
19. *Ibid.,* 66–67.
20. *Report of Bombing Attack on Enemy Shipping and Shore Establishments in Salamaua-Lae Area,* 4–6.
21. *Ibid.,* 4–6.
22. Wills, Richard K., "Dauntless in Peace and War: A Preliminary Archaeological and Historical Documentation of Douglas SBD-2 Dauntless BuNo 2106," *Midway Madness,* vol. 1 (Washington, D.C.: Research Analysis, Naval Historical Center, Underwater Archaeology Branch, 1997), 41–42.
23. *Report of Bombing Attack on Enemy Shipping and Shore Establishments in Salamaua-Lae Area,* 6–7; Cressman, *That Gallant Ship,* 67–68.
24. Cressman, *That Gallant Ship,* 67.
25. *Report of Bombing Attack on Enemy Shipping and Shore Establishments in Salamaua-Lae Area,* 6–7; Cressman, *That Gallant Ship,* 67–68.
26. Cressman, *That Gallant Ship,* 68.
27. Lundstrom, *The First Team,* 131–132.
28. Nimitz "Graybook," vol. 1, 286; Lundstrom, *The First Team,* 132–133.
29. *VF-42 Aircraft Trouble Report (Ens. W.A. Haas)* 15 March 1942, Correspondence with RADM W.N. Leonard; Lundstrom, *The First Team,* 132–134.
30. Lundstrom, *The First Team,* 134–135.

31. *Early Raids in the Pacific Ocean*, 67; Lundstrom, *The First Team*, 131.
32. *Interrogation Nav No. 97, USSBS No. 446, Air Operations by Japanese Naval Air Forces Based at Rabaul, Japanese Naval Planning*, United States Strategic Bombing Survey ([Pacific] Naval Analysis Division), vol. 1, 412.
33. *Attack made by Yorktown Air Group against Enemy Forces at Salamaua and Lae, New Guinea*, Commanding Officer USS Yorktown (serial 022), dated March 12, 1942, 5-7.
34. *Ibid.*, 6.
35. *Report of Bombing Attack on Enemy Shipping and Shore Establishments in Salamaua–Lae Area*, 11-12.
36. *Ibid.*, 10-12.
37. *Report of Attack on Enemy Forces in Salamaua–Lae Area*, 5-6.
38. *Cruise of Task Force Eleven*, 9.
39. *Ibid.*, 10.
40. *Ibid.*, 10-11.
41. *Ibid.*, 12-13.
42. *Ibid.*, 11-12.
43. *Ibid.*, 8.
44. *1st Endorsement, Report of Attack on Enemy Forces in Salamaua–Lae Area, 10 March 1942*, Commander-in-Chief, U.S. Pacific Fleet, Serial 01094, 8 April 1942, 1.
45. Cressman, *That Gallant Ship*, 69; Lundstrom, *The First Team*, 132.
46. *Lae and Salamaua Raid, 10 March 1942*, Naval History and Heritage Command, history.navy.mil/history; Hoyt, 71.
47. Potter, *Nimitz*, 44.
48. *Early Raids in the Pacific Ocean*, 57-66.
49. Edwin, 266-267.

Chapter 6

1. Glines, Carroll V., *The Doolittle Raid* (Atglen, PA: Schiffer Military/Aviation History, 1991), 10.
2. *Ibid.*, 12-13.
3. *Ibid.*, 12-13.
4. Glines, 13-15; *The Tokyo Raid, April 18, 1942*, U.S. Army Air Forces, Director of Intelligence Service, Informational Intelligence Summary (Special) No. 20, October 25, 1942 (College Park, MD: NARA), 2; Chun, Clayton, *The Doolittle Raid 1942* (New York: Osprey, 2006), 31-32.
5. Glines, 16.
6. *Ibid.*, 15-16.
7. *Ibid.*, 17.
8. Clutter, Lt. Col. Stephen, *Jimmy Doolittle: Famed Airpower Pioneer*, Air Force Print News, April 16, 2007, www.af.mil/News/Article-Display/Article/127211/jimmy-doolittle-famed-airpower-pioneer/.
9. Chun, 13-16; Glines, 17-18.
10. Glines, 17-20.
11. *Ibid.*, 21.
12. Taylor, Theodore, *The Magnificent Mitscher* (Annapolis: Naval Institute Press, 1954), 112.
13. Rose, Lisle Abbott, *The Ship that Held the Line: The USS Hornet and the First Year of the Pacific War* (Annapolis: Bluejacket Books, Naval Institute Press, 2002), 39-41.
14. Glines, 22.
15. Rose, 39.
16. Glines, 23.
17. Chun, 33-34; *The Tokyo Raid*, 2-3.
18. Glines, 23-27; *The Tokyo Raid*, 2-3.
19. Glines, 28-30.
20. *Ibid.*, 30-31.
21. *Ibid.*, 32, 35-36.
22. *Ibid.*, 35.
23. Rose, 39-41, 40-42.
24. *Ibid.*, 39-41, 49.
25. *Ibid.*, 50.
26. Halsey and Bryan III, 32.
27. Glines, 40.
28. Rose, 42-47.
29. *Ibid.*, 51.
30. Chun, 35.
31. Glines, 40-42.
32. Rose, 50.
33. Potter, *Bull Halsey*, 56-57.
34. Glines, 43-44.
35. *Ibid.*, 45.
36. *Ibid.*, 47.
37. *Ibid.*, 45.
38. Glines, 49; Rose, 52.
39. Glines, 49.
40. *Ibid.*, 50.
41. Potter, *Bull Halsey*, 57-58.
42. *Ibid.*, 58.
43. Rose, 54-55.
44. *Action Report USS Hornet (CV-6) Captain Marc A. Mitscher to Admiral Chester A. Nimitz*, April 28, 1942; *CINCPAC Report of Action in Connection with the Bombing of Tokyo on April 18, 1942*, dated May 4, 1942.
45. Potter, *Bull Halsey*, 57-58; *Action Report USS Enterprise, Captain George D. Murray to CINCPAC*, April 23, 1942.
46. *War Diary*, USS *Enterprise*, for April 1942.
47. Anonymous military historian, *Yomiuri Shimbun*, March 25, 1950, 2.
48. Glines, 61-62.
49. Chun, 38.
50. *Action Report USS Hornet (CV-6)*.
51. Potter, *Bull Halsey*, 58-59.
52. *War Diary*, USS *Enterprise*, for April 1942, 2.
53. *Ibid.*, 3.
54. Potter, *Bull Halsey*, 59.
55. Glines, 62-63; *Lieutenant (JG) Osborne Wiseman: Excerpts of War Diary, VB-3*, for April 1942, included with "The Navy's Share of the Tokyo Raid," Box 118, RG 38, NHHC, WWII Command Files, NARA.
56. *War Diary*, USS *Enterprise*, for April 1942, 2.
57. Rose, 61.
58. Glines, 53-55.
59. *War Diary*, USS *Enterprise*, for April 1942, 3.
60. Lundstrom, *The First Team*, 148.
61. *Action Report USS Enterprise*; Lundstrom, 147-148; *War Diary*, USS *Enterprise* for April 1942, 3.
62. *Action Report USS Hornet (CV-6)*; *Action Report USS Enterprise*; M.F. Leslie, Lt. Comdr., USN, Commanding Officer of VB-3, *War Diary VB-3* for April 1942; *War Diary*, USS *Enterprise*, for April 1942; *Report of Action in Connection with the Bombing of Tokyo on April 18, 1942*, Captain George D. Murray, April 23, 1942.
63. Glines, 66-67.
64. *Action Report USS Hornet (CV-6)*; *Action Report USS Enterprise*; M.F. Leslie; *War Diary*, USS *Enterprise*, for April 1942; *Report of Action in Connection with the Bombing of Tokyo*.
65. Glines, 71.
66. *Ibid.*, 71-72.
67. Chun, 43-45.

68. M.F. Leslie, 9–10.
69. *War Diary*, USS *Nashville*, for April 1942.
70. Glines, 67.
71. *Ibid.*, 67.
72. Greening, Charles R. Colonel, USAF *First Joint Action: A Historical Account of the Doolittle Tokyo Raid–April 18, 1942*, www.doolittleraider.com/first_joint_action.htm
73. Glines, 66–70; *Lieutenant (JG) Osborne Wiseman: Excerpts of War Diary, VB-3*, for April 1942.
74. Rose, 70–72; *War Diary*, USS *Enterprise*, for April 1942, 4.
75. M.F. Leslie, 10.
76. Doolittle, Brig. General James H., *Report on the Aerial Bombing of Japan*, to Commanding General of the Army Air Forces, Washington, June 5, 1942.
77. Chun, 51.
78. *The Tokyo Raid*, 3–7.
79. *Ibid.*, 10.
80. *Ibid.*, 7.
81. *Ibid.*, 7–8.
82. *Ibid.*, 7–8.
83. *Mission Report Filed By Doolittle in Chungking*, April 30, 1942, Headquarters, American Army Forces, China, Burma, and India.
84. Oxford, Edward, "Jimmy Doolittle and the Tokyo Raiders Strike Japan During World War II," *American History Magazine* (August 1997).
85. Glines, 158–169.
86. Potter, *Bull Halsey*, 62.
87. Chun, 83–89; Doolittle, *Report*; Glines, 85–86.
88. *Action Report USS Enterprise*.
89. *Ibid.*
90. *War Diary*, USS *Enterprise*, for April 1942.
91. Chun, 81, 83.
92. *War Diary*, USS *Enterprise*, for April 1942; Newton, 35; Lundstrom, *The First Team*, 151.
93. Potter, *Bull Halsey*, 65–66.
94. *Ibid.*, 64–66.
95. *War Diary*, USS *Hornet*, for April 1942; Newton, 35–36.
96. Newton, 35–36; Rose, 77–78; Lundstrom, *The First Team*, 150–153.
97. *War Diary*, USS *Enterprise*, for April 1942.
98. *The Tokyo Raid*, 2.
99. *Ibid.*, 9.
100. Oxford.
101. *Report of Action, April 18, 1942, with Notable Events Prior and Subsequent Thereto*, USS *Hornet*, M.A. Mitscher, April 28, 1942.
102. *The CINCPAC Report of the Action in Connection with the Bombing of Tokyo on April 18, 1942*, dated May 4, 1942 (College Park, MD: NARA).
103. Glines, 144.
104. *Ibid.*, 148.
105. *Ibid.*, 143–148.
106. *Ashi Shimbun*, April 18, 1942, "Raid on Tokyo," u-s-history.com.
107. *Record of Sea Battles: Diary of the Late Vice Admiral Matome Ugaki*, War History Office, April 18–19, 1942.
108. *Ibid.*
109. *Interrogation Nav No. 43*, 175.
110. *The Campaigns of MacArthur in the Pacific*, vol. 1 (U.S. Army, 1966), Chapter 1, "The Japanese Offensive in the Pacific Reports of General MacArthur," 1–3.
111. Stephen, John J., *Hawaii Under the Rising Sun: Japan's Plans for Conquest After Pearl Harbor*, 1st ed. (University of Hawaii Press, 1984), 92, 93, 109–111.
112. *Ibid.*, 111–112.
113. *Ibid.*, 113–11.
114. Chun, 89–90.
115. Stephen, 118–120.

Chapter 7

1. Chun, 89–90.
2. Haney, Admiral Cecil D., Commander, U.S. Pacific Fleet. *71st Anniversary of the Battle of Midway, Pearl Harbor, Hawaii, 07 June 2013*, www.cpf.navy.mil/leaders/cecil-haney/speeches/2013/06/battle-of-midway.pdf, 2.
3. *The Battle of Midway*, Office of Naval Intelligence; Keegan, John. *The Second World War* (New York: Penguin, 2005), 275.
4. *Early Raids in the Pacific Ocean*, 57–66.
5. Gustin, Emmanuel, *Grumman F4F Wildcat*, users.skynet.be/Emmanuel.Gustin/history/f4f.html.
6. Panko, Ray, *Douglas SBD Dauntless Scout/Dive Bomber*, Pacific Aviation Museum Pearl Harbor, www.pacificaviationmuseum.org/pearl-harbor-blog/douglas-sbd-dauntless-scout-dive-bomber.
7. Terzibaschitsch, Stefan: *Flugzeugtraeger der U.S. Navy*, 2nd ed. (Munich, Germany: Bernard & Graefe, 1986), 31.
8. Knott, R.C., *Black Cat Raiders of World War II* (Annapolis: Nautical & Aviation Publishing Company of America, 1981).
9. *Battle of Coral Sea, Combat Narratives*, NHHC, 2017, www.history.navy.mil/content/dam/nhhc/browse-by-topic/War%20and%20Conflict/WWII/Coral%20Sea%20170504.pdf, 8.
10. Lundstrom, 141.
11. *Ibid.*, 141, 449.
12. Barnes, 12–19.
13. Wukovits, John F., *Admiral "Bull" Halsey: The Life and Wars of the Navy's Most Controversial Commander* (New York: Palgrave Macmillan, 2010), xi–xii.

Bibliography

Action Reports

Action in the Marshall Islands, 1 February 1942, Commander Task Force Eight (Serial 006), dated 9 February 1942.

Action Report, Commanding Officer USS Hughes (serial 06), dated February 6, 1942.

Action Report USS Enterprise, Captain George D. Murray to CINCPAC, April 23, 1942.

Action Report USS Hornet (CV-6), Captain Marc A. Mitscher to Admiral Chester A. Nimitz, April 28, 1942.

Air Observations and Operations during Bombardment of Wake Island, Enclosure B, Report of Action with Enemy-Bombardment of Wake Island, Commanding Officer USS Northampton (serial 021), dated February 25, 1942.

Attack Made by Yorktown Air Group against Enemy Forces at Salamaua and Lae, New Guinea, CO USS Yorktown (serial 022), dated March 12, 1942.

Attack on Marcus Island, March 4, 1942, Enclosure C (Commander Bombing Squadron Six), Report of Attack Made by Enterprise Air Group on Marcus Island, Commander Enterprise Air Group (Serial 018), dated March 6, 1942.

Attack on Wake Island, February 24, 1942, Enclosure C, Commander Bombing Squadron Six (Serial 08), dated February 25, 1942.

Battle Engagement—1 February 1942, Commander Fighting Squadron Six (serial 001), dated February 2, 1942.

Bombardment of Wake and Withdrawal Therefrom, Commanding Officer USS Salt Lake City (serial 020), dated 9 March 1942.

CINCPAC Report of Action in Connection with the Bombing of Tokyo on April 18, 1942, dated May 4, 1942. College Park, MD: NARA.

Conduct of Ship's Company in Action Incident to Participation of Enterprise in Operations Against Wake Island on Tuesday, 24 February 1942 (Zone Minus Twelve), Enclosure D, Executive Officer USS Enterprise,

Cruise of Task Force Eleven, from January 31 to March 26, 1942, Commander TF 11, serial 0123, March 23, 1942.

Dolphin First War Patrol, COMSUBPAC, February 5, 1942.

Doolittle, Brig. General James H., Report on the Aerial Bombing of Japan, to Commanding General of the Army Air Forces, Washington, June 5, 1942.

Early Raids in the Pacific Ocean, February 1 to March 10, 1942, Publication Section, Combat Intelligence Branch, Office of Naval Intelligence, United States Navy, 1943.

Enclosure A, Report of Action on February 24, 1942 (Zone Minus Twelve) against Wake Island, Commanding Officer USS Enterprise (Serial 054), dated March 8, 1942.

Engagement Report, Task Force 17.1.1 Striking Group, CO, USS Louisville (serial 001), dated February 6, 1942, Report of Action, CO, Commander Destroyer Division Three (serial 07), dated February 7, 1942.

1st Endorsement, Commander Task Force Sixteen (Serial 033), dated 10 March 1942, Report of Action on March 4, 1942 (Zone Minus Eleven) against Marcus Island, Commanding Officer, USS Enterprise (Serial 055), dated March 9, 1942.

1st Endorsement, Commander Task Force Sixteen (Serial 037), dated 9 March 1942, Report of Action on February 24, 1942 (Zone Minus Twelve) against Wake Island, Commanding Officer, USS Enterprise (Serial 054), dated 8 March 1942.

Flight Leader's Report of Dawn Attack on Kwajalein Atoll, 1 February, 1942, Enclosure C, Attacks on Marshall Islands, 1 February 1942, Commander Bombing Squadron Six (serial 06), dated February 2, 1942.

Leslie, M.F., Lt. Comdr., USN, Commanding Officer of VB-3, War Diary, VB-3 for April 1942.

Lieutenant J.G. Osborne Wiseman: Excerpts of War Diary, VB-3, for April 1942, included with "The Navy's Share of the Tokyo Raid," Box 118, RG 38, NHHC, WWII Command Files, NARA.

Mission Report Filed by Doolittle in Chungking, April 30, 1942. Headquarters, American Army Forces, China, Burma, and India.

Narrative-Action 24 February 1942 (Wake Island), Enclosure C, Commander Fighting Squadron Six (Serial 08), dated 26 February 1942.

Narrative of Torpedo Attack on Vessels Anchored in Lagoon Adjacent to Island of Kwajalein in Kwajalein Atoll, XO Lieutenant Commander Massey, Enclosure D, Report After Battle, Commander Torpedo Squadron Six (serial 02), dated February 2, 1942.

Operation Order No. 2-42, Task Organization, Task Force 17, Commanding Officer, serial 0014(Y), dated January 25, 1942.

Report After Battle, Commander Torpedo Squadron Six (serial 02), dated February 2, 1942.

Report of Action, April 18, 1942, with Notable Events Prior and Subsequent Thereto, USS Hornet, M.A. Mitscher, April 28, 1942.

Report of Action of Task Force Eleven with Japanese Aircraft on February 20, 1942, CO TF 11 dated February 24, 1942. College Park, MD: NARA.

Report of Action on February 1, 1942, Commanding Officer USS *Enterprise* (serial 026), dated February 7, 1942.

Report of Action on February 24, 1942 (Zone Minus Twelve) against Wake Island, Commanding Officer, USS *Enterprise* (Serial 054), dated March 8, 1942.

Report of Action on March 4, 1942 (Zone Minus Eleven) against Marcus Island, Commanding Officer, USS *Enterprise* (Serial 055), dated March 9, 1942.

Report of Action 31 January 1942, Commanding Officer USS *Walke* (serial 02), dated February 5, 1942.

Report of Action with Enemy-Bombardment of Wake Island, Commanding Officer, USS *Northampton* (serial 021), dated February 25, 1942.

Report of Air Action at Jaluit, Enclosure A, *Report of Attack of Yorktown Air Group on Jaluit, Milli and Makin in Marshall and Gilbert Islands*, CO USS *Yorktown* (serial 07), dated February 5, 1942.

Report of Air Action at Makin, Enclosure B, *Report of Attack of Yorktown Air Group on Jaluit, Mili and Makin in Marshall and Gilbert Islands*, CO USS *Yorktown* (serial 07), dated February 5, 1942.

Report of Air Action at Milli, Enclosure C, *Report of Attack of Yorktown Air Group on Jaluit, Milli and Makin in Marshall and Gilbert Islands*, CO USS *Yorktown* (serial 07), dated February 5, 1942.

Report of Air Attack on Lexington on February 20, 1942, Enclosure A, CO *Lexington*, February 23, 1942. College Park, MD: NARA.

Report of Air Group Commander-USS Yorktown, Air Attacks on Marshall-Gilbert Islands, 31 January, 1942, Enclosure D, *Report of Attack of Yorktown Air Group on Jaluit, Milli and Makin in Marshall and Gilbert Islands*, CO USS *Yorktown* (serial 07), dated February 5, 1942.

Report of Attack Made by Enterprise Air Group on Marcus Island, Commander *Enterprise* Air Group (Serial 018), dated March 6, 1942.

Report of Attack of Yorktown Air Group on Jaluit, Mili and Makin in Marshall and Gilbert Islands, CO USS *Yorktown* (serial 07), dated February 5, 1942.

Report of Attack on Enemy Forces in Salamaua–Lae Area, March 10, 1942, Commander Task Force 11 (Serial 0125), March 25, 1942.

Report of Attack on Marcus Island, Enclosure C (Commander Scouting Squadron Six).

Report of Attack on the Marshall Islands, February 1, 1942, Commander, Scouting Squadron Six (serial 08-c), dated February 3, 1942.

Report of Attack on Wake Island, Enclosure C, Commander Scouting Squadron Six (serial 016-c), dated February 25, 1942.

Report of Attack on Wake Island, Enclosure C, Commander Torpedo Squadron Six (Serial 012), dated February 24, 1942.

Report on Attacks Made by Enterprise Air Group on Wake Island, Commander *Enterprise* Air Group (Serial 07), dated February 26, 1942.

Report of Bombardment of Wake Island on 24 February 1942, Commander Task Group 16.7 (serial 025), dated March 3, 1942.

Report of Bombing Attack on Enemy Shipping and Shore Establishments in Salamaua–Lae Area, March 10, 1942, Commander TG 11.5 (Commanding Officer USS *Lexington*) (Serial 008).

Report of Engagement, January 31, 1942, Commander Task Force 17 (serial 0018(Y), dated February 9, 1942.

Report on Attacks Made by Enterprise Air Group on Northern Marshall Islands, Commander *Enterprise* Air Group (Serial 01), February 4, 1942.

Report on Attacks Made by Enterprise Air Group on Wake Island, Commander *Enterprise* Air Group (Serial 07), dated February 26, 1942.

Report on Raid on Wake Island, USS *Maury*, Commanding Officer USS *Maury* (Serial 05), dated March 3, 1942.

2nd Endorsement, Commander-in-Chief, U.S. Pacific Fleet (Serial 0854), dated March 17, 1942, *Report of Action on March 4, 1942 (Zone Minus Eleven) against Marcus Island*, Commanding Officer, USS *Enterprise* (Serial 055), dated March 9, 1942.

2nd Endorsement, Commander-in-Chief, U.S. Pacific Fleet (Serial 0890), dated March 21, 1942, *Report of Action on February 24, 1942 (Zone Minus Twelve), against Wake Island*, Commanding Officer, USS *Enterprise* (Serial 054), dated 8 March 1942.

Ship Bombardment of Wake Island, Commander Destroyer Squadron Six (Serial 030), dated March 8, 1942.

The Tokyo Raid, April 18, 1942, U.S. Army Air Forces, Director of Intelligence Service, Informational Intelligence Summary (Special) No. 20, October 25, 1942. College Park, MD: NARA.

USS Tautog Patrol Report, 26 December 1941–4 February 1942, Commanding Officer, USS *Tautog*, February 4, 1942.

War Diary, USS *Enterprise*, for April 1942.
War Diary, USS *Hornet*, for April 1942.
War Diary, USS *Nashville*, for April 1942.
War Diary, VB-3 for April 1942.

General Sources

Admiral Ernest J. King (1878–1956), PBS American Experience, PBS, pbs.org/wgbh/amex/macarthur.

Ashi Shimbun, April 18, 1942, "Raid on Tokyo," u-s-history.com.

Astor, Gerald. *Wings of Gold: The U.S. Naval Air Campaign in World War II*. New York: Ballantine Books, 2004.

Attack at Pearl Harbor, 1941, eyewitnesstohistory.com.

Barnes, Major Gary I., USAF. *Great Warriors of World War II: Admiral Ernest J. King–Admiral Chester W. Nimitz*. Maxwell AFB, AL: Air Command and Staff College, Air University DTIC, February 12, 1949.

Battle of the Coral Sea, Combat Narratives, NHHC, 2017, www.history.navy.mil/content/dam/nhhc/browse-by-topic/War%20and%20Conflict/WWII/Coral%20Sea%20170504.pdf, 8.

The Battle of Midway, Office of Naval Intelligence.

Bauer, James L. *Fletcher, Task Force Commander: The Early Years of the Pacific War and a Former Sailor*. Marshalltown, IA: Manorborn Press, 2010.

Belote, James H., and William M. Belote. *Titans of the Seas: The Development and Operations of Japanese and American Carrier Task Forces During World War II*. New York: Harper & Row, 1975.

Bernstein, Marc D. "The Early Carrier Raids: Proving Japanese Vulnerability." *Naval Aviation News* (March–April 1992).

Blair Jr., Clay. *Silent Victory: The U.S. Submarine War against Japan*. Annapolis: Naval Institute Press, 2001.

Bowen, James. *The Pacific War 1942: The United States Strategy, Pacific War History*, kokodatreks.com/history/thepacificwar1942.

Brooks, Brenton. "The Carnival of Blood in Australian Mandated Territory." *Sabretache: Military Historical Society of Australia* 54 (4) (December 2013).

Budge, Kent G. "Brown, Wilson, Jr." *The Pacific War Online Encyclopedia.* Retrieved 4 August 2010.

Buell, Thomas. *Master of Sea Power: A Biography of Fleet Admiral Ernest J. King.* Annapolis: Naval Institute Press, 1980.

The Campaigns of MacArthur in the Pacific, vol. 1. U.S. Army, 1966. Chapter 1, "The Japanese Offensive in the Pacific Reports of General MacArthur."

Chun, Clayton. *The Doolittle Raid 1942.* New York: Osprey, 2006.

Command Summary of Fleet Admiral Chester W. Nimitz, USN. Nimitz "Graybook," vol. 1.

Cressman, Robert J. *A Magnificent Fight: Marines in the Battle for Wake Island.* Washington, D.C.: History and Museums Division, Headquarters, U.S. Marine Corps.

_____. *That Gallant Ship: USS Yorktown (CV-5).* Missoula, Pictorial Histories Publishing Company, 1989.

Damage to United States Naval Forces and Installations as a Result of the Attack, Report of the Joint Committee on the Investigation of the Pearl Harbor Attack. Washington, D.C.: United States Government Printing Office, 1946.

Dear, I.C.B., and M.R.D. Foot. "Admiral Ernest J. King." *The Oxford Companion to World War II*, 2001.

Edwin, Layton T. "Earlier Carrier Raids during World War II." Naval History: The Sixth Symposium of the U.S. Naval Academy. Wilmington, DE: Scholarly Resources, 1987.

Evolution of Aircraft Carriers. Washington, D.C.: Department of the Navy, Naval Historical Center.

Fall of Rabaul. Australian Government, Department of Veterans' Affairs, ww2australia.gov.au/japadvance/rabaul.

1st Independent Company, Second World War, 1939–1945 units. Australian War Memorial.

Fleet Admiral Chester William Nimitz. Washington, D.C.: Department of the Navy, Naval Historical Center.

Fleet Admiral Ernest Joseph King. Washington, D.C.: Department of the Navy, Naval Historical Center.

Fleet Admiral William Frederick Halsey, Jr. Washington, D.C.: Department of the Navy, Naval Historical Center.

Glines, Carroll V. *The Doolittle Raid.* Atglen, PA: Schiffer Military/Aviation History, 1991.

Greening, Charles R. Colonel, USAF. *First Joint Action: A Historical Account of the Doolittle Tokyo Raid—April 18, 1942*, www.doolittleraider.com/first_joint_action.htm.

Gustin, Emmanuel. *Grumman F4F Wildcat*, users.skynet.be/Emmanuel.Gustin/history/f4f.html.

Halsey, Fleet Admiral William F., and Lieutenant Commander Joseph Bryan III. *Admiral Halsey's Story.* New York: McGraw-Hill, 1947.

Haney, Admiral Cecil D., Commander, U.S. Pacific Fleet. *71st Anniversary of the Battle of Midway, Pearl Harbor, Hawaii, 7 June 2013.* www.cpf.navy.mil/leaders/cecil-haney/speeches/2013/06/battle-of-midway.pdf.

Heinl, Lieutenant Colonel R.D., Jr., USMC. *Marines in World War II. Historical Monograph: The Defense of Wake.* Chapter 4: "The Fall of Wake." Washington, D.C.: Headquarters USMC, 1947.

Hodges, Ian. *The Sinking of Montevideo Maru, 1 July 1942.* Remembering 1942. Australian War Memorial.

Hoyt, Edwin P. *How They Won the War in the Pacific: Nimitz and His Admirals.* Guilford, CT: The Lyons Press, 2002.

Interrogation Nav No. 43, USSBS No. 192, Japanese Naval Planning United States Strategic Bombing Survey. [Pacific] Naval Analysis Division, vol. 1.

Keegan, John. *The Second World War.* New York: Penguin, 2005.

Knott, R.C. *Black Cat Raiders of World War II.* Annapolis: Nautical & Aviation Publishing Company of America, 1981.

Lae and Salamaua Raid, 10 March 1942. Naval History and Heritage Command, history.navy.mil/history.

Lundstrom, John B. *Black Shoe Carrier Admiral: Frank Jack Fletcher at Coral Sea, Midway, and Guadalcanal.* Annapolis, MD: Naval Institute Press, 2006, Ch. 1.

_____. *The First Team: Pacific Naval Air Combat from Pearl Harbor to Midway.* Annapolis: Naval Institute Press, 2005.

Micallef, Joseph V. *The First Attack: Pearl Harbor, February 7, 1932.* Military.com.

Moore, Stephen L. *Pacific Payback: The Carrier Aviators Who Avenged Pearl Harbor at the Battle of Midway.* New York: NAL Caliber-Penguin Group, 2014.

Moremon, John. *Rabaul, 1942, Campaign History.* Australian War Memorial, 2003. Archived from the original on August 31, 2008.

Morton, Louis. *Strategy and Command: The First Two Years, US Army in World War II, The War in the Pacific.* Center of Military History, 1960. Chapter 6: "The First Weeks of War, 7–26 December."

Newton, David. *Journal of the Pacific War: From the Wartime Diary of Clarence W. Olive, M Division, USS Enterprise.* bookemon.com.

Offner, Larry. "The Butch O'Hare Story." *St. Louis Magazine* (July 29, 2006).

Oxford, Edward. "Jimmy Doolittle and the Tokyo Raiders Strike Japan During World War II." *American History Magazine* (August 1997).

Panko, Ray. *Douglas SBD Dauntless Scout /Dive Bomber*, Pacific Aviation Museum Pearl Harbor, www.pacificaviationmuseum.org/pearl-harbor-blog/douglas-sbd-dauntless-scout-dive-bomber.

Parillo, Mark. "The United States in the Pacific." Chapter 10 of Robin Higham and Stephen Harris, *Why Air Forces Fail: The Anatomy of Defeat.* Lexington: University Press of Kentucky, 2006.

Parshall, Jonathan, and Anthony Tully. *Shattered Sword: The Untold Story of the Battle of Midway.* Dulles, VA: Potomac Books, 2007.

A Pearl Harbor Fact Sheet. Census, U.S. Department of Commerce, U.S. Census Bureau, census.gov/history/pdf/pearl-harbor-fact-sheet-1.pdf.

Potter, E.B. *Bull Halsey.* Annapolis: Naval Institute Press, 1985.

_____. *Nimitz.* Annapolis: Naval Institute Press, 1979.

Prange, Gordon W. *At Dawn We Slept.* New York: McGraw-Hill, 1981.

Record of Sea Battles: Diary of the Late Vice Admiral Matome Ugaki, April 18–19, 1942. War History Office.

Reynolds, Clark J. *The Fast Carriers: The Forging of an Air Navy.* New York: McGraw-Hill, 1968.

Rickard, J. *Battle of Wake Island, 8–23 December 1941.* historyofwar.org.

Rose, Lisle Abbott. *The Ship that Held the Line: The USS Hornet and the First Year of the Pacific War.* Annapolis: Bluejacket Books, Naval Institute Press, 2002.

Skates, John Ray. *The Invasion of Japan: Alternative to the Bomb.* University of South Carolina Press, 2000.

Stafford, Edward P. *The Big E: The Story of the USS Enterprise*. Annapolis: Bluejacket Books, Naval Institute Press, 1962.

Stanley, Peter. *The Defense of the 'Malay barrier': Rabaul and Ambon, January 1942*. Remembering 1942, Australian War Memorial.

Stefan Terzibaschitsch: *Flugzeugtraeger der U.S. Navy*, 2nd edition. Munich, Germany: Bernard & Graefe, 1986.

Stephen, John J. *Hawaii Under the Rising Sun: Japan's Plans for Conquest After Pearl Harbor*. University of Hawaii Press, 1984.

Taylor, Theodore. *The Magnificent Mitscher*. Annapolis: Naval Institute Press, 1954.

Tillman, Barrett. "William Bull Halsey: Legendary World War II Admiral." *World War II Magazine* (July/August 2007).

Tucker, Spencer C. "Brown, Wilson, Jr. (1882–1957)." *World War II at Sea: An Encyclopedia*, vol. 1. ABC-CLIO LLC, 2012.

2/22nd Battalion, Second World War, 1939–1945 units. Australian War Memorial.

"Unravelling the Full Scope of Japan's Midway Operation." pacificwar.org.au/Midway/ScopeofMidwayOp.html.

USS *Enterprise* CV-6. "Marshall Islands Raid, February 1, 1942." cv6.org/1942/marshalls.

USS *Enterprise* CV-6 Association. "Account of Jack Leaming, RM 2/c: Prisoner of War." www.cv6.org/company/accounts/jleaming/default.htm.

VF-42 Aircraft Trouble Report (Ens. W.A. Haas) 15 March 1942. Correspondence with RADM W.N. Leonard.

Wallin, Vice Admiral Homer N., USN. *Pearl Harbor: Why, How, Fleet Salvage and Final Appraisal*. Department of the Navy, Naval History Division, 1969.

Wigmore, Lionel. *The Japanese Thrust: Australia in the War of 1939–1945*, vol. 4, 1st ed. Canberra: Australian War Memorial, 1957. "Chapter 18: Rabaul and the Forward Observation Line."

Willmot, H.P. *Empires in the Balance: Japanese and Allied Pacific Strategies to April 1942*. Annapolis: Naval Institute Press, 1982.

Wills, Richard K. "Dauntless in Peace and War: A Preliminary Archaeological And Historical Documentation of Douglas SBD-2 Dauntless BuNo 2106." *Midway Madness*, vol. 1. Washington, D.C.: Research Analysis, Naval Historical Center, Underwater Archaeology Branch, 1997.

Wukovits, John F. *Admiral "Bull" Halsey: The Life and Wars of the Navy's Most Controversial Commander*. New York: Palgrave Macmillan, 2010.

Index

Numbers in *bold italics* indicate pages with illustrations

Abercrombie, Lt. Comdr. Laurence A. 171
Academic Board (Naval Academy) 8
HMNZS *Achilles* 69
ACNB communications channel 67
Adams, Ensign John P. 61, 62
Adams, Lt. Sam 47, 48, 49, 50, 118
Advanced Raiding Force 2
Aeronautical Engineering Course 129
Aeronautical Organization 98
Agidyen Island 48, 49
Aichi E 13A1 Type 0 reconnaissance floatplane (Jake) 42, 77
Ailinglapalap Island 23
"Air Admiral" 14
Air Group 8, 135, 159
Air Group Commander 25, 46, 99, 123
Air Service Mechanical School 129
Aircraft, Battle Group 14
Aircraft Scouting Force 2
AK (cargo ship) 43
Akagi 68, 139
Alameda 134, 136
Alameda, California 129
Alameda Naval Air Station 135
Alameda Pier 137
Alaska 12, 67
Aleutian Islands 22, 162, 163
USS *Allen* 21
Allen, Lt. E.H. 77, 78, 79
American Embassy 17
American Naval Forces 13
Amphibious Force 125
Anacostia Naval Air Station 129
Andaman Islands 162
USS *Anderson* (DD-411) 84, 109, 110, 173

Anderson, Lt. (JG) E.L. 38
Anderson, Lt. Cmdr. William L. 130
Annapolis 7, 14, 17, 20, 125
ANZAC 66, 120, 124
ANZAC Force (COMANZAC) 66, 67
ANZAC squadron 67, 69, 70, 82, 108, 109, 110, 172
AO (oiler) 43
Ara Waterway 149
Arcadia Agreement 13
Arcadia Conference 127, 128
Argentine Embassy in Tokyo 161
USS *Arizona* 5, 6
Armstrong, Lt. Cmdr. Robert G. 46, 47, 48, 49, 50, 112, 118, 169, 172
Army Air Force 128, 131, 132, 137, 159
Army Air Force Action Intelligence Summary 148
Army Air Force bomber 81
Army Air Forces Intelligence Summary (Special) No. 20, 159
Army Arsenal 149
Army War College 21
Arndt, Lt. R.W. 147
Arno Island 23
Arnold, Lt. Gen. Henry "Hap" 127, 128, 129, 130, 132, 133, 134, 155
Asanagi 113, 118, 121
Ashford, Flag Lt. 158
Ashi Shimbun 161
Ashizurizaki 162
Ashkhabad 156
Asia 156
Asiatic Fleet 9
Asiatic Torpedo Flotilla 21
USS *Astoria* (CA- 34), 14, 22, 84, 108, 110, 173

Athletic Association (Annapolis) 17
Atlantic Submarine Flotilla 8
Atsuta Factory 149
Atsuta munitions firm 148
USS *Augusta* 9
Ault, Cdr. William B. 111, 112, 170, 172
Australia 11, 12, 15, 66, 67, 69–70, 108, 111, 120, 121–122, 124, 164
HMAS *Australia* (D-84) 69, 110, 173
Australia-New Zealand shipping corridor 10
Australian Army 68
Australian Chiefs of Staff 68
Australian government 68
Australian Imperial Force 68
Australian RAAF flying boat 68
Ayers, RM 3c R.L. 56
USS *Aylwin* (DD-355) 67, 80, 171
Azores 21

B-17 Boeing Flying Fortress bomber 68, 111, 120, 123
B-18 Douglas Bolo bomber 127, 128
B-23 Douglas Dragon bomber 128
B-24B Consolidated Liberator bomber 133
B-25 North American Mitchell bomber 131, 133, 134, 136, 140, 145, 146
B-25B North American Mitchell bomber 132, 141, 142, 146, 148, 150, 156, 159, 174
B-25B Special Project 132, 135
Baba, PO 2c 76
USS *Bagley* (DD-386) 67, 108, 171, 173

187

Index

Balboa 133
USS *Balch* (DD-363) 23, 39, 84, 85, 86, 91, 93, 94, 95, 96, 136, 138, 170, 172, 174
USS *Baltimore* 8
USS *Batch* 140
Barber's Point 6
Barr, observer RM 1c Joseph Alonzo 60
Bassatt, Ensign 119
Bassett, Ensign Edgar R. 19
Bataan Peninsula 63
Batangas Harbor 8
Batdiv Three 12
Battle Fleet 15
Battle of Coral Sea 71
Battle of Midway 163, 164, 166
Battle of the Coral Sea 167
Battleship Row 6
Baumeister, Lt. John 102, 104
Bayers, Gunner B.H. 42, 91
Bayers, Radioman Electrician E.H. 35
Beck, Lt. Comdr. Edward L. 109, 171, 173
Bellinger, Lt. G.L. 47, 56
Bellinger, Vice Adm. Patrick N.L. 5
USS *Benham* (DD-397) 21, 136, 138, 174
Benham class Destroyer 174
Berger, Ensign H.L.A. 49
Berkeley 9, 129
Berlin, Germany 17
Berry, Ensign David R. 49, 50
Best, Lt. Richard H. 34, 89, 102, 103
Betty G 4M1 Mitsubishi 75, 76, 77
Bigej Channel 31
Bigelow, Ensign L.M. 51, 52
Bismarck Archipelago 22, 108
"Black Forces" 2
"black-shoe" 21
Blackmer, Aviation Machinist's Mate 2nd Class 142
USS *Blakeley* 69
Blanche Bay 68
Blitch, Lt. J.D. 89, 102
Bloch, RAdm. Claude 15
USS *Blue* (DD-387) 18, 84, 85, 86, 169, 172
"Blue Forces" 2
Board of Submarine Design 9
Bode, Capt. Howard D. 108, 173
Boettcher, Ensign Robert R. 143
Bofors 10
Bombing Squadron 8 (VB-8) 135
Bombing Squadron Five (VB-5) 56, 58, 107, 118
Bombing Squadron Six (VB-6) 25, 29, 85, 87, 88, 89, 101, 103, 157

Bombing Squadron Three (VB-3) 143
Bombing Squadron Two (VB-2) 116
Bonins 99
BOQ 11
Borneo 14, 83
Boston 8
Bottjer, Ensign G.E. 52, 53
Bower, 1st Lt. William M. 132, 146, 149
Braemer, Sgt. 155
Brassfield, Lt. (JG) Arthur J. 120
Bremerton Navy Yard 18
Brett, Lt. Comdr. James H., Jr. 112, 115, 170, 172
British 13, 67, 83, 161
British-American policy (Germany first) 164
British consulate (Iran) 156
Brooke Army Medical Center 163
Brooklyn class Light Cruiser 174
Brown, Marine Col. Julian P. 83
Brown, Vice Adm. Wilson 8, 12, 14, 16, 62, 67, 69, 70, 72, 73, 77, 80, 81, 107, 108, 109, 110, 111, 120, 121, 123, 125, 168, 170, 172
Browning, Miles 23, 24, 63, 83, 134, 136, 137, 138, 158
Browning machine gun 41
Buckmaster, Capt. Elliott C. 60, 61, 62, 120, 121, 122, 169. 172
Buka Island 108
"Bull Halsey" 63
Buna, New Guinea 108, 110
Burbank, California 130
Burch, Lt. Comdr. William O., Jr. 56, 57, 62, 112, 118, 169, 172
Bureau of Aeronautics 166
Bureau of Navigation 9
Bureau of Navigation Circular Letter No. 1–42 80
Bureau of Ordnance 97, 166
Burroughs, Lt. Comdr. S. Everett, Jr. 26
Butaritari 58
Butler, Ensign J.C., A- V(N) 147

CAC Wirraway training aircraft 68
Caldwell, Lt. T.F. 57
California 135
USS *California* 5, 6, 69
Callaghan, Capt. Daniel J. 109, 171, 173
Calvert, Lt. Comdr. Allen P. 169, 172
Calvinist 13
Campbell, Ensign R.K., A/V(N) 147
Canal Zone 66
Canton Island 12, 15, 62, 66, 67, 84, 107

CAP (Combat Air Patrol) 18, 27, 32, 40, 41, 42, 45, 60, 61, 70, 73, 77, 81, 86, 95, 101, 104, 112, 120, 147
Caribbean 1
Caroline Islands 11, 68
Carrier Air Group 12 (CVG-12) 19
USS *Cassin* 6
Catalina PBY 5, 84, 137
Cavite submarine base 21
Celebes 14, 83
Central Air Corps Procurement District 130
Central Pacific 84, 167
USS *Chancey* 21
Chandler, Capt. William D. 170, 171, 173
Chantiny, Radioman 3c F.J. 55
Chekiang Province 156
Chennault, Gen. Claire 156
USS *Chester* (CA-27) 23, 39, 43, 170
USS *Chicago* (CA-29) 69, 108, 110, 111, 173
Chief of Naval Operations 127
Chief of Staff of the Combined Fleet 161
Chief of the Army Air Forces (AAF) 127
Chief of the Navy General Staff 163
Chikamasa, Lt. Comdr. Igarashi 23
Chile 129
Chillingworth, Lt. Comdr. Charles F., Jr. 109, 171, 173
China 21, 137, 143, 150, 155, 156, 157, 160, 162
China Maru 113
Chinese Medal of Honor for Meritorious Service 157
Chitose Air Group 23, 32
Chitose flight crews 42
Chitwood, AMM 1c (NAP) J.C. 56
Christiana, Norway 17
Christie, Lt. (JG) 47, 51, 52
Christmas Day 1941, 5
Christmas Harbor 35
Christmas-Palmyra line 13
Chuchow 143, 155
Chung-shui 162
Chungking, China 150, 157
Chungking Embassy 155
Churchill, British Prime Minister Winston 13, 125
USS *Cimarron* (AO-22) 133, 136, 138, 140, 159, 174
Cimarron Class Fleet Oiler 169, 170, 172, 174
CINCPAC 11, 13, 16, 66, 67, 70, 77, 80, 81, 82, 83, 99, 107, 108, 120, 125, 133, 134, 138, 160, 164

Index

CINCPAC Op-Ord 39–41, 22
CINCPAC Operational Plan 20–42, 138
Clarey, Lt. Bernard Ambrose 23
USS *Clark* (DD-361) 67, 108, 171, 173
Clark, Lt. (JG) Howard F. "Spud" 74, 78
Clark, Capt. J.J. ("Jocko") 61
Clark, AMM 3c Milton Wayne 28
Cleveland, Ohio 130
Cole, Lt. 155
Cole, Richard E. "Dick" 163
USS *Colorado* 12, 21
Columbia, South Carolina 132
Columbia Army Air Base 132
Columbus Evening Dispatch 160
COMANZAC 67, 69, 77, 81, 107, 110, 111
COMANZACFOR 107
Combat Information Center (CIC) 165
Combined Fleet 139, 144
COMINCH *see* Commander in Chief U.S. Fleet (COMINCH)
Commander Air Operations Order No. 3–42 110
Commander Aircraft, Atlantic Fleet 105
Commander Aircraft, Battle Force 98, 106
Commander Aircraft Squadrons 1
Commander Army Group 160
Commander Battle Division One 9
Commander Battleships, Battle Force 5
Commander Cruiser Division Two 9
Commander Destroyer Squadron Six 95
Commander Destroyers, Battle Force 10
Commander in Chief Atlantic Fleet 14
Commander in Chief of the Asiatic Fleet 21
Commander in Chief Pacific Fleet (CINCPAC) 5, 7
Commander in Chief U.S. Atlantic Fleet 21
Commander in Chief U.S. Fleet (CINCUS) 7
Commander in Chief U.S. Fleet (COMINCH) 7, 11, 12, 66, 67, 84, 107, 109, 120, 127
Commander in Chief, U.S. Pacific Fleet 160
Commander of the Battle Fleet 9
Commander of the Fleet Aircraft Battle Force 17

Commander Scouting Force-Pacific Fleet 69
Commander Submarine Division 20, 9
Commander Submarine Force Atlantic (COMSUBLANT) 9
COMTASKFOR 11, 16, 82, 107, 108, 110, 160
COMTASKFOR Eleven Secret Operation Order 5–42 (Serial 0105) 110
Connally, Ensign Clem B. 117
Conolly, Capt. Richard L. 172
Continental Divide 133
Coolidge, Pres. Calvin 69
Copenhagen, Denmark 17
Coral Sea 120, 159, 166
Corbin, Lt. Comdr. Frank 25, 27, 40, 41, 101
Corregidor Island 63
Costello, RM 1c L.W. 56
County Class Heavy Cruiser 173
Covington, Ensign F.H. (spotter for USS *Maury*) 91
Crace, RAdm. John Gregory, RN 67, 69, 110, 111, 120, 121, 124, 172
Cranford, Ensign J.T. 52, 53, 54
USS *Craven* (DD-382) 24, 84, 86, 169, 172
Craven, Capt. F.S. 144
Criswell, Ensign David W. 32
Cruiser Division (Crudiv) Three 22
Cruiser Division Five 85, 101, 171
Cruiser Division Six 22
Cruisers, Battle Force, U.S. Fleet 22
cruising disposition 7V formation 140
Cunningham, Navy Cmdr. Winfield S. 5
USS *Curtiss* 6, 67
Curtiss biplanes 135
Curtiss R 3C 129
Curtiss SOC-3 floatplane 60, 61, 91, 120
CXAM radar 70, 73, 75, 165

USS *Dale* (DD-353) 21, 67, 109, 121, 171, 173
Daly, Ensign Joseph R. 95, 96
Dalzell, RM 1c J.W. 56
Daniels, Lt. (JG) J.G., III 35, 42
Darden, Lt. Comdr. T.F. 174
Darwin, (Australia) 12
Dayton, Ohio 129
Deacon, Lt. (JG) E.T. 28, 29
USS *Decatur* 8
de Havilland DH-4 129
Dennis, RM 3c O.L. 28
Denniston, Lt. (JG) R. 51, 55
DESDIV 22, 136
Destroyer Division Three 60–61

Destroyer Squadron SIX 126, 172
Detroit 130
USS *Dewey* (DD-349) 67, 109, 171, 173
Dickenson, Lt. C.E., Jr. 28
Director of Intelligence Service 151, 152, 153, 154
Director of the Branch Government of Western Chekiang Province 155
Distinguished Flying Cross 78, 129, 157
Distinguished Service Medal 63
Dixon, Lt. Comdr. Robert E. 70, 112–113, 170, 172
Dobson, Ensign C.J. 28, 38, 103
Dolliver, Sen. Jonathan 20
USS *Dolphin* 23, 24
Dominguez Field 129
Donnell, Ensign E.R., Jr. 28
Doolittle, James H. "Jimmy" 129, 130, 131, 132, 133, 134, 135, 136, 137, 142, 145, 146, 148–150, 156, 157, 159, 160, 161, 163, 164, 174
Doolittle's Raiders 163
Douglas DC-3 127
Dow, Lt. Comdr. Leonard J. 41
USS *Downes* 6
Downing, Lt. (JG) A.L. 58, 59
Draemel, RAdm. Milo F. 8, 10, 11
USS *Drayton* (DD-366) 67, 171
Duckworth, Cmdr. Herbert S. 73, 78, 118
Dufilho, Marion 75, 76
Duncan, Capt. Donald B. "Wu" 128, 130, 131, 133, 134, 135, 137
USS *Dunlap* (DD-384) 23, 35, 36, 37, 38, 84, 85, 86, 170, 172
Dutch 83
Dutch East Indies 70

Eagle Boat (PE) 134
Earle, Cmdr. Ralph, Jr. 169, 172
East Asia War 157
East China Sea 143, 156
East Coast 9
East Coast of Japan 64
East Loch (anchorage) 5
East Marshall Islands 23
Eastern Army Command 144
Eastern Marshall Islands 12, 16
Ebeye Island 31, 42
Eder, Ensign Willard E. 74, 78
Eglin Field, Florida 132, 133
Egmedio Island 35, 36
8th Air Force 157
Eighth Cruiser Division (Japanese) 14
89th Reconnaissance Squadron 132
Eiji, RAdm. Goto 22

Elder, Ensign R.M., A-V(N) 147
Electric Light Plant 149
USS *Ellet* (DD-398) 136, 138, 174
Ellice Islands 11–12
Ellison, Lt. (JG) T.B. 52, 53, 54
Ely, Lt. 31
Emidji Island 47, 49, 56
Employment of Carrier Task Forces in January 11
Ene Cherutakku Island 35, 36
England 21, 157
Enijun Channel 39
Eniwetok Island 83
USS *Enterprise* (CV-6) 3, 6, 11, 14, 16, 17, 18, 22, 23, 24, 25, **26**, 27, 29, **30**, 31, 32, 33, 34, 35, 38, 39, 40, 41, 42, 43, 62, 64, 65, 83, 84, 85, 86, 87, **89**, 91, 93, 95, 96, 99, 101, 102, 104, 106, 135, 136, 138, 140, 142, 143, 144, **145**, 147, 157, 158, 159, 164, 166, **169, 171, 173**
Enterprise Air Group 6, 44, 62, 64, 85, 86, 91, 96, 97, 98, 99, 106, 138
Enterprise Air Group Commander (CEAG) 27, 29
Enterprise plan of attack 25
Enterprise Task Group 16, 84
Enubuj Island 29
Enybor Island 15, 47, 49, 51, 56
Erikub Atoll 36
SS *Esperanza* 21
Espiritu Santo 99
Essex class carrier 166
Europe 130
Eversole, Lt. (JG) Thomas 38, 85
Ewa Air Station (Barber's Point) 159

F2A-1 Brewster Buffalo fighter 116
F3F Grumman biplane 76
F3F-2 Grumman biplane 24
F3F-3 Grumman biplane 165
F4F Grumman Wildcat fighter 19, 24, 33, 34, 36, 40, 41, 42, 43, 61, 70, 73, 74, 75, 77, 84, 85, 86, 90, 95, 96, 98, 101, 111, 112, 119, 143, 147, 165, 173
F4F-3 Grumman Wildcat fighter 27, 32, 44, 79, 112, 119, 120, 158, 169, 170, 171, 172
F4F-3A Grumman Wildcat fighter 24
F4F-4 Grumman Wildcat fighter 135, 144, 165, 166, 171, 174
Fahrion, Capt. Frank G. 61
Fairmont Hotel 136
Faktor, Corporal Leland D. 156
USS *Fanning* (DD-385) 136, 138, 174
Fanning Class Destroyer 170, 172

Far East 8, 11, 12
Farncomb, Capt. H.P., R.A.N. 108, 173
Farragut Class Destroyer 171, 173
Farrow 1st Lt. William G. 146, 147, 149, 156
Fawcett, Photographer Second Class H.S. 71
Fenton, Lt. Comdr. Charles R. 61, 112
15th Air Force 157
55th Division Imperial Japanese Army 68
Fifth Fleet 162
5th Squadron 132
Fighter Director Officer (FDO) 41, 70, 78, 165
Fighting Forty-Two (VF-2) 119
Fighting Squadron Six (VF-6) 24, 25, 34, 85, 98, 143
Fighting Squadron Three (VF-3) 71, 78, 113
Fighting Squadron Two (VF-2) 71
Fiji Islands 11, 15, 162
Filipino 63
First Air Group (Japanese) 82
1st Division (Chutai) 77
1st Marine Division 168
First Submarine Flotilla 8
Fishel, Lt. (JG) M.P. 56
Fitch, RAdm. Aubrey W. "Jakey" 14, 106, 125
Fitzgerald, Lt. John E. 131
Fleet Problem IX 1
Fleet Problem VII 1
Fleet Problem XIII 1
Fletcher, RAdm. Frank Friday 21
Fletcher, RAdm. Frank Jack 5, 8, 12, 14, 17, 19, **20**, 21, 22, 23, 45, 61, 62, 63, 84, 107, 108, 109, 110, 120, 121, 168, 169, 172
Florida 133
USS *Florida* 21
Fogg, Lt. (JG) C.T. 22, 28
Ford Island 6, 32, 43, 62, 159
Forman, Ensign Percy W. 29, 96
Fosha, ACMM(PA) C.T. 56
14th Naval District 15
4th Air Group 70, 73, 77, 121
4th Fleet (Japanese) 22
Fox-George sector (of YE signal) 54
Fraser, Lt. Comdr. Thomas E. 109, 170, 173
Fredericksburg, Texas 7
French North Africa 127
Fuchida, Cmdr. Mitsuo 6
Fueling Group (TG 17.3) 23
Fujiro, Capt. Ohashi 23
Furer, Lt. A.H. 52, 53, 54

G 3M Type 96 land attack plane 41
Gaillard (Culebra) Cut 133
Gallagher, RM 2c T.A. 159
Gallagher, Lt. Comdr. Wilmer Earl 29, 38, 86, 88, 103, 173
Gasmata 108, 109, 110, 111, 121
Gayler, Lt. Noel A.M. 73, 74, 78, 79, 115
Gee Bee R-1 racer 130
Geiselman, Lt. Comdr. E. H. 174
"Germany First" policy 13
Gilbert Islands 11, 14, 16, 23, 57, 62
Gill, Lt. Frank F. "Red" 70, 72, 73, 75, 76, 78
Ginder, Lt. Cdr. John Kenneth Burkholder 109, 173
Gizo Islands 108
Gleaves class Destroyer 174
Golden Gate Bridge 135
Gooch, Seaman 1c Lonnie C. 60
Goto, RAdm. 73
Government Pier 58
Graetz, ARM 2c Ronald 38
Gray, 1st Lieutenant 146, 156
Gray, James S., Jr. 25, 32, 33, 41, 42, 86, 104, 173
Gray, Lt. Robert Manning 149
USS *Grayling* 11
USS *Grayson* (DD-435) 136, 174
Great Britain 9
Great Lakes 13
Greening, Capt. Charles Ross 132, 146, 148
Grew, Joseph C. 161
USS *Gridley* 21
Gridley Class Destroyer 169, 171, 172, 173
Grogg, AMM 3c D.F. 28
Grumman F 4F-3 "Wildcat" fighter 24, **71**
Grumman F 6F Hellcat fighter 19
Grumman SBD dive bomber 121
Grumman TBF Avenger torpedo bomber 19
Guadalcanal 99, 168
USS *Guadalupe* 84, 108, 123
USS *Gudgeon* 101
Guest, Lt. William S. 51, 118
Gugegwe Island 30
Gulf of Papua 110, 111, 112, 114, 115, 120
Gullen, Ensign Earle C. 18
USS *Gwin* (DD-433) 136, 174

Haas, Ensign Walter A. 19, 146
Hallmark, 2nd Lt. Dean Edward 146, 149, 156
Halsey, Ensign Delbert W. 90
Halsey, Vice Adm. William Frederick, Jr. 8, 12, 14, 16, 17, **18**, 22, 23, 24, 25, 27, 41, 42,

62, 63, 64, 67, 83, 84, 85, 95, 99, 101, 104, 105, 106, 107, 124, 133, 134, 135, 136, 137, 138, 140, 141, 143, 144, 145, 147, 150, 157, 158, 159, 160, 165, 167, 168, 169, 171, 173
Hamilton, Lt. Comdr. Weldon L. 112, 116, 117, 170, 172
USS *Hammann* (DD-412) 84, 109, 110, 173
Hampton Roads 130
Hang Chow Bay 155
Hanson, Ensign A.W. A-V(N) 143
Hanson, Capt. Edward W. 108, 171, 173
Harman, Miff 133
Harmon Trophy 130
Hartwig, Lt. Comdr. Glenn R. 109, 170, 173
Hawaii 2, 7, 10, 12–14, 66, 136, 137, 162, 163, 164, 167
Hawaii-Mainland line 12
Hawaii-Samoa line 12
Haynes, Ensign Leon W. 72, 78
Heck, Ensign 38
Hein, Ensign Herbert R. (AVN) 53, 56
Heisel, Lt. (JG) Harold N. 32
USS *Helena* 6
Henke, Anna 7
Henkle, Capt. Ralph H. 169
Henry, Lt. Walter F. 75, 78
Hickam Field 6, 62
Hiebert, Ensign W.J. 35, 158
Higashikuni, Gen. Prince 144
Hilger, Maj. John A. 132, 136, 146, 149
Hilton, Lt. (JG) Hart Dale 28, 29, 103
Hipple, William H. (Associated Press war correspondent) 112, 119
Hirohito, Emperor 134, 163
Hiroshima 144
Hiryu 139
Hodges, Ensign 38
Hodson, Ensign Norman 41, 85
Hollingsworth, Lt. Comdr. William R. 33, 87, 88, 102, 169, 171
Holstrom, 1st Lt. Everett W. 146, 149
Holt, Ensign William M. 32
Honolulu 80, 137
USS *Honolulu* 6
Hoover, 1st Lt. Travis 132, 146, 147, 149, 150, 155
Hoover, Pres. Herbert 69
Hopkins, Harry 127
Hopkins Hotel 137
Hopping, Lt. Comdr. Halsted L. 27, 28, 169, 171
Horii, Maj. Gen. Tomitaro 68

Horn Island 111
USS *Hornet* (CV-8) 128, 130, 131, 133, **134**, 135, 136, 137, 138, 140, **141**, 142, 143, 144, 145, 146, 147, 157, 158, 159, 160, 174
Hotel Nimitz 7
Howland Island 23, 24
Hoyle, Lt. (JG) Ronald J. 35, 41, 42
Hubbard, Lt. Cdr. Harry Ensor 174
USS *Hughes* (DD-410) 19, 22, 23, 45, 60, 61, 109, 110, 170, 173
USS *Hull* (DD-350) 67, 75, 108, 171, 173
Huon Gulf 113, 117, **119**
Hyman, Lt. Comdr. Wilford M. 109, 170, 173

I-6 (Japanese submarine) 18
IFF (Identification-Friend or Foe) 10, 41, 44, 64, 165
IJN (Imperial Japanese Navy) 2, 6, 82, 139, 143, 144, 145, 150, 157, 162, 164, 167
Imperial General Headquarters 163
Imperial Japanese Army 164
Imperial Navy Marines 163
"Imperial Navy Operational Plans for Stage Two of the Greater East Asia War" 163
Imperial Palace 142
Indian Ocean 139, 144
Indianapolis 130
USS *Indianapolis* (CA-35) 67, 108, 171, 173
Inoue, Vice Adm. Shigeyoshi 22, 68, 70, 73
"Int Corpen" signal 54
International Date Line 24, 85, 140, 159
Inubo Saki 140, 144, 146, 147
Inubo Shuma 155
Ishibe, Hinosuke 161
Ito, Lt. Comdr. Takuzo 75, 76, 77, 82

Jabor Island 56
Jaluit Island 13, 14, 15, 23, 45, 47, **48**, **49**, 50–51, 52, 53, 54, 56, 59, 60, 61, 63
Japan 6, 9, 11, 13, 68, 82, 99, 125, 127, 128, 130, 132, 136, 137, 140, 146, 155, 156, 157, 159, 163, 168
Japanese Army Air Force 162
Japanese Army General Staff (Operations Section) 163
Japanese Army transport 113
Japanese Coast 148
Japanese Combined Fleet Radio Intelligence 139
Japanese 1st Fleet 12, 144

Japanese 4th Fleet (South Seas Force) 14, 68
Japanese JN-25 code 164
Japanese metal auxiliary vessel 147
Japanese Naval Academy 82
Japanese naval forces 22
Japanese Navy 14, 113, 163
Japanese Navy Order Number 18, 163, 164
Japanese picket ship 144
Japanese 2nd Fleet 144
Japanese Steel Company 148, 149
Japanese Type 97 fighter 34, 43
Japanese Type 96 fighter 27, 28, 34
USS *Jarvis* 21
Java 81
Jeter, Commander T.P. 26, 99
Jewel, Radioman 3rd class James Buford 114
Jinks, Radioman-Gunner RM 3c E.P. 86, 96
Johnson, Lt. (JG) E.V. 58
Johnson, Lt. Harland T. 51, 53, 56
Johnson, Maj. Harry 132
Johnson, Lt. (JG) Howard L. 74
Johnson, Ensign Joseph Philip 114
Johnson, Lt. Cdr. Robert R. 174
Johnston Island 12, 13, 162, 163
Johnston-Midway line 13
Johnston-Palmyra line 12
Joint Chiefs of Staff 127
USS *Jones* 131
Jones, Capt. David M. 132, 146, 148, 149
Joyce 1st Lt. Richard Outcalt, 146, 148
Junghans, Lt. Comdr. E.A. (spotter two for USS *Northampton*) 91
USS *Jupiter* (AK-43) 19

Kabbenbock Island 47
Kaena Point 6
Kaga 68, 139
Kahiro, Capt. Moritama 73
Kai-shek, Madame Chiang 157
Kamio 123
Kamoi 118
Kanagawa 148
Kaneohe 6
USS *Kaskaskia* (AO-27) 19, 108, 110, 120, 121, 123
Kate horizontal bomber 6
Kavieng 108, 109
Kawanishi H 6K4 Type 97 flying boat (seaplane), (code named "Mavis") 23, 57, 58, 60, 61, 70, 72, 73, 90, 120
Kawasaki Aircraft Factory 149

Kawasaki Dockyard Company Aircraft Works 148, 149
Kazuo, Lt. Nakai (division leader) 23
USS *Kearsarge* 21
Kelly, Lt. (JG) John C. "Jack" 102
Kelly Field, Texas 129
Kenney, Brig. Gen. George C. 132
Kerr, U.S. Representative 13
Kiangwan Prison 156
Kieta, Bougainville Island 108
Kimmel, RAdm. Husband E. 5, 6, 7, 8, 11, 15, 22
King, Adm. Ernest J. 8, 11, 13, 14, *15*, 16, 66, 67, 73, 84, 108, 125, 127, 128, 128, 133, 134, 166, 167
Kinkaid, RAdm. T.C. 69
Kirarazu unit 161
Kiso 143
Kiyokawa Maru 121
Kiyokawa Maru Air Unit 77
Kiyoshi, W.O. Hayashi 72
Kleiss, Lt. (JG) N.J. 28, 29
Knobloch, Lt. Dick 145
Knox, Navy Sec. William Franklin 7, 13, 127
Knox Island 59
Kobe 132, 142, 148, 161
Kogiku, PO1c 76, 77
Kokai Maru 113, 114, 118, 121
Kongo Maru 113, 114, 118, 121
Kurakane, Lt. 32
Kure anchorage 64
Kuroshima, Capt. Kameto 162
Kwajalein Island 23, 24, 25, 27, 28, 29, 30, 31, 42–43, 64, 99

Lackey, Ensign John H. 74, 78
Lae 82, 107, 110, 111, 113, 114, 115, 118, 119, 120, 121, 122, 124, 125
Lae Field 121
Lae-Salamaua Raid *113*, 121, 125, 165, 166, 172
Laird Super Stallion biplane 130
Lake Erie 13
USS *Lamson* 69
Lane, Ensign C.F. A/VN(N) 143
USS *Langley* 1
Lark Force 68
USS *Lassen* (AE-3) 19
Lavelle, commercial attaché, Ramon M. 161
Lawhon, ACMM George F. 18
Lawson 1st Lt. Ted W., 136, 146, 148, 157
Layton, Lt. Comdr. Edwin T. 11
League of Nations 11
Leaming, ARM 2c Jack, 103
HMNZS *Leander* 69
Leary, Vice Adm. Herbert Fairfax 12, 14, 18, 66, 67, 70, 73, 107

Lee, Capt. W.A., Jr 10
Leigh, Adm. Richard 2
Lemmon, Lt. (JG) Rolla S. 74, 78
Leonard, Lt. William N. 121
Leonard, Sgt. 155
Lerew, Squadron Leader John 68
Leslie, Lt. Cdr. Maxwell Franklin 173
USS *Lexington* (CV- 2), 1, 2, 3, 11, 14, 16, 62, 67, 69, 70, 72, 73, 74, 75, 76, 77, 79, 81, 82, 84, 108, 109, 110, 111, 112, *113*, *114*, 115, *116*, 118, 120, 121, 122, 123, 125, 165, 167, 170, 172
Lexington Air Group 78, 111, 112, 113, 122
Lexington Class Aircraft Carrier 170, 172
Lindsay, Asst. LSO Robin 142
Lindsey, Lt. Comdr. Eugene Elbert 29, 30, 32, 87, 90, 169, 171, 173
Ling, Gen. Ho Yang 155
Lockheed Hudson light bomber 68
Logan, Capt. 8
London 69
Lorain, Ohio 13
Lorain High School 13
Los Angeles 129
Los Angeles City College 129
Los Angeles International Air Meet 129
Los Angeles Times 160
Louisiades 108, 110
USS *Louisville* (CA-28) 19, 23, 45, 60, 61, 84, 108, 109, 110, 170, 173
Lovelace, Lt. Comdr. Donald A. 73, 74, 75, 76, 78
Low, Capt. Francis S. 127, 128, 130
Lowe, Capt. Frank L. 109, 171, 173
Lowry, Capt. Frank J. 109, 171, 173
LSO (Landing Signal Officer) 158
USS *Ludlow* 131
Luke Field 2
Lurline (Matson liner) 19
Luzon 69

USS *MacDonough* (DD-351) 67, 108, 171, 173
Mackay Trophy 129
MacKillop, RM 1c D. 56
Maeda, CPO Gisaku 143
Maeda, PO 1c 76, 77
Mahan 8
USS *Mahan* (DD-364) 23, 24, 45, 170

Mahan class Destroyer 170, 171, 174
Maher, Lt. F.X. 56
Makalapa 6
Makin Island 11, 12, 13, 14, 23, 45, 56, *57*, 58, 59, 60, 62
Malay 64
Malay Barrier 12
Malaya 162
Malaysia 12
Maloelap Bombardment Group 170
Maloelap Island 23, 25, 27, 32, 36
Manchuria 21
mandates 11, 14, 43, 84
Manila Bay 8
Maples, Cmdr. Houston L. 170, 172, 174
March Field 135
Marcus Island 84, 99, *100*, 101, 102, 103, 104, 105, 106
USS *Margaret* (SP-527, yacht) 21
Marianas 11, 99
Marine air group 10
Marine airfield (Ewa) 63
Marine Parade (waterfront Street on Enybor Island) 15
Marine transports 17, 18
Mark-12 bomb 59
Marshall, Gen. George C. 127, 137
Marshall and Gilbert Islands 13, 15, 16, 17, 22, 45, 57, 59, 64
Marshall and Gilbert Islands Raid 63, 165, 167, 169
Marshall-Gilbert attack plan 23
Marshall Islands 11, 12, 14, 15, 22, 24, 26, 35, 43, 62, 64, 83, 124
Marshalltown, Iowa 20
Marshalltown High School 20
Martin B-26 Marauder bomber 128
Martin MB-2 twin-engine bomber 1
USS *Maryland* 12
Masayoshi, Lt. Nakagawa 73, 74, 75
Massau Island 108
Massey, Lt. Comdr. Lance E. 31, 38
Matsonia (Matson liner) 19
Matsuhigecho Oil Storage 149
Matsumura, Toshiko 161
Matsushige Oil storage site 148
USS *Maumee* 8
USS *Maury* (DD-401) 23, 39, 84, 85, 86, 91, 92, 93, 94, 95, 96, 170, 172
McCain, John S. 8
USS *McCall* (DD-400) 96, 99, 169
McCarthy, Lt. James F. 131

McClellan Field 133, 135
McClusky, Lt. Comdr. Wade 25, 34, 35, 41, 42, 84, 87, 90, 91, 103, 104, 169, 171, 173
McCook Field 129
McCormack, Lt. Vince 61
McCuskey, Ensign E. Scott 61, 62
McDowell, Ensign H.M. 51
McElroy, 1st Lt. Edgar E. 146, 148
McIsaac, Lt. Comdr. John M. 108, 171, 173
McMorris, Capt. Charles H. 11, 83
McPherson, Ensign 38
Medal of Honor 21, 78, 157
Meder, 2nd Lt. Robert J. 156
Mediterranean 157
Mehle, Lt. Roger 34, 41, 42, 91, 95
Melbourne 67
USS *Meredith* (DD-434) 136, 138, 159, 174
Mexico 15
Mid-Continental Airlines 132
Midway Island 12, 13, 18, 66, 96, 130, 136, 159, 162, 163, 164, 167
Midway-Hawaii line 12, 67
Midway/Hawaii Plan 162, 163, 164
Mille Island 13, 23, 45, **57**, 58, 59, 60
Miller, Lt. Henry L. 132, 135, 136, 137, 146
Milli Atoll 58, **59**
Milli Attack Group 58
Mills, Lt. Col. William C. 132
Minami Tori Shima 99
Minneapolis 132
USS *Minneapolis* (CA-36) 22, 67, 109, 171, 173
USS *Missouri* 168
MIT 129
Mitani, PO 1c Masashi 76
Mitchell, Billy 1, 2
Mitchell, Lt. Cdr. Samuel G. 174
Mitchell Field, Long Island, New York 129
Mitscher, Adm. Marc A. 127, 130, 131, 133, 135, 136, 137, 138, 140, 143, 145, 150, 174
Mitsubishi A 5M4 Type 96 carrier fighter 23, 32, 33, 43, 73, 166
Mitsubishi A 6M2 Zero fighter (Zeke) 6, 73
Mitsubishi Aircraft Factory 160
Mitsubishi Aircraft Works 148, 149
Mitsubishi F 1M2 Type 0 reconnaissance floatplane 118
Mitsubishi G 2M2 Type 96 "Nell" medium bomber 23

Mitsubishi G 4M "Betty" bomber 73, 74, 144
Miwa, Cmdr. Yoshitake 64
Miyazaki, Capt. Takashi 121
Miyo, Commander Tatsukichi 162, 163
Mk. XIX nose fuse 97
Mk. XXIII tail fuse 97
Model TBS 61
Model TBX 61
Model YE radio equipment 111
Model ZB radio equipment 111
Moffett, RAdm. William A. 14
Molokai, Hawaii 5
USS *Monssen* (DD-436) 136, 158, 159, 174
Monterey (Matson liner) 19
Montevideo Maru 69
Moore, Lt. J.C. 56
Moosbrugger, Cmdr. Frederick 169
Morgan, Lt. (JG) Robert J. 74, 78
Mori, PO 2c, 76, 77
Morrison, Samuel Eliot 158
Moscow 156
Motohiro, Reserve Ensign Makino 73
Mott, Lt. Comdr. E.B. 41
Mount Chapman 111, 112
Mount Lawson 111, 112
Murray, Capt. George D. 41, 42, 44, 98, 104, 105, 142, **144**, 166, 169, 171, 173
Mutsuki 113
MX 13 air-launched torpedo 165, 166

Nagano, Adm. Osami 163, 164
Nagata Maru 57
Nagoya 132, 142, 148, 149, 161
Nagoya Castle 149
Nagoya Second Temporary Army Hospital 161
Nagumo, Vice Adm. Chuichi 6, 144
Nakagawa, Lt. Comdr. Masayoshi 77, 82
Nakai, Lt. 32, 40, 41, 42
Nakajima E 8N2 Type 95 reconnaissance floatplane, 91, 118
Namir Island 27
Namorick Island 23
Namur Island 28
Nanking 156
USS *Narwhal* 8
USS *Nashville* (CL-42) 133, 136, 140, 142, 144, 145, 157, 160, 174
National Ensign 137
Nauru Island 12
Naval Academy 7, 8, 13, 14, 17, 20, 21, 25, 69, 125
Naval Air Station, Pearl Harbor 62

Naval Air Station Pensacola 14, 17, 25
Naval Air Station, Kaneohe, Oahu, Hawaii 71
Naval cadet 14
Naval Reserve Officer Training Corps 9
Naval Test Board 129
Naval War College 9, 17, 21, 69
Navy auxiliary field 131
Navy Blimp L-6 137
Navy Bureau of Navigation (Bureau of Naval Personnel) 7
Navy Commendation Medal 63
Navy Cross 21, 78, 80, 118
Navy Department 7, 133
Navy wings of gold 25
Navy Yard 106
Navy's Bureau of Aeronautics 14
Navy's War Instructions Manual (1934) 2
NC-4 (flying boat) 21
USS *Neches* (AO) 13
USS *Neosho* (AO) 62, 69, 110, 120, 121, 123
Netherlands East Indies (N.E.I.) 12, 63, 64, 82, 162
New Britain 67, 68, 108, 162
New Britain (New Guinea) 66
New Britain-Solomon Area 107
New Caledonia 66, 110
New Guinea 12, 67, 68, 83, 108, 109, 110, 112, 117, 121, 125, 162
New Guinea Volunteer Rifles 68
New Hebrides 66, 69, 108, 121, 124
New Ireland 68, 77, 109
New London, Connecticut 14
New London Submarine Base 69
USS *New Mexico* 22
USS *New Orleans* 22
New Orleans Class Heavy Cruiser 171, 173, 174
New York Times 160
New Zealand 22
Newport, Rhode Island 9, 21
Nicholson, Ensign H.W. 58
Nielsen, Lt. J.L. 49
Nihoa Island 138
Niigata 161
Nimitz, Adm. Chester W. 5, 7, **8**, 9, 11, 13, 14, 15, 16, 17, 18, 39, 62, 63, 65, 66, 67, 81, 84, 99, 105, 107, 125, 133, 134, 138, **144**, 164, 165, 166, 167
1931 Bendix Trophy Race 130
19th Air Group (Japanese) 42
Nippon Electric Corporation 148
Nitsu oil wells 161
Nitto Maru (No. 23) 143, 144, 145, 150
Nixon, Capt. Elliott B. 61, 109, 170, 173

Noboru, Lt. (JG) Sakai 70
Nome, Alaska 129, 160
Norden bombsight 132
Norfolk 128, 130, 131, 133
Norfolk pier 131
North Africa 128, 157
North American B-25 bomber 130
North American B-25 Mitchell bomber 128
North Atlantic 21
North Island Naval Air Station 135
North Pacific 10
USS *Northampton* (CA-26) 23, 35, 36, 37, 38, 63, 84, 86, 91, **92**, 94, 95, 96, 101, 104, 136, 138, 142, 170, 171, 173
Northampton Class Heavy Cruiser 170, 171, 173
Northern Gilbert Islands 17
Noumea, New Caledonia 69, 108, 124
Noumea-Suva line 67
No. 24 Squadron 68

Oahu 2, 5, 6, 10, 12, 13, 14, 18, 66, 84, 121, 138, 159
Ocean Island 12
Oerlikon 10
Office of Naval Intelligence 17
Office of the Chief of Naval Operations 9
USS *Oglala* 6
Ogura Oil Company 148
Ogura Refinery 149
USS *O'Hare* (DD-889) 79
O'Hare, Lt. Edwards H. "Butch" 70, 75, 76, 77, 78, 167
O'Hare International Airport 79
Ohashi, Captain 40
Ohio 129
USS *Ohio* 8
Ohmae, Capt. Toshikazu 162
Oite 113
Okhansk 156
USS *Oklahoma* 5, 6
Okuna 156
Olive, Clarence W. 85
Ollet (also known as Olliot, or Ollot) Island **33**, 34, 43
Omo, AOM 1c H.F. 56
Ono, PO 1c 76
Operation MI 163
Orchard Depot Airport 79
Oregon 132
Ormed Island 35, 36
Osaka 142, 148
Osaka Mainichi 82
Osborne, Lt. Edgar G. 146
Ostfriedland (German battleship) 1
Owen Stanley Mountains 111, 117

P-1 Hawk 129
Pablo Beach, Florida 129
Pacific Fleet 5, 6, 7, 9, 11, 12, 15, 43, 66, 67, 84, 162, 167
Pacific War 1, 2, 3, 7, 10, 13, 127, 162, 163, 164, 167, 168
Packard, AMM 1c Howard 158
Palau Island 81
Palmyra Island 12, 13, 163
Pan American Airways 90
Pan American Clipper 67, 135, 138
Pan American pier 90
Panama Canal 1, 133
USS *Panay* 8
Papuan Peninsula 110, 111
USS *Parker* 69
Parker, Lt. E.B. 53, 54
Patriarca, Lt. F.A. 28, 29
USS *Patterson* (DD-362) 67, 75, 80, 171
PBY 6
Peale Island 85, 86, 87, 88, 91, 92, 93, 95, 96
Pearl Harbor 1, 2, 3, 5, 6, 7, 9, 10, 11, 12, 13, 15, 16, 17, 18, 22, 23, 24, 26, 45, 62, 63, 64, 65, 68, 73, 74, 82, 83, 84, 94, 99, 106, 107, 120, 121, 127, 133, 135, 137, 138, 158, 159, 160, 162, 165, 167, 168
"Pearl Harbor Avenged!" 63
Pearle Island 90
Pederson, Lt. Comdr. Oscar 112, 119, 172
Pendleton, Oregon 132
USS *Pennsylvania* 12
Pensacola 132
USS *Pensacola* (CA-24) 67, 80, 109, 171, 173
Pensacola Class Heavy Cruiser 170, 171, 173
USS *Perkins* 69
Peterson, Ensign Dale W. 74, 78
USS *Phelps* (DD-360) 67, 74, 109, 171, 173
Phelps, Radioman 1c O.R. 51
Philadelphia 69
Philippines 8, 10, 12, 63, 64, 162
Phoenix 135
Phoenix Island Group 11
Photographic Section of Scouting Six 103
USS *Platte* (AO-24) 67, 74, 109, 169
USS *Plunger* 8
Point Loma 135
Point Option 50
"point pig" 110, 111, 120
point "TRUK" 54
Polloc, Mindanao 8
Port Moresby 82, 108, 110, 111, 120, 124, 126
Port Rhin anchorage 58

Porter Class Destroyer 170, 171, 173, 174
Portland Class Heavy Cruiser 171, 173
Postgraduate School (Naval Academy) 14
Potter, Lt. 155
Powers, Lt. J.J. 49, 52
Pratt, Vice Admiral 1
Preston, Ensign B.G. 50
Primorsky Province 156
HMS *Prince of Wales* (British battleship) 2
Public Cemetery Number 1 (Shanghai) 156
Puget Sound 18
Pukapuka Island 18
Purple Heart 157
Pye, Vice Adm. William S. 5, 6, 8, 9, 10, 11, 15, 16, 67, 84

Quady, Lt. (JG) Frank B. 41, 158

RAAF air reconnaissance 110
Rabaul 22, 64, 66, 67, 68, 69, 70, **71**, 73, 75, 77, 81, 82, 84, 107, 108, 109, 110, 111, 120, 121, 125, **167**, **170**
Rainbow War Plan 167
Rainer, Lt. Comdr. Gordon Benbow "Dizzy" 23
USS *Raleigh* 6
USS *Ralph Talbot* (DD-390) 84, 86, 95, 169
Ramsey, Lt. Comdr. Donald J. 109, 170, 173
Randall, Lt. G.D. 159
USS *Ranger* (gunboat) 8
Rangoon 12, 63
Rawie, Lt. (JG) Wilmer E. 32, 41, 42
RDF (radio direction finding) 86
Reeves, Lt. M.C. (spotter one for USS *Northampton*) 91
Reeves, Ensign T.A. 60
Reeves, Rear Admiral 1
Regular Army 129
Rend, Cmdr. Charles J. 170, 172, 174
Repair Basin 121
HMS *Repulse* 2
Respess, Aviation Chief Machinist's Mate Tom 146
Reuters (British news agency) 141
Rich, Ensign Ralph M. 32, 95
Richardson, Comdr. Myron T. 108, 171, 173
Rickover, Lt. Hyman G. 22
Riefkohl, Capt. Frederick Lois 174
USS *Rigel* 9
Riley, Lt. 38

Ring, Lt. Cdr. Stanhope C. 174
Roane, Lt. Comdr. Virginius R. 170, 172
Roberts, Lt. Cdr. James S. 174
Roberts, Ensign J.Q., A- V(N) 144
Rochefort, Cmdr. Joseph J. 164
Rockwell Field, California 129
Rodee, Lt. Cmdr. Walter F. 174
Rogers, Lt. Comdr. Robert H. 171
Rogers Field 2
Roi Island 23, 25, *27*, 28, 29, 40, 43
Rombach, Ensign Severin 38
Rood, Capt. George A. 170
Roosevelt, Pres. Franklin D. 7, 13, 14, 78, 125, 127, 157, 160
Roosevelt, Pres. Theodore 8
Rorschach, Lt. Comdr. Anthony L. 109, 171, 173
Rossel Island 108, 110, 111
Rountree, Bruce, ARM 1c 75, 77, 78, 80
Rowell, Ensign Richard M. 74
Royal Australian Air Force (RAAF) 68
Royal Australian Navy (RAN) 173
Royal Hawaiian Hotel 62, 63, 106, 121
USS *Russell* (DD-414) 19, 23, 45, 60, 109, 170, 173
Rutherford, Lt. R. 29, 38, 102

USS *Sabine* (AO-25) 23, 24, 45, 84, 85, 96, 99, 101, 136, 138, 159, 170, 172, 174
Sacramento 133, 135
USS *Sacramento* (gunboat) 21
Sacramento Air Deport 135
Sadamichi, RAdm. Kajioka 5, 113
USS *St. Louis* (CL-49) 19, 23, 45, 170
St. Louis class Light Cruiser 170
Sakai, Lt. Noboru 82
Sakura 148
Salamaua 82, 107, 108, 110, 111, 112, 115, 116, 118, 119, 120, 122, 123, 124, 125
Salamaua-Lae Air Strike Group 112
Salamaua-Lae Raid 114, *115*, *119*
Salamaua Roads 118
USS *Salt Lake City* (CA-25) 18, 23, 35, 36, 37, 38, 60, 84, 86, 91, *92*, 93, 94, 95, 96, 101, 104, 136, 138, 139, 140, 142, 170, 171, 173
Samoa 11, 12, 13, 15, 16, 17, 18, 20, 22, 23, 66, 162
Samoa Bay 115
San Antonio 135, 163

San Diego Harbor 11
San Diego, California 3, 9, 12, 14, 15, 19, 22, *116*, 125, *129*, *135*
San Francisco 134, 135, 136, 137
USS *San Francisco* (CA-38) 14, 22, 67, 80, 109, 120, 171, 173
San Francisco Bay 136, 137
Sanemiro, Lt. Comdr. Koizumi (division leader) 23
USS *Saratoga* (CV-3) 1, 2, 5, 11, 13, 14, 16, 17, 18, *19*, 22, 25, 126
SBD Douglas Dauntless dive bomber 18, *19*, 25, 28, 29, 33, 34, 38, 40, 41, 43, 44, 45, 46, 51, 53, 56, 58, 59, 60, 70, 73, 74, 75, 77, 86, 87, *88*, *89*, 101, 104, 107, 108, 114, 116, 117, 118, 120, 122, 139, 142, 143, 147, 157, 159, 165
SBD-2 Douglas Dauntless dive bomber 96, 112, 116, 166, 169, 172
SBD-3 Douglas Dauntless dive bomber 27, 46, 56, 59, 60, 96, 112, 113, 118, 135, 159, 166, 169, 171, 172, 174
SBD-5 Douglas Dauntless dive bomber 166
SBDPs (photographic plane with built-in camera) 25
Scanlan, Lt. Col. John 68
Scanland, Capt. Francis W. 108, 173
Schneider Marine Cup 129
Schonberg, RM 3c H.C. 56
Schultheis, Ensign A.J. 54, 55
Scout Patrol 21
Scouting Force, U.S. Fleet 22
Scouting Squadron 8 (VS-8) 135
Scouting Squadron Five (VS-5) 56, 58
Scouting Squadron Six (VS-6) 17, 22, 25, 29, 85, 86, 88, 89, 90, 96, 101, 102, 103
Scouting Squadron Two (VS-2) 70, 75, 77, 78, 113
Second Carrier Division (Japanese) 14
Second Fleet 162
2/1st Independent Company 68
2nd Marine Brigade 19
2/10th Field Ambulance 68
Secretary of the Navy 63, 98, 127
Secretary of War 127
Seid, Ensign Eugene D. 28
Sellstrom, Ensign Edward R. "Doc" 70, 72, 75, 76, 78
Seto, Lt. Comdr. Yogoro 82
17th Bombardment Group 132, 174
Shanghai 156
Shangri-La 160

USS *Shaw* 6
Shell Oil Company (Aviation Department) 130
Shell Speed Dash 130
Sherman, Capt. Frederick C. 70, 73, 74, 76, 77, 78, 79, 80, 110, 111, 120, 122, 123, 172
Shiba Ward 148
Shimazaki, Lieutenant Commander 6
Shipman, Ensign C.A. (spotter for USS *Balch*) 91
Shirah, Radioman 1c A.M. 53
Shock, Capt. Thomas M. 23, 32, 170
Short, Lt. Wallace C., Jr. 58, 118
Siberia 148, 156, 162
Signal Corps' Aviation Section 129
Signal Corps Reserve 129
Silver Lifesaving Medal 8
Silver Star 157
Simpson, Lt. Comdr. Rodger W. 170
Simpson Harbor 68, 70, 73, 77
USS *Sims* (DD-409) 19, 23, 45, 60, 84, 109, 110, 170, 173
Sims, Adm. William S. 1, 69
Sims Class Destroyer 170, 173
Sinclair, Lt. Comdr. George A. 108, 171, 173
Singapore 9, 63, 83
USS *Skipjack* 8
Slonim, Lt. Gilven 145
Smiley, Cmdr. Curtis S. 45, 46, 55, 56, 59, 60, 169
Smith, Lt. Donald G. 148
Smith, Capt. Frederick C. 111
Smith, Lt. L.A. 157
Smith, 1st Lieutenant 146
Smith, Radioman 3c C.L. 52
Smith, Capt. William W. (chief of staff to Kimmel) 5
Smoot, Cdr. Roland Nesbit 174
USS *Snapper* 8
Snare, Lt. Comdr. Elmer D. 172
SOC plane 93
Solomon Islands 68, 69, 70, 83, 108, 124, 168
Solomons-Bismarck area 67
Soryu 139
South America 129
USS *South Carolina* 9
South Pacific 10, 167
South Seas Force 22
Southern Marshall Islands 17
Southwest Pacific 66, 67, 81, 107, 125, 162
Spaatz, Brig. Gen. Carl 132
Spanish-American War 14
Spatz, Sergeant Harold 156
Special Letters of Commendation 78
Specialist Reserve Corps 130

Spruance, RAdm. Raymond A. 8, 15, 23, 36, 37, 63, 85, 91, 94, 96, 95, 170, 171
Stalin, Joseph 156
Stanley, Radioman/Gunner ARM 2 Forest G. 116
Stanley, Lt. Onia Burt, Jr. 70, 72, 78
Stark, Adm. Harold R. 8, 127
Station Hypo 164
Stilwell, Gen. 137
Stimson, Henry 127
Stinzi, Capt. Vernon L. 133
Stockholm, Sweden 17
Stokes, Cdr. Thomas Murray 174
Stout, Lt. Comdr. Richard F. 108, 171, 173
Strahl, AOM 3c J.D. 56
Strike Force 17.1.1 61
Striking Group (TG17.1) 23
Strong, Lt. Stockton B. 57
USS *Sturgeon* 69
Suekichi, S 2c Nakamura 143
Sugiyama, Chief of Army General Staff General 164
Sugiyama, General 163, 164
"Suicide Fleet" 21
Sumrall, ACMM (NAP) H.M. 142
Support Group (TG 17.2) 23
Suva 12, 13, 15, 67, 69, 121, 124
Swiss Minister 161
Sybrant, Aviation Ordnanceman 3c H.E. 55
Sydney 99

Tactical Method Number 3 144
Taiwan 64
Takuzo, Lt. Comdr. Ito 73
Tanaka, Maj. Gen. Shin'ichi 163
USS *Tangier* 67
Tank and Truck Factory 149
Tarawa Island 64
Taroa Bombardment Group 32, 39
Taroa Island (Maloelap Atoll) 23, 24, 27, 32, **33**, 34, 39, 42, 43
Task Force 13 (combined TF-8 and TF-17) 83
Task Force Commander 99
Task Force Eight 12, 13, 14, 16, 17, 18, 22, 23, 24, 39, 41, 42, 43, 84, 165, 169
Task Force Eighteen 136, 137, 140, 159
Task Force Eleven 12, 13, 14, 62, 66, 67, 69, 70, 73, 74, 77, 80, 107, 108, 111, 120, 121, 170, 172
Task Force Fourteen 12, 13, 14, 18, 22
Task Force Nine 5
Task Force Seventeen 12, 13, 14, 16, 17, 18, 19, 20, 22, 45, **57**, 60, 62, 107, 108, 109, 111, 120, 121, 169
TASK Force Sixteen 16, 84, 104, 107, 135, 138, 140, 143, 144, 147, 150, 157, 159, 171, 173
Task Group 8.1 23
Task Group 8.3 23
Task Group 16.1 173
Task Group 16.2 140, 174
Task Group 16.4 (Desron Six) 158
Task Group 17.1 Striking Group 45
Task Group 17.2 Support Group 45
Task Group 17.3 Fueling Group 45
USS *Tautog* 23, 24
Taylor, Lt. Comdr. Joe 112, 118, 169, 172
Taylor, Lt. Comdr. Jon 51, 52, 53, 55
Taylor, Lt. K.E. 50, 52, 55
Taylor, Adm. Montgomery Meigs 21
TBD-1 Douglas Devastator torpedo bomber 18, 25, 27, 31, 38, 45, 46, 47, 51, 52, 53, 54, 55, 85, 87, **88**, 112, 115, **116**, 117, 118, 120, 122, 169, 171, 172, 173, 174
TBS (talk between ships) 111
Teaff, Lt. (JG) Perry L. 28, 38, 86, 87, 96
USS *Tennessee* 12
Tenyo Maru 113, 114, 118, 121
USS *Terry* 14
TG 16.1 138
TG 16.2 136, 137
TG 16.7 99
Thach, Lt. Comdr. John S. "Jimmy" 70, 72, 73, 74, 75, 76, 78, 112, 114, 121, 170, 172
Thatcher, Corporal David J. 157
Theobald, RAdm. Robert A. 62
3rd Division Military Headquarters 148
Third Submarine Fleet 161
34th Squadron 132
37th Squadron 132
Thomas, Lt. (JG) 38
Thomas, RM 1c H.R. 28
Thompson Trophy Race 130
USS *Thresher* 130, 138, 140
Timor Island 81
Tinian Air Group 121
Tinian Flying Group 121
Tjan Island 32
Tokowa Island 58
Tokyo 99, 127, 132, 134, 136, 137, 139, 140, 141, 142, 143, 148, 150, 155, 156, 157, 158, 160, 161, 162, 164
Tokyo Bay 106, 140, 148, 149
Tokyo Gas & Electric Company 148, 149
Tokyo radio 65, 104
Tokyo Raid **144**, **145**, **151–154**, 148, 162, 163, 173
Tol Plantation 69
Tomioka, Capt. Sadatoshi 162, 163
Torpedo Squadron Five (VT-5) 46, 52, 56, 118, 123
Torpedo Squadron Six (VT-6) 18, 25, 27, 30, 85, 88, 90, 101
Torpedo Squadron Three (VT-3) 18
Torpedo Squadron Two (VT-2) 115, 116
Townsville, Australia 111, 120, 124
Train, Capt. Harold C. (chief of staff to Pye) 5
Training Command 25
Training Squadron Scouting Force-Atlantic Fleet 69
Travis, AMM 2c A.J. 28
Treasury Department 8
Troemel, Lt. (JG) B.H. 28, 38
Trott, Radioman 1c J.W., 46, 48
USS *Trout* 138, 140
True, Comdr. Arnold E. 109, 173
Truk 14, 22, 64, 68, 70, 73, 81, 82
Tsugaru 113, 116, 121
Tulagi Island 82, 108, 168
12th Air Force 157
25th Air Flotilla 121
24th Air Flotilla 23, 40, 70, 73, 77, 120
24th Air Flotilla (Japanese) 22
26th Air Flotilla 139, 144

Uchiyama, PO 1c 76
Ugaki, RAdm. Matome 64, 99, 106, 125
Ugaki, Vice Adm. Matome 139, 161, 162
Ukiannan Point 58
United States 2, 3, 5, 6, 13, 16, 21, 24, 34, 37, 40, 41, 61, 63, 64, 65, 66, 68, 73, 83, 104, 110, 120, 121, 123, 125, 127, 129, 130, 139, 144, 157, 159, 160, 161, 162, 164, 168
U.S. Ambassador to Japan 161
U.S. Army Air Corp 123
U.S. Army Air Forces 151, 152, 153, 154
U.S. Asiatic Naval Forces 12
U.S. Naval forces 69
U.S. Naval Intelligence 139
U.S. Navy Pacific carrier raids 164
U.S. Pacific Fleet 3, 163

Index

U.S. Pacific Fleet Estimate of the Situation 9
University of California 9, 129
University of California School of Military Aeronautics 129
USAAF B-25B bomber 141
USSR 156
USS *Utah* 5
Uyenoshita Steel Works 149

V-formation 73
Val dive bomber 6
VB-8 159, 174
VB-5 45, 46, 49, 50, 51, 52, 53, 55, 56, 112, 169, 172
VB-6 27, 30, 33, 34, 38, 40, 43, 88, 101, 102, 103, 169, 171
VB-3 147, 173
VB-2 75, 112, 116, 117, 170, 172
V-E Day 167
Vee of Vees formation 74, 76, 79
Veracruz, Mexico 21
USS *Vestal* 6
VF-8 174
VF-42 19, 45, 61, 112, 120, 121, 169, 172
VF-1B Squadron ("High Hats" renamed Bombing Three, VB-3) 25
VF-6 27, 32, 33, 35, 36, 37, 40, 42, 43, 44, 84, 85, 86, 87, 101, 104, 138, 169, 171, 173
VF-3 70, 74, 112, 114, 115, 120, 121, 170, 172
USS *Vincennes* (CA-44) 133, 136, 138, 142, 174
Virginia 1
Vixen (former German yacht) 127
Vladivostok 148, 156
VMF-221 5
Vorse, Lt. Albert O. "Scoop" 74, 78
VS-8 174
VS-5 60, 112, 118, 169, 172
VS-6 27, 28, 33, 38, 43, 86, 88, 89, 90, 101, 169, 171, 173
VS-2 112, 113, 114, 170, 172
VT-8 174
VT-5 45, 46, 47, 51, 52, 53, 54, 55, 56, 111, 112, 122, 169, 172
VT-6 29, 31, 32, 33, 38, 44, 64, 86, 90, 96, 139, 169, 171, 173
VT-2 112, 116, 117, 170, 172
Vulcan Beach 68
Vunakanau 68, 77
Vunakanau Airfield 70, 73

Waikiki 62
Waitavalo Plantation 69
Wakayama 161
Wake and Marcus Island Raid 171
Wake Island 5, 12, 13, 16, 22, 83, 84, 85, 86, **87**, **88**, 90, 91, 92, 93, 94, 96, 97, 99, 105, 107, 158
Wake Island Raid 88
Wake Relief Force (Task Force 14) 5
Waldron, Lt. Cdr. John C. 174
USS *Walke* (DD-416) 19, 22, 23, 45, 60, 84, 109, 170, 173
Walker, Comdr. Frank R. 171
Wall, Aviation Machinist's Mate Robert W. 146
Walsh, Fireman 2nd Class W.J. 8
Walter Reed Army Hospital 129
War Cabinet 68
War Department 2
War Plans office 83
Ware, Lt. C.R. 58, 59
Washington (state) 132
Washington, D.C. 5, 7, 9, 17, 67, 129, 130, 133, 137, 167
Washington Arcadia Conference 13
Washington Navy Yard 127
Watanabe, Cmdr. Yasuji 162
Watson, Harold Francis 146, 149
Wellington, New Zealand 99
Wen Chow Bay 155
West, Lt. (JG) J.N. 29, 38
West, Ensign W.F. 28, 29
West Coast 2, 10, 12, 13, 22, 128, 133
West Point 7
USS *West Virginia* 5, 6
Western Pacific 9
Western Sea Frontier 137
Wheeler, Keith (war correspondent) 86
Wheeler Field 2, 6
White, Doc 145
White, Lt. 38
White, 1st Lt. Thomas 157
White House 7, 127
Whittier, Lt. (JG) Mark Twain 116, 117
Wilkes Island 85, 88, 90
Williams, Commander Harold N. 169, 172
Willingham, Lt. Comdr. Joseph H., Jr. 24
Willows Field 135
Wilson, Ensign John W. 74, 75
Wilson, Capt. William W. 174
Winchester, Radioman-Gunner, AMM 2c J.E. 96
Windham, Sea 1c M.E. 56
Wiseman, Lt. (JG) O.B. 143
Withers, RAdm. Thomas, Jr. (Commander Submarines, Pacific Fleet) 23
Woodhull, Lt. R.B. 58
Woollen, Ensign William S. 19

World War I 1, 9, 11, 21, 69, 129
World War II 2, 8, 69, 78
Worthington, Lt. Edward Hicks 60, 61
Wotje Atoll 33, 36
Wotje Bombardment Group 170
Wotje Island 24, 25, 27, 33, 34, **35**, 36, 38, 41, 43, 64
Wright, Ensign Richard L. 19
Wright Field, Ohio 132
USS *Wyoming* 17

Yaki Shima 155
Yamagata, Vice Adm. Seigo 139, 144
Yamamoto, Admiral 64, 65, 82, 99, 162, 163, 164
Yamato 64
Yarnell, RAdm. Harry 2
Yawata class ship (Japanese) 31, 28, 43
Yayoi 113
YE signal 52, 53, 54, 60, 95
"Yoke Easy" radio transmissions 102
Yokohama 121, 132, 140, 142, 148
Yokohama Air Group 23, 61, 70, 72, 73, 77, 121
Yokohama Dock Yards 149
Yokohama Flying Group 121
Yokohama Maru 113, 115, 121
Yokosuka 144, 161
Yokosuka Navy Yard 148
York, Capt. Edward J. "Ski" 132, 136, 146, 148, 156
USS *Yorktown* (CV-5) 9, 11, 14, 15, 16, 18, 19, 22, 23, 45, **46**, 51, 52, 54, 56, 59, 60, 61, 62, 65, 83, 84, 107, 108, 109, 111, 112, 113, 114, **115**, 118, 119, 120, 121, 123, 164, 169, 172
Yorktown Air Group 45, 55–57, 59, 63, 112, 115, 118, 120, 121, 122
Yorktown Class Fleet Aircraft Carrier 169, 171, 172, 173, 174
Yoshio, Lt. Kurakane (division leader) 23
Young, CEAG Commander Howard L. 27, 29, 31, 38, 44, 64, 87, 90, 91, 97, 98, 101, 102, 103, 104, 169, 171
Youth's Companion Magazine 13
Yubari 114, 118, 121, 126
Yunagi 113, 118, 121

Zacharias, Capt. Ellis M. 94, 170, 171, 173
ZB signal 55
Zed Baker receiver 104
"ZED YOKE EASY" message 55
Zeke fighter 6
Zero 6, 34, 43, 166
Zhejiang-Jiangxi Campaign 156

www.ingramcontent.com/pod-product-compliance
Lightning Source LLC
Chambersburg PA
CBHW060344010526
44117CB00017B/2954